○FUNCTION	○KEY
Cancel character formats	Alt-spacebar, Alt-Z (5)
Case toggle	Ctrl-F4
Center text	Alt-C
Change disk drives	Esc T O
Character format	Esc F C
Clear document	Esc T C
Color (boxes and lines)	Esc F B (5)
Color (display)	Esc O (5)
	Esc W O (4)
Color (printing)	Esc F C (5)
Columns	Esc F D L
Copy text	Alt-F3
Cross reference	Esc F K
Cursor movement	
Bottom of document	Ctrl-PgDn
Bottom of screen	Ctrl-End
Left margin	Home
Next screen	PgDn
Next window	F1
Previous screen	PgUp
Right margin	End
To footnote	Esc J F
To page	Esc J P
Top of document	Ctrl-PgUp
Top of screen	Ctrl-Home
Delete	
Document on screen	Shift-F10 Del
File	Esc T D
Line	Shift-F9 Del
Not to scrap	Backspace or Shift-Del
Paragraph	F10 Del
Sentence	Shift-F8 Del
Text to scrap	Del or Esc D
Word	F8 Del
Division break	Ctrl-⏎
Document retrieval	Esc L D
Double space	Alt-2
Double underline	Alt-D

○FUNCTION	○KEY
Draft print	Esc P O
Font size	Esc F C
Font type	Alt-F8
Footer	Alt-F2
Footnote position	Esc F D L
Footnotes	Esc F F
Foreign characters	Alt-code-number (keypad)
Format	Esc F
Frame position/size	Esc F O (5)
Glossary	
Clear glossary	Esc T G C
Delete to	Esc D
Expand entry	F3
Insert from	Esc I
Load glossary	Esc T G L (5)
Merge glossary	Esc T G M
Print glossary	Esc P G
Save glossary	Esc T G S
Go to page	Alt-F5
Graphic link	Esc L L G (5)
Graphic mode	Alt-F9
Hanging indentation	Alt-T
Header	Ctrl-F2
Help	Esc H or Alt-H
Hidden text	Alt-E
Hyphen	
Optional	Ctrl-- (hyphen)
Required	– (minus on keypad)
Hyphenate	Esc L H
Indent	
Both margins	Alt-Q
Decrease	Alt-M
First lines	Alt-F
Increase	Alt-N

ADVANCED
TECHNIQUES
IN
MICROSOFT
WORD

ADVANCED TECHNIQUES IN MICROSOFT® WORD

SECOND EDITION

ALAN R. NEIBAUER

SAN FRANCISCO · PARIS · DÜSSELDORF · LONDON

Acquisitions Editor: Dianne King
Developmental Editor: Marilyn Smith
Technical Editor: Scott Campbell
Word Processors: Scott Campbell and Chris Mockel
Book Designer: Ingrid Owen
Screen Graphics: Sonja Schenk
Typesetter: Winnie Kelly
Proofreaders: Ami Knox and Vanessa Miller
Indexer: Anne Leach

Cover Designer: Thomas Ingalls + Associates
Cover Photographer: Michael Lamotte
Screen reproductions produced by XenoFont

Bitstream is a registered trademark of Bitstream, Inc.
Cooper Black is a registered trademark of Kingsley-ATF Type Corporation.
dBASE III Plus and dBASE IV are registered trademarks of Ashton-Tate Inc.
IBM is a registered trademark of International Business Machines Corporation.
LaserJet + is a registered trademark of Hewlett-Packard Corporation.
Lotus and PIC are registered trademarks of Lotus Development Corporation.
Microsoft Word, Pageview, and Windows are registered trademarks of Microsoft
Corporation.
PC Paintbrush is a registered trademark of ZSoft Corporation.
PostScript is a registered trademark of Adobe Systems, Inc.
Softcraft Laser Graphics, Spinfont, and Font Solution Pack are registered trademarks of
Softcraft Corporation.
Times is a registered trademark of Linotype Corporation.
XenoFont is a trademark of XenoSoft.

SYBEX is a registered trademark of SYBEX, Inc.

SYBEX is not affiliated with any manufacturer.

An earlier version of this book was published under the title *Practical Techniques in Microsoft
WORD*, copyright 1987 SYBEX Inc.

First edition copyright 1988 SYBEX Inc.

Library of Congress Card Number: 89-61524
ISBN 0-89588-615-4
Manufactured in the United States of America
10 9 8 7 6 5 4 3 2 1

To BARBARA

oACKNOWLEDGMENTS

Completing a new edition of a book such as this is no less difficult than producing the original. Fortunately, the very professional staff at Sybex was well equipped for the task.

The bulk of my thanks goes to Marilyn Smith, who reprised her role as editor of the first edition. She has the skills needed to tell an author his writing needs editing without touching any raw literary nerve.

Special thanks to technical editor Scott Campbell. His job wasn't easy in the early stages, working with beta versions of the software, but Scott made sure the instructions and information in this book are accurate and effective.

Recognition must also go to those responsible for the finished product: Chris Mockel, word processing coordinator; Winnie Kelly, typesetter; Sylvia Townsend, proofreading coordinator; Ingrid Owen, designer; and everyone else at Sybex who worked on the book. Of course, my sincere thanks to Microsoft Corporation for providing early versions of the software so we could complete this book in a timely fashion.

Finally, my deepest appreciation goes to Barbara Neibauer, Philadelphia College of Pharmacy and Science. I don't know how, or why, she puts up with me.

x

○CONTENTS AT A GLANCE

○TABLE OF CONTENTS

CHAPTER 3

FORMATTING YOUR DOCUMENTS

CHAPTER 6

FORMATTING WITH
INDENTATIONS

CHAPTER 7

PRODUCING QUICK AND
EASY LETTERS

CHAPTER 8

CREATING MULTIPAGE DOCUMENTS AND PRINTING ON LETTERHEAD

CHAPTER 9

PRODUCING QUICK AND EASY MEMOS

CHAPTER 10

CREATING, EDITING, AND MANIPULATING TABLES

CHAPTER 11

PRODUCING FINANCIAL DOCUMENTS

CHAPTER 12

PRODUCING REPORTS
AND PAPERS   239

PART THREE   **POWER-USER APPLICATIONS**   **283**

CHAPTER 13

**USING GLOSSARIES FOR
BOILERPLATE**   **285**

CHAPTER 14

BUILDING APPLICATIONS
WITH MACROS   301

CHAPTER 15

**USING DATABASE
MANAGEMENT
FUNCTIONS**

CHAPTER 16

**PRODUCING FORM
DOCUMENTS USING DATA
FILES**

CHAPTER 17

PERFORMING ADVANCED MERGING OPERATIONS

CHAPTER 18

USING SPECIAL CHARACTERS

CHAPTER 19

CREATING
MULTICOLUMN PAGES

CHAPTER 20

USING GRAPHICS AND
DESKTOP PUBLISHING
WITH WORD

CHAPTER 21

MANAGING YOUR SYSTEM   421

APPENDIX

USING THE SPELL AND
THESAURUS COMMANDS   439

∘INTRODUCTION

Microsoft Word is special. It is quite unlike other word processing programs in many ways. It even has capabilities beyond many "dedicated" machines—expensive computers built solely for word processing. Word fits comfortably in a busy office, on a college campus, or in a home. Its uses range from simple letter writing to desktop publishing. And, unlike learning to use many so-called "industry standards," it is easy to master even the most sophisticated of Word's powers.

And, just like Word, this book is special. It is designed to let you get the most from Word. Instead of spending your valuable hours memorizing keystrokes, you will follow practical, step-by-step techniques for conquering that mountain of paperwork quickly. You will learn how to use the special features of Word so that you can handle even the most complex word processing problems.

Are you a new Word user? This book quickly builds your skills from the simple to the complex. Have you already become familiar with Word? Are you upgrading to the newest version? Use this book to solve the word processing problems that you are facing today. Since this book is application oriented, you don't have to read the first 200 pages to use the techniques for the application on page 201. Each application provides the quickest and easiest way to handle specific problems.

Of course, you'll want to work through all the exercises. Each explains how specific word processing chores can be tackled with the least amount of work.

∘WHAT THIS BOOK CONTAINS

The book is divided into three parts. Part 1 (Chapters 1 through 3) reviews Word basics. These chapters explain how Word operates, how to enter and edit text, and how to use Word's formatting features to make your documents look good.

If this is your first experience with Word, read Chapters 1 through 3 carefully for a complete introduction. If you have already begun using Word, review these chapters briefly before going on to the specific applications that follow.

Part 2 presents techniques for typical applications. Chapter 4 describes how to customize Word for your own needs. You'll learn how to change Word's built-in defaults so that every document is automatically printed in the format that you want.

Chapter 5 presents methods for creating simple form letters and documents, including printing envelopes. You'll learn how to create templates and how to use multiple windows to create form documents and manage simple mailing lists.

Chapter 6 explains how special formats are created, such as paragraph indentations, hanging indentations, right-aligned text, and outlines.

Chapters 7 through 12 present techniques for specific word processing tasks. In Chapter 7, you'll learn how to streamline the production of letters. Creating multipage letters using preformatted templates is discussed in Chapter 8. Chapter 9 explains how to use these techniques for memos. Tables, from the simple to complex, are covered in Chapter 10. Financial documents, such as balance sheets and income statements, are the subject of Chapter 11. In Chapter 12, you'll learn how to plan and write a research report or major paper, including footnotes, page numbers, an index, table of contents, and detailed formatting.

In Part 3 (Chapters 13 through 21), you'll learn how to use Word for "power-user" applications. Chapter 13 details how to use glossaries to store boilerplate text. With boilerplate, you can create a multitude of "individualized" documents from standard paragraphs. In Chapter 14, you'll learn about Word's powerful macros and how to have Word perform even complex tasks in a few keystrokes.

Chapters 15 through 17 form a unit on data-management techniques. Chapter 15 presents some unique techniques for using Word as a file manager, and Chapter 16 shows how to use your database to print form letters and invoices. Chapter 17 explains how to extend these merging capabilities to include entire documents.

The next three chapters, 18 through 20, concentrate on graphics and desktop publishing. In Chapter 18, you'll learn how to access special characters and create simple line graphics and boxes (using a compatible graphics printer). Chapter 19 explains how to create newsletters and other multicolumn documents. Chapter 20 describes how to add graphics to your documents, including spreadsheet charts, drawings, scanned images, and laser fonts. Chapter 21 discusses using Word in a network or office environment, where multiple authors collaborate on a single document. You'll also see how to manage those long lists of documents on your hard disk.

Finally, the appendix covers the use of the Spell and Thesaurus commands to correct and add sparkle to your writing.

○HOW TO USE THIS BOOK

Depending on your system, you'll be using a mouse, the keyboard, or both to interact with Word. You may have either version 5.0 or version 4.0 of the software.

VERSIONS COVERED

This book concentrates on Word version 5.0 for the IBM PC, XT, and AT, and compatible computers. However, complete instructions are presented for version 4.0 in the margin, next to the 5.0 instructions.

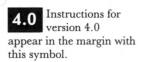 Instructions for version 4.0 appear in the margin with this symbol.

If you have version 4.0, look for the 4.0 margin note to see if instructions or features differ from those presented in the chapter.

All the screen images in the book are taken from version 5.0. If you have an earlier version, be aware that your own screen may look slightly different.

USING THE MOUSE

Many readers will be using the mouse to edit documents and navigate through Word's menus and commands. Instructions for the mouse are presented in the text.

Whenever you're in Word, you'll see a special pointer—either an arrow, a rectangular block, or some other symbol—on the screen (the pointer's appearance is discussed in Chapter 1). The pointer is always used along with the mouse to edit your document or perform some special function by either clicking or dragging.

If you're new to using the mouse, review the following sections, which define some of the terminology you'll be seeing throughout the text.

Note that even if you have a mouse, some functions can still be performed quicker using function keys or combinations of keys. So look for the special keyboard notes in the margin, as explained in the next section.

Clicking

To click the mouse, position the pointer where the instruction indicates, then press and release one or both of the mouse buttons, as indicated in the text. For example, this instruction:

Click left on Search

means to position the mouse pointer on the command Search, and then press down and release the left mouse button. (Note that, in this book, the first letters in command and option names are capitalized, although they do not always appear that way on the screen.)

Here is how we will indicate which button to press:

Click left   Click with the left button

Click right   Click with the right button

Click both   Click with both buttons at the same time

If no button is given, you can click with either (but not both).

To perform some functions, you have to click on more than one word in sequence. These instructions look like this:

Click left on Format Division Margins

This means to click with the left button on the words Format, Division, and Margins (in that order) as they appear on the screen.

Dragging

To drag the mouse, position the pointer where instructed, and then press and *hold down* the mouse button as you move the pointer. As with clicking, if no button is specified, you can hold down either button. Dragging is used to select text that you want to delete, move, copy, or format, and for moving tab stops from one position to another.

Instruction for using the keyboard appear in the margin with this symbol.

USING THE KEYBOARD

In the first chapters, there are several special sections devoted to keyboard users. But in most cases, the instructions for the keyboard appear in the margin next to the mouse instructions in text.

If you're not using a mouse, don't assume that it will take you longer to perform tasks. In many cases, you'll be able to accomplish a task much faster using special key combinations.

Special Keys

The computer keyboard includes some keys not found on a regular typewriter. These might be labeled with an arrow, some other symbol, or by an abbreviation like Alt or Ctrl. You will be using these keys often:

 This is the Tab key. When an instruction says to press Tab, press this key. With Word, the Tab key serves two purposes. When you're typing, Tab inserts blank spaces in the line to align your entries with a set tab stop—just like a typewriter. But when you're working with command menus, you can use the Tab key to select the options that you wish to change.

 This is the Shift key. When an instruction says to press Shift, press this key. You can press either one of the two Shift keys on the keyboard.

 This is the Enter key—one of the most important keys you will be using. When an instruction says to press Enter, press this key. You will use the Enter key to end paragraphs and to insert blank lines in the text. You will also use the Enter key to select options from Word's message lines and menus.

 When an instruction says to press Esc, press this key. The Esc key is used to enter the command area. From there, you can format, print, save, or otherwise manipulate your text.

 When an instruction says to press Ins, press this key. It inserts text at the position of the cursor.

When an instruction says to press Del, press this key. It deletes text at the position of the cursor.

Key Combinations

In many instances, you will have to press more than one key to perform a certain task. These key combinations can be of two types:

o You might have to press two keys at the same time.

o You might have to press several keys in sequence.

The instructions in this book indicate that you should press the keys at the same time by showing a hyphen between the two key names. For example, if an instruction says to press Alt-P, this means that you should press and hold down the Alt key while you press the P key.

Other key combinations must be pressed in sequence, one after the other. In this book, these keys are separated by blank spaces. For example, if an instruction says to press Esc F P, this means that you should press and release the Esc key, then press and release the F key, then press and release the P key.

Cursor-Movement Keys

The cursor is a small box, the size of one character. When you're working on a document, the cursor indicates where the next character typed will appear on the screen. If the cursor is at the end of your document, the characters that you type will be added to the end of your text. You can move the cursor anywhere in your document. If you want to add words to the middle of some paragraph, move the cursor to that spot.

You move the cursor by pressing special keys called cursor-movement keys. Most of these are located on the right side of the keyboard. If you press a cursor-movement key and a number appears on the screen, press the key marked Num Lock.

The four most basic keys are the directional arrows.

 This is the up arrow key. When you press this key, the cursor moves up one line.

 This is the down arrow key. When you press this key, the cursor moves down one line.

 This is the right arrow key. It moves the cursor one character to the right.

 This is the left arrow key. It moves the cursor one character to the left.

To move more than one line or character at a time, hold down the directional arrow key.

Four other cursor-movement keys are very useful:

 This key moves the cursor to the left margin.

 This key moves the cursor to the right margin.

 This key displays the next 18 lines of text.

 This key displays the previous 18 lines of text.

Use the cursor-movement keys to move the cursor around the screen, either to insert text or as the first step in selecting text.

Function Keys (F1 through F10 or F12)

The function keys have been programmed by Microsoft to perform special functions. They provide an easy way to perform some complex task. When an instruction says to press F5, just press the key marked F5. Some instructions combine function keys with Ctrl, Alt, or Shift. So when an instruction says Press Ctrl-F10, press and hold down the Ctrl key, then press F10.

As you use Word, you will quickly learn the function keys and their combinations.

SPECIAL NOTES

Throughout this book, you'll see special notes in the margin. These notes contain hints or reminders for getting the most out of Word—whether you're using the mouse or keyboard. They appear next to related topics in the text, marked with a special notes symbol.

Notes that provide further information or reminders appear in the margin next to this symbol. For example, make sure you've installed Word using the Setup program before going on to Chapter 1.

PART ONE

AN OVERVIEW OF MICROSOFT WORD

The following three chapters review how Word works and how basic documents are edited and formatted for printing. If you are new to Word—or to version 5 of Word—read these chapters carefully. Sit down by your computer with this book and your Word disks. Practice each function as you read about it.

Even if you are an experienced Word user, you should at least quickly scan this section. Although you are already using Word, the review may show you some easier techniques, and it will prepare you for the applications that follow.

CHAPTER 1

- HOW
- WORD
- WORKS

4.0 KEY

This chapter summarizes the basic way that Microsoft Word operates. It reviews the different areas of the Word screen, how to use the mouse and keyboard, and how to create and print documents.

Because Word is different than more commonplace word-processing programs, it is important that you fully understand these fundamental concepts. Don't rush through this chapter unless you're already very familiar with Word.

○WORKING WITH FLOPPY DISKS

If you have a hard disk, use the Setup program to copy the necessary files onto it.

If you have not yet done so, use the Setup program supplied with Word to prepare the program for use on your floppy disk system. Setup will create a "working" copy of the program and a formatted, blank disk to hold your documents. If your computer has 360-KB disk drives, the Setup program will create two Word disks, Word Program 1 and Word Program 2. For higher capacity systems, it produces just one disk, Word Program. The program disks, which contain Word itself, the printer file for your particular printer, and some other programs used by Word, always go in drive A.

Stylesheets are special files containing formatting information. Glossaries hold boilerplate text that you can quickly insert in documents.

The blank, formatted disk, which goes in drive B, will store your documents, custom stylesheets, and glossaries. If you don't put the Help and Hyphenation programs on the disk when you run the Setup program, it can store about 140 pages or more, depending on the disk's size and type. But you can have as many document disks as you need. One disk can hold documents regarding a particular client, and another can store your presentation notes. You can have a separate disk for each subject you take, or one for each class you teach. When you use Word, just insert the appropriate document disk in drive B.

With floppy disk systems, Word automatically saves documents on drive B. You don't have to type B: when you're naming documents because Word assumes that you are using that drive as long as there is a disk in there. You can tell the program to store text on drive A, but that disk doesn't have much room for documents.

oUSING AUTOMATIC BACKUP COPIES

There may be times when you want to add to or change a document that you have already typed and saved onto your disk. You just recall it to the screen, make your changes, and then save the edited copy. As a safety feature, every time that you save an edited document, Word makes a backup copy of the original file.

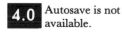 Word automatically adds the DOC extension when you save a document.

Suppose that you want to change a document you've named LETTER.DOC. You recall it from the disk and make the appropriate changes. When you save the new version, Word stores it under the same name, LETTER.DOC. However, before doing so, Word changes the name of the original file to LETTER.BAK.

Files with the BAK extension are backup copies of documents that you have edited. These backup files are for your protection. If you decide that you do not want the changes that you made, or if you accidentally erase your DOC file, the backup version is there. Of course, backup files do take up a lot of room on the disk. So, when you have printed the final version of a file, you may want to delete the backup copy by using the DOS command DEL or Word's document retrieval function (discussed in Chapter 20).

4.0 Autosave is not available.

For more protection, you can have Word save a temporary copy of your text as you are typing. This copy will be erased when you save your document or exit Word, but it will remain on the disk if your computer locks up or someone accidentally turns off your computer. The next time you start Word, you'll be given a chance to restore the backup file to a normal Word document. You turn on this feature, which is called Autosave, through the Options menu, discussed a little later in this chapter.

oWHAT YOU SEE IS . . .

Word is a screen-oriented program. This means that, with a few exceptions, the text on the screen (in graphics mode) looks exactly like the text on the printed page. You will see underlines, boldface, italics, small capital letters, and other effects right on the screen, as shown in Figure 1.1. This lets you experiment with various styles until you see just the one that you want in the printed copy.

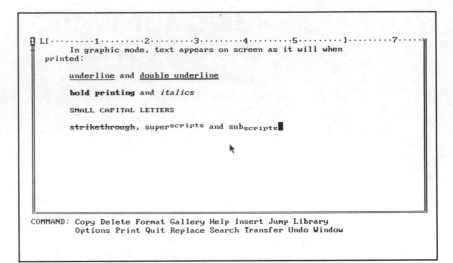

o **Figure 1.1:**   *Text appears as it will be printed*

There are only a few exceptions to this rule. But these actually add to the power of Word. Footnotes, for example, appear in their own separate window, even though they will print at the bottom of the appropriate page. And different sized fonts, such as those produced by laser or some dot-matrix printers, will appear normal size on the screen (unless you have special graphics hardware).

oWORD'S DEFAULT SETTINGS

Each time that you start Word, the standard page size, line spacing, and other formats are automatically set. These *default* settings are provided so you can type and print average documents without worrying about such matters. But, as you will soon learn, you can change these settings to meet your own specifications.

The following are Word's default settings:

o Page size of 8½ by 11 inches

o Top and bottom margins of 1 inch

o Left and right margins of 1¼ inch

- One column
- Single spacing
- 10-point font (single-strike)
- Tab stops every ½ inch
- No page numbers
- No paragraph indentation

These settings result in a page with 55 lines of text, each line 60 characters (or 6 inches) wide. The text will appear neatly arranged on standard business stationery, with all text aligned at the left margin. Figure 1.2 illustrates Word's default settings.

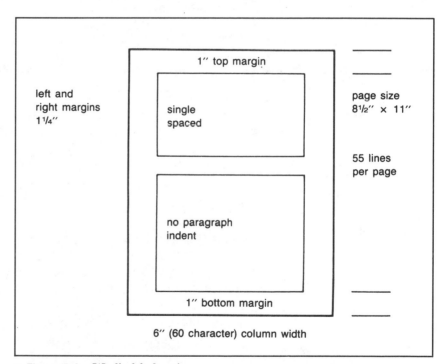

o **Figure 1.2:** *Word's default settings*

By the way, don't bother looking for the Normal stylesheet on your disk. All of the default formats are stored as part of Word itself. The Normal stylesheet is only made an actual disk file, called NORMAL-.STY, when you add your own styles to it or modify the default settings.

The formatting information that Word uses to control the appearance of your documents is contained on stylesheets. The default settings are on the Normal stylesheet, which is loaded automatically when you start Word. You can change the Normal stylesheet and create custom stylesheets, as described in Chapters 4 and 7.

oTHE WORD SCREEN

When you start Word, the screen is divided into four sections: the text window surrounded by a border, the command area, the message line, and the status line. Figure 1.3 shows these areas. There's actually a lot of information contained on the Word screen, so take the time to understand each element.

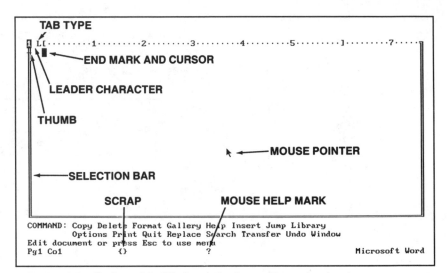

o **Figure 1.3:** *Sections of the Word screen in the graphics mode using the mouse*

THE TEXT WINDOW

The *text window*, also called the *typing window*, is where your document will appear as you type. Think of the window as a blank piece of paper in a typewriter.

You can increase the number of lines displayed in the text window through the Options menu selections. These allow you to remove the display of the command area (until Esc is pressed), remove the window borders, and with high-resolution systems, change display modes.

Mouse Pointer

If you have a mouse, you'll notice the mouse pointer somewhere on the screen. The shape of the pointer depends on whether you're in text or graphics mode, and where the pointer is located. When the pointer is in the text window, it will be either a small arrow (in graphics mode) or a rectangle (in text mode). The pointer will change shape when you move it to other locations. Table 1.1 shows the various mouse pointer shapes in graphics mode.

o **Table 1.1:** *Mouse Pointer Shapes in Graphics Mode*

Shape	Position	Action
‣	Text window	Moves cursor and highlights (selects)
‣	Command area	Activates commands and registers choices
⁄	Inside window, far left	Highlights
↕	Left window frame	Ready to scroll up or down
↑	Left window frame	Scrolls up
↓	Left window frame	Scrolls down
↔	Bottom window frame	Ready to scroll left or right
◂	Bottom window frame	Scrolls left
▸	Bottom window frame	Scrolls right
□	Top or right window frame	Ready to split or close a window
⊟	Right window frame	Splits a window horizontally
⊞	Top window frame	Splits a window vertically
⊡	Top or right window frame	Closes a window
|||	Upper-right corner of window	Turns ruler line (at top) on and off
✛	Lower-right corner of window	Moves a window's border
►	Left window frame	Jumps to a position
Y	Command area	Confirms a command
X	Command area	Cancels a command

Ruler Line

KEY To display the ruler, press Esc O (with version 4.0, press Esc W O), use the arrow keys to select the Show Ruler option, and then press Y. To turn the ruler off, press N after you select the option.

At the top of the text window is a *ruler line*. The ruler line can be turned off and on, and may not appear automatically when you first start Word. To display the ruler using the mouse, click on the upper-right corner of the window. To turn the ruler off, click both buttons on the right corner. The ruler indicates the left-margin position with the [symbol and the right-margin position with].

The character at the left of the ruler (which only appears when you are using the mouse) indicates the type of the next tab to be set. In Figure 1.3, the L represents a left-aligned tab. You can use the mouse to change the tab type at any time.

4.0 No character appears at the left of the ruler to indicate the next type of tab.

The ruler line does not show the default tab stops, which are set every 1/2 inch. Any additional tab stops that you set will be shown on the ruler, indicated by the first letter of the type of tab, as explained in the section on tab stops in Chapter 3.

Each dot across the ruler line represents one character position with a standard 10-pitch type style. Ten pitch means that ten characters will fit in 1 inch of space. You can think of the ruler line as an actual ruler laying across the top of your paper. Use it to visualize how your document will appear when it is printed.

Window Number

To the left of the ruler line, in the upper-left corner of the border, is the *window number*. When you start Word, the window will always be numbered 1. But if you divide the screen into several different windows, say to edit more than one document at the same time, each will have its own number. The number of the active window—the one in which the cursor is located—will be highlighted. When an instruction says to click on the window number, place the mouse pointer directly on the number, and then click the button indicated in the prompt.

Other Text Window Elements

The area in the text window between the left margin and the border (under the tab letter) is called the *selection bar*, which is used with the mouse to select specific portions of text. In graphics mode, the mouse pointer's arrow will change direction when you move it into this area.

The name of the document you're working on (if it has one) will appear on the lower-right border line. This is particularly useful when you're working with multiple windows that each contain a different document. Refer to the document name to make sure you're working on the correct file.

The diamond-shaped object in the upper-left corner is the *end mark*. This represents the end of your document. The end mark moves down as you enter characters and up as you delete them. You can't delete the end mark, place the cursor after it, or use formatting commands when only the end mark is selected.

The end mark you see in a new window is superimposed over the *cursor*, a small rectangle that indicates the position of the next character that you type. You can use the arrow keys or the mouse to move the cursor anywhere in the document, but the end mark will always remain at the very end.

Finally, the small horizontal line on the left border is called the *thumb*. The thumb indicates the approximate location in the document of the text displayed on the screen. For example, if the thumb is in the center of the border, you're viewing text midway through your document.

THE COMMAND AREA

Underneath the text window is the *command area*, also called the *command line*. It contains options for formatting, editing, printing, moving, and searching within your document. Table 1.2 summarizes Word's commands. You'll be using the command area constantly, with either the mouse or the keyboard, as you create documents.

o **Table 1.2:** *Word Commands*

Command	Function
Copy	Copies selected (highlighted) text into the scrap or glossary.
Delete	Deletes selected text from the screen and into the glossary.
Format	Displays options for formatting characters, paragraphs, or divisions (pages).

o **Table 1.2:** *Word Commands (continued)*

Command	Function
Gallery	Lets you view or change the current stylesheet.
Help	Displays comprehensive, context-sensitive information on how Word works.
Insert	Inserts glossary text into the document.
Jump	Positions the highlight at a specific page, footnote, annotation, or bookmark.
Library	Lets you perform special functions such as spelling tasks, sorting, linking graphics or spreadsheets, and creating an index or table of contents.
Options	Displays a menu to control the Word environment, including removing the window borders and command line to display more lines, changing the screen mode from text to graphics, and specifying certain formats and parameters.
Print	Displays the Print menu. From here, the document can be printed, paginated, saved on the disk as a print file, or viewed in graphics mode. Alternative printers and printing options may also be selected.
Quit	Exits Word and returns to DOS. If you have not saved your work, Word will ask if you want to quit without saving your changes. Quitting without saving will erase any changes made.
Replace	Automatically replaces characters that you specify with others.
Search	Scans the document for specific characters that you enter.
Transfer	Displays a menu for saving, recalling, or merging documents. Additional transfer options are provided.
Undo	Cancels your most recent typing. If you "undo" text by mistake, use Undo a second time to replace it.
Window	Divides the screen into a number of text windows. After the screen is divided, you can display and edit more than one document at a time.

Selecting Commands

Every command line, menu, and prompt you'll use with Word has a *command line title* in all uppercase letters preceding the list of options. In some cases, the title is one word, such as COMMAND or INSERT; other times it will be two or more words, such as TRANSFER SAVE or FORMAT DIVISION MARGINS. You can click the mouse, with either button, on the capitalized command line title to have Word perform that command immediately.

To use one of the options listed in the command area, simply click on the command word. The mouse button you press depends on what type of action you want to perform. Clicking with the right button always performs some action immediately, as you'll soon learn. What happens when you click with the left button varies. In some cases, such as with Help and Undo, clicking with the left button also performs the function immediately. With other commands, pressing the left button displays another command line (called the second-level command line), a menu, or a prompt. In this book, we will refer to clicking on an option with the right mouse button as *click right*, clicking with the left button as *click left*, and clicking with both buttons as *click both*.

From a menu, prompt, or command line, click on the command line title to accept your selections and return to the last menu or text window. To leave the command line or menu without accepting any changes, press both mouse buttons.

Second-Level Command Lines

Click left on the Format, Gallery, Jump, Library, Print, Transfer, and Window commands to display a second-level command line. For example, click left on Print to display

PRINT: Printer Direct File Glossary Merge Options Queue Repaginate preView

This second-level command line looks very similar to the first one, and you select options from it in the same way; click right to perform some action or click left to either perform the function (as with Printer), display a prompt (as with File), or show a menu (as with Options).

If you originally clicked right on Print, however, you would immediately activate the first option on the second-level command line, Printer, without seeing those choices. So clicking right on Print performs the same function as clicking left on Print and then clicking on Printer.

Clicking left on Jump displays the command line

Jump to: Page Footnote Annotation bookmarK

Clicking right on Jump selects the Jump to Page option, which is the first choice on the second-level command line.

Remember, you can also perform the highlighted option by clicking on the capitalized command line title, such as PRINT or JUMP.

Prompts

Other command line choices, such as Copy, Delete, and Insert, display prompts requesting information. Click left to display the prompt; click right to perform an action without being prompted.

For example, clicking left on Insert displays the prompt

INSERT from { }

The program is asking you to type the name of a glossary entry to be inserted into the text. Clicking right on Insert automatically reinserts the last deleted text (no prompt will appear).

With Insert and other commands, such as Copy and Transfer, you'll also see a prompt at the bottom of the screen that includes the message

press F1 to select from list

This means that you can have the program display a list that you can select from, rather than typing the name at the prompt. Click right to the right of the command line title to see a list of possible selections. Click left on an option to select it and remain at the prompt line; click right to execute your selection immediately and return to the document.

For example, suppose that you want to insert a boilerplate paragraph that you added to your glossary, but you don't remember what you named it. You would click left on Insert to display the prompt, and then click right to the right of the command line title INSERT to display a list of boilerplate paragraphs. Click right on your selection to insert it into the text and return to the document.

Transfer commands, such as those used to save a document or glossary, may already display a document name at the prompt. If that is the document name you want to select, just click on the command line title

---

KEY Press Esc J (Jump) to display the second-level command line. Press Esc J P (Jump Page) to move to a specific page.

4.0 The Annotation and Bookmark options are not available.

KEY Press Esc I (Insert) to display the prompt. Press Esc I Enter to automatically insert the last deleted text.

KEY Press F1 to display available alternatives. Use the arrow keys to make your selection, and then press Enter to return to the document.

 Press Enter to accept the displayed file name.

to perform the action. If not, click right to the right of the command line title to display selections (if the F1 message is displayed), or type the new name and then click on the command line title.

Menus

Menus are combinations of command lines and prompts. When a command displays a menu, click on the options you wish to change. Where specific choices are given, such as in the option

bold:Yes(No)

click left on your choice to select it and stay in the menu, or click right to select it and return to the document.

Where some keyboard entry is required, such as in the option

left indent: 0"

click on the option with either button, and then type your entry. If the F1 message is displayed, click right on the option to display a list of alternatives.

For example, suppose that you want to display the ruler line through the Options menu (rather than clicking on the corner of the window) and turn on the Autosave feature. The Options menu is shown in Figure 1.4.

KEY Use the Tab key or arrow keys to select an option. Depending on the option, type your setting or entry, press the first letter of your choice, or press F1 to see available alternatives. Press Enter to accept your selections, or press Esc to cancel.

4.0 The selections on this single Options menu are divided into two menus, Options and Window Options. Click left on Window, then on Options. Autosave is not available, so click right on Yes for the Show Ruler option to make the change and return to the text window.

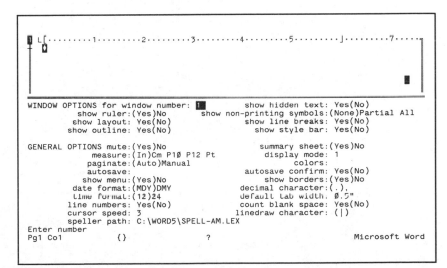

o **Figure 1.4:** *The Options menu*

KEY Press Esc O (with version 4.0, press Esc W O) to display the menu. Use the arrow keys to select the Show Ruler option, and then press Y. With version 4.0, press Enter (the Autosave feature is not available). Press ↓ six times to reach the Auto-save option, and then type **15**. Press Tab to reach the Autosave Confirm option, and then press N. Press Enter to return to the document.

Start by clicking on Options with either button to display the Options menu. Click left to select Yes for the Show Ruler option. If you click right on Yes, the Options menu will disappear and the text window will return, even though you want to make more selections from the menu.

Now click with either button on the Autosave option, which is blank (turned off) by default. There are no choices to select from; you have to enter your own setting. Type **15**, which will have Word save a backup version of your work every 15 minutes.

The Autosave Confirm option allows you to have Word ask you to confirm if the file should be saved. Since this is the last selection you want from the menu, click right on No for this option. The menu disappears, retaining your selections.

You could have also clicked left on No, and then clicked with either button on the word WINDOW or OPTIONS. Remember, click with both buttons anywhere in the menu to cancel your selection.

THE MESSAGE LINE

The words under the command area on the *message line* tell you what to do next. While you're typing a document, the message line reads

Edit document or press Esc to use menu

Figure 1.5 shows this display on the message line.

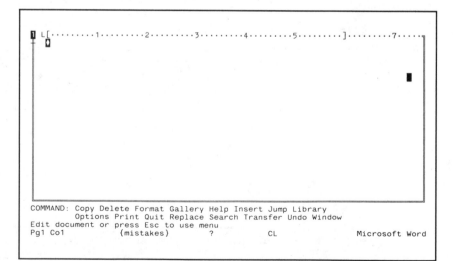

o **Figure 1.5:** *The message line while typing and the status line with text in the scrap and Caps Lock on*

When you're in the command area, the message line tells you the type of functions the highlighted command performs. For example, if you highlight Format by using the keyboard, you'll see the message

Sets all document formats. Applies and records styles

If you click left on Format, the second-level command line appears with the first option, Character, already highlighted. The message line now reports the functions of the Format Character command:

Set character format (bold, italic, hidden, etc.) and fonts

When a menu or prompt is displayed, the message line tells you what type of action is expected. Common messages are

Select option

and

Enter measurement

Other message lines tell you to press certain keys, as in

Enter Y to replace, N to skip and continue, or Esc to cancel

KEY Press Y (Yes), N (No), or Esc.

Press either mouse button on the message line to select Y (Yes), press the N key to select N (No), or click both to cancel.

THE STATUS LINE

As the name implies, the *status line* gives you information about the current status of Word and your document. The status line displays the following information:

4.0 The page number will always be 1 until you print or paginate your document.

o **Page number:** Following the characters *Pg*, you'll see the number of the page displayed on the screen.

o **Column position:** The number after *Co* is the column position of the cursor, or the number of spaces the cursor is from the left margin.

o **Scrap:** Enclosed in the brackets {} are the first and last several characters of the text you last deleted or copied. This area is called the scrap.

o **Key status:** The area between the scrap and the words *Microsoft Word* indicates the status of certain keys or modes. If you see any of the following characters, it means that the mode is turned on. Characters not displayed mean the mode is off.

CL	Caps Lock
CS	Column select mode
EX	Extended mode
LY	Show layout mode
NL	Num Lock
OT	Overtype mode
RM	Record macro mode
SL	Scroll Lock
ZM	Zoom window mode

Depending on your system and document, you may also see two other indicators on the status line:

D   The division number appears between the Pg and Co indicators. A division is a section of text conforming to specific page formats, such as page size or margins. If you change these formats through the Format Division menu, you create another division. The number of the current division appears in the status line.

(?)   This is a help mark. It will appear after the scrap if you are using a mouse. Click the help mark with either button to display Help screens.

USING FUNCTION KEYS

Many of the commands can also be selected by pressing combinations of function keys (the numbered keys, either on the left side or top row of the keyboard) with either the Alt, Shift, or Ctrl key. These are called *speed keys* because they perform some complex function with just one key combination. For example, pressing Ctrl-F2 is the same as clicking left on Format Running-Head, and then clicking right on Top.

If your hands are already on the keyboard, these few keystrokes are quicker and easier than using the mouse or manually working though menus with the keyboard. So, even if you have a mouse, watch the keyboard margin notes for speed keys as you follow the steps in this book.

○**HELP!**

If you need help when typing or editing, take advantage of Word's comprehensive Help facility. Word can display screens of useful information explaining each command and function.

You can get help in one of three ways.

4.0 The Help function is not context sensitive. The main Help window is displayed when you press Alt-H. The functions are the same as the ones described for version 5.0 (Resume exits Help).

- ○ If you are using a mouse, place the pointer on the question mark (?) or the command Help, then click.

- ○ From the text window, a prompt, or in a menu, press Alt-H. Remember to hold down the Alt key, then press H. When you use Alt-H, the help function is context sensitive. That means that it will display information on the function, menu, or command that you were on when you requested help.

- ○ From the command area, press H. (You are in the command area if you pressed Esc and one of the options is highlighted.) You'll see the first of three screens explaining how to use help.

Each Help screen includes the command line

HELP: Exit Next Previous Basics
Index Tutorial Keyboard Mouse

KEY Press the first letter of option desired, or select it with the arrow keys, and then press Enter.

Click on an option to select it. The options perform the following functions:

Exit	Exits the Help function and returns you to your document.
Next	Displays the next Help window in the sequence. A message in the top window shows the number of screens in the sequence, such as Screen 1 of 6.
Previous	Displays the previous window in the sequence.
Basics	Shows how to use the Help function.
Index	Displays an index of Help topics. From the index, you can select the function for which you need help.
Tutorial	Begins the tutorial lessons.
Keyboard	Lists editing and formatting functions available from the keyboard.
Mouse	Gives instructions on using the mouse with Word.

oPAGINATION

4.0 No line or other indication appears to let you know when one page ends and another begins until you print or paginate the document.

As you type, you don't have to worry about ending one page and starting another—just continue typing. When you reach the end of the page, Word will insert a dotted line across the screen and increment the page-number indicator on the status line by one.

oTHE DOCUMENT-CREATION CYCLE

There is a pattern that is common to all word-processing programs—whether on microcomputers or mainframes:

Enter—Edit—Format—Save—Print—Review

Follow this pattern, and your documents will look attractive, will be organized, and will be effective. Don't follow it, and you'll find yourself wasting time, paper, and disks.

The steps in this process and how to accomplish them with Word are described below:

KEY Press Ctrl-F7 (Transfer Load F1), use the arrow keys to highlight (select) the document you want to edit, and then press Enter.

1. **Enter**: Start Word when you see the A> or C> prompt on the screen. Type the text. Make any obvious format changes as you type, such as underlining or boldfacing, but don't let the task of formatting distract you from concentrating on the content. If you already started the document and saved it on the disk, recall it for editing or addition. To recall text, click right on Transfer. Then click right to the right of TRANSFER LOAD and click right on the document you want to recall. When you start Word, you can automatically recall the last document that you worked on by typing **word/L** at the A> or C> prompt.

KEY Press Ctrl-F10 to save the document.

2. **Edit**: Make any corrections to the text. Check your spelling and grammar. Does it say what you want it to say? Use the Del and Ins keys and other editing techniques, such as Library Spell.

KEY Press Ctrl-F8 to print a document.

3. **Format**: Check the appearance of the text. Are the margins correct? Should certain words be underlined or boldface? Are the page breaks correct? Format the text by using speed keys or the Format menu selections (click on Format).

KEY Press Esc Q to quit, or press Ctrl-F7 to load another document.

4. Save: Store the document on disk. Click left on Transfer Save, type the document name or, if it appears on the screen, click on TRANSFER or SAVE. With version 5.0, you can save the document and its associated stylesheet and glossary by using the Transfer Allsave command. When you save a document for the first time, a summary sheet menu is displayed, as explained in the next section.

5. **Print**: Print the draft or final document. Select printing options, and then click right on Print.

6. **Review**: Take a good look at the finished product. If any corrections or additions are needed, go back to step 1 and repeat the cycle. If no changes are needed, quit Word (click on Quit), recall another document, or start a new one.

USING SUMMARY SHEETS

The first time you save a document, you have the option of filling in a summary sheet. The sheet is not displayed on the screen with the document, but you can display, edit, and print it separately through various command menus. But more important, summary sheets can be used as the basis for a document-management system using the Library Document-Retrieval command, which we'll cover in Chapter 20.

The summary sheet menu that appears after you enter the document's name to save it is shown in Figure 1.6. The summary sheet is entirely optional, and you can click on the command line title SUMMARY INFORMATION when it is first displayed to leave the menu blank. If you decide to use the summary sheet, click on the items you want to enter and fill in the information. Click on the command line title when you've made all your entries to save both the document and the summary sheet.

The file name, creation date, and revision date fields will be filled in automatically by Word. Use the other fields to identify the document and help you manage your files.

For instance, while you cannot have two documents with the same name as far as the disk is concerned, you can have many with the same summary sheet title. That way, you can easily keep track of several revisions of the same document. Each revision will have a different file

KEY To leave the summary sheet menu blank, press Enter when it is first displayed. To make entries, press Tab or the arrow keys to reach the items you want to fill in. Make your entries, and then press Enter to save both the document and summary sheet.

```
1 L[·········1·········2·········3·········4·········5·········]·········7·····┐
  Dear Sir:

       Please send me a copy of your 199Ø Annual Report.

                        Sincerely,

                        Adam M. Chesin█

                              █



SUMMARY INFORMATION
   title: █                           version number:
   author:                           creation date: Ø4/11/9Ø
   operator:                         revision date: Ø4/11/9Ø
   keywords:
   comments:
Enter text
Pg1 Co45            {}              ?                  Microsoft Word
```

o **Figure 1.6:** *Summary sheet for a new document*

name. Enter the same title in the summary sheets but use a new revision number for each one. You can use the title, as well as other fields in the summary sheet, to retrieve or print selected documents.

The author and operator fields are useful in an office to identify the originator of the document and the typist who completed it. In the comments field, you can type up to 220 characters. You can use this to store notes or special instructions about the document.

The keywords field may be the most useful one. Here you can enter words or phrases that further identify the document (up to a total of 80 characters). For example, suppose that you type a page of notes for a research paper about martial arts. Since the notes refer to Tae Kwon Do, you could enter *Tae Kwon Do* and *Korea* in the keywords field of the summary sheet menu when you save the notes. Later, when you want to add information about this martial art to your paper, you can use the Library Document-retrieval command to quickly locate all documents that contain those words.

You can print the summary sheet with the document or by itself. To print it with the document, select Yes for the Summary Sheet option on the Print Options menu. The summary sheet will print on a separate sheet of paper, with 1-inch margins, after the document is printed. You can also print the summary sheet, by itself or with the document, through the Library Document-Retrieval command.

Before going on to the next chapter, make sure that you have prepared your disks properly. Hard disk users should log onto the subdirectory containing the Word program. Floppy disk users should insert the Word program disk in drive A and a blank, formatted disk in drive B.

CHAPTER 2

- EDITING
- TEXT

If we could type without ever making mistakes, few people would need word processors. But words are misspelled, punctuation is ignored, and information is left out or organized incorrectly. In short, much of the time that we spend at the keyboard is in changing what has already been typed.

This chapter reviews editing techniques to use with Word. You will learn how to move the cursor, delete unwanted characters and insert new ones, manipulate large sections of text, search your document for specific text, and split the screen into two or more text windows.

○MOVING THE CURSOR

As you fill your screen, text at the top of the window will scroll up out of view to make room for new text at the bottom. You can move the cursor anywhere in the document, using either the mouse or the cursor-movement keys, to scroll text back into view. The end mark will always stay after the last line of text.

Using Cursor-Movement Keys

When Num Lock is on, you'll type numbers when you press the keys on the numeric keypad.

If you have only one set of cursor-movement keys, they are combined with the numeric keypad. To use the keypad for cursor movement, turn the Num Lock key off. Check that the characters NL are not on the status line. If they are, press Num Lock once.

Some keyboards have a separate set of cursor-movement keys between the keyboard and the numeric keypad. The Num Lock key has no effect on these.

The four most basic keys are the directional arrows. Each time you press an arrow key, the cursor moves one character or line in that direction. Hold down the key to move several characters or lines at a time.

You can also use the following keys to move the cursor:

Home	Moves to the beginning of the line
End	Moves to the end of the line
PgDn	Displays the next screen full of text
PgUp	Displays the previous screen full of text

Ctrl-PgUp	Moves to the start of your document
Ctrl-PgDn	Moves to the end of your document

Another way to move the cursor is to use the Jump command to go quickly to a specific page in your document. Press Alt-F5 (or Esc J P), type the page number, and then press Enter.

USING THE MOUSE

You don't have to use the keyboard to move through your document if you have a mouse. You can position the cursor anywhere in the displayed text by pointing to it with the mouse pointer and clicking left.

Scrolling with the Mouse

To scroll beyond the displayed text, point to the left window border with the mouse pointer. The pointer will change shape. Click left to scroll the text on the screen down (displaying text that was above the top border); click right to scroll up.

Where you place the mouse pointer determines how much text scrolls with each click. The closer the pointer is to the top of the window, the less text will scroll. For example, clicking with the pointer just under the window number scrolls a line at a time. Clicking on the bottom corner scrolls a full screen at a time (like pressing the PgDn and PgUp keys).

By clicking with both buttons, you can move to the relative position of the pointer. For example, display the start of your document by pointing just under the window number and clicking both. Reach the end by clicking both on the lower-left corner. Want to reach the middle of your text? Point halfway down the border and click both.

If you set the margins so the line width is wider than the screen, or divide the screen into smaller vertical windows, text may scroll off to the left or right. To scroll that text into view, point to the bottom border with the mouse pointer, and then click left to scroll left or click right to scroll right.

But beware, scrolling with the mouse does not move the cursor, only the displayed text and the mouse pointer. Until you click left in the window, the cursor remains where you left it. If you scroll through your document and then start typing, the original position will pop into view, and your characters will be inserted there.

oDELETING CHARACTERS

The most basic and common editing function is deleting characters. There are many ways to erase characters with Word, but the simplest methods are to use the Backspace and Del keys.

As you type, press the Backspace key to delete characters to the left of the cursor. Hold the key down to erase several characters. Press the Del key to erase characters that are highlighted by the cursor. Hold the Del key down to delete several characters to the right of the cursor.

When you delete a character by using the Del key (not the Backspace key), it is temporarily stored in the scrap. The first and last few characters of the contents of the scrap are displayed on the status line between the brackets. If you last deleted the letter *j* in *mistakje*, for instance, the status line would display {j}. The contents of the scrap are replaced each time that you use the Del key.

To delete a character without placing it in the scrap, press Shift-Del (hold down the Shift key, then press the Del key). The contents of the scrap will be unchanged. Use this method if you already have something in the scrap that you want to insert elsewhere.

Don't hold down the Backspace or Del key too long, or you'll delete characters you really want. If you do make this mistake, however, you can "undo" it, as explained shortly.

oTWO TYPING MODES: INSERT AND OVERTYPE

As you type, characters are inserted into the text. While you're first creating a document, characters are inserted between the last character typed and the end mark. However, you can insert characters anywhere in the document by moving the cursor where you want them to go, and then typing.

When you type new characters within a document, two things can occur. Usually, new characters will be inserted between existing ones. The words to the right of the cursor will move over, and down if necessary, to make room for the new ones. This is *insert mode*, which is the default mode used by Word.

But you can also overtype characters. In *overtype mode*, the new characters that you type replace the existing ones—each new character takes the place of one already there. To enter overtype mode, press the F5 key. The characters OT will appear on the status line.

F5, by the way, is called a toggle key. You press it once to turn on a function; press it again to turn the same function off. So, to get back into insert mode, press F5 again, and the characters OT will disappear from the status line.

Overtype is a fast way to change mistakes. However, it has limited value. Use overtype mode when you are replacing characters with the same number of new ones. This way, you will not erase words accidentally as you continue typing. Actually, you can change a single character just as fast in insert mode—simply type the new character, then press Del to erase the old character, which is now under the cursor.

oEDITING LARGER AMOUNTS OF TEXT

If you have words, sentences, or paragraphs to change, the Backspace and Del keys are not very efficient. Fortunately, Word provides special methods that let you manipulate any amount of text. To work with larger amounts of text, you must first *select* the characters that you want to delete, copy, or move, and then perform the action. When you select text, by using the keyboard or the mouse, it becomes highlighted on the screen.

Highlighted characters appear dark on a light background. Unfortunately, because of the way that screen images are captured, Figure 2.1 shows the opposite effect, but it does give you some idea of how selected text appears.

You can select any amount of text, from a single character to the entire document, as explained in the following sections.

SELECTING TEXT WITH SPEED KEYS

Any text highlighted on the screen is selected, and characters selected in groups are called *blocks*. To select a block to be manipulated, position the cursor near the text that you wish to change. Then use a combination of the function keys and the arrow keys to highlight the block.

```
 ▌L[·········1·········2·········3·········4·········5·········]·········7·····
    Dear Sir:

         Please send me a copy of your ▐1990 Annual Report▌. I
    will be using the report for my final term paper in Business
    Management.

                        Sincerely,


                        Adam M. Chesin♦




                                                          ═══REQUEST.DOC═══
    COMMAND: Copy Delete Format Gallery Help Insert Jump Library
             Options Print Quit Replace Search Transfer Undo Window
    Edit document or press Esc to use menu
    Pg1 Co53          {·}                  ?              EX      Microsoft Word▐
```

o **Figure 2.1:** *Selected text*

Use the speed keys shown below to quickly select text:

F7	Selects the word on the left
F8	Selects the word on the right
F9	Selects current or previous paragraph
F10	Selects the current or next paragraph
Shift-F7	If the cursor is between two sentences, selects the sentence on the left
Shift-F8	If the cursor is between two sentences, selects the sentence on the right
Shift-F9	Selects the line
Shift-F10	Selects the entire document

It is important that you understand the distinction between a sentence and a line. Word considers a *sentence* to be the text between the first period (not surrounded by numbers), question mark, exclamation point, or paragraph return to the left and the right. In most cases, this will be a entire grammatical sentence, but not in

I met Mrs. Jones in the theater.

If you press Shift-F7 at the end of the sentence, you would just highlight *Jones in the theater*.

A *line* is the text between the left and right margins. In many cases, a sentence is more than one line long.

SELECTING TEXT BY CLICKING THE MOUSE

The mouse has its own version of speed keys: clicking. By pointing to certain locations with the mouse pointer and pressing a mouse button, you can quickly select words, lines, sentences, paragraphs, and even the entire document.

With the pointer in the text:

o Click right to select a word.

o Click left to select a character.

o Click both to select a sentence.

With the pointer in the selection bar (between the window border and the text):

o Click left to select a line.

o Click right to select a paragraph.

o Click both to select the entire document.

SELECTING BLOCKS BY DRAGGING THE MOUSE

Unfortunately, we do not always want to delete text in such neat grammatical divisions. We might want to erase a word and a half or just three words on the line. To select any amount of text with the mouse, drag the mouse pointer over it while pressing one of the mouse buttons.

 To select less than a word with the mouse, such as a few characters or parts of a word, drag with the left button pressed.

Which button you press while dragging depends on how you want to select text. Dragging across a line with the left button pressed selects text a character at a time. Dragging with the right button pressed selects a word at a time, including the blank space following the word. When the right button is down, as soon as the pointer reaches the first letter of the word, the entire word becomes selected. Both buttons work the same when dragging down through your document: they select a line at a time.

When you drag the pointer down, all the text from the original position to the new pointer position is selected. Figure 2.2 shows the effects of placing the pointer in the middle of a line and dragging straight down.

SELECTING TEXT BY EXTENDING WITH THE KEYBOARD

The keyboard equivalent to dragging is extending. Place the cursor at one end of the block you want to select, and then press F6. The characters EX (for extend) will appear on the status line. Press the arrow keys to extend the selection in any direction. Press the up or down arrow key to select more than one line. Press the left or right arrow key to select more than one character to the left or to the right. Press the F7 or F8 key to select more than one word to the left or to the right.

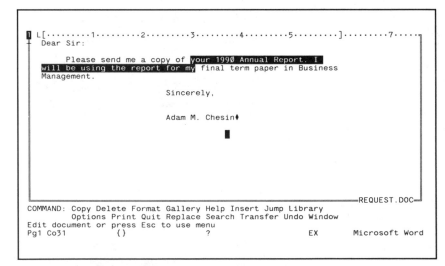

○ **Figure 2.2:** *Effects of dragging down*

TURNING OFF THE HIGHLIGHTING

When you select text by extending or dragging, the original position of the cursor acts like an anchor. If you move the cursor with the arrow keys or drag the pointer (before releasing the mouse button) back past where you originally started the selection, the text becomes highlighted in the other direction. So, if you select more text than you want, move the cursor or pointer back over the text.

With the mouse, you can quickly get rid of all the highlighting by releasing the mouse button and then clicking left. Using the keyboard, press F6 again to toggle off the extend function, and then move the cursor.

All highlighting disappears (and the extend function turns off) after you perform some action on selected text.

DELETING SELECTED TEXT USING THE DEL KEY

To delete a block of text, select it and press the Del key. The first and last few characters of the deleted text will appear in the scrap. Any text already in the scrap will be erased.

To delete a block of text and not place it in the scrap, select the block and press Shift-Del. The highlighted text will be erased from the screen. This will have no effect on the contents of the scrap.

KEY Use the scrap to move or copy sections of text from one location to another. To move text, select it and press Del. (Do not press Del again until you have completed the move operation, or the characters saved in the scrap will be erased.) Position the cursor where you want the text to appear, and press Ins to insert the text in the scrap at the cursor's position. To copy text, select it and press Alt-F3 to place it into the scrap. Move the cursor to the new position, and then press Ins.

oMOVING AND COPYING TEXT QUICKLY

With the mouse, it is easy to move and copy text. *Move* means to delete the text from its original position and place it elsewhere. *Copy* leaves the text intact and makes a copy of it somewhere else in the document.

To move text, select it, place the pointer at the new location, hold down the Ctrl key, and then press either button. You can quickly move text to the start of the document by selecting the text, holding down the Ctrl key, and then clicking both mouse buttons on the selection bar.

To copy text, select it, place the pointer at the new location, hold down the Shift key, and then press either mouse button. To quickly copy text to the start of the document, select the text, hold down the Shift key, and then click both mouse buttons on the selection bar.

INSERTING THE SAME TEXT USING THE SCRAP

The contents of the scrap do not change when you insert them into the text. The only way to change the scrap is to delete or copy something else into it. As long as a word, phrase, or any other amount of text is in the scrap, you can insert it by pressing Ins. This means that you can use the scrap as a quick way of inserting a word or phrase that you use often.

If you want to insert text this way, the first time that you want to use the word or phrase, type it normally. Then, copy it into the scrap, select it, and press Alt-F3 (or Esc C Enter). The next time that you want to use the word or phrase, press Ins. If you delete some text between uses, just copy the word or phrase into the scrap again.

oMOVING AND COPYING TEXT THROUGH THE GLOSSARY

Use the glossary method when you have a number of blocks of text that you want to move or copy within your document. Several blocks can be stored in the glossary at one time, and they will not be erased when you press the Del key.

A *glossary* is a collection of one or more blocks of text stored in the computer's memory or on the disk. Each block has a name, and you can use its name to insert the block into the document. Unlike the scrap, deleting or copying other text does not affect text already saved in the glossary. Glossaries are very powerful features of Word, and they will be discussed in detail in Chapter 13. In this section, you will learn how to use the glossary as a temporary storage area for text that you want to copy or move.

MOVING TEXT

To move text through the glossary, select the block of text to be moved, and click left on Delete to see the prompt

DELETE to { }

in the command area. Type a short name for the block. If you are moving your name and address, for example, type Name. The only names that you cannot give a block are those reserved for special Word functions: Page, Footnote, Date, Time, Dateprint, Timeprint, and Nextpage (not in version 4.0).

After you've named the block of text, click on DELETE or press Enter. The highlighted block will be erased from the screen and saved in the glossary, but not placed in the scrap.

When you want to insert that block of text into a document, click left on Insert. The prompt

INSERT from { }

will appear in the command area. Type the name of the block, and then click on INSERT or press Enter. The text saved in the glossary with that name will appear at the position of the cursor. As with the scrap, inserting text from the glossary does not remove it from the glossary.

If you forget the names that you gave blocks of text, when the prompt

INSERT from { }

appears on the screen, click right to the right of INSERT. This displays a list of the names in the glossary. Point to the name of the block you want to insert, and then click right.

COPYING TEXT

To copy text through the glossary, select the block of text to be copied and click on Copy. If you click right, the text will be placed into the scrap immediately. Click left to see the prompt

COPY to { }

Type a short name for the block, and then click on COPY. A copy of the text will be saved in the glossary, and the highlighted text will remain in its original position.

KEY Press Esc I, type the glossary name, and then press Enter. Press F1 to see a list of glossary names.

The procedure for inserting copied text from the glossary is the same as the procedure for inserting moved text: click left on Insert, type the name of the block at the prompt, and click on INSERT. If you forget the name, click right to the right of INSERT when you see the Insert prompt, and Word will display a list of glossary names.

QUITTING DOCUMENTS AFTER USING THE GLOSSARY

Before saving or quitting a document after using the glossary, Word displays the prompt

Enter Y to save changes to glossary, N to lose changes, or Esc to cancel

Since you are just using the glossary as a temporary storage area when you move or copy blocks, press N in response to this prompt. In Chapter 13, you will learn how to use the glossary for storing boilerplate paragraphs, which are sections of text that you add to the glossary so you can use them at any time.

oCHANGING "INVISIBLE" CHARACTERS

Some keys that you press do not leave characters on the screen. The most common ones are the spacebar, Tab, and Enter keys. You can delete and insert spaces created by pressing the spacebar in the same way that you delete and insert other characters. The Tab and Enter keys, however, actually insert invisible codes. While you can make these codes visible through the Options menu, you don't have to see them to change them.

This section describes how to delete tab stops and how to insert and delete return codes in order to split and combine paragraphs.

DELETING TAB STOPS

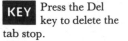 **KEY** Press the Del key to delete the tab stop.

To delete a tab stop, position the cursor in the blank space of the tab area. The entire blank space (five characters wide) will be highlighted, as

shown in Figure 2.3. Click right on Delete, and the tab stop will be deleted. The text will shift five spaces to the left, and a small arrow (the tab symbol) will appear in the scrap.

CHANGING RETURNS TO SPLIT AND COMBINE PARAGRAPHS

The key for splitting a paragraph into two, or joining two into one, is Enter. When you press the Enter key—to begin a new paragraph or insert blank lines—you are really inserting a return code in the text. By deleting the code that separates two paragraphs, you can join them together. By inserting a return code in a paragraph, you divide it into two.

Splitting a Paragraph

To split one paragraph into two, position the cursor at the beginning of the sentence that you want to start the new paragraph (as in Figure 2.4) and press Enter. The text of that paragraph, from the cursor position down, will move down to the next line. Press Tab to indent text, press Enter again to double space between paragraphs, or otherwise adjust the spacing, if necessary.

```
1 L[ · · · · · · · · 1 · · · · · · · · 2 · · · · · · · · 3 · · · · · · · · 4 · · · · · · · · 5 · · · · · · · · ] · · · · · · · · 7 · · · · ·
  Dear Sir:

        ███Please send me a copy of your 1990 Annual Report. I
  will be using the report for my final term paper in Business
  Management.

                      Sincerely,

                      Adam M. Chesin♦




                                                        REQUEST.DOC
COMMAND: Copy Delete Format Gallery Help Insert Jump Library
         Options Print Quit Replace Search Transfer Undo Window
Edit document or press Esc to use menu
Pg1 Co1            {·}               ?              Microsoft Word
```

o **Figure 2.3:** *Selecting a tab stop*

```
█ L[·········1·········2·········3·········4·········5·········]·········7·····
  Dear Sir:

        Please send me a copy of your 1990 Annual Report. █
  will be using the report for my final term paper in Business
  Management.


                        Sincerely,


                        Adam M. Chesin◆




                                                        ═══════REQUEST.DOC═
COMMAND: Copy Delete Format Gallery Help Insert Jump Library
         Options Print Quit Replace Search Transfer Undo Window
Edit document or press Esc to use menu
Pg1 Co56              {·}                    ?                Microsoft Word█
```

o **Figure 2.4:** *The cursor position for splitting a paragraph*

Combining Paragraphs

KEY Press the Del key to delete the return code.

To combine two paragraphs, position the cursor at the end of the first paragraph that you want to combine (as in Figure 2.5), and click right on Delete. The paragraph below will move up one line. If you double spaced between paragraphs by pressing Enter twice, you must click right on Delete twice.

oSEARCHING FOR AND REPLACING TEXT

Have you ever misspelled the same word several times in a letter or paper or realized that you entered the wrong information at several places? Word allows you to correct this type of error quickly and easily. You can simply have Word automatically locate any text and replace it with something else, no matter how many times it appears. On the other hand, you may just want to search through a document to see if a certain word or phrase has been used.

The text to be searched for can be any number of characters, including letters, numbers, spaces, and punctuation marks. It can be just one letter, part of a word, or several words.

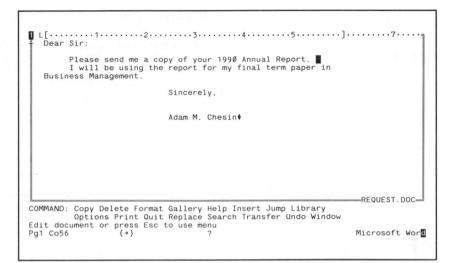

```
█ L[·········1·········2·········3·········4·········5·········]·········7·····┐
  Dear Sir:

          Please send me a copy of your 199Ø Annual Report. █
          I will be using the report for my final term paper in
  Business Management.

                              Sincerely,


                              Adam M. Chesin◆




                                                        └REQUEST.DOC┘
COMMAND: Copy Delete Format Gallery Help Insert Jump Library
         Options Print Quit Replace Search Transfer Undo Window
Edit document or press Esc to use menu
Pg1  Co56              {→}                  ?               Microsoft Word█
```

○ **Figure 2.5:** *The cursor position for combining two paragraphs*

SEARCHING FOR TEXT

Press Esc S to see the Search menu. Type the characters, and then press Enter to use the default values or select options and press Enter.

You search through a document to find specific text that may appear anywhere in that document. To search the entire document, start at either the start or end of the document, and then click on Search to see the menu

SEARCH text:
direction: Up(Down) case: Yes(No) whole word: Yes(No)

Type the characters that you want to locate. Click on SEARCH to use the default values, or select from the search options (described below), and then click on INSERT.

Word will scan the document searching for the first occurrence of the specified text. The search will start at the position of the cursor and stop at either the end (if you chose to search down) or beginning (if you chose to search up) of the document. When Word finds the characters, it will highlight them on the screen. If Word cannot find the text in the part of the document that it searched through, it will beep and the cursor remains where you started the search.

To find the next occurrence of the text, press Shift-F4.

Search Options

Word provides the following search options:

o **Direction of Search**: To search upward (from the position of the cursor to the start of the document), click on Up for the Direction option. A downward search (from the cursor position to the end of the document) is the default direction.

o **Case Matching**: To locate characters only if they match the cases (uppercase or lowercase), click on Yes for the Case option. The default option is not to match only cases. This means that if the text to search for is *Word*, for example, the search will also locate *word* and *WORD*.

o **Whole Word Matching**: To locate a word only if it is a whole word (not merely part of a longer word), click on Yes for the Whole Word option. The default option is not to match only whole words. This means that if the text to search for is *Miss*, for example, the search will locate *mission*, *Mississippi*, *emissary*, or any word with the four characters *miss*. A whole word search will only locate the word *Miss* or *miss*.

REPLACING TEXT

When you want to replace the text that you are searching for with other text, click on Replace to see the menu:

REPLACE text: **with text:**
confirm : (Yes)No case: Yes(No) whole word: Yes(No)

Type the text that you want to replace, click on the With Text option, and then type the text that you want to insert in its place. Select from the replacement options (described below) or click on REPLACE to use the default options.

Using the default options, Word will scan the document searching for the first occurrence of the specified text, from the position of the cursor to the end of the document. When the text is found, Word highlights it on the screen, and displays the message

Enter Y to replace, N to skip and continue, or Esc to cancel

Press Y to replace and continue, N to skip this occurrence, or Esc to skip and stop searching.

Click on REPLACE (or the message line) to make the change and continue searching, press N to skip this occurrence and continue searching, or click both to skip this occurrence and stop the search.

If Word can't find the text, it will beep and return the cursor to its original position.

To search the entire document, start at the beginning of the document; there is no upward option for replacing text.

Using Replace to Delete Text

You can use the Replace command to delete text by leaving the With Text option blank. For example, suppose that you write a letter referring several times to *Dr. Wilma Smith*, only to find out that she has not yet graduated from medical school. To delete the title without replacing it with something else, enter *Dr.* for the Replace Text option, but leave the With Text option blank.

Replace Options

The Case and Whole Word options in a replace operation work the same as they do in a search operation. The Confirm option is specific to replacements. The default for this option is Yes, which means that Word will stop at each occurrence of the specified text and display a message asking you to confirm the replacement.

 Press Tab N to select No for the Confirm option.

If you select No for the Confirm option by clicking on No, Word will make all the replacements without stopping for a confirmation. This is a potentially dangerous method since replacements—especially those not matching cases or whole words—can lead to unfortunate results. For example

REPLACE text: his   with text: her

will change *History* to *Hertory* and *this* to *ther*. Use continuous replacement with caution.

oUSING THE UNDO COMMAND

Press Shift-F1 or Esc U to undo.

Another editing method that Word provides is the Undo command. To cancel your last insertion or deletion, click on Undo. If you just deleted text, it will be reinserted, even if you did not place it in the scrap. If you just typed text, it will be completely removed—it will not be placed in the scrap.

Just how much typing will be undone? If you use the Undo command, all the characters that you typed since last moving the cursor will be erased.

If you undo too much, you can even undo your last undo! Don't move the cursor and click on Undo if you want your last undo restored.

oUSING THE REPEAT EDIT COMMAND

As you type or edit documents, Word stores your keystrokes in a buffer. In fact, this is the same area that saves your work for the Undo command. When you move the cursor and start editing, Word clears everything out of the buffer and starts saving your keystrokes again.

 Press F4 to replay the keystrokes in the buffer.

When you click on COMMAND, Word replays all of the keystrokes in the buffer, repeating the typing or other editing you just performed (including the last deletion or insertion).

oMANAGING WINDOWS

With Word, you can divide the screen into as many as eight text windows, both horizontally and vertically. One advantage of this is that you can work with more than one document at a time. For example, you may be typing a letter and find that you need to refer back to a letter that you typed last week. You can divide the screen into two text windows and load the existing letter right alongside the new one. Then you can switch back and forth between windows and scroll either document. You can even copy text from one letter to another.

Splitting the screen into two or more windows is particularly helpful when you are editing long documents. It can be tedious scrolling back and forth through the document to copy or move portions or to refer to some text on another page. With two windows, you can work with different parts of the same document simultaneously.

SPLITTING WINDOWS

KEY Press Esc W S and choose the direction for the split. The next menu shows the line number for the split, which depends on the cursor position. Press Enter to accept the position, type another position number, or press F1. When you press F1, the cursor moves to the selection bar. Use the up or down arrow key to reach where you want the window split, and press Enter. To create a blank window, select Yes for the Clear New Window option. If you forget to select Yes, or have a version earlier than 5.0, press Esc T C W.

To create a horizontal window holding the current document, point to the right border with the mouse pointer, at the position where you want to new window to start, and then click left. The new window will contain the same document that was already on the screen. To create a blank horizontal window, perhaps for starting a new document or recalling another from the disk, point and click right.

To create a vertical window for the current document, point to the ruler line, hold down the Alt key, and then click left. For a blank window, click right. (If the ruler line isn't displayed, point to the top border and click without holding down the Alt key.)

USING WINDOWS TO EDIT LONG DOCUMENTS

Let's work through an example to show how you can use multiple windows to work with a long document. You will create a document longer than one screen, then edit the beginning of the document, referring to several numbers near the end. Follow these steps:

1. Start Word.
2. Type the following document.

   MEMORANDUM

To:	**William Morely, Purchasing**
From:	**Sigmund Wilcox, Pharmacy**
Subject:	**Laboratory Equipment**
Date:	**October 1, 1990**

   We are preparing our program for the new year and, as usual, have a large number of items which must be ordered. Below is a list of those items which require priority handling. These items are needed no later than January 2 if we are to complete several key research projects.

   Because of the unusual rush with this order, please contact any of our regular vendors. I recommend the following because of their excellent delivery history:

   Virginia Biological Supply, Wellsprings, VA
   Morris Scientific Supply Corp., Philadelphia, PA
   Chesin Laboratory, Inc., New Hope, PA
   Supplies, Inc., New York, NY

Please contact me if you anticipate any delays.

QUANTITY	ITEM	REFERENCE NUMBER
1	Coulter Counter	5623A43
1	Centrifuge	6ACT45209-8
2	Spectrophotometer	SPTR-U6543
100	Test Tubes - #3	654f58
5	Microscope - Oil Immersion	7655
45	Beakers - 1 Lt.	82341L
45	Beakers - .5 Lt.	8235.5L
45	Counting Chambers	CBE-4a1
900	Cover Plates	09002

KEY Press Esc W S H, type **12**, and then press Enter.

KEY Press Ctrl-PgDn, and then press the up arrow to view the last several lines.

KEY Press F1 to move the cursor to the top window.

KEY Press Ctrl-PgUp, and then press the down arrow until the first paragraph is displayed.

KEY Press F1 to switch to the bottom window. Press PgUp until you see the first paragraph.

3. Point on the right border, at about line 12, and then click left. The window will divide into two typing areas, both containing the current document.

4. Point at the bottom-left corner of the bottom window, click both to reach the end of the document, and then click left on the left border to view the last several lines. (Notice that the text in the top window did not scroll.)

5. Click left anywhere in the top window (window 1) to select that window.

6. Point just under the window number, and then click both to reach the start of the document. Click right on the border until the first paragraph is displayed, as shown in Figure 2.6.

7. With the reference numbers displayed in the bottom window, add the following text to the end of the first paragraph.

    We are particularly concerned with items

8. Refer to the bottom window, and then complete the line with the reference numbers for both size beakers, the counting chambers, and the cover plates. The final line should read as follows.

    We are particularly concerned with items 82341L, 8235.5L, CBE-4a1, and 09002.

9. Click left in window 2, and then click left on the left border until you display the first paragraph. Notice that the new text inserted in window 1 also appears in window 2, as shown in Figure 2.7.

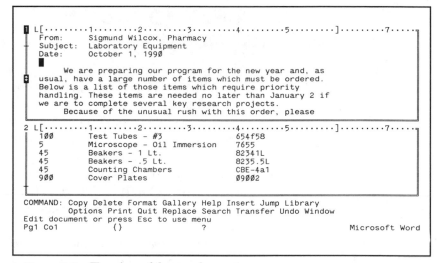

o **Figure 2.6:** *Two views of the same document*

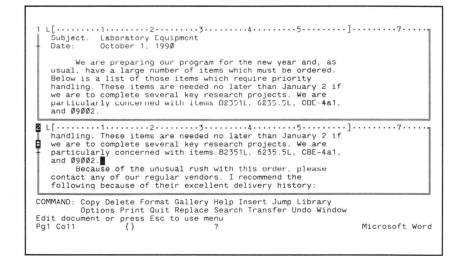

o **Figure 2.7:** *The new text appears in both windows*

KEY Press Esc W C
Enter to close the
second window. Press Esc
Q, then press N to quit
without saving.

10. Close the bottom window by pointing to its right border, and then clicking both. Click left on Quit, and then press N to exit Word without saving the document.

A FEW POINTS ON WINDOWS

When you split the screen into two or more windows, each text window is smaller, and you'll see less of your document at one time. When you split text into vertical windows, you will have to scroll right and left to see the ends of the line. When you split the text into horizontal windows, you will see fewer lines. Simply scroll up and down by clicking or using the arrow keys, as usual.

When two or more windows have different documents in them, they act as two separate Word programs. What you type in one window has no effect on the other document, unless you move or copy text between windows.

The situation changes when the same document is in all the windows. In this case, keep in mind a few important points:

o Each window scrolls independently. Scrolling one window will not scroll the text in another.

o Format changes (character, paragraph, or division) made in one window will affect the text in other windows. For example, if you make a word boldface in one window, it will become boldface in the other windows as well.

o Editing performed in one window will automatically be duplicated in the others. Words added or deleted to the text in window 2, for instance, will automatically be added or deleted in window 1.

As a rule of thumb, remember that scrolling is the only action that is not duplicated in all windows when the same document is displayed.

ZOOMING WINDOWS

 Press Ctrl-F1 to zoom the window.

 Press F1 to display the next window full size. Press Ctrl-F1 to return the windows to their original size.

If you find it difficult working with a small window area, you can quickly resize it to the full screen, or *zoom* the window display, by clicking right on its window number. The active window fills the screen, and the characters ZM appear in the status line.

When zoom is active, click left on the window number to display the next window using the full screen. This is very useful when you are working on more than one document and the smaller windows are not efficient. Click right on the window number again to return the windows to their original size, displaying all of them on the screen once more.

Zooming is a useful technique to keep prying eyes from your documents. When working with confidential material, split the screen into a second, clear, window. Click on the first window, and then click right on the window number to zoom it to full size. If someone approaches who should not see your document, click left on the window number to zoom the clear window on the screen.

oCOMBINING DOCUMENTS

Word lets you combine, or *merge*, documents that are stored separately on the disk. With this ability, you can write and store long documents in sections.

To merge documents, follow these steps:

1. Start Word.
2. Recall the document that you want to appear first. Click right on Transfer, click right of the command line title, point to the document name, and then click right.
3. Position the cursor where you want the next document to be placed.
4. Click left on Transfer Merge to display the prompt

   TRANSFER MERGE filename:

5. Type the name of the document that you wish to merge, click right of the command line title, and then click right on the document name.

If you tried this using Transfer Load instead of Transfer Merge, the first document would be cleared from the screen when the second one was recalled.

As you've seen, Word's editing commands are very powerful. When you use these commands in conjunction with the program's formatting commands, described in the next chapter, you have full control over your document.

KEY Create a second, clear, window. Press F1 to return to the first window, press Ctrl-F1 to zoom it full size and then press F1 to "hide" the window from prying eyes.

KEY Press Ctrl-F7, select the document you want to load, and then press Enter.

KEY Press Esc T M to display the prompt.

KEY Press Enter after you type the document's name.

CHAPTER 3

- FORMATTING
- YOUR
- DOCUMENTS

4.0 KEY

Editing assures that the content of a document is correct—that you're saying what you want to say. Formatting makes the document attractive and adds visual effect. It is a fact of life that the appearance of a document is frequently almost as important as its contents. So if you want someone to read what you have written, it must be appealing to the eyes as well as the mind. In fact, formatting can add impact and emphasis to what you think is important.

Since Word is a screen-oriented program, you can adjust the format on the screen until you are pleased with it. Print the document only when you are sure that its format is correct.

This chapter reviews some ways to change the appearance of your documents using Word's built-in formatting options. You will learn how to change the format of characters, paragraphs, and entire pages; how to set tab stops; and how to hyphenate at the ends of lines. Finally, you will learn some details about your options for printing text.

Most formatting can be performed quickly with speed keys. So even if you have a mouse, pay particular attention to the keyboard margin notes and sections of the chapter dealing specifically with these keys.

oCHANGING THE APPEARANCE OF CHARACTERS

In this section, you will learn how to add underlining, boldfacing, italics, small capital letters, strike through, superscripts, and subscripts to your document. You will also learn how to quickly convert lowercase letters to uppercase and change the font type and size. While Word will display all the effects on the screen, your printer may not be capable of printing them all on paper. If it cannot, the characters will be printed normally.

You can change the appearance of characters either as you type them or by selecting them afterward. In either case, they can be changed by using speed keys or the Format Character menu.

USING SPEED KEYS FOR ADDING CHARACTER STYLES

To add character styles, hold down the Alt key and press the appropriate key. The Alt-key combinations and their effects are as follows:

Alt-U	underline
Alt-D	double underline
Alt-B	**boldface**
Alt-I	*italics*
Alt-K	SMALL CAPITAL LETTERS
Alt-S	~~strike through~~
Alt- +	superscript $^{\text{letters and numbers}}$
Alt--	subscript $_{\text{letters and numbers}}$
Alt-E	hidden text—characters that you can choose to not display or print (discussed in Chapter 12)
Alt-spacebar	normal character style (cancels all other styles)
Alt-Z	cancels all styles except font type and size

Styles can be combined by pressing two or more Alt-key combinations. For example, you can add

underlined italics or

BOLDFACE SMALL CAPITAL LETTERS

To format characters as you type them, press the Alt-key combination, and then type the characters. For example, here's how to type

I subscribe to the New York Times**.**

1. Type **I subscribe to the** to begin the sentence.
2. Press Alt-U.
3. Type **New York Times**, and the words will be underlined as they appear on the screen.
4. Press Alt-spacebar to turn off the underlining.

If you want to add formatting after you have typed the characters, select the characters, and then press the appropriate key combination. The highlighted characters will change to the new style.

ADDING STYLES THROUGH THE FORMAT CHARACTER MENU

4.0 You cannot change the printed color. Also, the Position, Annotation, and Bookmark formatting options are not available.

As an alternative, you can add the same character styles by using the mouse or keyboard to access the Format Character menu from the command area. This menu also allows you to change the character type style and size, convert lowercase letters to uppercase, and change the printed color if you have a capable printer.

To use the Format Character menu, select the characters to be formatted, or type until you are ready to enter formatted characters, and then click right on Format. You will see the menu shown in Figure 3.1.

KEY Press Esc F C, or Alt-F8, to display the Format Character menu with the Font Name option selected. Use Tab or the arrow keys to reach the options desired, and then press the first letter of your choice. For the Font Name, Font Size, and Font Color options, press F1 to see alternatives, and then use the arrow keys to highlight your choice. Press Enter after making your selections.

If you click left on Format, you will see the command line

FORMAT: Character Paragraph Tab Border Footnote
Division Running-head Stylesheet
sEarch repLace revision-Marks pOsition Annotation bookmarK

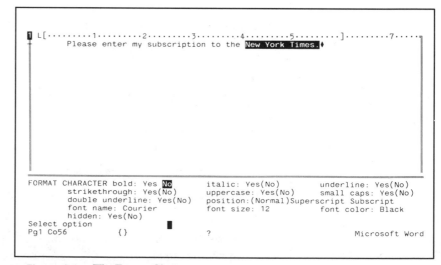

o **Figure 3.1:** *The Format Character menu*

Click on Character to display the Format Character menu.

Select from this menu as you would any other: click on your choices or, for the Font Name, Font Size, and Font Color options, click right on the option to display alternatives. For example, to change the font type and size, click right on the Font Name option. This will display a list of optional fonts, as shown in Figure 3.2. The list will vary depending on your printer. Click left on the desired font if you want to make other selections from the menu; click right on the font to select it and return to the document.

If you highlighted text, it will take on the format selected in the menu. If you are about to type, the new characters will be formatted accordingly.

CHANGING CASES

KEY Press Esc F C, select the Upper-case option, press Y, and then press Enter.

The Uppercase option on the Format Character menu lets you quickly change lowercase letters to uppercase. Select the characters, click right on Format, then click on Yes for the Uppercase option. You can return these letters to lowercase by changing the selection to No.

When you change cases by using the Uppercase option, you are inserting invisible format codes into the text. So, as with the speed-key styles, you can press Alt-spacebar to cancel the format and return the

```
Courier (modern a)              CourierLegal[H] (modern b)
Prestige[D/H/J/M] (modern c)    PrestigeLegal[G] (modern d)
LetterGothic[E/N/Q/W/X] (modern e)  LinePrinter (modern h)
HELV[B] (modern i)              OCR-A[W] (modern o)
OCR-B[X] (modern p)             TMSRMN[B] (roman a)
Danish/Norwegian[C] (foreign a) UnitedKingdom[C] (foreign b)
French[C] (foreign c)           German[C] (foreign d)
Italian[C] (foreign e)          Swedish/Finnish[C] (foreign f)
Spanish[C] (foreign g)          PiFont[J] (symbol a)
LineDraw[G/H/W/X] (symbol b)    Math7[J] (symbol c)
Math8[J] (symbol d)             Bar3of9[W] (symbol e)
EAN/UPC[X] (symbol f)

FORMAT CHARACTER bold: Yes(No)     italic: Yes(No)        underline: Yes(No)
     strikethrough: Yes(No)        uppercase: Yes(No)     small caps: Yes(No)
     double underline: Yes(No)     position:(Normal)Superscript Subscript
     font name: Courier            font size: 12          font color: Black
     hidden: Yes(No)
Enter font name or press F1 to select from list
Pg1 Co56            {}                    ?              Microsoft Word
```

o **Figure 3.2:** *Optional fonts listed on the screen*

 Ctrl-F4 is not available.

characters to their original state. But Alt-spacebar will not change the case of capital letters entered using the Shift or Caps Lock key, and you cannot make these letters lowercase through the Format Character menu.

Another way to change cases is to press the Ctrl-F4 speed-key. Select the text you wish to change, and then press Ctrl-F4 until the characters appear in the case you want.

Each time you press this speed key, the selected text will cycle between lowercase, uppercase, and initial capitals (the first letter of each word is uppercase). The cycle follows the pattern lowercase to uppercase to mixed. The first time you press Ctrl-F4, the characters will change to the next format in the cycle, then the next, and then back to their original condition (except for mixed characters). For example, if the text is all lowercase, press Ctrl-F4 to change them to uppercase, Ctrl-F4 again for initial capitals, and then Ctrl-F4 once more for all lowercase.

Ctrl-F4 changes the characters without inserting format codes, so pressing Alt-spacebar will have no effect. Also, Ctrl-F4 has no effect on characters made uppercase through the Format Character menu.

Mixed characters cannot be returned to their original state, even if you cycle all the way through. If you selected a sentence such as

We requested a meeting with Mr. Peterson.

the first time you pressed Ctrl-F4, it would cycle to all lowercase:

we requested a meeting with mr. peterson.

The second time you pressed the speed key, you would see

WE REQUESTED A MEETING WITH MR. PETERSON.

And the third time, it would be mixed:

We Requested A Meeting With Mr. Peterson.

The only way to return such characters to their exact original condition is to manually change them (edit the text).

oCHANGING THE APPEARANCE OF PARAGRAPHS

Paragraph formatting affects the placement of entire paragraphs on the screen and on the printed page. Paragraphs, like characters, can be formatted as you type them or by selecting them afterward. In either case, you can format them by using speed keys or through the Format Paragraph menu.

USING SPEED KEYS FOR PARAGRAPH FORMATTING

Word defines a paragraph as all the text between two presses of the Enter key. To format a paragraph, hold down the Alt key and press the appropriate key. The Alt-key combinations and their effects are as follows:

Alt-Q is not available.

Alt-C	centered between the margins
Alt-L	flush left
Alt-R	flush right
Alt-J	justified (even left and right margins)
Alt-F	indented first line of every paragraph
Alt-N	indent increased by ½ inch (moves the left margin in ½ inch each time that it is pressed)
Alt-M	indent decreased by ½ inch (moves the left margin out ½ inch each time that it is pressed)
Alt-Q	indent both margins by ½ inch
Alt-T	hanging indentation
Alt-1	single-spaced lines
Alt-2	double-spaced lines
Alt-O	double-spaced between paragraphs
Alt-P	normal paragraph format (cancels all other formats)

If you press the speed key while the cursor is in existing text, the paragraph will immediately adjust to the format. To format more than one paragraph, select them first (as explained in Chapter 2), and then press the speed key. To format text before you enter it, press the speed key, and then type.

For example, here's how to center text between the margins:

1. Press Alt-C.
2. Type the text to be centered.
3. Press Enter.
4. Press Alt-P to cancel the centered format.

If you already typed the title at the left margin, place the cursor anywhere in the line, and then press Alt-C.

FORMATTING THROUGH THE FORMAT PARAGRAPH MENU

You can also select paragraph formats by using the mouse or keyboard to access the Format Paragraph menu from the command area. The speed keys are faster, but the Format Paragraph menu provides more flexibility for indentation and line spacing settings.

To use the Format Paragraph command, select the text to be formatted, or type until you are ready to enter the formatted paragraphs, and then click left on Format Paragraph. The Format Paragraph menu appears, with the Alignment option highlighted, as shown in Figure 3.3.

KEY Press Esc F P, and then press the first letter of your choice to select alignment: L for left, R for right, C for centered, or J for justified. Press Tab or the arrow keys to highlight any other options that you wish to change, press Y or N, or enter a measurement. Press Enter after you've made all your changes.

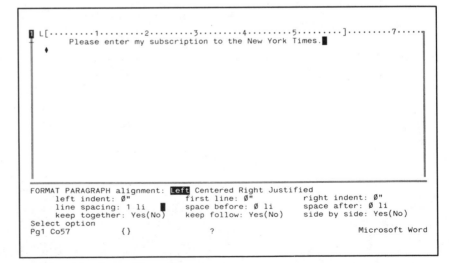

o **Figure 3.3:** *Format Paragraph menu*

Click on your choice to change the alignment, or click on any of the Yes (No) choices. Click right on the choice to select and exit the menu; click left to select and remain in the menu.

Where measurements are needed, as with the Left Indent option, click on the option with either button and type your setting in either inches (such as .25") or lines (such as 3 li). If you just type a number, Word assumes you mean inches for the indentation options, and lines for spacing. So you could enter 1.5 to indent 1½ inches or 2 for double-spacing.

Click on the command line title to accept your changes and return to the document, or click both to cancel your changes.

oSETTING TAB STOPS THROUGH THE KEYBOARD

The quickest way to set tab stops is to press Alt-F1 to display the menu

FORMAT TABS SET position:
alignment (Left)Center Right Decimal Vertical   leader char:(Blank). - _

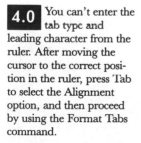

If the ruler is not on the screen, it will appear when you press Alt-F1.

Notice that there are two cursors: one on the ruler line, and another on the Position option on the menu. If you know where you want the new tab stop, type the position, the first letter of its type, then the leading character desired (a period, hyphen, underline, or B for blank). Spaces before the tab stop will be filled in with the leading character you selected. For example, press 5R. to set a right-aligned, dot-leader tab stop at 5 inches. Figure 3.4 illustrates the types of tab stops and leading characters.

Keep entering tab stops this way, and then press Enter to return to the document, or press Esc to cancel.

If you're not sure exactly where to place the tab stop, press the right or left arrow key until the cursor reaches the correct position on the ruler. Then enter the tab type and leader character.

4.0 You can't enter the tab type and leading character from the ruler. After moving the cursor to the correct position in the ruler, press Tab to select the Alignment option, and then proceed by using the Format Tabs command.

You can also display the Alt-F1 menu by pressing Esc F T (Format Tabs). This displays the command line

FORMAT TAB: Set Clear Reset-all

Press S (Set) to display the menu. To enter tabs from the ruler, first press F1. Otherwise, from the command line, type the measurement in inches

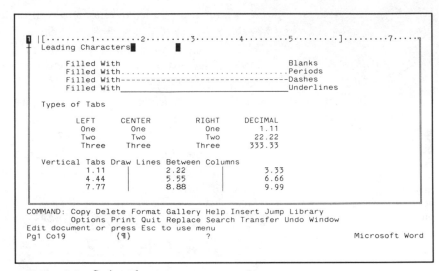

```
1 |[·········1·········2·········3·········4·········5·········]·········7·····
  Leading Characters█          █

      Filled With                                    Blanks
      Filled With................................Periods
      Filled With------------------------------Dashes
      Filled With_____Underlines

  Types of Tabs

      LEFT        CENTER        RIGHT        DECIMAL
      One         One           One          1.11
      Two         Two           Two          22.22
      Three       Three         Three        333.33

  Vertical Tabs Draw Lines Between Columns
      1.11      |       2.22      |       3.33
      4.44      |       5.55      |       6.66
      7.77      |       8.88      |       9.99


COMMAND: Copy Delete Format Gallery Help Insert Jump Library
         Options Print Quit Replace Search Transfer Undo Window
Edit document or press Esc to use menu
Pg1 Co19          {¶}                ?                    Microsoft Word
```

o **Figure 3.4:** *Setting tab stops*

for the tab stop, press Tab to highlight the Alignment option, and type the first letter of your choice. Press Tab again to select the Leading Character option and type your choice. Press Enter if you are finished setting tab stops, or press Ins to accept that tab stop and set another.

CLEARING AND MOVING TAB STOPS

There are several ways to delete tab stops through the keyboard:

o Press Esc F T C (Format Tabs Clear). Enter the measurement of the tab stop, or press F1 then the right arrow key until the measurement appears, and then press Enter.

o Press Alt-F1, then the up or down arrow key until you highlight the tab stop you want to remove, and then press Del.

o To delete all new tab stops, press Esc F T R (Format Tabs Resetall). This will not erase the default ½-inch tab stops, just any new ones that you set.

To move a tab stop, press Alt-F1, then the up or down arrow key to highlight the tab. Press Ctrl-right arrow or Ctrl-left arrow to reach the new position, and then press Enter. If you move over another existing tab, it will be deleted. So if you have other tab stops set, it may be more efficient to delete and reset the tab instead of moving it.

oSETTING TAB STOPS WITH THE MOUSE

 You must display the Format Tab Set menu first. Click left on the desired alignment and leader character, and then click left on the ruler.

If you have a mouse, you can set tab stops using the ruler without having to display the Tab Set menu. As explained in Chapter 1, the letter at the left of the ruler indicates the next type of tab to be set, and the space to its left shows the leading character.

To set a tab stop, first click on the upper-right corner of the screen if the ruler isn't displayed. Next click the alignment letter at the left end of the ruler until the tab type appears: L for left, C for centered, D for decimal, or | for vertical. Click the space to the left of the letter to select a leader character: blank, period, dash, or underline. Then point to the desired setting on the ruler and click left.

To clear a tab, click both on the letter in the ruler. To clear all tabs, click left on Format Tab Reset-All. If you want to move a tab, point to the tab, hold down either button, then drag the pointer to the new location.

oREPEATING AND COPYING FORMATS

KEY Press F4 after you select the text.

To immediately repeat your last formatting, as long as you haven't typed or edited any text in between, select the text you want to format, and then click on COMMAND.

With the mouse, you can also copy character or paragraph formats from location to location. To copy character formats, select the text you want to format, point to the already formatted text, hold down the Alt-key, and then click left. The characters you selected will be formatted just like those you are pointing to.

To copy paragraph formats, select the text you want to format, and then point to the selection bar next to the paragraph whose format you want to copy. Hold down the Alt-key and click right.

○CHANGING PAGE FORMATS

Page formats, or *divisions* in Word's terminology, affect the margins, page size, and number of columns printed on the page. You can use the Format Division menu options to quickly change any of these divisions. However, you should avoid changing division styles just to adjust the left margin. Instead, use the speed keys or Format Paragraph menu indentation options.

The general procedure for using the Format Division command is described in this section. Specific applications for different page formats are covered in detail in later chapters.

To change page formats, click left on Format Division to see the menu

FORMAT DIVISION: Margins Page-numbers Layout line-Numbers

Click on Margins to display another menu for setting the top, bottom, left, and right margins; the page length and width; the gutter width; and the running head (header and footer) position. In version 5.0, you can also choose to mirror margins or use the current division formats as the new defaults. Another way to set these options is to click left on Format; then click right on Division.

Click on Page-Numbers to set page-numbering options. Click on Line-Numbers to print line numbers down the left margin of the printed document.

By clicking on Layout, you can set the footnote position, the number and spacing of columns, and the type of division break. The division break options on the Layout menu are as follows:

- **Page**: The division break also serves as a page break. The new division format takes effect immediately. (This is the default option.)

- **Continuous**: The division break does not serve as a page break. As long as the new division does not have different margins or page size, the new settings start at that point on that page. Use this to combine single and multiple columns of text on the same page. If the margins or page size is different in the new division, the settings take effect on the next page.

- **Column**: The column starts a new page using the division settings.

KEY Press Esc F D to see the menu. Press M to set margins, P to set page numbering, L to set layout, or N to print line numbers.

4.0 Continuous breaks always take effect on the next page.

o **Odd**: Starts the new settings on the next odd-numbered page.

o **Even**: Starts the new settings on the next even-numbered page.

 KEY Press Enter to exit the menu.

After you've made your selections from the Format Division menu, click on the command line title to return to the document. Two dotted lines, called the *division mark*, will appear across the screen, as shown in Figure 3.5. All text above the division mark will have the page formats you just selected.

CHANGING PAGE FORMATS AFTER TYPING

Remember the basic document-preparation cycle: enter, edit, format, and print. Format Division menu options are designed primarily to be added to your document after the entry and editing stages. The division mark stores the format characteristics of all the text above it, up to the next division mark. So, the following is the easiest way to change the page format for a document:

1. Type and edit the entire document.

2. Make any Format Character or Format Paragraph menu changes.

3. Make all the Format Division menu changes.

```
█ L[·········1·········2······3·········4·········5·········]·········7·····┐
  Morris Scientific Supply Corp., Philadelphia, PA
  Chesin Laboratory, Inc., New Hope, PA
  Supplies, Inc., New York, NY

        Please contact me if you anticipate any delays.
  :::::::::::::::::::::::::::::::::::::::::::::::::::::::::::::::::::::::::::::::
  █

  QUANTITY          ITEM              REFERENCE NUMBER

  1               Coulter Counter         5623A43
  1               Centrifuge              6ACT45209-8
  2               Spectrophotometer       SPTR-U6543
  100             Test Tubes - #3         654f58
  5               Microscope - Oil Immersion  7655
  45              Beakers - 1 Lt.         82341L
  45              Beakers - .5 Lt.        8235.5L
  45              Counting Chambers       CBE-4a1
  900             Cover Plates            09002

  COMMAND: Copy Delete Format Gallery Help Insert Jump Library
          Options Print Quit Replace Search Transfer Undo Window
  Edit document or press Esc to use menu
  P2 D2 C1              {}                ?                Microsoft Word
```

o **Figure 3.5:** *Dotted lines mark the division*

If you want to use differently formatted divisions in a document, move the cursor to each division-break location and press Ctrl-Enter. See the next section for details.

The cursor does not have to be at the end of the document when you change Format Division settings. Wherever it is located, a division mark will be added to the end of your document. The text above the division mark will print according to the format that you just created.

CHANGING PAGE FORMATS BEFORE TYPING

You can also make division changes before typing the document. In this case, use the following procedure:

4.0 The cursor is under the division line. Press the up arrow to select the division line.

1. Change the Format Division menu settings as desired.

2. Exit the menu, and the division line will appear and be highlighted on the screen.

3. Type your document. The division mark will move down as you enter text. All text above the division line will be formatted according to your division changes.

MULTIPLE DIVISIONS IN ONE DOCUMENT

Let's say that you just typed three pages using the default division formats. You want the fourth page, however, printed on 14-inch paper with 2-inch left and right margins.

Here's what you should do:

KEY With the cursor anywhere in the document, press Esc F D, and then press Enter twice. Press Ctrl-PgDn, type the fourth page after the division mark, and press Esc F D M. Press Tab twice to reach the Left option and type **2**. Press Tab to reach the Right option and type **2**. Press Tab to reach the Page Length option and type **14**, and then press Enter.

1. Place the cursor at the end of the last page, and then press Ctrl-Enter to insert a division line. Since you did not change any of the options, the first three pages will print with all the default settings, and a new page will begin after the division line. As an alternative, with the cursor anywhere in the document, click left on Format, click right on Division, and then click on the command line title. The division mark will appear after the last page.

2. Place the cursor after the division mark, and then type the fourth page.

3. Click left on Format, and then click right on Division.

4. Click on the Left option and type **2"**.

5. Click on the Right option and type **2"**.

6. Click on the Page Length option and type **14"**.

7. Click on the command line title.

All the text between the two division marks will be adjusted to print on 14-inch paper with 2-inch margins.

oSEARCHING FOR AND REPLACING STYLES

One of Word's greatest assets is its ability to format characters, paragraphs, and pages in a wide variety of styles. Wouldn't it be useful if you could quickly change all underlined characters to italic, or automatically change all 12-point Times Roman characters to 16-point, no matter where they appear in the document? Well, you can do this by searching for styles rather than text. You can also move directly to centered titles, indented quotations, or formulas with subscripts or superscripts. These tasks can be performed from the Format menu.

SEARCHING FOR FORMATS

KEY Press Esc F E to display the command line. Select the type of format, choose from the next menu, and press Enter when you are finished making selections.

Click left on Format Search to display the command line

FORMAT SEARCH: Character Paragraph Style

Select the type of format that you want to locate. After you make this selection, another menu appears listing the possible formats, with a choice for either a forward (down) or backward (up) search. The menu for a character search resembles the Format Character menu. The menu for a paragraph search resembles the Format Paragraph menu. Select the types of formats you wish to search for, and click on the command line title.

The Style option refers to one of your own gallery format styles identified by a key code combination, as described in Chapter 4. If you are searching for a style, enter the key code that identifies the style, and then click on the command line title.

KEY Press Esc F E P,
select Centered
for the Alignment option,
and press Enter.

For example, to locate a centered title, click left on Format Search Paragraph, and then click right on Centered. The cursor will move to the first instance of the selected format. Press Shift-F4 to find the next occurrence.

REPLACING FORMATS

The Format Replace option allows you to locate a specific occurrence of a format and replace it with something else. You can replace one character style with another or return text to the default format.

Begin by clicking left on Format Replace to display

KEY Press Esc F L to
display the menu.
Make your selections and
press Enter. Next select
the replacement format,
and then press Enter.

FORMAT REPLACE: Character Paragraph Style

Select the type of format to replace from this menu. Select either a confirmed or automatic replacement, the specific style, and then click on the command line title. From the next menu that appears, select the type of format you want as the replacement, and then click on the command line title.

To remove a style, select all the default options on the Replace menu.

For example, suppose that you wrote a document, and then printed it using a dot-matrix printer. Because of the limitations of the printer, you simply double-underlined all the subtitles. But now you have purchased a laser printer with built-in fonts, and you would like to change all the double-underlined titles to 16-point Times Roman.

KEY Press Esc F L C,
select Yes for the
Double Underline option,
and press Enter to display
the Replace with Character Format menu. Set
Double Underline to No,
enter **TMSRMN** as the
font name, enter **16** as
the font size, and then
press Enter.

To change the style, click left on the Character option on the Format Replace menu, and then click right on Yes for the Double Underline option. When the Replace with Character Format menu appears, click left on No for the Double Underline option. Click right on the Font Name option, and then click left on TMSRMN. Click right on the Font Size option, and then click right on 16.

As with text replacement, if you selected to confirm format replacement, Word will locate the first occurrence and prompt you. Click either button, and the characters will be formatted as you requested.

KEY Press Y to
confirm the
replacement.

Note that you have to be very explicit about the replacement format. Not selecting Yes for a format will not remove that format if it exists. To delete a format, even if you are selecting a new style, you must select No.

oHYPHENATING WORDS

Word wrap (or auto-carrier return) lets you type without pressing Enter at the end of each line. But at times, such as when long words are carried to the next line, a paragraph can have an extremely uneven right margin. This is especially apparent with short columns:

> **Word wrap**
> **automatically**
> **returns the carrier**
> **return to the left**
> **when the right**
> **margin is reached.**

The situation is worse when columns are justified:

> **Word   wrap**
> **automatically returns**
> **the carrier return to the**
> **left   when   the   right**
> **margin   is   reached.**

The large, unsightly gaps between words or an uneven margin can be corrected by hyphenation.

> **Word wrap automati-**
> **cally returns the carrier**
> **return to the left when**
> **the   right margin is**
> **reached.**

Although you can hyphenate manually, another option is to use the Library command to have Word hyphenate for you. Word will hyphenate long words that would normally be carried down to the next line, creating a more even paragraph.

To hyphenate the entire document, place the cursor at the start of your text. To hyphenate specific text, select it. Otherwise, Word will hyphenate from the cursor location to the end of the document.

Next, click left on Library Hyphenate to display the prompt line

LIBRARY HYPHENATE confirm: Yes No   hyphenate caps: (Yes)No

The Confirm option determines if you want Word to let you verify the position of the hyphen or proceed automatically.

KEY Press Esc L H to display the prompt line. Press Enter after you make your selections. Insert the hyphenation disk in drive B if necessary, and then press Enter.

The Hyphenate Caps option determines if Word will hyphenate words with capital letters, such as proper names that are generally not divided between sentences.

4.0 Hyphenate Caps is not available.

Make your selections from the menu and then click on the command line title. With a floppy disk system, you'll see the message

Insert disk with Hyphenation file HYPH.DAT. Press Y when ready

Insert the hyphenation disk in drive B, and then click on the message line.

If you choose No for Confirm, Word will hyphenate the text without stopping. If you choose Yes, each suggested hyphenation point will be highlighted, and the command line will read

Enter Y to insert hyphen, N to skip, or use directional keys

KEY Press Y to insert a hyphen and continue or N to skip the word and continue. To change the hyphenation point, use the arrow keys, and then press Y. Press Esc to cancel.

Click on the message line to insert the hyphen and continue to the next word, press N to skip that word and continue to the next word, or use the arrow keys to change the hyphenation point, and then click on the message line. You can also click both on the message line to cancel the hyphenation process.

When Word has worked its way through the selected area, the message

XX Words Hyphenated

will appear on the screen. This lets you know how many words (*XX*) were hyphenated.

○PREVIEWING DOCUMENTS

KEY Press Ctrl-F9 or Esc P V to see the preview.

If your computer is equipped with a graphics adapter and monitor, click left on Print Preview to display a detailed facsimile of how your document will look when printed. (The resolution of the displayed image will depend on your computer system.) This feature is similar to the display of Microsoft Pageview, an optional program that can be added to earlier versions of Word.

4.0 Print Preview is not available.

While you may not be able to read the text, it will appear formatted exactly as it will when printed, even showing underlines, italic, and

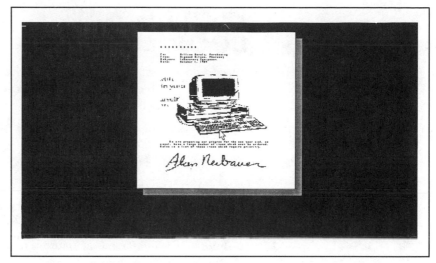

o **Figure 3.6:** *Graphics document in the preview mode*

other character formats. You'll also see graphic files linked with the Library Link Graphics command (discussed in Chapter 20). Figure 3.6 shows how a complex document may appear in preview mode. This document includes text, a graphic figure created with a drawing program, and a scanned signature.

The command line at the bottom of the screen lists the options available in preview mode:

- o **Exit**: Returns to the document.
- o **Jump**: Lets you preview another page or move directly to a bookmark (a location marked elsewhere in the document).
- o **Options**: Controls the number of pages displayed on the screen. You can display a single page, two pages (the current page will be on the left of the screen, the one following on the right) or facing pages (odd numbered page on the right, even on the left).
- o **Print**: Lets you print the current document and select from the printing options.

With a multipage document, press PgUp and PgDn to move from page to page. When you exit preview mode, the page displayed on the left side of the screen will be in the text window.

oPRINTING YOUR DOCUMENTS

To print a document using all the default settings, click right on Print. But let's take a look at some of the printing options that Word offers.

When you click left on Print, you will see the Print command line:

PRINT: Printer Direct File Glossary Merge Options Queue Repaginate preView

These options have the following effects:

o **Printer**: The document will begin printing.

o **Direct**: Every character typed will be sent directly to the printer, rather than added to your document—the "typewriter" mode.

o **File**: Word will request the name of a disk file to which the "printed" copy of the document will be sent. The document will not be printed on paper but saved on the disk, complete with all the codes needed to control your printer. Use this option if you later want to print the document by using the DOS Print command. Because of the codes, it is not practical to retrieve the file into Word. Word, by the way, does not add its own extensions to these files.

o **Glossary**: Prints a directory of the name and text in the glossary. This is explained in detail in Chapter 13.

o **Merge**: Produces form letters and other documents.

o **Options**: A new menu will be displayed:

PRINT OPTIONS printer:	**setup: LPT1:**
model:	**graphics resolution:**
copies: 1	**draft: Yes(No)**
hidden text: Yes(No)	**summary sheet: Yes(No)**
range: (All) Selection Pages	**page numbers:**
widow/orphan control: (Yes)No	**queued: Yes(No)**
Paper feed:	**duplex: Yes(No)**

Printer is the name of your printer.

Setup indicates the printer port being used: parallel ports LPT1, LPT2, or LPT3, or serial ports COM1 or COM2.

Model is the model name or number of your printer.

Graphics Resolution selects the dot-per-inch resolution of graphic images. The higher the resolution, the sharper the image. But beware, some laser printers may not have enough memory to print a whole page of text and graphics at high resolution.

Copies determines the number of copies to be printed.

Draft prints characters without special formats.

Hidden Text indicates whether text designated as hidden (not normally displayed on the screen) will be printed or not.

Summary Sheet determines whether you want to print the summary sheet with the document.

Range indicates if you want to print the entire document, specific pages (enter them in the page numbers option), or just selected text.

Page Numbers indicates the page numbers to print if Pages was chosen in Range.

Widow/Orphan Control, if active, prevents widows (the first line of a paragraph appearing by itself at the bottom of the page) and orphans (the last line of a paragraph appearing by itself on the top of a page).

Queued prints the document while you edit or create another (if you select Yes).

KEY Select Paper Feed and press F1 to see alternatives. With version 4.0, select the Feed option; then press the spacebar to highlight your selection.

Paper Feed indicates the source of paper. Click right on the option to display possible alternatives, which will vary depending on your printer. Click on **Manual** for individual sheets; **Continuous** for continuous, perforated pages; **Bin1** for the top drawer of a multidrawer printer; **Bin2** for the second drawer of a multidrawer printer; **Bin3** for the third drawer of multidrawer printer; **Mixed** for the first sheet from one drawer and the remainder from the second drawer of a multidrawer printer; or **Envelope** for an optional envelope feeder.

4.0 Click on Manual, Continuous, Bin1, Bin2, Bin3, or Mixed.

Duplex prints text on both sides of the page (if your printer is capable).

○ **Queue**: Documents in the print queue will be manipulated.

○ **Repaginate**: The document will be divided into pages.

○ **Preview**: Displays a graphic representation of the printed document.

This completes our review of basic Word techniques. You know how Word operates, and how to enter, edit, format, and print documents. Now you're ready to learn how to harness Word's powers for practical and advanced applications.

PART TWO

GENERAL APPLICATIONS

You should now be familiar with the basic way that Word works. One of the outstanding features of Word is its simplicity. You can start using it with very little training or reading. But the software has many powerful features that make word processing every kind of document, even long and complex ones, more efficient.

The following chapters detail specific applications, presented in easy-to-follow, step-by-step instructions. Each chapter explains how Word's advanced functions can be used to prepare every-day correspondence and typical business and academic documents.

CHAPTER 4

- CUSTOMIZING
  - WORD
    - FOR
  - YOUR
- OFFICE

4.0

KEY

If you prefer the default settings provided by Microsoft, just start Word and begin typing. You can always change these settings temporarily for a specific document by using the Format commands or speed keys.

But you just can't please everybody. Some people prefer 65 characters on each line instead of 60, always use 8- by 14-inch legal paper, or want every document to include page numbering. Still others want justified text, which is aligned on both the left and right margins (like newspaper columns).

Rather than go through the trouble of setting the same format every time you start Word, you can change the default values to suit your own tastes. You can also create custom styles to use for particular projects. This chapter describes how to change the default settings and how to create and load custom styles.

oMODIFYING THE NORMAL STYLESHEET

A *stylesheet* is a special file containing formatting information. When you begin a session, Word automatically uses the Normal stylesheet, which contains all the default settings. When you change the Normal stylesheet, you change the default values Word uses automatically.

The modified Normal stylesheet controls the format of every document that does not have its own custom stylesheet attached. Even existing documents that were formatted by the original Normal stylesheet will take on the new characteristics of the modified stylesheet.

There are several ways to change the Normal stylesheet:

- o Using the Use as Default option on the Format Division Margins menu
- o Through the Gallery
- o Recording styles by example

SAVING DIVISION FORMATS AS THE DEFAULTS

You can quickly save your division margin settings as the new default values. First, set your margins through the Format Division Margins menu. Then on the same menu, select Yes for the Use as Default option. As long as you don't use the Transfer Clear All command (or manually change the division), these settings will be recorded on your disk and used for every document you type.

KEY Press Esc F D M to adjust the division. Press Esc T C A to return to the original Word defaults.

If you want to use other settings for a particular document, click left on Format, right on Division, and then adjust the division as desired. But unless you want these new settings as the default, select No for the Use as Default option. To return to the original Word default settings, click left on Transfer Clear All.

Unfortunately, you can only use this method to change division margin defaults. For other settings, you make changes through the Gallery.

USING THE GALLERY TO CHANGE DEFAULTS

You enter Word's Gallery to view and alter the settings of the current stylesheet. If you want to change the default font type or size, line spacing, or indentation of your documents, you need to modify the standard paragraph format on the Normal stylesheet. If you want to change the side margins, set up columns, or number the pages, you need to adjust the standard division format.

CHANGING THE DEFAULT FONT AND SIZE

Even though Word takes full advantage of your printer's features, it assumes you want to use the default font, or typestyle. If your printer has a NLQ (near-letter quality) mode or can accept downloaded fonts, you may want to change to another font.

NLQ is not the same as boldface (Alt-B). With boldface printing, each character is printed twice, but the spaces between dots are not filled in.

In NLQ mode, for example, dot-matrix printers add extra dots to the image, making it darker and more defined, closer to the output of a letter-quality printer. Figure 4.1 shows the same line of text printed in single-strike and NLQ.

With laser printers, you can use downloadable fonts (also called *softfonts*) to print in a variety of styles and sizes. The fonts are stored on your disk and transferred to the printer's memory when needed. Figure 4.2 illustrates some common softfont typestyles and sizes. Softfonts are discussed in Chapter 20.

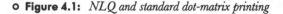

```
NLQ dot-matrix printing

Standard dot-matrix printing
```

o **Figure 4.1:** *NLQ and standard dot-matrix printing*

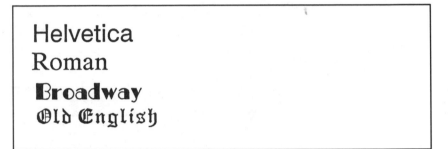

Helvetica
Roman
Broadway
𝔒𝔩𝔡 𝔈𝔫𝔤𝔩𝔦𝔰𝔥

o **Figure 4.2:** *Downloadable font styles*

If you have not yet run the Setup program to tell Word what printer you have, quit Word, Insert the Word utilities disk in drive A, type **Setup**, and designate the printers that you will be using. After Setup copies the appropriate files, you'll be able to choose a printer from within Word.

KEY Press Esc G, and then press I. Press Tab to reach the Usage option and press P for Paragraph. Press Tab to reach the Variant option, and then press F1 to see alternatives. Standard is already highlighted, so press Enter.

To change the Normal stylesheet to use NLQ or a softfont as the default, you enter the Gallery and change the standard paragraph font. If your printer doesn't have NLQ mode, you can switch to double-strike, as explained below.

Follow these steps:

1. Start Word.

2. Click on Gallery to display the Gallery menu, as shown in Figure 4.3. Notice that NORMAL.STY appears on the bottom right of the screen. The Gallery window is blank because only the built-in functions (obtained by pressing the speed keys) and default formats are now active—you haven't yet added your own.

3. Click left on Insert to display the Insert menu, as shown in Figure 4.4. To designate a style as the default, you leave the Keycode option blank. This tells Word to make the style available without any special Alt-key command. We'll go directly to the Usage option.

4. Click left on Paragraph. Printer fonts are controlled by paragraph formats.

5. Click right on the Variant option to display alternatives. The variant Standard is already selected on the top of the screen.

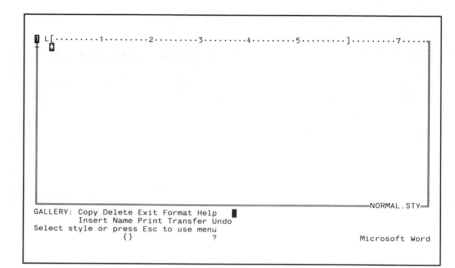

o **Figure 4.3:** *The Gallery window*

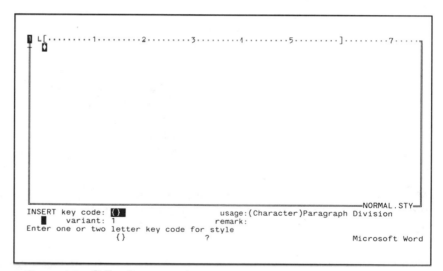

o **Figure 4.4:** *Gallery Insert menu*

6. Click on the command line title, or click right on Standard at the top of the screen.

The Gallery window will reappear, and the default standard paragraph style will be displayed. Depending on your printer, it should look something like:

1   Paragraph Standard
Pica (modern a) 12. Flush left.

KEY Press F C to
display the menu.
Press the down arrow
three times to reach the
Font option, and then
press F1.

7. You are now ready to set the default font. Click right on Format to display the Format Character menu.

8. Click right on the Font option to list possible fonts. This list will vary depending upon your printer. Figures 4.5 and 4.6 show two typical font lists.

```
Pica (modern a)                       PicaD (modern b)
Elite (modern c)                      EliteD (modern d)
NLQ (modern e)                        PS (roman b)




FORMAT CHARACTER bold: Yes(No)     italic: Yes(No)        underline: Yes(No)
         strikethrough: Yes(No)    uppercase: Yes(No)     small caps: Yes(No)
         double underline: Yes(No) position:(Normal)Superscript Subscript
         font name: Pica          font size: 12          font color: Black
         hidden: Yes(No)
Enter font name or press F1 to select from list
              {}                        ?                 Microsoft Word
```

o **Figure 4.5:** *Fonts available on common dot-matrix printers*

KEY Use the arrow
keys to select the
font and press Enter.
Press T S, and then press
Enter. Press E, and then
press Esc Q.

9. If you have a dot-matrix printer, look for the NLQ font. If your printer doesn't have that mode, it should list one called PicaD. The PicaD font is usually double-strike—each character is printed twice, the second time at a slight offset. The offset makes the character appear darker and crisper than standard print, but not as sharp as NLQ.

10. Click right on the font of your choice. The standard paragraph format in the Gallery will now show the new font default.

1 Paragraph Standard
NLQ (modern a) 12. Flush left.

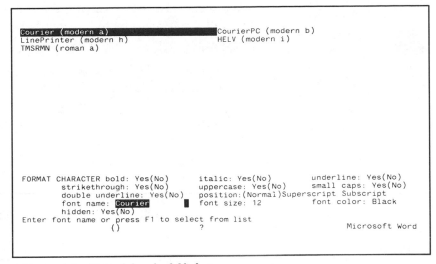

o **Figure 4.6:** *Typical downloadable fonts*

11. Click left on Transfer; then click right on Save. The adjusted Normal stylesheet is now saved on your disk under the name NORMAL.STY. Your printer will use this font with every document that doesn't have a custom stylesheet attached.

12. Click on Exit to leave the Gallery.

13. Click on Quit to quit Word.

Using the same basic procedure, you can change the default setting to any of your printer's fonts or font sizes. Click left on the font name, instead of right, then click right on the Font Size option. A list of sizes for that font will appear. Point to the size you want, and then click right.

KEY Highlight the fonts with the arrow keys, and then press Tab to highlight the Font Size option on the menu. Press F1 to display alternative sizes. Select the size and press Enter.

CHANGING THE PAGE-SIZE DEFAULT

You also can change the page-size defaults by modifying the settings on the Normal stylesheet.

As an example, let's change the Normal stylesheet to the default values found in some other word-processing programs: a 65-character line with 1-inch right and left margins, page numbers centered at the bottom of the page, and text justified at both margins.

You justify text by modifying the standard paragraph. The other defaults are controlled by the standard division. Follow these steps:

 Press Esc G to enter the Gallery. Press F P, press the space-bar three times to highlight Justify and then press Enter.

1. Start Word.

2. Click on Gallery. You should see the Gallery window with the modified standard paragraph displayed. If the window is blank, your document is currently using all the default settings chosen by Microsoft—you didn't save the stylesheet after changing the font. In this case, follow steps 3 to 6 in the previous section before you continue.

3. Click left on Format Paragraph to display the Format Paragraph menu, and then click right on Justified. The standard paragraph in the Gallery will show the new default alignment.

 Press I, and then Tab D. Press Tab to reach the Variant option, press F1 to display alternatives (Standard is already selected), and then press Enter.

4. Create a new standard division.

   a. Click left on Insert to display the Insert menu.

   b. Click left on Division.

   c. Click right on the Variant option to see a list of possible division variants. Standard will be highlighted.

   d. Click on the command line title, or click right on Standard at the top of the screen. The Gallery reappears, and the default standard division style is displayed in the window, as shown in Figure 4.7.

5. Now let's add page numbers centered at the bottom of each page.

 Press F P to see the Format Page-Numbers menu. Press Y to highlight the Yes option. Press Tab to reach the From Top option and type **10.5**. Press Tab to reach the From Left option, type **4.25**, and press Enter. (Press Esc to cancel the changes.)

   a. Click left on Format Page-Numbers to display

   **FORMAT DIVISION PAGE-NUMBERS: Yes(No) from top: 0.5"
   from left: 7.25"
   numbering:(Continuous)Start   at: number format:(1)I i A a**

   By default, page numbers, when turned on, will print in the top-right corner of the page, $1/2$ inch from the top, $7^1/4$ inches from the left.

   b. Click left on Yes to turn on page numbering.

   c. Click on the From Top option and type **10.5**.

   d. Click on the From Left option and type **4.25**.

e. Click on the command line title. (Remember, you can click both to cancel the changes.) The new default page numbering will be reflected in the standard division definition shown in the Gallery window.

6. Finally, let's change the left and right margins.

 Press F M to select Format Margins. Press the down arrow to reach the Left Margin option and type **1**. Press the right arrow to highlight the Right option and type **1**. Press Enter to confirm the changes (or Esc to cancel them).

a. Click right on Format to display the Format Margins menu.

b. Click on the Left option and type **1**.

c. Click on the Right option and type **1**.

d. Click on the command line title. The Gallery now displays your adjusted standard paragraph and division formats, as shown in Figure 4.8.

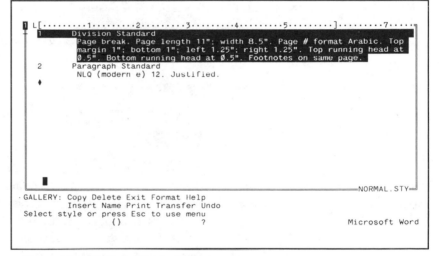

o **Figure 4.7:** *Standard division style*

 Press T S Enter to save the stylesheet. Press E to exit the Gallery, and then press Esc Q to quit.

7. Click left on Transfer; then click right on Save. The adjusted Normal stylesheet will be saved.

8. Click on Exit to leave the Gallery.

9. Click on Quit to quit Word.

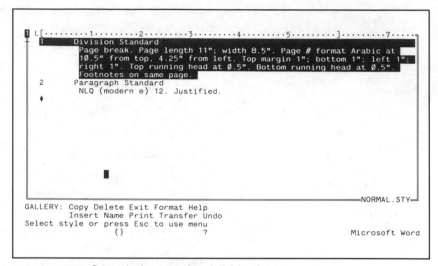

o **Figure 4.8:** *Customized paragraph and division formats*

RETURNING TO THE DEFAULT NORMAL STYLESHEET

In the exercise above, we changed the Normal stylesheet used with every document. If you find that you prefer the original default styles after you've made changes, you can erase the NORMAL.STY file that's now on your disk. All the default styles will be available when you start Word, even though this file was deleted.

You can also use the Gallery command to delete some or all of the new styles. Just remember to save the adjusted stylesheet before leaving Word.

Here's how to use the Gallery command:

1. Start Word.

2. Click on Gallery. One of the new styles is highlighted on the screen.

3. Click on Delete. The style will be deleted, and the next style will move up and become highlighted.

4. Continue clicking on Delete until all your custom styles have been removed from the Gallery.

KEY Press Esc G to enter the Gallery; then press D until all the styles have been erased. Press T S to save the Normal stylesheet in its original form. Press E, and then press Esc Q.

5. Click left on Transfer; then click right on Save. The Normal stylesheet will be saved in its original form.

6. Click on Exit.

7. Click on Quit.

RECORDING STYLES BY EXAMPLE

As you already know, there are three ways to format text: using speed keys (such as Alt-N), through the Format menu, and by changing or creating styles in stylesheets. While the speed keys and Format menus are faster, stylesheets provide much more flexibility.

But you can take advantage of the best points of both methods by recording styles by example. Here's how to use this technique:

1. Format a character, paragraph, or division the way you want it to appear. You can use any of the speed keys or Format menus.

2. Place the cursor on the characters, paragraph, or in the division whose style you want to add to a stylesheet.

3. Click left on Format Stylesheet to see the command line

   FORMAT STYLESHEET: Attach Character Paragraph Division Record

4. Click on Record. The Format Style Record menu appears:

   FORMAT STYLESHEET RECORD key code: usage:
   Character Paragraph Division
   variant: remark:

Notice that the menu looks exactly like the Gallery Insert menu that you used earlier in this chapter.

5. To record a new standard style, click on either Paragraph or Division for the Usage option.

6. Click right on the Variant option.

7. Click on the command line title, or click right on Standard at the top of the screen.

KEY Press Esc F S R to record the style. Press Tab to reach the Usage option, and then press either C, P, or D for the type of format you want to record. Press Tab to reach the Variant option, press F1, and press Enter to accept the Standard variant.

You cannot record a new standard character style this way. To set a new default character style, enter the Gallery and use the Format Character command on the standard paragraph.

The style is now part of the Gallery, and you didn't have to enter the Gallery and manually select the formatting option. If you display the Gallery window now, you'll see that the format has already been inserted.

But just like any other stylesheet, you still have to save it to the disk by using Transfer Save from the Gallery before leaving Word.

○CREATING CUSTOM STYLESHEETS

While most of us use one format (or style) for a majority of our typing, occasionally we need other formats for special projects. A law office, for example, may switch back and forth between printing on standard (8- by 11-inch) and legal (8- by 14-inch) paper. Through custom stylesheets, you can make these changes in just a few keystrokes.

In fact, you can create a whole series of custom stylesheets, each having its own default values. Then you just *attach* the stylesheet to the document when needed—the new defaults will be in effect immediately.

So the same law office, for instance, could set up several stylesheets—one for printing two-column leases, another for printing legal documents with wide margins, and a third for producing financial reports.

CREATING A STYLESHEET FOR LEGAL-SIZE PAPER

As an example, let's create a custom stylesheet for printing documents on legal-size paper. First, you'll use the Format Stylesheet command to attach a new stylesheet to a document. Then, you'll enter the Gallery and insert a new standard division format. But instead of saving these changes as the Normal stylesheet, you'll create a custom stylesheet called Legal.

Follow these steps:

1. Start Word.

2. Click left on Format; then click right on Stylesheet to display

    FORMAT STYLESHEET ATTACH: C:\WORD\NORMAL.STY

3. Type **Legal**, the name for the new stylesheet. LEGAL replaces NORMAL.STY on the screen.

KEY Press Esc F S A to
display the
prompt. Type **Legal**, and
then press Enter. Press Y
to create the stylesheet;
then press Esc G to enter
the Gallery. Press I, press
Tab D, and then press Tab
to highlight the Variant
option. Type **Standard**, or
press F1 to display a list of
division variants. Press
Enter to select Standard
division. Press F to display
the Format Division menu.
Press M for Margins.
Press Tab four times to
reach the Page Length
option, type **14**, and press
Enter to confirm the
changes. Press T S Enter
to save the stylesheet, E to
exit, and Esc Q to quit.

4. Click on the command line title. Since there is no stylesheet with that name, you'll see the prompt

File does not exist. Enter Y to create or Esc to cancel

5. Click on the message line.
6. Click on Gallery.
7. Click left on Insert. The Insert menu appears.
8. Click left on Division for the Usage option.
9. Click right on the Variant option to display alternatives, and then click on the command line title to accept Standard.
10. Click right on Format to display the Format Division Margins menu.
11. Click on the Page Length option and type **14**.
12. Click on the command line title to accept the changes and return to the document.
13. Click left on Transfer, then right on Save to save the stylesheet.
14. Click on Exit.
15. Click on Quit.

USING CUSTOM STYLESHEETS

If you type and save a document immediately after creating a custom stylesheet, that text will be in that custom format. But other new documents will still be formatted by the Normal stylesheet. To use the Legal (or any other) custom stylesheet with a new file, you must attach it by using the Format Style Sheet command. Here's how to attach custom stylesheets:

KEY Press Esc F S A,
type **Legal**, and
press Enter. Press F1 to
display a list of stylesheet
names to select from.

1. Start Word.
2. Click left on Format; then click right on Stylesheet.
3. Type **Legal** (or the name of another stylesheet). If you don't remember the name, click right to the right of the command line title and click right on the stylesheet name at the top of the screen.
4. Click on the command line title. The custom stylesheet will be recalled from the disk, and its format will be applied to the document.

KEY Press Esc F S A, and then press Del Enter Y.

To return that document to the format of the Normal stylesheet:

1. Click left on Format; then click right on Stylesheet.
2. Press Del to erase the stylesheet name from the screen.
3. Click on the command line title. If you've made any changes to the stylesheet, you'll see the prompt

   Enter Y to save changes to old style sheet, N to lose them, or Esc to cancel

4. Click on the message line to save the stylesheet before removing it from the Gallery.

oSAVING OTHER DEFAULTS

Stylesheets only store default or custom formats. Other Word settings, such as displaying the ruler line or turning on Autosave, as well as any other changes you make to the Options menu, are in a file call MW.INI.

Take some time to look over the Options menu to see if you would like to customize other Word features. For example, Figure 4.9 shows the Word screen without the ruler, border, or menus in high-resolution mode, displaying 43 lines—almost a whole page in one screen.

```
  ¯
  M E M O R A N D U M
  ■
  To:        William Morely, Purchasing
  From:      Sigmund Wilcox, Pharmacy
  Subject:   Laboratory Equipment
  Date:      October 1, 1990
       We are preparing our program for the new year and, as
  usual, have a large number of items which must be ordered.
  Below is a list of those items which require priority
  handling. These items are needed no later than January 2 if
  we are to complete several key research projects. We are
  particularly concerned with items 82351L, 6235.5L, CBE-4a1,
  and 09002.
       Because of the unusual rush with this order, please
  contact any of our regular vendors. I recommend the
  following because of their excellent delivery history:

  Virginia Biological Supply, Wellsprings, VA
  Morris Scientific Supply Corp., Philadelphia, PA
  Chesin Laboratory, Inc. New Hope, PA▸
  Supplies, Inc., New York, NY

       Please contact me if you anticipate any delays.

  QUANTITY         ITEM                    REFERENCE NUMBER
  1            Coulter Counter             5623A43
  1            Centrifuge                  6ACT4509-8
  2            Spectrophotometer           SPTR-U6543
  100          Test Tubes - #3             654f58
  5            Microscope - Oil Immersion  7655
  45           Beakers - 1 Lt.             82341L
  45           Beakers - .5 Lt.            8235.5L
  45           Counting Chambers           CBE-4a1
  900          Cover Plates                09002
  ◆
  Pg1 Co1              {}            ?                      Microsoft Word
```

o **Figure 4.9:** *EGA screen customized to display the maximum number of lines*

4.0 You cannot
change the
default path.

In addition, you can change the default path where Word will store and retrieve files. Select Transfer Options to see the menu

TRANSFER OPTIONS setup: c:\WORD5
save between sessions: Yes(No)

Your own default path will be listed for the Setup option. Enter the new directory path here, and then select Yes. This is particularly useful if you're storing your documents on a subdirectory on a hard disk. Whenever you recall or save a document, Word will automatically use the path you specified.

Using the techniques described in this chapter, you can change Word's default settings to your own specifications. Next, you will learn how to use the program's features to quickly create form documents.

CHAPTER 5

- ○ **CREATING**
- ○ **SIMPLE**
- ○ **FORM**
- ○ **DOCUMENTS**
- ○ **AND**
- ○ **ENVELOPES**

4.0

KEY

Mr. Wilson, YOU can win $50 billion by just . . .
Form Letters—Junk Mail—Mass Mailings
Over the years, form letters have earned a bad reputation. They were pretty obvious in the old days. Some advertisement or letter was mass-produced, and then your name was just inserted (often in a different typeface) in a few places.

Businesses had the same problem. When a corporate office needed to send letters to every member of the board of directors, for example, there were two choices: They could duplicate the basic letter, then type in just the names and addresses, or a secretary could spend the day typing individual copies.

Word processing, and programs like Word, have changed all that. Form documents, whether letters, legal contracts, or any other type of communication, can be produced quickly, with each copy looking like it was individually typed.

Form documents consist of two parts: shell text and variable information. *Shell text* is the part of the document that does not change. *Variable information,* on the other hand, must be personalized with each printing. This might be a name and address, an amount due, or a quantity ordered. With modern word processing, after the shell text is created, only the variable information is typed for each letter.

oUSING TEMPLATES FOR FORM DOCUMENTS

Most people only think of using form documents when they must produce a large volume of letters. But form documents can be used in a variety of situations. You might be sending an announcement to only 25 customers, requesting information from 10 different companies, or preparing a new lease for 12 tenants. There might be a standard contract, agreement, or letter that you produce one or two copies of periodically throughout the year. Like the mass-produced letter, the wording generally remains the same, while a few words or phrases vary with each use. In all these cases, form documents can save you the trouble of typing the same document many times.

There are several methods of creating form documents with Word. The most efficient way to produce the types of form documents described above—those that you need only a relatively small number of or those that you will produce periodically, a few copies at a time—is to create a template. For larger productions, it's more efficient to use Word's Print Merge command, as described in Chapter 16.

A *template* is a document that contains all the shell text and formatting for the final copies. You add the variable information just before printing each copy.

CREATING A FORM-DOCUMENT TEMPLATE

We'll now create a model form document—a template. It will include the text that is needed for every copy of the document. At each place where some variable, or specific, information is needed, you will insert a variable name. When you're ready to personalize each letter, you'll replace the variable names with the appropriate information.

The example also includes a template for printing envelopes on a dot-matrix or letter-quality printer that's capable of feeding individual sheets of paper. Printing envelopes on laser printers is discussed later.

Follow this procedure to create the form-document template:

1. Start Word.

2. Type the body of the cover letter:

   DATE
   ADDRESS

   Dear SALUTATION:

   I want to welcome you to the growing family of companies entrusting their computer service to Emlen Electronics.
   Let me assure you, however, that FIRM will not become just another "client." Our goal is to do more than just respond to service calls. We want to maintain the total integrity of your computer system, preventing downtime and costly repairs. Toward this goal, I have asked REP to serve as your personal liaison with Emlen Electronics. FIRST will be calling you soon.

   Sincerely,

   John Emlen
   President

3. The cover letter and the envelope template require different margins, so press Ctrl-Enter to insert a division mark before beginning the envelope template. You screen should look like the one shown in Figure 5.1.

```
█ L[·········1·········2·········3·········4·········5·········]·········7·····┐
  Dear SALUTATION:
          I want to welcome you to the growing family of
  companies entrusting their computer service to Emlen
  Electronics.
          Let me assure you, however, that FIRM will not become
  just another "client." Our goal is to do more than just
  respond to service calls. We want to maintain the total
  integrity of your computer system, preventing downtime and
  costly repairs. Toward this goal, I have asked REP to serve
  as your personal liaison with Emlen Electronics. FIRST will
  be calling you soon.

  Sincerely,                                       █

  John Emlen
  President
  :::::::::::::::::::::::::::::::::::::::::::::::::::::::::::::::::::::::::::::::::
  ▯

  ─────────────────────────────────────────────────────────────────────────────
  COMMAND: Copy Delete Format Gallery Help Insert Jump Library
          Options Print Quit Replace Search Transfer Undo Window
  Edit document or press Esc to use menu
  Pg1 Co1              {}                    ?                    Microsoft Word
```

○ **Figure 5.1:** *The form letter, followed by a division mark*

4. Click left on Format; then click right on Division to display the Format Division Margins menu. You will create a division with no top margin and a 4-inch page length. This way, you can align the printhead exactly where you want the first line of the address to appear on the envelope.

5. Enter **0** for the Top Margin option.

6. Click on the Left Margin setting and type **3**.

7. Click on the Page Length option and type **4**.

8. Click on the command line title. A second division mark appears across the screen, as shown in Figure 5.2.

9. Press Enter to insert a blank line between the division marks.

10. Click left on Transfer Save.

11. Type **SERVICE**, click on the command line title, and then click on SUMMARY. This saves the letter and envelope template on the disk under the name SERVICE.DOC.

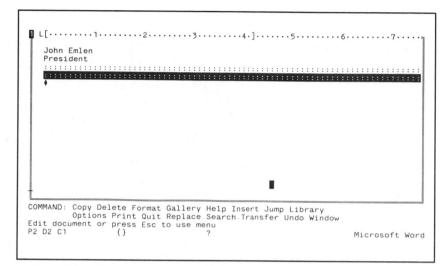

o **Figure 5.2:** *The second division mark after entering the envelope format*

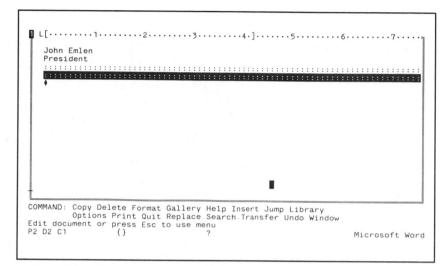

KEY Press Ctrl-F10, type **SERVICE**, and then press Enter twice to save the letter. Press Esc T C W to clear the screen.

12. Click left on Transfer, and then click right on Clear to clear the screen.

This letter contains variable names in six places. Specific information for DATE, ADDRESS, SALUTATION, FIRM, REP, and FIRST will be added when each copy of the form letter is printed.

PERSONALIZING FORM DOCUMENTS

Now that you've created the template for a form letter, you can easily personalize each one by inserting the appropriate variable information. To see how this works, we'll recall the SERVICE.DOC template from the disk and replace each variable with specific information. This is the procedure you use to produce each form letter from a template.

KEY Press Ctrl-F7, highlight Service, and press Enter to display the template. Place the cursor on Date, press F8 Del, and enter the date. Follow the same procedure to replace the rest of the variable information.

1. Click right on Transfer.

2. Click right to the right of the command line title to display file names, and then click right on SERVICE. The SERVICE.DOC template appears in the text window.

3. Click right on DATE; then click right on Delete to delete the variable name from the text.

4. Type **March 12, 1990**.

5. Click right on ADDRESS, and then click right on Delete.

6. Type the following address:

   Mr. William Hemmings
   345 Wacker Drive
   Chicago, IL 17652

7. Click right on SALUTATION; then click right on Delete.

8. Type **Mr. Hemmings**.

9. In the same manner, replace FIRM with **Hemmings Automotive**, REP with **Robert Foster**, and FIRST with **Bob**.

10. Move the mouse cursor to the address at the top of the letter, drag to select the three lines, and then click right on Copy. Note that if you include the space following the zip code in the selection, you will get an extra blank line when you copy the address to the envelope template.

11. Click both on the bottom-left border to reach the end of the document; then click between the two division marks, as shown in Figure 5.3.

KEY Place the cursor on the first line of the address, press F9 F6, and then press the down arrow key until the entire address is highlighted. Press Alt-F3 to copy it into the scrap. Press Ctrl-PgDn to reach the bottom of the document. Place the cursor between the division marks and press Ins.

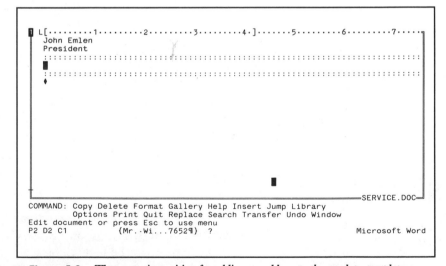

o **Figure 5.3:** *The cursor in position for adding an address to the envelope template*

12. Click right on Insert, and the address will appear between the division marks, as shown in Figure 5.4. Even though the envelope address appears to start at the far left margin, it will be printed 3 inches from the left edge.

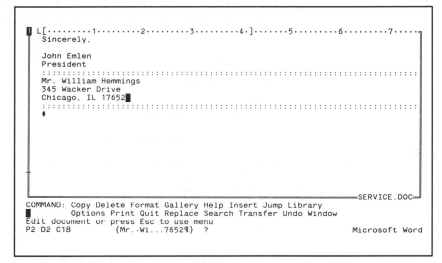

```
 L[·········1·········2·········3·········4·]·······5·········6·········7·····
  Sincerely,

  John Emlen
  President
  :::::::::::::::::::::::::::::::::::::::::::::::::::::::::::::::::::::::::::::::::
  Mr. William Hemmings
  345 Wacker Drive
  Chicago, IL 17652▮
  :::::::::::::::::::::::::::::::::::::::::::::::::::::::::::::::::::::::::::::::::
  ◆



                                                                  ┌SERVICE.DOC┐
 COMMAND: Copy Delete Format Gallery Help Insert Jump Library
 ▮        Options Print Quit Replace Search Transfer Undo Window
 Edit document or press Esc to use menu
 P2 D2 C18         {Mr.·Wi...7652¶}   ?                    Microsoft Word
```

o **Figure 5.4:** *An address copied into the envelope template*

PRINTING FORM LETTERS AND ENVELOPES

The next step is to print the form letter and envelope. As part of this procedure, you'll instruct Word to pause after printing the letter so that you can insert the envelope. (See the instructions for printing envelopes later in the chapter if you have a laser printer.)

1. Click left on Print Options.
2. Click right on the Paper Feed option to display alternatives, and then click right on Manual. (With version 4.0, just click right on Manual at the prompt line.)
3. Click on Printer. The message

   Enter Y to continue or Esc to cancel

   appears on the message line.

KEY Press Esc P O. Press the down arrow six times and type **Manual**. (With version 4.0, press the down arrow five times, and then press M.) Press Enter; then press P Y to print.

4. Make sure that the paper and printer are ready, and then click on the message line. The letter will print, and the continue or cancel message will appear again.

5. Insert a blank envelope in the printer. Roll it up so that the print-head is located where you want the first line of the address to print.

6. Click on the message line. The address will print on the envelope.

To print another copy of the form letter, you must first reload the original template. This ensures that the variable information from the first letter will not accidentally print on the next one. Follow the same procedure to load the Service template. After you select it (or enter its name), you will see the message

Enter Y to save changes to document, N to lose changes, or Esc to cancel

Press N, and the original template, without the variable information you just entered, will appear in the text window. In the next section, you'll learn how to use windows to store variable information so that you don't have to retype it for each mailing.

STORING THE TEMPLATE ON DISK

When you're finished printing form letters for the current work session, you'll either quit Word or begin a new document. In either case, you must be sure that the original version of the template is stored on disk.

KEY Press Esc Q N to quit and store the template on disk.

To quit Word without saving the personalized version of the template currently on the screen, Click left on Quit. Word displays the message prompting you to save or lose changes again. Press N, and you will be returned to the operating system. The template remains on disk, ready for the next time that you need to produce the form letter.

oUSING WINDOWS TO CREATE FORM LETTERS

If you need to produce form letters that are exactly the same except for the inside addresses and salutations, you can copy that information from one window to another instead of typing it in. This requires two separate documents: the form-letter template and the list of addresses and salutations. The file of addresses on disk is particularly useful if you will be using the same information for another group of form letters. In fact, later you'll learn how to create databases of such information for producing reports.

CREATING A TEMPLATE FOR COPIED INFORMATION

First we'll create the form-letter template that will receive variable information copied from another window. Since only the address and salutation differ for each letter, you don't have to enter variable names. Follow these steps:

1. Start Word.

2. Type the following template. Insert three blank lines between the date and body of the letter.

   July 23, 1990

   On behalf of the Faculty Council of the Philadelphia College of Pharmacy and Science, let me welcome you to our college.
   We appreciate the contribution made to our students by part-time instructors like yourself. Adjunct faculty add unique insights to the learning environment and contribute greatly to the overall academic program.
   Enclosed is the 1990-91 Faculty Handbook and Academic Calendar. Our first Faculty Council meeting will be September 5, 1990, in Whitecar Hall, at noon. I am looking forward to seeing you there.

   Sincerely,

   G. Victor Rossi
   Vice President

KEY Press Ctrl-F10, type **Faculty**, and press Enter twice.

3. Click left on Transfer Save.

4. Type **Faculty**, click on the command line title, and then click on SUMMARY.

CREATING A VARIABLE LIST DOCUMENT

In the previous example, you created form letters by adding information to the template. After printing each letter, you erased the variable information by reloading the template. This technique is fine if you will not need to use that personal information again. However, you might have a list of persons to whom you will be sending letters periodically. Rather than retyping the names and addresses each time, you can create a variable list document to be used with each group of form letters.

Follow these steps to create the variable list document that we'll use with our form-letter template:

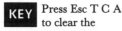 Press Esc T C A to clear the screen.

1. Click left on Transfer; then click right on Clear to clear the screen.
2. Type the following addresses and salutations:

> **Mr. John Williams**
> **3465 Lockhart Road**
> **Philadelphia, PA 19115**
>
> **Dear Mr. Williams:**
>
> **Dr. Maven Meyers**
> **569 Swallow Drive**
> **Brigintine, NJ 06251**
>
> **Dear Dr. Meyers:**
>
> **Dr. Ruth Opinski**
> **459 Willowdale Lane**
> **Meadowbrook, PA 19273**
>
> **Dear Dr. Opinski:**

 Press Ctrl-F10, type **List**, and press Enter twice.

3. Click left on Transfer Save.
4. Type **List**, click on the command line title, and then click on SUMMARY.
5. Click on Quit.

DISPLAYING THE TEMPLATE AND LIST

You now have two documents: a template of the shell text and a variable list. To insert the variable information into the template, you will

KEY Press Esc W S V and type **40**. Press Tab to reach the Clear New Window option, press Y, and then press Enter. Next, press Ctrl-F7, select List, and press Enter to load the variable list. Press F1 to move to window 1. (F1 moves the cursor from one window to another.) Press Ctrl-F7, select Faculty, and press Enter to load the template.

first divide the screen into two typing windows. One window will contain the template; the other will display the list of variables. Then you'll copy the variable information into each form letter. Follow these steps:

1. Start Word.

2. Click right on the 4 on the ruler line while pressing the Alt key to divide the window. (If the ruler isn't shown, click right on the upper-right corner.) The screen will divide into two vertical text windows, as shown in Figure 5.5. The window on the left is marked 1; the right window is 2. The number 2 is highlighted to indicate that it is the active window.

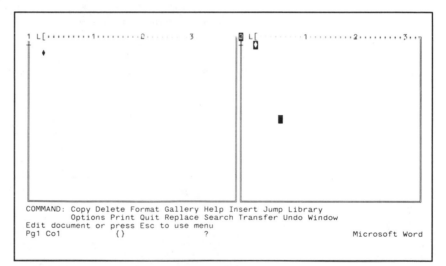

o **Figure 5.5:** *The screen split into two vertical text windows*

3. Click right on Transfer; then click right to the right of the command line title.

4. Click right on List. The variable list will be loaded into window 2.

5. Click left anywhere in window 1 to make it the active window. Figure 5.6 shows the variable list in the right window and the number 1 of the left window highlighted.

6. Click right on Transfer.

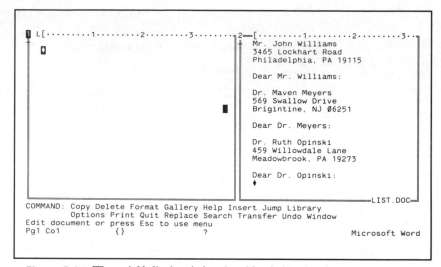

o **Figure 5.6:** *The variable list in window 2, with window 1 active*

7. Click right to the right of the command line title, and then click right on Faculty. The FACULTY.DOC template will be loaded into window 1, as shown in Figure 5.7.

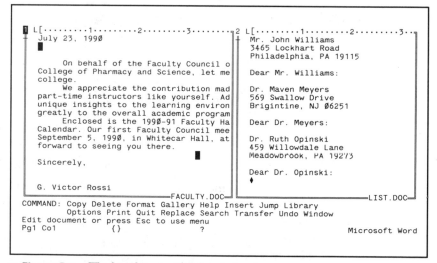

o **Figure 5.7:** *The form-letter template in window 1*

COPYING THE VARIABLE INFORMATION INTO THE TEMPLATE

Both the template and variable information are on the screen. Now let's copy an inside address and salutation from window 2 to window 1 and print the completed form letter. You'll repeat this process to produce each form letter.

KEY Press F1 to move to window 2. Select the first address, including the space after the salutation, and press Alt-F3 to copy it into the scrap. Press F1 to move to window 1, place the cursor one line down from the date, and press Ins.

1. Click left in window 2 to move the cursor into it.

2. Drag the entire first address and salutation until all five lines (including the space after the salutation) are highlighted, as shown in Figure 5.8.

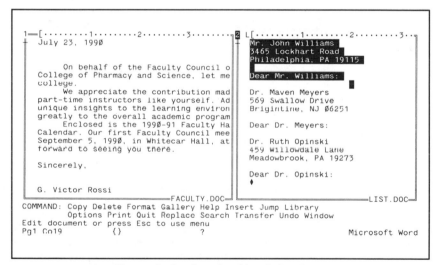

o **Figure 5.8:** *An address and salutation selected in window 2*

3. Point at the left margin, one line down from the date, in the first window.

4. Hold down the Shift key and click left to copy the address and salutation to the first window. Your screen should look like the one shown in Figure 5.9.

5. Click right on Print to print the form letter.

```
┌─────────────────────────────────────────────────────────────────────┐
│ 1 L[·········1·········2·········3········ 2 L[·········1·········2·········3···│
│  ┼ July 23, 1990                          Mr. John Williams           │
│  │                                        3465 Lockhart Road          │
│    Mr. John Williams                      Philadelphia, PA 19115      │
│    3465 Lockhart Road                                                 │
│    Philadelphia, PA 19115                 Dear Mr. Williams:          │
│                                                                    ■  │
│    Dear Mr. Williams:                                                 │
│    ■                                      Dr. Maven Meyers            │
│         On behalf of the Faculty Council o 569 Swallow Drive          │
│    College of Pharmacy and Science, let me Brigintine, NJ 06251       │
│    college.                                                           │
│         We appreciate the contribution mad Dear Dr. Meyers:           │
│    part-time instructors like yourself. Ad                            │
│    unique insights to the learning environ Dr. Ruth Opinski          │
│    greatly to the overall academic program 459 Willowdale Lane        │
│         Enclosed is the 1990-91 Faculty Ha Meadowbrook, PA 19273      │
│    Calendar. Our first Faculty Council mee                            │
│    September 5, 1990, in Whitecar Hall, at Dear Dr. Opinski:          │
│    forward to seeing you there.            ♦                          │
│  ══════════════════════════FACULTY.DOC══ ═════════════════════LIST.DOC══│
│ COMMAND: Copy Delete Format Gallery Help Insert Jump Library          │
│          Options Print Quit Replace Search Transfer Undo Window       │
│ Edit document or press Esc to use menu                                │
│ Pg1 Co1              {Mr.·Jo...ams:¶}  ?                Microsoft Word │
└─────────────────────────────────────────────────────────────────────┘
```

o **Figure 5.9:** *The address and salutation inserted in the template in window 1*

KEY Press Esc P P.
Press Ctrl-F7,
select Faculty, and press
Enter. Press N to load the
document without saving
the first form letter.
Repeat the steps for each
form letter, and then
press Esc Q to exit Word.

6. After the first letter is printed, click right on Transfer to replace the personalized template with the original. (As an alternative, you could just delete the address and salutation, rather than reloading the template.)

7. Click right to the right of the command line title, and then click right on Faculty. When prompted, press N to lose changes and load the original template into the typing window.

8. Repeat the steps above for each of the remaining inside addresses and salutations.

9. When you have finished, click left on Quit; then press N to quit Word without saving the edits. The original template and list will remain intact on the disk.

PRINTING ENVELOPES WITH VARIABLE DOCUMENTS

You can print envelopes if you have a friction-feed printer, if you purchase envelopes that are connected continuously, or if you have a laser printer that can print in the landscape (sideways) mode. Since you have already typed the addresses once in the variable list document, you don't have to type them again to address the envelopes. You just need to format the list properly. We will paginate the list so each address is on its own page. This way, each envelope will be printed separately.

You'll now create an envelope printer file using the variable list document. The file will print addresses on individual envelopes using a friction-feed printer. (The next section explains how to print envelopes on a laser printer.)

Follow these steps:

1. Start Word.
2. Click right on Transfer.
3. Click right to the right of the command line title, point to List, and click right. The list of addresses and salutations appears.
4. Click on Search.
5. Type **Dear**; then click on SEARCH. The first salutation is displayed.
6. Click right in the selection bar next to Dear to select the line, and then click right on Delete.
7. Press Enter to insert an extra line, leaving three blank lines between addresses.
8. Repeat the search-and-delete process until all the salutation lines are deleted. Click on Search, then SEARCH to repeat the same search.

Each address is now six lines long—three address and three blank lines—so we can automatically divide the document into one-inch pages. The addresses on your list may be four or five lines long, including a company name, title, or box number. Just make sure that the total number of lines from the first line of one address to the first line of the next is the same throughout the list.

9. Click left on Format; then click right on Division to display the Format Division Margins menu.
10. Click on the Left option and type 3.
11. Click on the Page Length option and type **6 li** for six lines.

KEY Press Ctrl-F7, select List, and press Enter. Press Esc S, type **Dear**, and press Enter. Press F10 Del to delete the line, and then press Enter for an extra line. Press Shift-F4 to repeat the search.

KEY Press Esc F D M to display the menu. Press the down arrow to reach the Left option and type **3**. Press the down arrow to reach the Page Length option and type **6 li**. Press Enter.

Where margin measurements are called for, Word assumes you mean inches unless you specify otherwise. Here you are telling Word that each division will be six lines long. (You can also enter measurements in points, such as 18 pt). If you later look at the page-length setting, you'll see that Word converted it to 1'', which you could have entered directly. So why use lines? Let's say that your addresses are seven lines long. How many inches would you enter for the Page Length option? Rather than calculate the measurement, enter 7 li. Word will convert it to 1.17''. Of course, all these measurements are based on a standard type size that fits six lines into every inch, since Word does convert everything to inches.

12. Click on the command line title. The variable document list now has the correct page length and left margin for envelopes. Figure 5.10 shows the modified variable list.

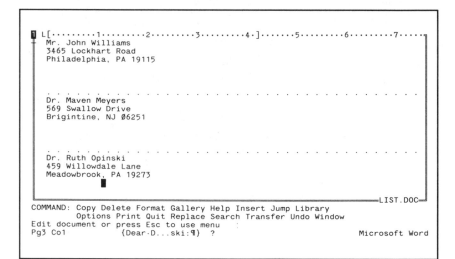

o **Figure 5.10:** *The modified variable list for printing envelopes*

13. If you're not certain that each address is the correct size, or if you have version 4.0, paginate the document, checking for proper spacing.

   a. Click left on Print Repaginate.

KEY Press Esc P R Y Enter to repaginate. Press Y at the prompt when each page break is correct.

b. Click right on Yes to paginate the document, confirming each page-break position. At each break, the message line will change to

Enter Y to confirm page break or use direction keys to reposition

c. If the page break is either on the first line of an address or between two addresses, click on the message line. If the page break is in the middle of an address, press the up arrow key. When the break is at the first line of an address, click on the command line. Repeat this step until the list is paginated.

KEY Press Esc P O. Press the down arrow key six times (five times with version 4.0) to reach the Paper Feed option. Type **Manual** (with version 4.0, press M), and then press Enter twice to start printing. Press Esc Q N to exit Word.

14. Set the paper feed to manual.

   a. Click left on Print Options.

   b. Click right on the Paper Feed option to display alternatives, and then click right on Manual. (With version 4.0, just click right on Manual at the prompt line.)

15. Insert each envelope. Align the printhead at the location where you want the first line of the address to print, click on Printer, and then click on the message line. Repeat this step to print all the envelopes.

16. Click left on Quit; then press N to quit Word without saving the edits. The original variable list document will remain intact for future use.

PRINTING ENVELOPES ON A LASER PRINTER

If you have a laser printer, you already know that it is unsurpassed in terms of both speed and print quality. Laser printers have several built-in fonts and type sizes, plus a wide variety of optional fonts in either cartridges or on disk. Most laser printers can also print in both the normal portrait mode and the landscape mode (sideways down the page).

If your laser printer has a landscape mode, you can easily print envelopes by selecting the proper printer options, and then inserting the envelopes individually into the printer's manual paper feeder.

In this section, we'll use the Hewlett-Packard LaserJet + printer as an example. The same technique can be used with any printer that has a landscape mode. You'll format the variable list document created in the previous section so that each address is on its own page. However, the division will be formatted to print correctly in landscape mode.

Follow these steps:

1. Start Word.

2. Click right on Transfer, then click right to the right of the command line title.

3. Point to List and click right. The list of addresses and salutations appears. The first step is to delete the salutations, leaving just the addresses.

4. Click on Search.

5. Type **Dear** and click on SEARCH. The first salutation is displayed.

6. Click right in the selection bar next to Dear; then click right on Delete.

7. Click on Search, then SEARCH to repeat the search.

8. Delete the text on the line.

9. Repeat the search-and-delete process until all the salutation lines are deleted.

10. Click left on Format; then click right on Division.

The division for printing envelopes will have 6-inch top and left margins, and 11-inch page length and width. You might want to adjust the margin settings for your own envelopes.

11. Type **6** for the top margin setting.

12. Click on the Left option and type **6**.

13. Click on the Width option and type **11**.

14. Click on the command line title to return to the document. The division format has been set, but now each address must be placed on its own page.

15. Place the cursor in the blank line following the first address and press Ctrl-Shift-Enter to insert a page break at that location.

16. In the same manner, insert a page break following each of the remaining addresses. Next you select the proper printing options.

KEY Press Ctrl-F7, select List, and press Enter. Press Esc S, type **Dear**, and press Enter. Press F9 Del to delete the line. Repeat the search-and-delete process until all the salutation lines are deleted.

KEY Press Esc F D M. Type **6** for the Top Margin option. Press the down arrow to reach the Left option and type **6**. Press the down arrow, then the right arrow to reach the Width option, type **11**, and press Enter.

KEY Press Esc P O.
Press the F1 key,
and select HPLASLAN,
but don't press Enter.
Press the down arrow key
six times (five times with
version 4.0) to reach the
Paper Feed option. Type
Manual (with version 4.0,
press M) and press Enter
twice to start printing.

17. Click left on Print Options; then click right on the Printer option to display a list of printer types, as in Figure 5.11. The PRD files listed will depend on how you set up Word. Look for the landscape PRD file, such as HPLASLAN. If it is not listed, save your work, quit Word, and then copy the PRD file from your Word disks.

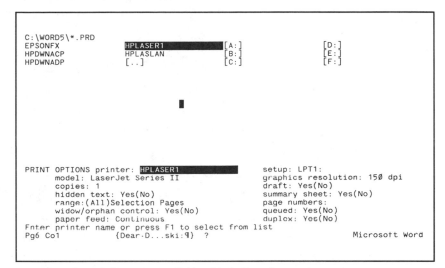

o **Figure 5.11:** *Printer types available with the LaserJet + printer*

18. Click left on HPLASLAN, the landscape mode.

19. Click right on the Paper Feed option. With version 4.0, click right on Manual for the Paper Feed option, and then skip step 20.

20. Click right on Manual. If your laser printer has an optional envelope feeder, the Envelope option should appear on the list of alternatives. Click on Envelope instead, and follow the directions for using the feeder that came with the attachment.

21. Click on Printer. The message line reads

   Enter Y to continue or Esc to cancel

Before printing, you must set the printer to manual feed and insert an envelope in the manual-feed tray. Remember, the following instructions are for the LaserJet +.

KEY Press Y after you
feed in the enve-
lope. Press Esc Q N when
you are finished printing.

22. Press the button marked On Line until the light on the button goes off.

23. Press the button marked Manual Feed until it goes on.

24. Press the On Line button again to bring the printer on line.

25. Place an envelope in the manual-feed tray in the back of the machine. Insert it so that the side to be printed on is facing up and the top of the envelope is facing toward the center of the tray, away from the alignment edge. Gently push the envelope in until it stops.

26. Click on the message line to start the printing process. The envelope will feed into the machine, and the address will print at the correct location. Again, you will be prompted to let Word know when you're ready to continue printing.

27. Feed another envelope into the printer and click on the message line.

28. Repeat the process until all the addresses have been printed.

29. Click left on Quit; then press N to exit Word without saving the edits.

USING LASER PRINTER CODES TO PRINT ENVELOPES

Because dot-matrix and letter-quality printers only have portrait orientation, just the margins have to be changed to print a form letter and envelope at one time. But printing the letter and envelope this way on a laser printer is more complicated because you can't change PRD files in the middle of your document. You can't select the portrait PRD for the letter, and then switch to a landscape PRD to print the envelope.

However, you can accomplish the same thing by using the printer's built-in programming language. Every function of the printer is controlled by a series of commands—the same commands that Word put into the PRD file. With the LaserJet family of printers, the commands form the PCL language.

You can insert the PCL directions directly in the document to tell the printer to print the letter in portrait mode using the sheet feeder, and then switch to landscape mode and manual feed for the envelope. As an example, we'll produce a sample letter and envelope. The commands shown here will work on any LaserJet-compatible printer.

1. Start Word. First we'll enter the codes to have the letter print in portrait orientation using the paper cassette.

2. Press and hold down the Alt key while you type **27** using the numeric keypad.

3. Release the Alt key, and you'll see a small left-pointing arrow on the screen. This arrow represents the Esc code, the special character that starts all PCL commands. (You can't use the Esc key to enter the code because Word uses that key for its own purposes.)

4. Type **&l0O**. Make sure that you enter a lowercase L, not a one, then a zero, followed by a capital O. This code, shown in Figure 5.12, is the PCL command for using portrait orientation.

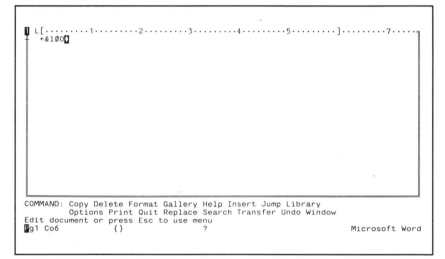

o **Figure 5.12:** *PCL commands for portrait orientation*

5. Now type your letter:

Mr. In Ho Kim
6531 Walnut Lane
Philadelphia, PA 19116

Dear Mr. Kim:

   Thank you for your interest in our services. I will be calling you soon to arrange an appointment.
   In the meantime, please review the enclosed literature.

Sincerely,

Alvin A. Aardvark

6. Press Ctrl-Enter to insert a division mark.

7. Enter the codes for printing the envelope. The code is rather long because you have to set the paper type, manual feed, and top and left margins. You'll be using PCL commands, not Word's division, to set the margins here.

   a. Press Alt-27 and type **&l1O**.

   b. Press Alt-27 and type **&l3h**.

   c. Press Alt-27 and type **&l38E**.

   d. Press Alt-27 and type **&a0R**.

   e. Press Alt-27 and type **&a42L**.

   f. Press Enter. Your screen should look like the one shown in Figure 5.13.

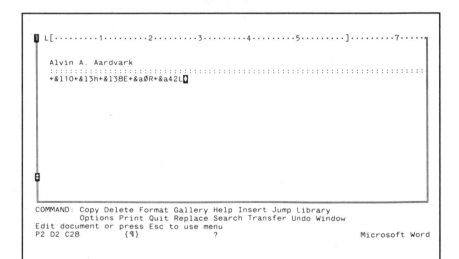

o **Figure 5.13:** *PCL commands for landscape orientation, envelope feed in the manual tray*

KEY Press Esc P P to print.

8. Copy the address from the first page onto the new division, beneath the codes.

9. Click right on Print. After the page is printed, a blank page will eject from the printer. Then you'll see the message PE on the printer's control panel, indicating that you should feed an envelope in the manual tray.

10. Insert the envelope as instructed in the previous section. The envelope will print in the landscape orientation.

Just in case you have to adjust the margins for your own envelopes, here's what the envelope codes do:

&l1O	Sets landscape orientation
&l3h	Sets envelope feed in the manual intake
&l38E	Sets the top margin to 38 lines; adjust this if necessary
&a0R	Activates the top margin
&a42L	Sets the left margin at 42 characters; adjust this if necessary

oUSING THE REPLACE COMMAND TO INSERT VARIABLE INFORMATION

In the form letter in the first example, each variable name was used only once. It was a short document—short enough for you to find each variable by scrolling through the text with the down arrow key. Most mass-mailing type form letters are like this.

But other form documents, such as contracts and proposals, may have the same variables repeated throughout. The name of the client, the company name, or specific terms might appear in several places. In these instances, the Replace command can be used to simplify the process of inserting the variable information.

CREATING A CONTRACT WITH REPEATED VARIABLES

To see how the Replace command works, we'll create a form document in which the same variable information is used several times. Follow these steps:

1. Start Word.

2. Type in the following text, underlining the variable name where you want the actual data underlined in the printed contract:

Agreement dated <u>DATE</u>, between Emlen Electronics, a Pennsylvania Corporation, and <u>CLIENT</u>.

<u>CLIENT</u> agrees to pay Emlen Electronics the sum of <u>$AMOUNT</u> within 30 days of <u>DATE</u>. In consideration for said payment, Emlen Electronics will provide repair services, including all parts and labor, for the following equipment maintained and operated at the offices of <u>CLIENT</u>:

ITEM   SERIAL NUMBER

<u>CLIENT</u> will contact Emlen Electronics when repair services are needed. Emlen Electronics will report on-site at the offices of <u>CLIENT</u> within 24 hours of contact.

If repair parts for equipment covered under this contract become unavailable, Emlen Electronics will notify <u>CLIENT</u> in writing. Thirty (30) days from said notice, Emlen Electronics will reimburse <u>CLIENT</u> a pro-rated share of the contracted service price. Said equipment will no longer be covered by the terms of this agreement.

_____

Emlen Electronics

_____

<u>CLIENT</u>

KEY Press Ctrl-F10, type **Contract**, and press Enter twice. Press Esc Q to quit Word.

3. Click left on Transfer Save and type **Contract**. Click on the command line title; then click on SUMMARY. The template, CONTRACT.DOC, is saved on the disk.

4. Click right on Quit.

INSERTING VARIABLE INFORMATION

Now we will load the contract into the text window and use the Replace command to insert the variable information. Follow these steps:

1. Start WORD.

KEY Press Ctrl-F7, select Contract, and press Enter. Press Esc R to see the Replace menu. Type **DATE**. Press Tab and type **May 12, 1990**. Press Tab N to make all the replacements without stopping, Tab Y to match only cases, or Tab Y to match only whole words. Press Enter.

KEY Press Ctrl-PgUp, and then press Esc R to start replacing at the beginning of the document.

KEY Press Tab N Enter to select No for Confirm.

2. Click right on Transfer; then click right to the right of the command line title. Click right on Contract. The CONTRACT.DOC template will appear in the text window.

3. Click on Replace to display the Replace menu.

4. Type **DATE**.

5. Click on the With Text option and type **May 12, 1990**.

6. Click left on No for the Confirm option.

7. Click left on Yes for the Case option to match only cases.

8. Click right on Yes for the Whole Word option. Each occurrence of the word DATE will be replaced with **May 12, 1990**.

9. Click on Replace.

10. Type **CLIENT**, press Tab, and type **Hemmings Automotive**.

11. Click right on No for the Confirm option. You must select No for the Confirm option for each variable; however, the Case and Whole Word options need only be selected once.

12. Click on Replace.

13. Type **AMOUNT**, press Tab, and type 1500.

14. Click right on No for the Confirm option.

15. Position the cursor under the column heading ITEM. Enter the following columns:

IBM PC	**358192**
IBM PC	**640950**
IBM PC	**429757**
IBM PC	**654287**

Although continuous replacement is often risky, you could use this option with the CONTRACT.DOC template because you took some precautions. First, you typed the variable names in the template in all uppercase letters. Then, when using the Replace command to insert the variable information, you chose Yes for matching only the same case and Yes for matching only whole words. If you had used the default selections for these options, the word *dated* in the first line would have been changed to *May 12, 1990d*.

PRINTING THE CONTRACT

Print this form document as you would any other. The next time that you need to produce the same type of contract, simply use the Transfer Load command to open the template (CONTRACT.DOC), and repeat the replacement procedure.

After printing the form letter, quit Word without saving the edits. This leaves the original template on disk, ready for the next session.

In this chapter, you learned a few different ways to use templates to create simple form documents. These methods are appropriate when you need to produce a small number of copies or when you will only produce one or two copies periodically.

By combining other Word commands with those that you learned in this chapter, you can create a variety of documents. If you have two templates that you sometimes use together, save them separately in two different files. Then when you want to combine the documents, use the Transfer Merge command. For example, a realtor may have a lease template and a transmittal letter and envelope template. When both documents must be sent to the same individual, the templates can be combined by using Transfer Merge, and then the variable information can be inserted at all the locations at one time with the Replace command.

In the next chapter, you'll learn how to use indentation formats to produce attractive, readable documents.

CHAPTER 6

- FORMATTING
  - WITH
- INDENTATIONS

The default format used by Word for paragraphs is the block style. Every line starts at the left margin, and sentences wrap around when they reach the right margin. It is a common format used in documents.

As with all of Word's settings, you can change the default paragraph style to suit your own needs. You can use the Tab key to indent paragraphs or type columns of numbers. You can change the left and right margins by using the Format Division command.

But in some documents, more frequent changes are required. Some paragraphs should be wide, some narrow. Long quotations, for example, are usually indented from both the left and right margins, while sections of legal contracts might be indented at several levels, each level representing a refinement of the point before it.

These formats are examples of indented paragraphs. In this chapter, you will learn how to quickly create various types of indented paragraphs. First, let's set up Word so that it automatically indents the first line of every paragraph, which is more efficient for typing the body of a long document.

oINDENTING THE FIRST LINE OF EVERY PARAGRAPH

Many people prefer paragraphs with indented first lines over the block style. This format is easier to read because each paragraph stands out from the rest and the extra spaces on the first line give a more pleasant appearance to the page.

Of course, you can create the indentation by simply pressing the Tab key at the beginning of each paragraph. Although this technique takes just a few seconds, Word provides an alternative that makes indenting paragraphs even easier.

To have Word indent the first line of every paragraph automatically, simply press Alt-F before typing the text. The first line of each paragraph (the text after you press Enter) will be indented ½ inch. When you want to return to the block style, press Alt-P to cancel the indented format.

Before you begin formatting with Alt-F, you should be aware of how it interacts with other formatting commands. You've probably noticed that some paragraph-formatting commands automatically cancel others. For example, you can type a paragraph, and then see how it looks different ways by pressing Alt-R (right justified), Alt-C (centered), Alt-J (justified along both margins), and Alt-L (left justified). None of these formats can exist in combination with another.

However, this isn't the case with Alt-F (and other indentation styles that you'll use). Alt-F can be applied in combination with Alt-C, Alt-J, Alt-R, and Alt-L. So if you're using Alt-F, or another indented format, and decide to format the paragraph with another command, just make sure that the final layout is what you had in mind.

The two lines below show what can happen:

CENTER
    CENTER

The first line contains a word centered using Alt-C. The second line was centered with Alt-C *after* Alt-F was used. Notice that it is several characters off center. If you press Alt-J or Alt-R after using Alt-F, Word will justify the lines but leave the Alt-F space.

CREATING A LETTER WITH INDENTED PARAGRAPHS

As an example, we'll type a standard letter with indented paragraphs. Follow these steps:

1. Start Word.

2. Press Alt-C to center the date between the margins.

3. Type the date **August 16, 1990**.

4. Press Enter twice.

5. Press Alt-P to cancel the centered format.

6. Type the inside address and salutation:

    Mr. Richard Simonns
    458 Merdi Lane
    Williamsport, WI 16543

    Dear Mr. Simonns:

7. Press Enter twice.

8. Press Alt-F. The cursor moves in ½ inch from the margin, and a broken vertical line (¦) appears on the status line. Every time that you press Enter, the cursor will move in ½ inch.

9. Type the following paragraph:

> **Thank you for your interest in Sigma Corporation and for sending us your resume and writing samples.**

10. Press Enter. The cursor moves into position for a paragraph.

11. Type the next paragraph:

> **While your credentials are excellent, we unfortunately have no positions currently available. We will, however, keep your materials on file. Our personnel department will be in touch if any positions become open.**

12. Press Enter twice after the last paragraph.

13. Press Tab to move to the center of the screen and type

> **Sincerely yours,**
>
> **Reginald Van Mop**
> **Personnel Director**

14. Press Enter, then Alt-P to cancel the paragraph-indent function.

15. Click right on Print to print the document.

16. Click left on Quit; then press N to exit Word without saving the edits.

KEY Press Esc P P to print. Press Esc Q N to quit.

oINDENTING ENTIRE PARAGRAPHS

The Alt-F command can be used when you want to indent the first line of a paragraph. But what about text where the entire paragraph should be indented?

> You might want to indent a whole paragraph, like this one, to make a specific point stand out. Because all the lines are indented, it catches the reader's eye. It adds impact to the text.
>
> > Or, you might need several indented levels to stress some relationship between the subject matter discussed at each level.

Here every line, not just the first, is indented from the left margin.

Rather than change the left margins for the entire document, you can create a temporary left margin for one or more paragraphs. You could use the Left Indent option on the Format Paragraph menu, but the speed keys are much faster.

The Alt-N command moves the left margin ½ inch to the right each time that it is pressed. For example, if you press Alt-N once, the left margin will move in ½ inch—just as if you entered .5 for Left Indent on the Format Paragraph menu. If you press Alt-N a second time, the left margin will be indented 1 inch. You can continue moving the left margin in by pressing Alt-N. The text will wrap at the indented margin until you press Alt-P to return to the default margin or use another paragraph-formatting speed key.

The Alt-M command moves the margin toward the left in ½-inch increments. If the margin is currently indented 2 inches, pressing Alt-M will place it at 1½ inches. Press Alt-M again for a 1-inch margin.

CREATING A DOCUMENT WITH INDENTED PARAGRAPHS

To see how easy it is to indent whole paragraphs with Word, you will create a document with several levels of indented paragraphs. Follow the procedure below:

1. Start Word.
2. Press Alt-C to center the heading.
3. Type the following heading:

   Classification of Living Things

4. Press Enter twice.
5. Press Alt-P to cancel the centered format.
6. Type the following paragraphs, using the default format. Press Enter between the paragraphs.

   Living things are classified to identify the groups to which they belong. The several levels of classification refine the group from general to specific.

> **The first level is Kingdom. This group is divided into plants and animals. It is the largest division of living things. Because it is so large, knowing the Kingdom of a living thing does not tell us much about the organism. The Kingdom of the anteater is Animal.**

7. Press Enter twice, and indent the next paragraph ½ inch by pressing Alt-N. Then type the following text.

> **The second level is Phylum. Phylum is the largest division of a Kingdom. It is based on specific traits from the appearance of the living thing. The Phylum of the anteater is Chordate.**

8. Press Enter twice; then press Alt-N to indent the next paragraph an additional ½ inch. Type the following text.

> **The third level is Class. Class is the largest division of a Phylum. The Class of the anteater is Mammal.**

9. Press Enter twice, press Alt-N, and type the following text.

> **The fourth level is Order. The members of this division possess body parts and structures that are very much alike. The Order of the anteater is Edentata.**

10. Press Enter twice, press Alt-N, and type the following text.

> **The fifth level is Family. This is a division within an Order. The Family of the anteater is Myrmecophagidae.**

11. Press Enter twice, press Alt-N, and type the following text.

> **The sixth level is Genus. These living things share closely related features. The Genus of the anteater is Myrmecophaga.**

12. Press Enter twice, press Alt-N, and type the following text.

> **The seventh level is Species. This is normally the lowest unit. It includes all organisms of similar kinds. The Species of the anteater is Tridactyla. The species of the octopus is Vulgaris.**

13. Press Enter twice; then decrease the indentation ½ inch by pressing Alt-M. Type the following text.

> **The Genus of the octopus is Octopus.**

14. Press Enter twice, and press Alt-M to decrease the indentation an additional ½ inch. Then type the following text.

> **The Family of the Octopus is Octopodidae.**

15. Press Enter twice, press Alt-M, and type the following text.

    The Order of the octopus is Octopoda.

16. Press Enter twice, press Alt-M, and type the following text.

    The Class of the Octopus is Cephalopod.

17. Press Enter twice, press Alt-M, and type the following text.

    The Phylum of the octopus is Mollusk.

18. Press Enter twice, and press Alt-M to move out to the default margin. Then type the following text.

    The Kingdom of the octopus is Animal.

KEY Press Esc P P to print. Press Esc Q N to quit.

19. Click right on Print.

20. Click left on Quit, and then press N to exit Word without saving the edits.

The Alt-N and Alt-M combinations give you the flexibility to vary the left margin quickly.

oINDENTING BOTH THE LEFT AND RIGHT MARGINS

4.0 Alt-Q is not available.

To indent a paragraph from both margins, use either the Alt-Q speed key or the Left Indent and Right Indent options on the Format Paragraph menu. Indentations made with Alt-Q, like all speed-key paragraph formatting, can be canceled by pressing Alt-P.

CREATING A DOCUMENT WITH AN INDENTED QUOTATION

Let's use Alt-Q to indent a quotation in a short document. Follow these steps:

1. Start Word.

2. Type the first paragraph using the default paragraph format, and then press Enter.

> **To a large extent, a Management Information System (MIS) is still largely an ideal. It is a concept of how computers and modern technology can be applied to the decision-making process of the corporate environment. While a very complex issue, MIS can be defined as follows.**

4.0 Click left on Format Paragraph, or press Esc F P, to display the Format Paragraph menu. Click on the Left Indent option, or press Tab to reach it, and type **1**. Click on the Right Indent option, or press Tab twice to reach it, and type **1**. Click on the command line title or press Enter.

3. Press Alt-Q twice to indent both margins one inch. The left and right margin markers will move on the ruler line. The left margin will be at the 1-inch position, and the right margin will be at 5 inches.

4. Type the following text, and then press Enter.

> **A management information system provides management with past, present, and projected information relating to the internal and external environments of the organization. The information supports the overall decision-making process.**

KEY Press Esc P P; then press Esc Q N.

5. Press Alt-P to return the paragraph format to the default margins.

6. Click right on Print.

7. Click left on Quit, and then press N to exit Word without saving the edits.

oHANGING INDENTATIONS

Normal paragraphs have only the first line indented with the remaining text flush on the left. *Hanging indentations* are just the opposite. Subsequent lines are indented to the right of the first line, which "hangs" out to the left. This is a common style for numbered paragraphs or paragraph outlines.

1. The lines in a numbered format such as this one are examples of paragraphs with hanging indentations.

   In this example, too, the first line hangs to the left of the remaining text in the paragraph.

To understand hanging indentations, first remember how normal indented paragraphs are formed: You press Enter to indent the first line at the tab stop, and word wrap continues long lines at the left margin.

With hanging indentations, the two actions are reversed: You press Enter to start long lines at the left margin, and word wrap continues long lines at the indentation.

You can create hanging indentations by pressing Alt-T. Each time that you press Alt-T, the margins of the indented lines (every line but the first one of the paragraph) move ½ inch to the right. The hanging first line remains at the left margin.

To see how hanging indentations can be used, you will type a short document of numbered paragraphs with several levels of hanging indentations. Here's the procedure:

1. Start Word.

2. Press Alt-T. Notice the change in the ruler line. The ¦ character marks the starting position of the hanging text, the current left margin for that paragraph. The [marks the location of a tab stop and the indented position of the remaining lines—now at ½ inch.

3. Type the number for the first paragraph.

   1.

4. Press Tab.

5. Type the rest of the text at that level.

   Kingdom is the first level of classification. It is so broad that many types of living things are included in this group.

6. Press Enter. Notice that all the lines are indented ½ inch from the position of the hanging character. Now you're ready to enter the next level of hanging indentation. If you press Alt-T, however, only the indented position will shift to the right (to 1 inch); the hanging position will stay at the margin.

7. Press Alt-N to shift everything in toward the right. Both the hanging position (indicated by ¦) and the indented position ([) move ½ inch.

8. Type the letter for the next level.

   a.

9. Press Tab.

10. Type the second paragraph.

    Animal is one Kingdom. Insects are the largest population of this Kingdom.

11. Press Enter. The indentation settings do not change, so we can enter another paragraph at this level.

12. Type the letter for next paragraph.

    b.

13. Press Tab.

14. Type the next paragraph.

    Plants comprise the other Kingdom.

15. Press Enter. Now let's return the settings to the first hanging indentation.

16. Press Alt-M. Both the hanging text and indentation positions move back ½ inch.

17. Type the next paragraph. Remember to enter the hanging number, and then press Tab.

    2. Phylum is the next level of classification. Since it is a small class, fewer living things belong to this group.

18. Press Enter.

19. Click right on Print.

20. Click left on Quit, and then press N to exit Word without saving the edits.

KEY Press Esc P P, and then press Esc Q N.

If you are using hanging indentations for numbered paragraphs, as in this example, you must press Tab after entering the hanging number. Remember that it is word wrap that starts each subsequent line at the indented position. Pressing Tab aligns the nonhanging characters in the first line with subsequent lines started by word wrap.

If you want a hanging indentation in something other than ½ inch increments, such as hanging text at ¾ inch with indented text at 1¼ inch, you have to use the Left Indent and First Line options on the Format Paragraph menu. Enter the position for the indented text (such as 1.25) as the Left Indent setting. Enter the hanging text's position as the First Line setting. For example, if you want the first line to start ½ inch to the right (back toward the left margin), enter − .5 for the position of the first line. Finally, set a tab stop at the indented position (1.25).

o**OTHER INDENTED FORMATS**

In the outline above, each paragraph aligns according to its level in neat $\frac{1}{2}$ increments. If you pressed Alt-T a second time, rather than Alt-N, then first two paragraphs would appear like this:

1. Kingdom is the first level of classification. It is so broad that many types of living things are included in this group.

a.   Animal is one Kingdom. Insects are the largest population of this Kingdom.

The first paragraph is a hanging indentation created by pressing Alt-T once. The second paragraph shows the format when Alt-T is pressed a second time, and Tab was pressed twice after the level number. This way, you can quickly create hanging indentations using larger spacing between the hanging and indented text.

By using combinations of the indenting techniques described in this chapter, you can create a variety of different formats. Take a look at the text below:

Speakers for each session are:

Morning
                                     Mrs. Barbara Neibauer
                   Philadelphia College of Pharmacy and Science

                                          Loretta Williams
                             Winston College, Philadelphia

                                        Mr. John B. Smiler
                   Philadelphia College of Textiles and Science

Afternoon
                                        Dr. Vince Gorman
                                       Princeton University

                                      Dr. Averil H. Boxiter
                                       Williamsport College

This format can be created a number of ways. One method is to press Alt-R for right alignment (or select the Right Alignment option from the Format Paragraph menu), and then press Alt-T to create the hanging indentations. Type the hanging text (*Morning* and *Afternoon* in the example) and press Tab. Type the remainder of that line and press Enter. Subsequent lines are aligned on the right.

Don't be afraid to experiment with different combinations of commands as you continue with the exercises in this book and with Word.

In the next chapter, you will learn how to facilitate your work with Word by creating your own speed keys.

CHAPTER 7

○ **PRODUCING**
○ **QUICK**
○ **AND**
○ **EASY**
○ **LETTERS**

4.0 KEY

In general, letters account for much of our word processing. At first glance, except for form letters, they all seem different—different content, addresses, and lengths. But in reality, every letter you type has many things in common. Most offices, in fact, have a standard format that all business letters follow. In this chapter, you'll learn how to use this to your advantage.

You have already seen that you can modify the Normal stylesheet to your own desired defaults. Using the same techniques, you can design your own custom stylesheets, including your own speed keys.

In this chapter, we will create and use two stylesheets: one for business letters and one for legal documents. You will learn how to customize the sample stylesheets to suit your own styles. We will also create several letter and envelope templates, and you will see how to use them in combination with stylesheets to make your letter writing more efficient.

oIDENTIFYING STANDARD FORMATS

Business letters have several common elements. They are usually on office stationery with the name and address of the firm already printed at the top. They all have the date that the letter was written, an inside address, and a salutation. If your company doesn't use the block style, the first line of each paragraph is indented. The closing always follows the final paragraph.

Special-purpose letters also have a designated format. For example, legal letters typically include a case reference following the inside address. The reference may be the docket number or official name of the case.

The only "trick" is to identify the types of letters that you write and their standard formats. Creating a stylesheet for each type of letter speeds up your letter production because you don't have to take the time to format each individual letter as you type it.

oDISPLAYING STYLES ON THE SCREEN

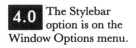 The Stylebar option is on the Window Options menu.

When you use your custom speed keys, you may want to have Word display the key code on the screen after you press it. Word will do this if you choose Yes for the Stylebar option on the Options menu. The ruler line will shift to the right ¼ inch, creating an area called the *stylebar*, where your key code characters appear. These indicate the type of format used for each style in the document.

This display is quite helpful when you are using custom stylesheets and templates. Before you enter text, you can tell which format it will take by the character displayed on the stylebar.

To turn the stylebar off, simply choose No for the Stylebar option on the same menu.

oA BUSINESS LETTER STYLESHEET

The importance of business letters cannot be overlooked. They often give clients (or prospective clients) their first impression of your company. Business letters represent you when you cannot be somewhere in person. They plead your case or make your demands. They also represent quite an investment. Word-processing experts estimate that the average business letter costs anywhere from $7 to $15 to produce. So, it's in your best interest to produce attractive letters as efficiently as possible.

CREATING THE BUSINESS LETTER STYLESHEET

Our example business letter stylesheet will take you some time to create and learn how to use, but you will find it worth the effort. It will save you more and more time with every letter that you write.

This stylesheet will include formats for the following parts of the letter:

o The date, centered 1 inch below the normal first line to leave room for a printed letterhead

o The inside address and salutation at the left margin

o Single-spaced paragraphs, with the first line indented

o Double spacing between paragraphs

o The closing

o The envelope address

You may want to adjust one or more of these formats for your own letters. For example, this stylesheet will insert six blank lines before the date to leave room for the printed letterhead. You may have to adjust this spacing for your own letterhead style. Just measure how far down on the page you want the date to appear. Subtract 1 inch (the normal top margin), then multiply the remainder by six. This will be the number of lines to leave before the date (in step 11 below).

Follow these steps to display the stylebar and then create the Business stylesheet:

1. Start Word.

2. Click on Options to display the menu

   WINDOW OPTIONS window number: 1 outline Yes(No) show hidden text: Yes(No) background color: 0 stylebar:Yes(No) ruler:(Yes)No

3. Click right on Yes for the Stylebar option. The window will display the stylebar to the left of the ruler line, as shown in Figure 7.1. The asterisk represents the standard paragraph.

4. Click left on Format; then click right on Stylesheet.

5. Type **BUSINESS,** and then click on the command line title. You'll see the message

   File does not exist. Press Y to create or Esc to cancel

6. Click on the message line. The text window will return to normal.

So that you can practice what you've learned, we'll create the styles two ways: by recording styles by example and by adding the formats directly into the Gallery. First we'll create the date format by example.

7. Click left on Format Paragraph.

4.0 Click left on Window Options to display the menu.

KEY Press Esc O (Esc W O with version 4.0). Press Tab seven times (four with version 4.0) to highlight the Stylebar option. Press Y, and then press Enter.

KEY Press Esc F S A, type **BUSINESS,** and press Enter. Press Y at the prompt.

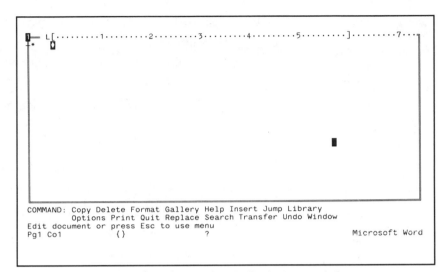

o **Figure 7.1:** *The stylebar to the left of the ruler line in the text window*

KEY Press F P, and
then press C for
the Alignment option.
Press the down arrow
twice, then the right
arrow to reach the Space
Before option, and type
6. Press Tab to reach the
Space After option, and
type 1; then press Enter.
Next press Esc F S R.
Type da, and then press
Tab three times to reach
the Remark option. Type
Date, and then press
Enter.

8. Click left on Centered.

9. Click on the Space Before option and type **6** (or the number of blank lines for your own letterhead style, as explained at the beginning of this section).

10. Click on the Space After option and type **1** (for one blank line after the date).

11. Click on the command line title.

12. Click left on Format Stylesheet Record to display the Format Style Record menu.

13. Type **da** for the Key Code option. Because you are entering a key code and will select a variant other than Standard, this style will not be the default. Instead, you will use it by pressing a new speed key, Alt-da.

14. Click on the Remark option. (Paragraph is already selected as the Usage option.)

15. Type **Date** and click on the command line title.

Now we'll enter the Gallery to make sure that the style was recorded and to create the remaining styles.

KEY Press Esc G. From the Gallery menu, press I. Type **in** for the Key Code option, press Tab, and then press P. Press Tab twice to reach the Remark option, type **Inside Address**, and press Enter. Next press F P. Press L for the Alignment option. Press the down arrow twice, then the right arrow twice to reach the Space After option and type **0**. Then press Enter.

KEY From the Gallery menu, press I. Type **sa** for the Key code option, press Tab, and press P. Press Tab twice to reach the Remark option, type **Salutation**, and press Enter. Next press F P. Press L for the Alignment option. Press the down arrow twice, then the right arrow once to reach the Space Before option, and type **1**. Press Tab to reach the Space After option, type **1**, and press Enter.

16. Click on Gallery. The Gallery displays the new date style, as shown in Figure 7.2.
17. Create the format for the inside address (aligned at the left margin and single spaced).
    a. From the Gallery menu, click left on Insert.
    b. Type **in** for the Key Code option.
    c. Click left on Paragraph for the Usage option.
    d. Click on the Remark option and type **Inside Address**.
    e. Click the command line title.
    f. Click left on Format Paragraph.
    g. Click on the Space After option and type **0**.
    h. Click on the command line title. The second style is added to the Gallery, as shown in Figure 7.3.
18. Create the format for the salutation (at the left margin, with one blank line before and after).
    a. From the Gallery menu, click left on Insert.
    b. Type **sa** for the Key Code option.
    c. Click left on Paragraph for the Usage option.

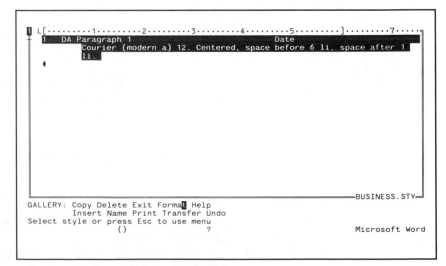

○ **Figure 7.2:** *Date style inserted in the Gallery*

d. Click on the Remark option and type **Salutation**.

e. Click on the command line title.

f. Click left on Format Paragraph.

g. Click on the Space Before option and type **1**.

h. Click on the Space After option and type **1**.

i. Click on the command line title. Figure 7.4 shows this style added to the Gallery.

19. Create the format for the body of the letter (aligned at the left margin, with the first line of each paragraph indented and a blank line between paragraphs).

a. From the Gallery menu, click left on Insert.

b. Type **bd** for the Key Code option.

c. Click left on Paragraph for the Usage option.

d. Click on the Remark option and type **Body**.

e. Click on the command line title.

f. Click left on Format Paragraph.

g. Click left on Left at the Alignment option.

h. Click on the First Line option and type **.5**.

KEY From the Gallery menu, press I. Type **bd**, press Tab P, press Tab twice to reach the Remark option, type **Body**, and then press Enter. Next press F P. Press L, press Tab twice to reach the First Line option, and type **.5**. Press Tab four times to reach the Space After option, type **1**, and press Enter.

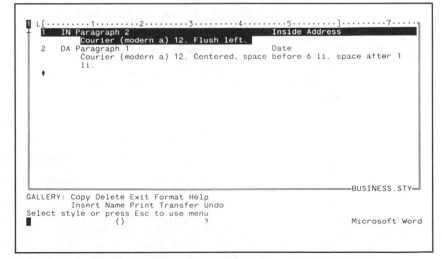

○ **Figure 7.3:** *The paragraph style for the inside address added in the Gallery*

```
1 L[·········1·········2·········3·········4·········5·········]·········7·····
  1   SA Paragraph 3                           Salutation
         Courier (modern a) 12. Flush left, space before 1 li, space after 1
         li.
  2   IN Paragraph 2                           Inside Address
         Courier (modern a) 12. Flush left.
  3   DA Paragraph 1                           Date
         Courier (modern a) 12. Centered, space before 6 li, space after 1
         li.
  ◆




                                                       ═BUSINESS.STY═
GALLERY: Copy Delete Exit Format Help
         Insert Name Print Transfer Undo
Select style or press Esc to use menu
■                    {}                   ?              Microsoft Word
```

o **Figure 7.4:** *The paragraph style for the salutation added in the Gallery window*

> i. Click on the Space After option and type **1**.
>
> j. Click on the command line title. Figure 7.5 shows our style-sheet at this point.

20. Now create the format for the closing (indented 3 inches from the left margin, with three blank lines after the closing). You will use the Keep Follow option to ensure that the closing and signature will print on the same page.

> a. From the Gallery menu, click left on Insert.
>
> b. Type **cl** for the Key Code option.
>
> c. Click left on Paragraph for the Usage option.
>
> d. Click on the Remark option and type **Closing**.
>
> e. Click on the command line title.
>
> f. Click left on Format Paragraph.
>
> g. Click on the Left Indent option and type **3**.
>
> h. Click on the Space After option and type **3**.
>
> i. Click right on Yes for the Keep Follow option. Figure 7.6 shows the result.

KEY From the Gallery menu, press I. Type **cl**, and then press Tab P. Press Tab twice to reach the Remark option, type **Closing**, and press Enter. Next press F P. Press L, press the down arrow to reach the Left Indent option, and type **3**. Press the down arrow once and the right arrow twice to reach the Space After option and type **3**. Press Tab to reach the Keep Follow option, press Y, and then press Enter.

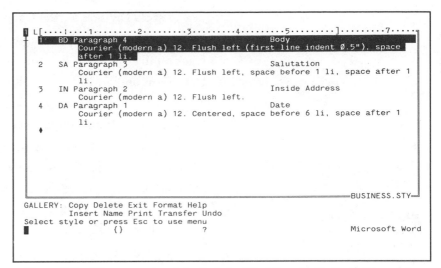

o **Figure 7.5:** *The paragraph style for the body of the letter added in the Gallery window*

```
1 LØ·········1·········2·········[·········4·········5·········]·········7·····
  1    CL Paragraph 5                     CLosing
       Courier (modern a) 12. Flush left, Left indent 3", space after 3 li
       (keep with following paragraph).
  2    BD Paragraph 4                     Body
       Courier (modern a) 12. Flush left (first line indent Ø.5"), space
       after 1 li.
  3    SA Paragraph 3                     Salutation
       Courier (modern a) 12. Flush left, space before 1 li, space after 1
       li.
  4    IN Paragraph 2                     Inside Address
       Courier (modern a) 12. Flush left.
  5    DA Paragraph 1                     Date
       Courier (modern a) 12. Centered, space before 6 li, space after 1
       li.
  ♦

                                                          ═BUSINESS.STY═
GALLERY: Copy Delete Exit Format Help
        Insert Name Print Transfer Undo
Select style or press Esc to use menu
█                     ()                 ?                 Microsoft Word
```

o **Figure 7.6:** *The paragraph style for the closing added in the Gallery window*

KEY From the Gallery menu, press I. Type **en**, and then press Tab D. Press Tab twice to reach the Remark option, type **Envelope**, and press Enter. Next press F M. Type **0** for the Top Margin. Press Tab to reach the Bottom Margin option and type **0**. Press Tab to move to the Left Margin option and type **3**. Press Tab to reach the Right Margin option and type **1**. Finally, press Tab to reach the Page Length option, type **3**, and then press Enter.

21. Now create the format for the envelope (a new division for the 3-inch left margin and different page size).

   a. Click left on Insert.

   b. Type **en** for the Key Code option.

c. Click left on Division for the Usage option.

d. Click on the Remark option and type **Envelope**.

e. Click on the command line title.

f. Click right on Format.

g. Type **0** for the Top Margin option.

h. Click on the Bottom Margin option and type **0**.

i. Click on the Left Margin option and type **3**.

j. Click on the Right Margin option and type **1**.

k. Click on the Page Length option and type **3**.

l. Click on the command line title. The finished Business style-sheet is shown in Figure 7.7.

KEY Press T S Enter to save the completed stylesheet. Press E to exit the Gallery; then press Esc Q to quit Word.

22. Click left on Transfer, then click right on Save.

23. Click on Exit, and then click on Quit to exit Word.

```
1 L[·········1·········2·········3·········4·········5·········]·········7·····
  1    EN Division 1                        Envelope
       Page break. Page length 3"; width 8.5". Page # format Arabic. Top
       margin 0"; bottom 0"; left 3"; right 1". Top running head at 0.5".
       Bottom running head at 0.5". Footnotes on same page.
  2    CL Paragraph 5                        CLosing
       Courier (modern a) 12. Flush left. Left indent 3", space after 3 li
       (keep with following paragraph).
  3    BD Paragraph 4                        Body
       Courier (modern a) 12. Flush left (first line indent 0.5"), space
       after 1 li.
  4    SA Paragraph 3                        Salutation
       Courier (modern a) 12. Flush left, space before 1 li, space after 1
       li.
  5    IN Paragraph 2                        Inside Address
       Courier (modern a) 12. Flush left.
  6    DA Paragraph 1                        Date
       Courier (modern a) 12. Centered, space before 6 li, space after 1
       li.
  ♦                                                         ═BUSINESS.STY═
GALLERY: Copy Delete Exit Format Help
         Insert Name Print Transfer Undo
Select style or press Esc to use menu
■                    {}                    ?                  Microsoft Word
```

o **Figure 7.7:** *The division style for the envelope, along with other formats, in the Gallery window*

oUSING THE BUSINESS STYLESHEET

With the Business stylesheet, you can produce business letters without worrying about formatting. You can use the stylesheet in two different ways:

- o Attach the stylesheet and format as you type.
- o Use a formatted template that contains all the styles.

First, let's use the stylesheet to format a letter as we type it.

FORMATTING AS YOU TYPE

In the following exercise, you will type a simple business letter using the Business stylesheet. For each element of the letter, press the appropriate speed key. To use a two-letter key code, hold down the Alt key while you press and release the first letter, and then press and release the second letter.

Follow these steps for formatting the letter as you type:

1. Start Word.
2. Click left on Format, and then click right on Stylesheet.
3. Click right to the right of the command line title, and click right on Business. The Business stylesheet will be recalled from the disk and attached to the document.
4. If it is not already on the screen, display the stylebar (select Yes for Stylebar on the Options menu) so that you can see the key codes as you use them. This is just for convenience; you don't have to display the stylebar to use the speed keys.
5. Press Alt-DA. The characters DA appear in the stylebar, and the cursor is centered six lines down from the top of the screen.
6. Type the date **January 16, 1990**, and press Enter. Word now assumes that the next paragraph will be in this style, and six blank

KEY Press Esc F S A, type **Business**, and press Enter.

lines appear after the date. But don't worry—they will be erased in the next step.

7. Press Alt-IN to change to the inside address format and type

Mr. William Randolph
10 Century Road
Madison, WI 16523

8. Press Enter.

Now let's say that you forgot the speed key to use for the salutation style. You could enter the Gallery to see the style, return to the document, and then use the speed key. But there is an easier way: You can "apply" the key code from the Format Stylesheet menu. Let's see how.

KEY Press Esc F S P, and then press F1 to list alternatives. Select style SA and press Enter.

9. Click left on Format Stylesheet Paragraph (because the format you want was assigned paragraph usage in the Gallery). You will see the prompt line

FORMAT STYLESHEET PARAGRAPH: Paragraph2

10. Click right to the right of the command line title to see a list of paragraph styles, along with their key codes and remarks, as shown in Figure 7.8.

```
   Paragraph Standard                     CL Paragraph 5 (Closing)
BD Paragraph 4 (Body)                     SA Paragraph 3 (Salutation)
IN Paragraph 2 (Inside Address)           DA Paragraph 1 (Date)




                                                                    ■




FORMAT STYLESHEET PARAGRAPH: Paragraph Standard
Enter paragraph style variant or press F1 to select from list
Pg1 Co1               {}                    ?              Microsoft Word
```

o **Figure 7.8:** *List of paragraph styles that can be applied*

11. Click right on style SA. Now the text you type in the document will be in this style.

12. Type **Dear Mr. Randolph:**.

13. Press Enter.

14. Press Alt-BD and type the body of the letter.

> **Your account has been overdue for 120 days in the amount of $129.96. If payment is not received within 14 days, we will be forced to cancel your credit status with our company and take legal action. Please remit the full amount.**

15. Press Enter.

16. Press Alt-CL and type the closing **Sincerely yours,**.

17. Press Enter. Figure 7.9 shows the letter at this point.

18. Type the name **Sigmond Smith, President**.

19. Press Enter.

20. Press Ctrl-Enter to insert a division mark after the letter.

KEY Select the inside address and press Alt-F3 to copy it to the scrap. Place the cursor after the division mark, and then press Ins to insert the address.

21. Move the mouse cursor to the inside address in the letter and drag to select the three lines. Then click right on Copy.

22. Point after the division mark, click left, and then click right on Insert.

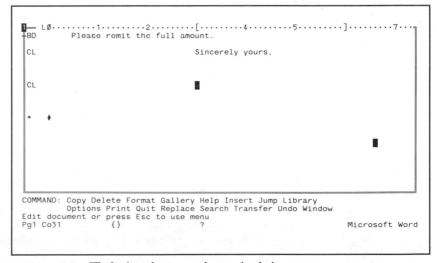

o **Figure 7.9:** *The business letter example up to its closing*

23. Press Alt-P (Alt-XP with version 4.0) to return to the normal paragraph format.

24. Position the cursor after the address that you just inserted, and then press Alt-EN. Another division mark will appear, as shown in Figure 7.10. The second address will be formatted for the envelope. The letter and envelope are ready to be printed. (To print these envelopes, your printer must be capable of feeding individual sheets of paper.)

25. Click left on Print Options.

26. Click right on the Paper Feed option to display alternatives, and then click right on Manual. (With version 4.0, just click right on Manual at the prompt line.)

27. Click right on Printer to print the letter, then the envelope.

28. Click left on Quit, and then press N.

You have just created an attractive letter, without using any formatting commands. Now you see how the time you spent creating the stylesheet will be rewarded.

KEY Press Esc P O. Press the down arrow six times and type **Manual**. (With version 4.0, press the down arrow five times and press M.) Press Enter, then P. Press Esc Q N to quit.

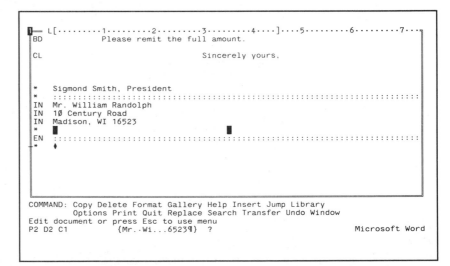

o **Figure 7.10:** *The envelope address between division marks*

USING A FORMATTED TEMPLATE

There is one problem with using custom stylesheets: You have to remember the speed keys. You can have Word display them on the screen by using the Format Stylesheet commands, but this can be tedious with long, complicated stylesheets.

An alternative is to use a *formatted template*, which is a special document made up of formatting information. In the template, the speed keys are in the same order as the styles will appear in the finished document. The stylebar shows which key codes have been used. To use the template, you simply place the cursor next to the appropriate code and type.

Creating a Formatted Template

To use a formatted template, you must first create it. Follow these steps to create the Business template.

1. Start Word.

2. Click on Format Stylesheet Attach.

3. Click right to the right of the command line title, and then click right on Business. The Business stylesheet will be attached to the document.

4. Press Alt-DA, then Enter.

5. Press Alt-IN, then Enter.

6. Press Alt-SA, then Enter.

7. Press Alt-BD, then Enter.

8. Press Alt-CL, and then press Enter twice.

9. Press Ctrl-Enter.

10. Press Alt-P (Alt-XP with version 4.0), then Enter.

11. Press Alt-EN. Your screen should look like the one shown in Figure 7.11.

12. Click left on Transfer Save and type **BusTem**. Click on the command line title, and then click on SUMMARY.

13. Click right on Quit to exit Word.

KEY Press Esc F S A, type **Business**, and press Enter.

KEY Press Esc T S, type **BusTem**, and press Enter twice to save the template. Press Esc Q to quit.

Typing with a Formatted Template

You use a formatted template as you would use any other type of template: Load it and enter the information. Unlike templates for creating form letters, however, the formatted template includes nothing but styles.

When you're using a formatted template, you must press the down arrow key to move from one format to the next. Press the Enter key only when you want to begin another paragraph with the same format as the previous one.

Let's use the Business template to type another typical business letter. Follow the procedure below:

1. Start Word.

2. Click right on Transfer.

Press Ctrl-F7, type **BusTem**, and press Enter.

3. Click right to the right of the command line title, then click right on BusTem.

4. Display the stylebar if it is not already on the screen.

5. With the cursor at the start of the document, type the date **November 16, 1990**. Do not press Enter. The date will be centered on the screen, in accordance with the preselected format.

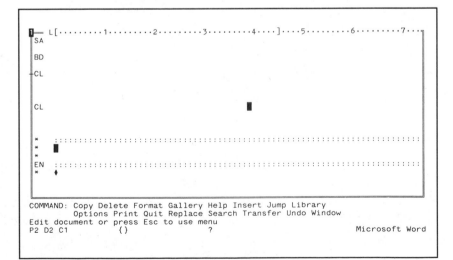

o **Figure 7.11:** *The formatted Business template*

6. Press the down arrow key. The cursor will be in position for the inside address.

7. Type the address. Press Enter after each line except the last one.

> **Ms. Robbin Mathews**
> **659 Sixth Street**
> **Berkeley, MN 38711**

8. Press the down arrow key. Then type the salutation. Do not press Enter when you're done.

> **Dear Ms. Mathews:**

9. Press the down arrow key and type the body of the letter. Press Enter between paragraphs, but not after the last one.

> **On behalf of our president, Mr. James B. Butlocks, I have the pleasure of offering you the position of MIS Director. The position starts on January 1, 1991.**
> **Please contact Mrs. Sandy Forman, Personnel Director, to formalize the appointment.**

10. Press the down arrow key. The cursor will be in position for the closing. (Don't worry if the cursor is at the far right margin—the closing will be formatted correctly as you type.) Type

> **Sincerely yours,**

Figure 7.12 shows the letter up to this point.

11. Press the down arrow key and type

> **Samual Smythe, Vice President**

12. Move the mouse cursor to the inside address, drag to select it, and then click right on Copy.

13. Point between the two division marks, click left, and click right on Insert. The inside address is inserted into the envelope template, as shown in Figure 7.13.

14. Click left on Print Options.

15. Click right on the Paper Feed option to display alternatives, and then click right on Manual. (With version 4.0, click right on Manual at the prompt line.)

KEY Select the inside address and press Alt-F3 to copy it to the scrap. Position the cursor between the two division marks at the bottom of the page, and then press Ins. Next press Esc P O. Press the down arrow six times and type **Manual**. (With version 4.0, press the down arrow five times, and then press M.) Press Enter, then P. Click left on Quit, and then press N.

16. Click right on Printer to print the letter, and then the envelope.

17. Click left on Quit; then press N to quit Word without saving the edits. This leaves the original template on the disk.

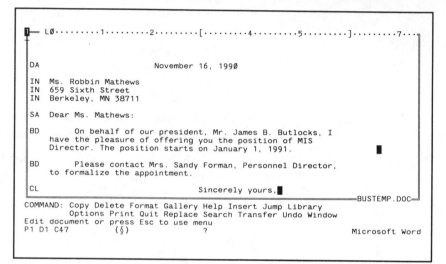

o **Figure 7.12:** *The business letter, up to its closing, typed with the template*

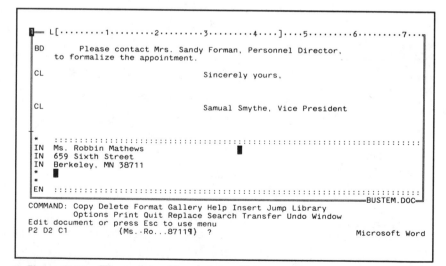

o **Figure 7.13:** *The envelope address in its template*

oA STYLESHEET FOR A LEGAL LETTER

The typical legal letter has the same elements as a business letter. It has the date, an inside address, a salutation, the body of the letter, and a closing. In addition, many legal letters have a heading following the inside address. The heading includes a file or docket number, case name, or some other reference number. Legal letters also often include indented paragraphs. These may state terms of settlement, references, or other text that the letter writer wants to stand out. Some legal documents have line numbers along the left margin to serve as references at some later date. These standard elements make the legal letter a good candidate for its own custom stylesheet.

CREATING THE LAW STYLESHEET

You will now create such a stylesheet for a typical legal letter, following the same basic procedure that you used to create the Business stylesheet in the previous example. This stylesheet will include formats for the following elements:

- o The date, centered six lines below the normal first line to leave room for a printed letterhead
- o An inside address at the left margin
- o A reference line, which is underlined, uppercase, and boldface
- o Block style, single-spaced paragraphs
- o An optional indented paragraph format
- o The closing
- o An optional division format to number each line along the left margin

Remember that you can customize any of these formats to suit your own needs.

Follow the steps below to create the Law stylesheet:

1. Start Word.

2. Click left on Format; then click right on Stylesheet.

KEY Press Esc F S A, type **LAW**, and press Enter Y.

3. Type **LAW** and click on the command line title.

4. Click on the message line to confirm that you want to create a new stylesheet.

5. Click on Gallery.

6. Create the format for the date.

KEY Press Esc G. Press I and type **da** for the Key Code option. Press Tab P Enter. Press F P C, press Tab five times to reach the Space Before option, and type **6**. Press Tab to reach the Space After option, type **1**, and press Enter.

    a. Click left on Insert.

    b. Type **da** for the Key Code option.

    c. Click right on Paragraph for the Usage option.

    d. Click left on Format Paragraph.

    e. Click left on Centered.

    f. Click on the Space Before option and type **6**.

    g. Click on the Space After option and type **1**.

    h. Click on the command line title.

7. Create the format for the inside address.

KEY From the Gallery menu, press I and type **in** for the Key Code option. Press Tab P Enter. Press F P L, press Tab six times to reach the Space After option, and type **0**. Press Enter.

    a. Click left on Insert.

    b. Type **in** for the Key Code option.

    c. Click right on Paragraph for the Usage option.

    d. Click left on Format Paragraph.

    e. Click on the command line title.

8. Create the reference number format.

KEY From the Gallery menu, press I and type **re**. Press Tab P Enter. Press F P C, press Tab six times to reach the Space After option, and type **0**. Press Enter. Press F C, press Tab twice to reach the Underline option, and press Y. Press Tab twice to reach the Uppercase option, press Y, and press Enter.

    a. Click left on Insert.

    b. Type **re** for the Key Code option.

    c. Click right on Paragraph for the Usage option.

    d. Click left on Format Paragraph.

    e. Click left on Centered.

    f. Click on the command line title.

g. Click right on Format to display the Format Character menu. Click left on Yes for the Underline option; then click right on Yes for the Uppercase option.

9. Now create the format for the salutation.

   a. Click left on Insert.
   b. Type **sa** for the Key Code option.
   c. Click right on Paragraph for the Usage option.
   d. Click left on Format Paragraph.
   e. Click on the Space Before option and type **1**.
   f. Click on the Space After option and type **1**.
   g. Click on the command line title.

10. Create the optional indented paragraph style. You don't have to set up the format for the block paragraph style of the body of the letter since it is the standard format, recalled by pressing Alt-P (with version 4.0, Alt-XP).

    a. Click left on Insert.
    b. Type **op** for the Key Code option.
    c. Click right on Paragraph for the Usage option.
    d. Click left on Format Paragraph.
    e. Click left on Left.
    f. Click on the Left Indent option and type **1**.
    g. Click on the Right Indent option and type **1**.
    h. Click on the Space Before option and type **1**.
    i. Click on the Space After option and type **1**.
    j. Click on the command line title.

11. Create the format for the closing.

    a. Click left on Insert.
    b. Type **cl** for the Key Code option.
    c. Click right on Paragraph for the Usage option.
    d. Click left on Format Paragraph.
    e. Click left on Left.

KEY From the Gallery menu, press I and type **sa**. Press Tab P Enter. Press F P L, press Tab five times to reach the Space Before option, and type **1**. Press Tab to reach the Space After option, type **1**, and then press Enter.

KEY From the Gallery menu, press I and type **op**. Press Tab P Enter. Press F P L, press Tab to reach the Left Indent option, and type **1**. Press Tab twice to reach the Right Indent option and type **1**. Press Tab twice to reach the Space Before option and type **1**. Press Tab to reach the Space After option and type **1**. Press Enter.

KEY From the Gallery menu, press I and type **cl**. Press Tab P Enter. Press F P L, press Tab to reach the Left Indent option, and type **3**. Press Tab five times to reach the Space After option and type **3**. Press Tab twice to reach the Keep Follow option and press Y. Press Enter.

     f. Click on the Left Indent option and type **3**.

     g. Click on the Space After option and type **3**.

     h. Click right on Yes for the Keep Follow option.

12. Create the optional division for numbering lines.

     a. Click left on Insert.

     b. Type **ln** for the Key Code option.

     c. Click right on Division for the Usage option.

     d. Click left on Format Line-Numbers to see the menu:

> **FORMAT DIVISION LINE-NUMBERS: Yes No**   **from text: 0.4"**
> **restart at: (Page)Division Continuous**   **increment: 1**

     e. Click left on Yes.

     f. Click right on Division for the Restart At option to number the lines consecutively through the whole division, starting at the division break. Figure 7.14 shows the completed Law stylesheet.

13. Click Left on Transfer; then click right on Save.

14. Click on Exit, and then click on Quit to quit Word.

USING THE LAW STYLESHEET

Whenever you want to prepare a legal letter using the styles on the Law stylesheet, follow the procedure below:

1. Start Word.

2. Click left on Format; then click right on Stylesheet.

3. Type **Law**, and then click on the command line title. The Law stylesheet will be attached to the document.

4. Press Alt-DA and type the date.

5. Press Alt-IN and type the inside address.

6. Press Alt-RE and type the reference.

7. Press Alt-SA and type the salutation.

8. Press Alt-P (Alt-XP with version 4.0) and type the body of the letter.

KEY From the Gallery menu, press I and type **ln**. Press Tab D Enter. Press F N, and then press Y. Press the down arrow to reach the Restart At option, press D, and press Enter.

KEY Press T S to save the stylesheet. Press E, then Esc Q to quit.

KEY Press Esc F S A, type **Law**, and press Enter.

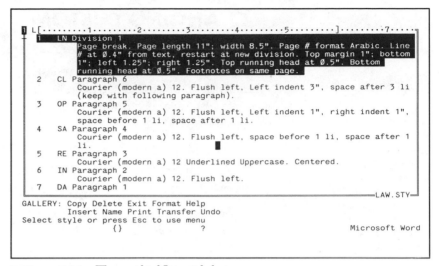

```
1 L[········1········2········3········4········5········]········7·····
  1   LN Division 1
          Page break. Page length 11"; width 8.5". Page # format Arabic. Line
          # at 0.4" from text, restart at new division. Top margin 1"; bottom
          1"; left 1.25"; right 1.25". Top running head at 0.5". Bottom
          running head at 0.5". Footnotes on same page.
  2   CL Paragraph 6
          Courier (modern a) 12. Flush left, Left indent 3", space after 3 li
          (keep with following paragraph).
  3   OP Paragraph 5
          Courier (modern a) 12. Flush left, Left indent 1", right indent 1",
          space before 1 li, space after 1 li.
  4   SA Paragraph 4
          Courier (modern a) 12. Flush left, space before 1 li, space after 1
          li.
  5   RE Paragraph 3
          Courier (modern a) 12 Underlined Uppercase. Centered.
  6   IN Paragraph 2
          Courier (modern a) 12. Flush left.
  7   DA Paragraph 1
                                                                    ═LAW.STY═
GALLERY: Copy Delete Exit Format Help
         Insert Name Print Transfer Undo
Select style or press Esc to use menu
              {}                    ?                         Microsoft Word
```

o **Figure 7.14:** *The completed Law stylesheet*

9. When you want to type an indented paragraph, press Alt-OP, and type the text.

10. When you're finished entering the letter, press Alt-CL and type the closing.

11. Press Enter, then Alt-P (Alt-XP with version 4.0) to cancel the closing style.

If you want to type a numbered document on the page following the letter, press Ctrl-Enter to insert a division break, type the document, and then press Alt-LN for the new division format. The numbers won't appear on the screen, but you will see them when the document is printed or when you view it in preview mode.

oYOUR OWN STYLESHEETS

The Business and Law stylesheets are for typical formats that you may find useful. You might want to modify these stylesheets to suit your needs or create entirely different ones.

CHANGING CUSTOM STYLESHEETS

You can add formats to your stylesheet or change the ones that are already there. To edit a stylesheet, first recall it, and then enter the Gallery. For example, if you want to change the Business stylesheet, follow these steps:

1. Click left on Format, and then click right on Stylesheet.
2. Type **Business** and click on the command line title.
3. Click on Gallery to display the stylesheet.
4. To change a format, press the up or down arrow key until that format is highlighted. Click left on Format; then select Character, Paragraph, Tab, Border, or Position, as appropriate, and make the changes.
5. To add a new format, click on Insert, and enter the Key Code, Usage, and Variant options, as appropriate. Click on the command line title, click left on Format, and then make the changes.

Note that you can assign a key code that is the same as a default speed key, such as Alt-C. However, you then must press X before you press the default speed key letter to have the command perform its normal (not customized) function. To center text, for example, press Alt-XC. (With version 4.0, you must press Alt-X to use any default speed key.)

6. When you're finished making changes, save the edited stylesheet. From the Gallery menu, click left on Transfer, and then click right on Save. To save the stylesheet under a new name, click left on Transfer Save, type the name, and then click on the command line title.

CREATING CUSTOM STYLESHEETS

You can create as many custom speed keys and stylesheets as you need. Design a series of formats that you use in one type of document,

KEY Press Esc F S A, type **Business**, and press Enter. Press Esc G to display the stylesheet. Highlight the style you want to change, and then press F. Press C, P, T, B, or O, and make the changes.

4.0 The Position option is not available.

KEY Press I; then enter the Key Code, Usage, and Variant options; and press Enter. Format the style to suit your tastes. Press T S to store the stylesheet on disk.

add them to a new stylesheet, and save the stylesheet with a name that is easy to remember.

The formats that you design can be different division, paragraph, as well as character styles. For instance, suppose that your legal office includes a reference to the relevant case in every letter. For emphasis, it is typed underlined and in all uppercase letters, such as <u>WELLINGTON VS. BEEF</u>. You could create a character style with the key code CA that specifies both underlining and uppercase letters, as shown in Figure 7.15. Then you merely have to press Alt-CA before typing the reference. After the reference, you can return to the standard style by pressing Alt-P (Alt-XP with version 4.0).

Custom stylesheets can be used for any type of document. But because letters account for a large part of general office word processing, their production should be a major application for stylesheet techniques.

If there is some information included in each letter, type it directly in the template. For example, the salutation line could appear as:

SA Dear

If you don't have printed letterhead paper, type your address at the top of the template. Then change the Spaces Before option (on the Format Paragraph menu) for the date style to 1.

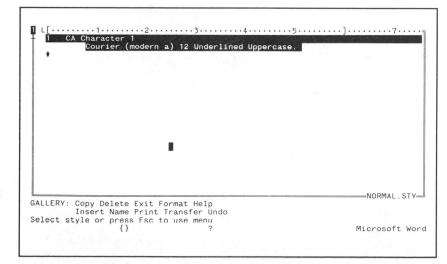

o **Figure 7.15:** *The format for underlined, uppercase characters*

oINSERTING DATES AND TIMES

Earlier in this chapter, you typed the date at the top of a letter. If your computer has a built-in clock circuit, or you enter the correct date and time at the DOS prompt, you can have Word insert the proper date or time for you automatically.

In fact, two separate date and time functions are available: Date and Time, and Dateprint and Timeprint. The Date and Time functions insert the current date and time in the document. Let's say that you typed a document on January 23, 1990, and used the Date function. Whenever you print the document, the date January 23, 1990, will appear.

The Dateprint and Timeprint functions insert a code into the text, which will appear as the actual date or time when the document was printed. If you enter the Dateprint code on January 23, 1990, the code

(dateprint)

appears in the document. But when you print the document, the current date appears.

All these functions are available in the normal glossary. The glossary will be discussed in Chapter 19, but you don't need the details to use the functions now. Follow one of these procedures:

- o To insert the current date into the document, type **date** and press the F3 key. The actual date will appear, in the form November 16, 1990.

- o To insert the current time, type **time** and press F3. The time will appear, in the form 11:16 AM.

- o To have the current date appear whenever the document is printed, type **dateprint** and press F3. The code (dateprint) will appear in the text.

- o To have the current time appear whenever the document is printed, type **timeprint** and press F3. The code (timeprint) will appear in the text.

You can change the format of the date and time through the Options menu. The date can either print in the default month-day-year (MDY) format, or in day-month-year (DMY) format such as 16 November

1990. The time can either use a 12-hour clock (the default) or 24-hour (military) time.

In this chapter, you've learned that you can create your own stylesheets and templates for the various kinds of documents that you produce. Next, we will take stylesheet applications one step further. You will learn how to create stylesheets to handle several problems unique to multipage documents.

CHAPTER 8

- CREATING
- MULTIPAGE
- DOCUMENTS
- AND
- PRINTING
- ON
- LETTERHEAD

4.0

KEY

When you're producing multipage letters and other documents, you must make some decisions:

o Should the pages be numbered? Where should the numbers be? On which page should numbering begin? Should it be at the same location on both odd- and even-numbered pages?

o Is the first page on letterhead paper? What about following pages? Does this mean that the margins have to be changed?

o Do you want a standard heading on every page? Should some text be printed at the bottom of each page?

Confusing? Well, fortunately, Word can accommodate whatever choices you make.

As examples of the ways that you can handle multipage documents, this chapter presents step-by-step procedures for printing on letterhead and plain paper, with numbered pages, and running heads (also called headers and footers) for odd- and even-numbered pages. You'll also see how to "mirror" margins, alternating indentation settings for odd- and even-numbered pages.

oPRINTING ON LETTERHEAD PAPER

One common application is printing a long document with the first page on letterhead paper, which has the name and address of your company preprinted on the top of the page. The following pages are normally printed on plain paper.

While the letterhead paper requires a top margin large enough to skip over the printed material, the plain paper should have the standard 1-inch top margin. So these documents need two divisions to start the text at the appropriate place, as shown in Figure 8.1. The first division formats the first page for letterhead paper. The second division returns the margin to normal for subsequent pages.

You could avoid the problem of setting up two divisions by pressing Enter a few extra times before typing the first page. Many typists do just that. But that method is inexact and easy to forget—something you might not notice until the letter starts printing right over the company

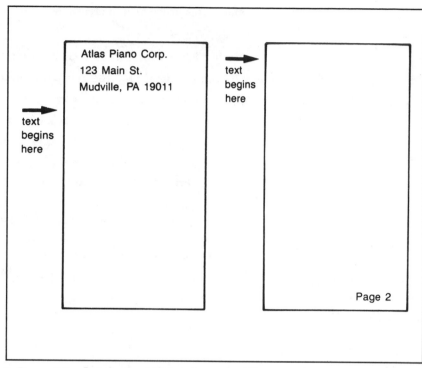

o **Figure 8.1:** *Letterhead and plain paper require different margins*

logo or address. The best way to print documents on letterhead and plain paper is to add two division styles to a stylesheet.

CREATING A LETTERHEAD STYLESHEET

In this exercise, you'll not only create a stylesheet for printing letters on two different types of paper, but you'll also format the divisions to print a page number at the bottom of each page. There are several ways to print page numbers with Word. In this example, we'll use the options on the Format Division menu.

First, you will create a new standard division to print on your letterhead paper. With this standard, you can use the stylesheet even if you're printing a single-page letter on letterhead paper. The second division will return the following pages to the normal top margin for printing on blank paper.

Follow this procedure to create the stylesheet:

1. Start Word.

2. Click left on Format; then click right on Stylesheet.

3. Type **LetHead**, and then click on the command line title.

4. Click on the message line to create a new stylesheet.

5. Click on Gallery, and then click left on Insert.

6. Click left on Division for the Usage option.

7. Click right on the Variant option; then click on the command line title to accept the Standard variant.

8. Create a new standard division for letterhead paper (2-inch top margin, with page numbers printed in the center, $1/2$ inch from the bottom of the page). If your letterhead requires more or less room, enter the appropriate measurement in step g below.

   a. From the Gallery menu, click left on Format.

   b. Click on Page-Numbers.

   c. Click left on Yes.

   d. Click on the From Top option and type **10.5**.

   e. Click on the From Left option and type **4.25**.

   f. Click on the command line title.

   g. Click right on Format and type **2** for the Top Margin option, which is already selected.

   h. Click on the command line title. Figure 8.2 shows the new standard division in the Gallery window.

9. Create the division for the following pages.

   a. From the Gallery menu, click left on Insert.

   b. Type **nx** for the Key Code option.

   c. Click right on Division for the Usage option.

   d. Click left on Yes for the Format Page-Numbers option.

   e. Click on the From Top option and type **10.5**.

   f. Click on the From Left option and type **4.25**.

   g. Click on the command line title. Figure 8.3 shows the completed stylesheet.

KEY Press Esc F S A, type **LetHead**, and press Enter. Next press Esc G I. Press Tab D, press Tab to reach the Variant option, type **Standard**, and press Enter.

KEY From the Gallery menu, press F P Y. Press Tab to reach the From Top option, and type **10.5**. Press Tab to reach the From Left option, type **4.25**, and then press Enter. Press F M. The Top Margin option is already selected. Type **2**, and then press Enter.

KEY From the Gallery menu, press I. Type **nx** for the key code. Press Tab to reach the Usage option, press D, and then press Enter. From the Gallery menu, press F P Y. Press Tab to reach the From Top option and type **10.5**. Press Tab to reach the From Left option, type **4.25**, and then press Enter.

KEY From the Gallery menu, press T S Enter to save the style-sheet. Press E to exit the Gallery, then Esc Q to exit Word.

10. Click left on Transfer; then click right on Save to save the style-sheet.

11. Click on Exit, and then click on Quit to exit Word.

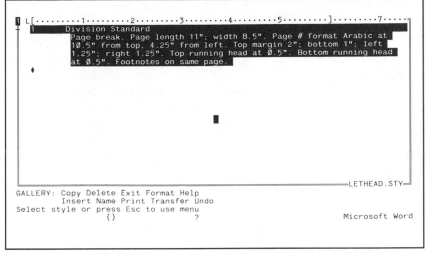

o **Figure 8.2:** *The new standard division for letterhead paper*

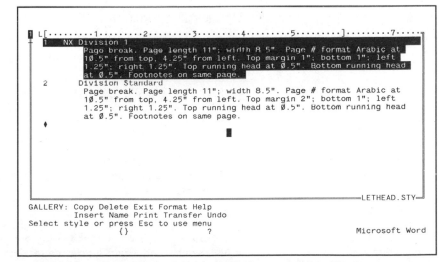

o **Figure 8.3:** *The completed stylesheet for letterhead paper and plain following pages*

If you always use letterhead paper, add these two divisions to your Normal stylesheet. Single-page letters will automatically be formatted with the new standard division. If you decide to use plain paper for every page of a specific document, simply type that document, and press Alt-NX when you're finished.

USING THE LETTERHEAD STYLESHEET

Now that the stylesheet is created, you can use letterhead paper without worrying about the margins. If you are typing a short cover letter as the first page, press Ctrl-Enter when you want that page to end and continue typing. Press Alt-NX after you finish the document.

If you're working on a long, continuous document, enter the text. When you're finished, place the cursor at the first page break, and press Ctrl-Enter to insert a division mark. Press Alt-NX to format the remaining pages to print on plain paper.

In the following exercise, you will type a two-page document consisting of a short cover letter formatted to print on letterhead paper followed by an enclosure to print on plain paper. Follow these steps:

4.0 Paginate the document before inserting the division mark.

1. Start Word.
2. Click left on Format; then click right on Stylesheet.
3. Click right to the right of the command line title to display alternative stylesheets, and then click right on LetHead at the top of the screen.

KEY Press Esc F S A, type **LetHead**, and press Enter to attach the Letterhead stylesheet.

4. Type the following cover letter:

   March 14, 1990

   Siravo Hobbies and Crafts
   573 Tudor Village Drive
   Landsend, MA 65439

   Dear Sirs:

   Our company is entering the hobby and craft market in Philadelphia. We would appreciate receiving your bid on the items listed on the attached sheet.

We will be ordering the items within the next 90 days and would appreciate a timely response.

Sincerely,

Wilson B. Witherspoon
President

5. Press Ctrl-Enter to insert a division mark. This represents the new standard division (with a 2-inch top margin).

6. Type the text of the enclosure.

Request For Bids

Quantity	Item
Balsa Wood	
50 each	**Balsa—1/2 by 1/2 by 36 inches**
50 "	**Balsa—1 by 1 by 36 inches**
100 "	**Balsa—1 by 2 by 36 inches**
50 "	**Balsa—2 by 2 by 36 inches**
100 "	**Balsa—4 by 4 by 12 inches**
75 "	**Balsa—2 by 4 by 36 inches**
Hobby Paint (in 2-ounce bottles)	
25 bottles	**Bright Red**
25 "	**Metallic Red**
25 "	**Dark Red**
25 "	**Baby Blue**
25 "	**Steel Blue**
25 "	**Navy Blue**
25 "	**Robin's Egg Blue**
25 "	**Sky Blue**
25 "	**Metallic Blue**
100 "	**White**
100 "	**Black**
100 "	**Battleship Gray**
100 "	**Silver**
100 "	**Bronze**
100 "	**Gold**

7. Press Alt-NX. Another division mark will be inserted into the text. This will format all the text between the two division marks to print on blank paper, with the normal 1-inch top margin.

8. Print a copy of the letter to confirm that the divisions are set correctly. If you're going to insert the individual pages into your printer, select Manual for the paper Feed option on the Print Options menu. If you have a multibin printer, place the letterhead paper in bin 1, put the plain paper in bin 2, and select Mixed for the Paper Feed option.

oPREPARING PUBLICATION-QUALITY DOCUMENTS

The quality of the printed image depends on your printer. We'll discuss this in detail in Chapter 20.

With Word and the correct printer, you can prepare publication-quality documents, or *camera-ready copy*. Producing documents this way is much quicker and less expensive than having them typeset.

You control the page size of your document, one of the main layout considerations, by changing the page length, width, and margin settings on the Format Division menu. But published documents require some other considerations. Two of these are the placement of page numbers and the inclusion of headers.

In bound books, for example, page numbers usually appear near the outer edge of the paper, on the left side of even-numbered pages and on the right side of odd-numbered pages. The numbering can be on the top or bottom of the page.

Printed documents also often include a header, which is some text printed on the top of every page. It may be the name of the book or report, company name, or author. Headers, like page numbers, are normally printed on the left side of even-numbered pages and on the right side of odd-numbered pages. Figure 8.4 shows the typical placement of page numbers and headers.

CREATING THE RUNNING HEADS

4.0 The default format places running heads at the edge of the paper, ignoring the right and left margin settings. You can change this placement by using the Format Paragraph menu options, as explained later.

In Word's terminology, *running head* refers to standard text printed at the top or bottom of every page. By default, Word prints running heads ½ inch from the top or bottom of the page, aligned with the margins, and on every page of the document formatted with them, except the first.

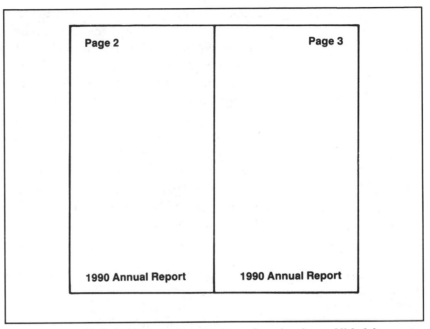

o **Figure 8.4:** *Typical placement of page headers and numbers in a published document*

If the default settings are suitable for your document, you can create running heads very easily by using speed keys. Place the cursor at the start of the document, type the text of the header, and then press Ctrl-F2. To create a footer, enter the footer text, and then press Alt-F2. The running heads will print on every page of that document but the first.

If you want to use different settings for your running heads—print them only on odd- or even-numbered pages, print one on the first page, or align them with the edge of the paper—use the options on the Format Running Head menu. Our next example shows how to set up running heads through this menu.

SETTING UP A RUNNING HEAD TEMPLATE

Now let's create a format suitable for publication in a bound document. Each page will be numbered at the bottom, on the right side of odd-numbered pages and the left side of even-numbered pages. Running heads will appear on the top of each page, also alternating between the left and right sides. The running heads will start on the first page. In this example, the running head will be your name, but you can, of course, use other text.

For extra effect, we'll include a line to neatly separate the running head from the rest of the text. Rather than simply typing an underline, however, we'll use Word's graphic commands. These commands are discussed in detail in Chapter 18; here you'll get an idea of their power. Figure 8.5 shows the format that you will set up.

Creating a template for running heads is a two-phase process. First, you enter the text of the running head, and then you designate its placement.

Follow these steps:

1. Start Word.

2. Type your name, but do not press Enter.

KEY Press Esc F B L. Press Tab six times to reach the Below option, press Y, and press Enter. Next press Esc F R T. Press Tab to reach the Odd Pages option, press N, and press Enter.

3. Click left on Format Border to display the menu shown in Figure 8.6. (The last line of the menu is not in version 4.0.) The powerful options on this menu let you draw lines and boxes.

4. Click left on Lines for the Type option.

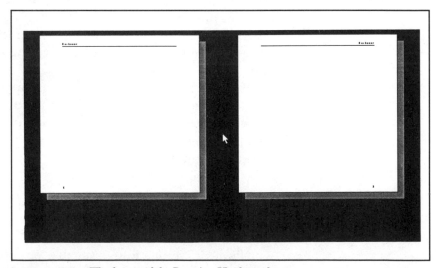

o **Figure 8.5:** *The format of the Running Head template*

5. Click right on Yes for the Below option. A line appears under your name. That line is now "linked" with the paragraph just above it; it's part of that paragraph, in fact, and can't be selected by itself. Since you'll be making that paragraph a running head, the line will print on each page.

6. Click left on Format Running-Head to display the menu

   FORMAT RUNNING-HEAD position: Top Bottom None
   odd pages:(Yes)No even pages:(Yes)No first page:Yes(No)
   alignment:(Left-margin)Edge-of-paper

The stylebar indicates running heads by their position: *te* for top even, *to* for top odd, *be* for bottom even, or *bo* for bottom odd.

7. Select a running head for even-numbered pages.

   a. Click left on Top.

   b. Click right on No for the Odd Pages option. A small caret appears next to the line of text to indicate that this is a running head, not regular text.

   ^Neibauer

8. Click left after the line.

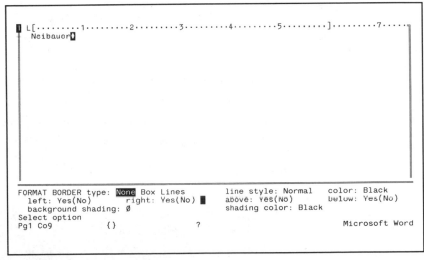

o **Figure 8.6:** *The Format Border menu*

KEY Press Esc F B L. Press Tab six times to reach the Below option, press Y, and press Enter. Next press Esc F R T. Press Tab twice to reach the Even Pages option, and then press N. Press Tab to reach the First Page option, press Y, and then press Enter.

9. Enter the text for the running head on odd-numbered pages.

   a. Press Alt-R to right align the text.

   b. Type your name.

   c. Click left on Format Border Lines.

   d. Click right on Yes for the Below option.

10. Select a running head for odd-numbered pages.

    a. Click left on Format Running-Head.

    b. Click left on Top.

    c. Click left on No for the Even Pages option.

    d. Click right on Yes for the First Page option. The running head will be marked with a small caret at the end of the line.

   ^   **Neibauer**

   _____

KEY Place the cursor on the line beneath the last running head, type **page**, and press F3. Next press Esc F R B. Press Tab to reach the Odd Pages option, press N, then press Enter.

11. Enter the text for the page number on the bottom of even-numbered pages.

    a. Click left under the last running head and type **page**.

    b. With the cursor in the space immediately after the Word *page*, press the F3 key. F3 changes this word to a special glossary entry: *(page)*. After you make this a running head, the proper page number will print at this location.

12. Format the page number as a running head on the bottom of even-numbered pages.

    a. Click left on Format Running-Head.

    b. Click left on Bottom.

    c. Click right on No for the Odd Pages option. The running head will be marked

   ^(page)

13. Click left after the footer.

14. Enter the text for the page number on the bottom of odd-numbered pages.

    a. Press Alt-R.

 b. Type **page**, and press F3. The screen will display

(page)

15. From the Format Running-Head menu, select a running head for the bottom of odd-numbered pages.

 a. Click left on Format Running-Head.

 b. Click left on Bottom.

 c. Click left on No for the Even Pages option.

 d. Click right on Yes for the First Page option. The running head will be marked:

 ^

 (page)

The text for the running heads is completed, as shown in Figure 8.7.

16. Save the template. Click left on Transfer Save and type **Running**.

17. Click on the command line title, and then click on SUMMARY.

USING THE TEMPLATE

 When you want to enter a document using the Running Head template, follow this procedure:

1. Start Word.

2. Click left on Transfer Merge.

KEY Press Esc F R B. Press Tab twice to reach the Even Pages option, and then press N. Press Tab to reach the First Page option, press Y, and then press Enter.

KEY Press Ctrl-F10, type **Running**, and press Enter twice.

```
L[·········1·········2·········3·········4·········5·········]·········7·····
^Neibauer¶

^                                                              Neibauer¶

^(page)¶
^                                                              (page)¶
  ♦



                                                              ▊




COMMAND: Copy Delete Format Gallery Help Insert Jump Library
         Options Print Quit Replace Search Transfer Undo Window
Edit document or press Esc to use menu
Pg1 Co61          {}                  ?                    Microsoft Word
```

o **Figure 8.7:** *The completed text for the running heads*

KEY Press Esc T M. At the prompt, type **Running**, and then press Enter.

3. Click right to the right of the command line title.

4. Click right on Running at the top of the screen.

5. Position the cursor after the final running-head format.

6. Type your document as usual.

When you print the document, the top and bottom running heads will appear on the appropriate pages.

OTHER OPTIONS FOR RUNNING HEADS

Through the Format Running-Head menu, you can customize your running heads. Let's briefly review the options:

o **Position** determines if the running head will be a header (Top) or footer (Bottom). You can select None to change a running head to regular text.

o **Odd Pages**, **Even Pages**, and **First Page** determine the pages on which the running head appears. By default, the running head will print on every page but the first.

4.0 The None selection for Position is not available. To convert a running head to text, select No for the Even Pages, Odd Pages, and First Page options. Also, there is no Alignment option on the menu, and edge of page is the default. To align running heads with the margins, use the Format Paragraph menu to format each running-head paragraph with a 1.25" left indent and a 1.25" right indent. The heads will not appear in the correct position when you add text to the template, but they will print correctly.

o **Alignment** determines if you want the running head to be even with the margins (aligning with the text) or all the way at the edges of the paper.

To convert a running head to regular text, place the cursor on it, and then select None for the Position option. The caret will disappear, and the text will print just on one page.

If you want the running heads to print at the far edge of the page, as shown in Figure 8.8, place the cursor on each running head, and then select Edge-of-Paper for the Alignment option.

You can customize running heads to suit specific documents. Business proposals might be headed by the client's name. Academic papers might include the document's title, date, or professor's name. You can even have different text in the running heads for odd- and even-numbered pages.

For long documents, you can change the running head at each chapter or section break. For example, they might read *Chapter 1, Section 4* or *Personnel Requirements*. Just create a new running head at the top of the page where you want it to start.

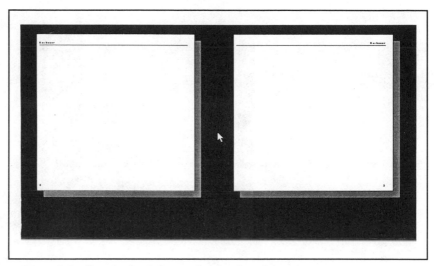

o **Figure 8.8:** *Running heads formatted at the edges of the paper*

Page numbering can also include some text. Instead of just 1, it might appear as *Page 1* or *Page 3.1*. In these cases, the running head would appear on the screen as

Page (page)

or

Page 3.(page)

4.0 The Mirror Margins option is not available. Create two different divisions with the speed keys Alt-LF and Alt-RT, and format them with the opposite margin settings. For example, create Alt-LF for even-numbered pages with a left margin of 2 inches and a right one of ½ inch. Format Alt-RT for odd-numbered (right) pages with a ½-inch left margin and a 2-inch right one. Then enter the appropriate speed key at the end of the corresponding pages.

oMIRRORING MARGINS

Many bound books alternate the position of the text as well as the running heads. Extra margin space appears on the outside edges of each page—the left side of even-numbered pages, the right side of odd-numbered ones, as shown in Figure 8.9. Other formats add the extra space to the inside margin of alternating pages.

This is easy to accomplish in Word. Simply set the appropriate left and right division margins on the Format Division menu, and then select Yes for the Mirror Margins option on that menu.

In the next chapter, you'll see how to use stylesheets and templates for another common office document: the memo.

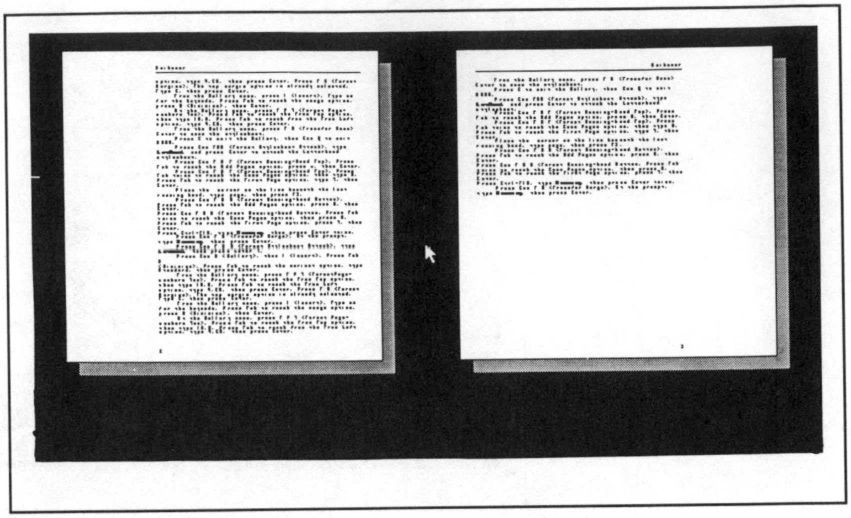

○ **Figure 8.9:** *Mirrored margins*

CHAPTER 9

- PRODUCING
- QUICK
- AND
- EASY
- MEMOS

In most offices, memos play an important role. They carry our requests and commands, as well as our inquiries and proposals. They serve as transmittal and cover letters, reminders, and announcements. Thus, memos require the same care as any other written communication. Their form and content should be organized to achieve maximum impact.

In this chapter, you'll learn how to apply the formatting powers of Word to memos. You'll create templates and stylesheets for preparing memos and for using preprinted memo forms. These templates and stylesheets will help you create effective memos with the least amount of time and effort.

○ELEMENTS OF A MEMO

Although there are an unlimited number of forms that a memo can take, the typical memo includes at least six elements:

- ○ Title—Usually MEMORANDUM on the top of the page
- ○ Recipient—Most often following TO:
- ○ Sender—Usually following FROM:
- ○ Subject—Headed by the formal SUBJECT: or the informal RE:
- ○ Date—After DATE: (what else?)
- ○ Body—The text of the memo

Many companies have blank memo forms printed in quantity. They're either on company letterhead or plain paper. Usually, the element headings are preprinted on the form. Using preprinted forms adds some complexity to the word processor's task. Later in this chapter, you'll learn how to align text at exact locations on the page. First, let's see how to format a memo on blank paper.

○CREATING A MEMO FORM FOR BLANK PAPER

If you do not use preprinted memo forms, you must decide on a style before you create a stylesheet or template. Figure 9.1 shows some examples of memo form styles. In the following exercise, you'll create a form that has the word MEMORANDUM centered at the top and the headings TO, FROM, DATE, and SUBJECT listed along the left margin.

CREATING THE MEMO STYLESHEET

The first step is to create a stylesheet that contains the formats of the major elements of the memo. Our stylesheet will include a hanging-paragraph format for the memo's headings, a standard paragraph format with an indented first line, optional indented and hanging-indentation paragraph formats, and provisions for page numbering on the bottom of pages following the first one. The actual headings for the memo form (TO, FROM, etc.) will not be on the stylesheet; they'll be entered on the template that we'll create next.

After this exercise, you will have a number of custom stylesheets on your disk. To help organize your work, you will take advantage of the Gallery's Remark option and enter a line of information explaining the purpose of each format.

Follow this procedure to create the Memo stylesheet:

1. Start Word.

2. Click left on Format; then click right on Stylesheet.

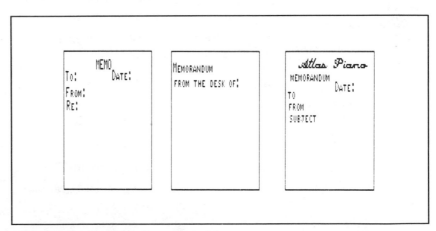

o **Figure 9.1:** *Examples of memo form styles*

KEY Press Esc F S A, type **Memo**, press Enter, and then press Y. Press Esc G, and from the Gallery menu, press I. Type **hd** for the Key Code option, press Tab to reach the Usage option, and press P. Press Tab twice to reach the Remark option, type **Memo Headings**, and press Enter.

KEY From the Gallery menu, press F P. Press Tab to reach the Left Indent option and type **1**. Press Tab to reach the First Line option, type **– 1**, and press Enter. Next press F T S, type **1**, make sure Alignment is set to Left, and then press Enter.

KEY From the Gallery menu, press I. Type **in** for the Key Code option, press Tab to reach the Usage option, and press P. Press Tab twice to reach the Remark option, type **Indented Paragraph**, and press Enter. Press F P, press Tab twice to reach the Left Indent option, and type **.5**. Press Tab twice to reach the Right Indent option, type **.5**, and press Enter.

3. Type **Memo**, click on the command line, and then click on the message line.

4. Click on Gallery.

5. Insert a new paragraph format.

   a. Click left on Insert.

   b. Type **hd** for the Key Code option.

   c. Click left on Paragraph for the Usage option.

   d. Click on the Remark option and type **Memo Headings**.

   e. Click on the command line title.

6. Create the format for the TO, FROM, DATE, and SUBJECT headings: a hanging paragraph, with the first line at the left margin and a tab stop at 1 inch. The hanging-paragraph format is for entries that are more than one line, such as a list of memo recipients.

   a. Click left on Format Paragraph.

   b. Click on the Left Indent option and type **1**.

   c. Click on the First Line option and type **– 1**.

   d. Make sure that the tab type character in the ruler is L. If not, click on the character until the L appears.

   e. Point at the 1-inch setting on the ruler and click left.

   f. Click on the command line title. Figure 9.2 shows the style for the memo headings.

7. Create a format for indented paragraphs (left and right margins indented ½ inch).

   a. Click left on Insert.

   b. Type **in** for the Key Code option.

   c. Click left on Paragraph for the Usage option.

   d. Click on the Remark option and type **Indented Paragraph**.

   e. Click on the command line title.

   f. Click left on Format Paragraph.

   g. Click on the Left Indent option and type **.5**.

h. Click on the Right Indent option and type **.5**.

i. Click on the command line title. Figure 9.3 shows the style for indented paragraphs added in the Gallery window.

4.0 Set the tab stop by clicking left on the command line title, left on Format, then right on Tab. Click left on the 1 on the ruler. Follow the same procedure to set tab stops at the specified position throughout the exercise.

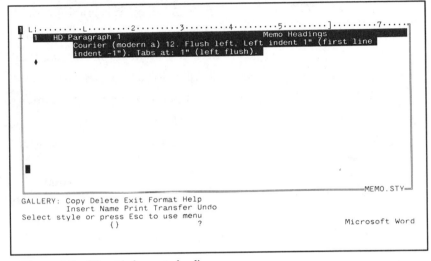

o **Figure 9.2:** *The style for memo headings*

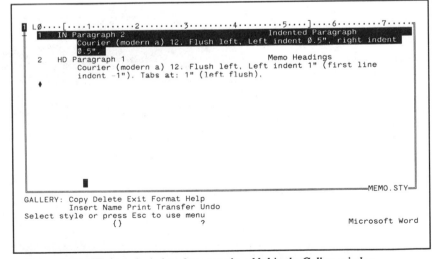

o **Figure 9.3:** *The style for indented paragraphs added in the Gallery window*

8. Create a hanging-paragraph format (first line at the ½-inch position, remaining lines indented 1 inch).

KEY From the Gallery menu, press I. Type **hi** for the Key Code option, press Tab to reach the Usage option, and press P. Press Tab twice to reach the Remark option, type **Hanging Indent,** and press Enter. Press F P, press Tab twice to reach the Left Indent option, and type **1.5**. Press Tab to reach the First Line option, type **– 1**, and press Enter. Press F T S, type **1.5**, and press Enter.

   a. Click left on Insert.

   b. Type **hi** for the Key Code option.

   c. Click left on Paragraph for the Usage option.

   d. Click on the Remark option and type **Hanging Indent**.

   e. Click on the command line title.

   f. Click left on Format Paragraph.

   g. Click on the Left Indent option and type **1.5**.

   h. Click on the First Line option and type **– 1**.

   i. Point halfway between the 1 and 2 on the ruler, and then click left to set the tab stop.

   j. Click on the command line title. Figure 9.4 shows the style for paragraphs with hanging indentations added in the Gallery window.

9. Create a standard paragraph format with an indented first line.

   a. Click left on Insert.

   b. Click left on Paragraph for the Usage option.

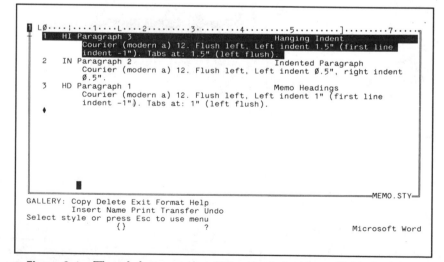

○ **Figure 9.4:** *The style for paragraphs with hanging indentations added in the Gallery window*

KEY From the Gallery
menu, press I.
Press Tab to reach the
Usage option and press P.
Press Tab to reach the
Variant option and type
Standard. Press Tab to
reach the Remark option,
type **Normal Paragraph**,
and press Enter. Press
F P. Press Tab twice to
reach the First Line
option, type **.5**, and press
Enter.

KEY Press T S Enter to
save the style-
sheet. Press E to exit the
Gallery.

   c. Click right on the Variant option. Standard, the first variant in
       the list will be selected.

   d. Click on the Remark option and type **Normal Paragraph**.

   e. Click on the command line title.

   f. Click left on Format Paragraph.

   g. Click on the First Line option and type **.5**.

   h. Click on the command line title. Figure 9.5 shows the style for
       standard paragraphs added in the Gallery window.

10. Click left on Transfer; then click right on Save to save the style-
    sheet.

11. Click on Exit.

CREATING THE MEMO TEMPLATE

The stylesheet only defines the format of paragraphs in the memo.
Now you'll create the template for typing memos, complete with the title
and headings in their proper format.

```
 L[....|....1.........2.........3.........4.........5.........].........7.....
 1     Paragraph Standard                      Normal Paragraph
       Courier (modern a) 12. Flush left (first line indent Ø.5").
 2  HI Paragraph 3                             Hanging Indent
       Courier (modern a) 12. Flush left, Left indent 1.5" (first line
       indent -1"). Tabs at: 1.5" (left flush).
 3  IN Paragraph 2                             Indented Paragraph
       Courier (modern a) 12. Flush left, Left indent Ø.5", right indent
       Ø.5".
 4  HD Paragraph 1                             Memo Headings
       Courier (modern a) 12. Flush left, Left indent 1" (first line
       indent -1"). Tabs at: 1" (left flush).


                                                            ═MEMO.STY═
 GALLERY: Copy Delete Exit Format Help
          Insert Name Print Transfer Undo
 Select style or press Esc to use menu
              ()                    ?              Microsoft Word
```

o **Figure 9.5:** *The style for standard paragraphs added in the Gallery window*

You should still be in Word with the Memo stylesheet attached. If you quit Word at the end of the last section, start Word and use the Format Style Sheet command to attach the Memo stylesheet. Then follow the steps below to create the template:

1. Enter the page number for the bottom running head.

   a. Press Alt-C (Alt-XC with version 4.0).

   b. Type **Page page**.

   c. With the cursor immediately after the second page, press F3. This inserts the glossary page-numbering code.

   d. Press Alt-F2.

2. Move the cursor to the line under the running head.

3. Enter the memo headings.

   a. Press Alt-C, then Alt-U (Alt-XC, then Alt-XU with version 4.0).

   b. Type **M E M O R A N D U M** and press Enter twice.

   c. Press Alt-spacebar, then Alt-P (Alt-XP with version 4.0).

   d. Press Alt-HD.

   e. Type **TO:** and press Enter twice.

   f. Type **FROM:** and press Enter twice.

   g. Type **DATE:** and press Enter twice.

   h. Type **SUBJECT:** and press Enter twice.

   i. Press Alt-P (Alt-XP with version 4.0).

 Press Ctrl-F10, type **Memo**, and press Enter twice to save the template. Press Esc Q to quit Word.

4. Click left on Transfer Save and type **Memo**.

5. Click on the command line title; then click on SUMMARY. Figure 9.6 shows the completed template.

6. Click right on Quit.

USING THE MEMO TEMPLATE

You've taken some time to create a stylesheet and template for typing memos. So that you can see that the time was well spent, let's type a

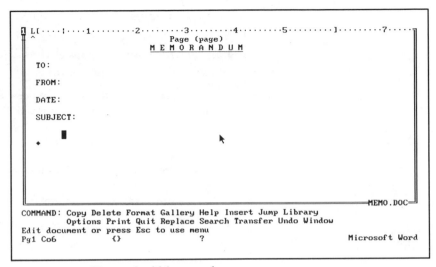

```
 L[····¦····1·······2·······3·······4·····5········]········7····¦
 ^                              Page (page)
                             M E M O R A N D U M

   TO:

   FROM:

   DATE:

   SUBJECT:

      ▪                                        ▸
   ◂

                                                              ⌐MEMO.DOC⌐
 COMMAND: Copy Delete Format Gallery Help Insert Jump Library
            Options Print Quit Replace Search Transfer Undo Window
 Edit document or press Esc to use menu
 Pg1 Co6              {}                ?                  Microsoft Word
```

o **Figure 9.6:** *The completed Memo template*

memo using the Memo template. Follow these steps:

1. Start Word.

2. Click left on Transfer Load.

3. Type **Memo** and click on the command line title. The Memo template and stylesheet will be recalled.

4. Position the cursor after the heading TO:, using the mouse or arrow keys. Do not use the Enter key to position the cursor unless you want to add another line to an entry. The blank lines between headings arc already entered.

5. Press Tab to reach the 1-inch tab stop.

6. Type **Ms. Rose Savage**. Then, to add another line under the name, press Enter.

7. Press Tab to reach the 1-inch tab stop and type **Purchasing Clerk**.

8. Position the cursor after the heading FROM:, press Tab, and type **George Wilson**.

9. Position the cursor after the heading DATE:, press Tab, and type **June 23, 1990**.

10. Position the cursor after the heading SUBJECT:, press Tab, and type **New Purchasing Forms**.

KEY Press Esc T M, type **Memo**, and press Enter. Use the arrow keys to position the cursor after the headings.

11. Position the cursor on the end mark.

12. Type the following memo. Press Alt-HI to format the listing as hanging-indentation paragraphs. Figure 9.7 shows how the different elements of the memo appear on the screen.

> **We have changed the format of our standard purchase order forms. They are now color coded to represent the major requisition classes.**

> **Red** **Consumable supplies and equipment less than $250 and a usable life of less than one year**
> **Blue** **Equipment and furniture less than $250 and a usable life of ten years or less**
> **Green** **Any other equipment and furniture**

13. Click right on Print to print a copy of the memo.

14. Click left on Quit, and then press N to exit Word without saving the memo.

KEY Press Ctrl-F8 to print a copy of the memo. Press Esc Q to quit.

Since the Memo template's stylesheet includes a standard paragraph with the first line indented, a hanging-indentation paragraph, and a paragraph indented on both sides, you can quickly type properly formatted memos.

```
 LΘ····!·····1··L···2·········3·········4·········5·········]·········7·····
 ^                      Page (page)
                        M E M O R A N D U M

   TO:      Ms. Rose Savage
            Purchasing Clerk

   FROM:    George Wilson

   DATE:    June 23, 1990

   SUBJECT: New Purchasing Forms

        We have changed the format of our standard purchase
   order forms. They are now color coded to represent the major
   requisition classes.
        Red         Consumable supplies and equipment less than
                    $250 and a usable life of less than one year.
        Blue        Equipment and furniture less than $250 and a
                                                        ————MEMO.DOC———
 COMMAND: Copy Delete Format Gallery Help Insert Jump Library
          Options Print Quit Replace Search Transfer Undo Window
 Edit document or press Esc to use menu
 Pg1 Co60            {}                  ?              Microsoft Word
```

o **Figure 9.7:** *The Memo template with text*

oCREATING A TEMPLATE FOR PREPRINTED MEMO FORMS

Many word processors recoil in horror when they think about working with preprinted forms. But, in reality, these forms are merely another type of template in which the headings are already printed. You just have to add the formatting.

CREATING AN ALIGNMENT GRID

In Chapter 17, you'll see how you can further streamline using preprinted forms by designing an input form directly on your screen.

The major objective in using preprinted forms is aligning the appropriate information with the preprinted headings. One way to accomplish this is with an *alignment grid*, which is a special document that shows the line and column positions for each of the preprinted elements on the form.

Let's create an alignment grid to use for our template for preprinted memo forms. Since the memo form is normally preprinted only on the top, we need a grid for just the top one-third of the page. Follow these steps:

1. Start Word.

2. Use the Format Division command to set the division to the same page size as the memo form. If the preprinted memo form is $8^{1}/_{2}$ by 11 inches, you can use the default settings. As a guide, check for the following items.

   a. Is the memo form bigger or smaller than $8^{1}/_{2}$ by 11 inches? If so, measure the form and set your division to match.

   b. Does the memo form use less than 1-inch margins? If so, you must change the division to match them.

   c. Does the memo form use less than a 1-inch top margin? If so, set the division to match.

3. Starting at the top of the screen, type an entire line of numbers until it reaches the right margin, and then press Enter.

12345678901234567890123456789012345678

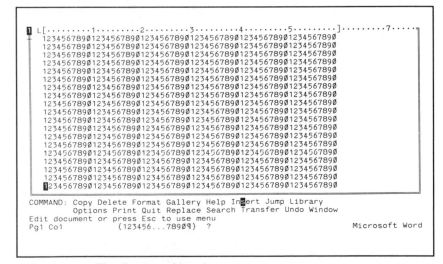

KEY Press F10 to select the line. Press Alt-F3 to copy it into the scrap, and then press Ins until the screen is full. Press Ctrl-F10, type **Grid**, and press Enter twice to save the alignment grid. Insert a memo form in your printer, and then press Ctrl-F8 to print the grid.

4. Click right on the selection bar next to the line; then click right on Copy.

5. Click right on Insert to duplicate the line.

6. Continue clicking right on Insert until at least one entire screen is filled with the same line, as shown in Figure 9.8.

7. Click left on Transfer Save and type **Grid**.

8. Click on the command line title; then click on SUMMARY.

9. Insert a copy of the memo form into your printer.

10. Click right on Print to print the grid.

11. The lines and characters on the alignment grid indicate where your printed information should appear. On the grid printed on your memo form, place a circle on the number directly following each heading and at the beginning of the third line past the last heading. Figure 9.9 shows an example of a grid marked for a memo.

o **Figure 9.8:** *The alignment grid on the screen*

CREATING THE STYLESHEET FOR PREPRINTED MEMO FORMS

You will use your marked alignment grid to create the stylesheet for preprinted memo forms. On the grid, count down the number of lines to the first circle. The number of lines must be added to the normal top margin of Word. Then count over the number of characters to that circle. Add 2 to the number of characters, and treat each number as one-tenth (e.g., 6 would be .6 and 43 would be 4.3).

The number of characters represents the size of the paragraph indentation. Repeat this process for each circle on the grid. In the exercise below, these measurements are based on the marked alignment grid shown in Figure 9.9. Adjust the measurements that you enter to match your grid.

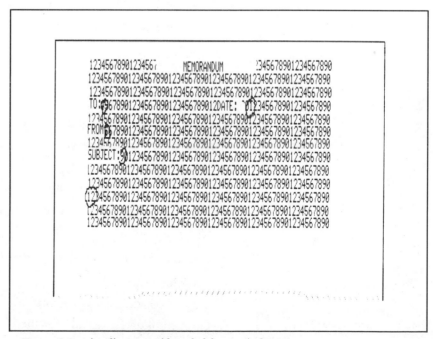

o **Figure 9.9:** *An alignment grid marked for a typical memo*

Follow these steps to create the stylesheet:

1. Start Word.

2. Click left on Format; then click right on Stylesheet.

3. Type **Preprint**.

4. Click on the command line title; then click on the message line.

5. Create a style for the top margin. Since the first typing line is four lines beneath the top margin, another 1/2 inch must be added to the normal margin.

   a. Click on Gallery.

   b. Click left on Insert.

   c. Click left on Division for the Usage option.

   d. Click right on the Variant option.

   e. Click on the command line title to accept Standard.

   f. Click right on Format and type **1.5**.

   g. Click on the command line title.

6. Create a paragraph format for the TO heading. This heading aligns with position 4 on the grid, so we'll make the left indentation .6 inch. We'll also set a tab stop at 4.3 inches for the date on the same line.

   a. Click left on Insert.

   b. Type **to** for the Key Code option.

   c. Click right on Paragraph for the Usage option.

   d. Click left on Format Paragraph.

   e. Click on the Left Indent option and type **.6**.

   f. Point at the third dot after the 4 on the ruler and click left.

   g. Click on the command line title.

7. Create a paragraph format for the FROM heading.

   a. Click left on Insert.

   b. Type **fr** for the Key Code option.

   c. Click right on Paragraph for the Usage option.

   d. Click left on Format Paragraph.

KEY Press Esc F S A, type **Preprint**, press Enter, and then press Y. Press Esc G I. Press Tab to reach the Usage option and press D. Press Tab to reach the Variant option, type **Standard**, and press Enter. Press F M, type **1.5**, and press Enter.

KEY From the Gallery menu, press I and type **to** for the Key Code option. Press Tab to reach the Usage option, press P, and then press Enter. Press F P, press Tab to reach the Left Indent option, type **.6**, and then press Enter. Press F T S, type **4.3**, and press Enter.

4.0 Set the tab by clicking left on the command line title, left on Format, then right on Tab. Click left on the third dot after the 4 on the ruler.

e. Click on the Left Indent option and type **.7**.

f. Click on the command line title.

8. Create a paragraph format for the SUBJECT heading.

   a. Click left on Insert.

   b. Type **su** for the Key Code option.

   c. Click right on Paragraph for the Usage option.

   d. Click left on Format Paragraph.

   e. Click on the Left Indent option and type **1.1**.

   f. Click on the command line title. Figure 9.10 shows the completed stylesheet.

9. Click left on Transfer; then click right on Save to save the stylesheet.

10. Click on Exit.

KEY From the Gallery menu, press I and type **fr** for the Key Code option. Press Tab to reach the Usage option, press P, and then press Enter. Press F P, press Tab to reach the Left Indent option, type **.7**, and then press Enter.

KEY From the Gallery menu, press I and type **su** for the Key Code option. Press Tab to reach the Usage option, press P, and then press Enter. Press F P, press Tab to reach the Left Indent option, type **1.1**, and then press Enter.

KEY Press T S Enter to save the stylesheet. Press E to exit the Gallery.

CREATING A TEMPLATE FOR PREPRINTED MEMO FORMS

The stylesheet now contains the necessary division and paragraph formats. The division includes a top margin large enough to begin the

```
  LØ·········1[·······2·········3·········4··▪·····5·········]·········7·····
1    SU Paragraph 3
        Courier (modern a) 12. Flush left, Left indent 1.1".
2    FR Paragraph 2
        Courier (modern a) 12. Flush left, Left indent Ø.7".
3    TO Paragraph 1
        Courier (modern a) 12. Flush left, Left indent Ø.6". Tabs at: 4.3"
        (left flush).
4       Division Standard
        Page break. Page length 11"; width 8.5". Page # format Arabic. Top
        margin 1.5"; bottom 1"; left 1.25"; right 1.25". Top running head
        at Ø.5". Bottom running head at Ø.5". Footnotes on same page.
◆

                                                              ═PREPRINT.STY═
GALLERY: Copy Delete Exit Format Help
         Insert Name Print Transfer Undo
Select style or press Esc to use menu
            ()                      ?
                                                              Microsoft Word
```

o **Figure 9.10:** *The completed stylesheet for preprinted memos*

memo's first line at the first printed heading. The paragraphs contain the proper indentations to enter the information that you type after each of the appropriate headings.

You should still be in Word with the Preprint stylesheet attached. Follow this procedure to create the template for preprinted memo forms:

1. Press Alt-TO.
2. Press Enter once; then press the down arrow key to place the cursor on the next line.
3. Press Alt-FR.
4. Press Enter once; then press the down arrow key to place the cursor on the next line.
5. Press Alt-SU.
6. Press Enter once; then press the down arrow key to place the cursor on the next line.
7. Press Enter one more time.
8. Click left on Transfer Save and type **Preprint**.
9. Click on the command line title; then click on SUMMARY.
10. Click on Quit.

KEY Press Ctrl-F10, type **Preprint**, and press Enter twice to save the template. Press Esc Q to quit.

USING THE TEMPLATE FOR WRITING MEMOS

The stylesheet and template are now completed. When you need to use a preprinted memo form, follow the steps below. Remember to use the down arrow key to go from one formatted paragraph to the next. Press Enter only when you want to type another paragraph using the same format as the previous one.

1. Start Word.
2. Click left on Transfer Load.
3. Click right to the right of the command line title; then click right on Preprint at the top of the screen.

KEY Press Esc T M, type **Preprint**, and press Enter.

4. Display the stylebar by selecting Yes for the Style Bar option on the Options menu (the Window Options menu in version 4.0). Figure 9.11 shows the template with the style codes.

5. Place the cursor on the line with the TO code in the stylebar, and type the name of the recipient of the memo.

6. Press Tab and type the date.

7. Press the down arrow key to reach the line with the FR code in the stylebar and type your name.

8. Press the down arrow key to reach the line with the SU code in the stylebar and type the subject of the memo.

9. Press the down arrow key to reach the line beginning the standard paragraph format (marked by the * on the stylebar) and type the body of the memo.

KEY Press Ctrl-F8 to print the memo. Press Esc Q to exit Word.

10. Click right on Print to print the memo. You may have to adjust the starting position of the memo to align it correctly. A little trial and error may be needed.

11. Click on Quit.

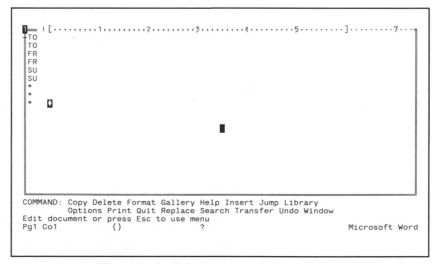

o **Figure 9.11:** *The completed template for preprinted memos*

oOTHER MEMO FORMATS AND PREPRINTED FORMS

Now that you know how to set up stylesheets and templates for memos, you don't have to limit yourself to one memo format. You can have one form for informal memos and another for more formal ones. You can even create "form" memos to use when you will be distributing the same information to a number of people.

In addition, the techniques for working with preprinted memo forms that you just learned can be applied to preprinted forms of all types. Just prepare an alignment grid the same size as the form, with the same margins. Use the grid as an aid in locating the line and character positions where your text must be entered. Then use the Format commands to create the appropriate division and paragraph styles.

This section dealt with printing your information on an existing preprinted form. Creating your own custom forms will be covered in Chapters 17 and 18.

CHAPTER 10

- CREATING,
- EDITING,
- AND
- MANIPULATING
- TABLES

Tables are an excellent means of presenting detailed information—even the simplest table can convey information that would require several pages of writing. Look at the table below:

	First Quarter	Second Quarter	Third Quarter	Fourth Quarter
Sales	40,000	20,000	35,000	37,500
Cost	25,000	22,000	24,000	26,000
Profits	15,000	– 2,000	11,000	11,500

You can tell at a glance how this company is doing. It is clear that the second quarter was the company's weakest period and that the first quarter was its strongest.

In this chapter, you'll create, edit, and manipulate typical tables. First, you'll learn how to set and use the various types of tab stops and make format changes without retyping information. Then we'll cover the techniques for sorting the information in the table and performing calculations.

oCREATING TABLES

Creating a table takes planning—you must set the correct types of tabs at the proper locations. Before you start typing, you should have some idea of how you want the completed table to look. You should know the number of columns, the way each column is to be aligned, the number of spaces between each column, and the total width of the table.

Word can format documents to print on paper up to 22 inches wide. However, typical printers are only wide enough for 8½- or 13-inch paper. Additionally, it's harder to work with tables wider than the 7½ inches that appear on the screen because you must scroll the screen horizontally to view the columns.

4.0 The tab type and leader you specify through the Format Tabs Set menu only apply to the tab stop you are setting. When you exit the menu and later set another tab stop, the default options (left aligned, no leaders) will be selected.

TAB OPTIONS

When you set tab stops with the mouse, you can always tell the alignment and leader type by the characters on the ruler. Whether you set a tab stop on the ruler or through the Format Tabs Set menu, the type and leader you select will remain until you change them again. If you set the alignment to right, for example, it will stay that way until you change it, or it will revert back to left alignment when you clear the screen or exit Word.

ENTERING A TABLE

Now let's create a sample table using both right and decimal tab stops. Figure 10.1 shows the table we will set up.

Follow this procedure to enter the table:

1. Start Word.

2. Press Alt-C to center the two title lines.

3. Type the title.

   Aardvark Seed Company
   Outstanding Salesperson Competition

4. Press Enter twice, then Alt-P.

5. To set the right tab stop for the first column heading, click on the tab type letter until an R appears. Then click left on the 4 on the ruler. (With version 4.0, click left on Format, click right on Tab, and then click left on Right for the Alignment option. Click left on the 4 on the ruler.)

   The letter R will appear at the 4-inch position on the ruler line. Now we need to set the right tab stop for the second column heading. The tab type is still Right. (With version 4.0, you should still be in the Format Tabs Set menu.)

6. Click left on the first dot before the right margin indicator on the ruler. (With version 4.0, finish by clicking on the command line title to exit the menu.)

KEY Press Alt-F1 and type **4R**. (With version 4.0, press Alt-F1, then the right arrow key until 4" appears at the Position option. Next press Tab to reach the Alignment option, press R, and then press Ins.)

KEY Type **5.9R** and press Enter. (With version 4.0, type **5.9**, press Tab R, and then press Enter.)

```
┌─────────────────────────────────────────────────────────────┐
│                  Aardvark Seed Company                        │
│             Outstanding Salesperson Competition               │
│                                                               │
│                         Regional Total      National Total    │
│                                                               │
│      James R. Armitage     1,004,765.00      1,043,876.00     │
│   Wilson C. Landsmokker        98,654.00         99,864.00    │
│         Joseph Millkie         92,765.00         96,764.00    │
│      Rosalie Butchalski        91,765.00         93,762.00    │
└─────────────────────────────────────────────────────────────┘
```

o **Figure 10.1:** *The printed sample table*

The letter R will appear at the 5.9-inch position on the ruler line. The default left tab stops are cleared.

7. Press Tab and type **Regional Total**.

8. Press Tab and type **National Total**. Figure 10.2 shows the screen so far.

9. Press Enter twice. The headings are aligned at the 3.9-inch and 5.8-inch positions.

Next we must clear the right tab stops. We need to do this before setting the decimal tab stops because the decimal numbers will not align properly if they encounter a right tab stop to their left.

10. Click left on Format Tabs Reset-All to clear the two right tab stops.

11. Set the tab stops for the columns.

a. Click left on the second dot past the 2 on the ruler.

b. Click on the tab type letter until a D appears.

c. Click left on the third dot before the 4 on the ruler, at position 3.7.

d. Click left on the sixth dot past the 5 on the ruler, at position 5.6.

KEY Press Esc F T R to clear the tab stops. To set the tabs for the columns, press Alt-F1. Type **2R**, **3.7D**, and **5.6D**. Then press Enter. (With version 4.0, press Alt-F1, type **2**, press Tab R, and then press Ins. Type **3.7**, press Tab D, and then press Ins. Type **5.6**, press Tab D, and then press Enter.)

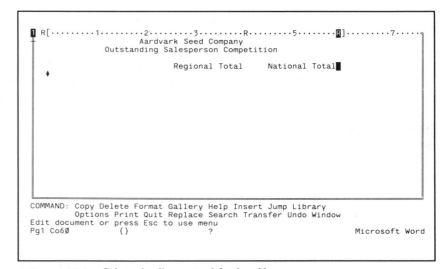

o **Figure 10.2:** *Column headings entered for the table*

(With version 4.0, click left on Format, click right on Tab, and then click left on Right for the Alignment option. Click left on the second dot past the 2 on the ruler. Next click left on Decimal for the Alignment option, click left on the third dot before the 4 on the ruler, and then click left on the sixth dot past the 5 on the ruler. Click on the command line title.)

Your screen should look like Figure 10.3 at this point. Notice the R and D characters marking the tab stops on the ruler line.

12. Enter the first row of the table. Press Tab before each entry. Do not press Enter after the last number.

   James R. Armitage 1,004,765.00 1,043,876.00

13. Press Shift-Enter. This moves the cursor to the next line without ending the paragraph.

14. Enter the second row. Press Tab before each entry. Do not press Enter after the last number.

   Wilson C. Landsmokker 98,654.00 99,864.00

15. Press Shift-Enter to move the cursor to the next line.

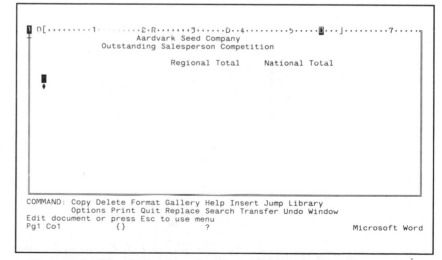

o **Figure 10.3:** *The ruler line shows the right and decimal tab stops*

16. Enter the third row. Press Tab before each entry. Do not press Enter after the last number.

   Joseph Millkie 92,765.00 96,764.00

17. Press Shift-Enter to move the cursor to the next line.

18. Enter the fourth row. Press Tab before each entry. Press Enter after the last number.

   Rosalie Butchalski 91,765.00 93,762.00

   Figure 10.4 shows the completed table on the screen.

19. Click left on Transfer Save and type **Table**.

20. Click on the command line title, and then click on SUMMARY. We will use this table again in the next exercise.

KEY Press Ctrl-F10, type **Table**, and press Enter twice to save the table.

```
D[·······1·······2·R·····3·····D··4·········5·····█···]·········7·····
                    Aardvark Seed Company
                 Outstanding Salesperson Competition

                              Regional Total     National Total

          James R. Armitage     1,004,765.00      1,043,876.00
      Wilson C. Landsmokker         98,654.00         99,864.00
          Joseph Millkie            92,765.00         96,764.00
          Rosalie Butchalski        91,765.00         93,762.00
    █
    ♦



COMMAND: Copy Delete Format Gallery Help Insert Jump Library
            Options Print Quit Replace Search Transfer Undo Window
Edit document or press Esc to use menu
Pg1 Co1              {}                 ?                    Microsoft Word
```

o **Figure 10.4:** *The completed table*

oEDITING TABLES

Editing tables only differs from editing other text in that tables contain tab characters. Deleting and inserting tab stops and characters in an existing table will change the placement of the columns. For example, take a look at the two numbers below. They were entered using decimal tab stops at the 2-inch and 4-inch positions.

123.45   1234.56

If the 4-inch tab stop were deleted, the numbers would appear as:

123.45   1234.56

The number that had its decimal point aligned at the 4-inch position shifted to the nearest preset left tab stop. However, the tab character is still in the text. If you set a new tab stop at the 5-inch position, the second number would automatically shift to that tab position—you wouldn't have to place the cursor in front of the number and press the Tab key. The tab character already in the text would make the number conform to the new tab stop.

The ability of Word to have entries conform to new tab settings makes it easier to reformat tables. We used Shift-Enter to end each line in our example table so that we could take advantage of this feature and manipulate the entire table as a single paragraph.

DISPLAYING FORMAT CODES

KEY Press Esc O. Press Tab three times to reach the Show Non-Printing Symbols option. Press A, and then press Enter. (With version 4.0, press C, then Enter.) To turn off the display, press N at the Show Non-Printing Symbols option.

You might find it easier to edit tables with all the format codes displayed on the screen. This is a personal choice. To display the codes, click on Options. Then click right on All for the Show Non-Printing Symbols option. (With version 4.0, click right on Complete.) Figure 10.5 shows our sample table with its format codes displayed on the screen.

To turn off the code display, follow the same procedure, but click on None for the Show Non-Printing Symbols option.

REFORMATTING AND EDITING THE TABLE

We'll now change our table so that it looks like Figure 10.6. As you can see, the decimal places have been removed from all the numbers, yet the columns are still right aligned under the headings. The second row (the one for Wilson C. Landsmokker) has been deleted. The last two rows were moved up, and a new one was added at the end. All the format changes were made without retyping existing information.

You should still be in Word with the table on your screen. If not, start Word and load the Table document. Follow these steps to make the changes:

1. Place the cursor on the first line of data (the James R. Armitage line).

2. Delete the decimal points and zeros after each number.

   a. Click on Replace.

   b. For the Replace Text option, type **.00**.

   c. Click right on No for the Confirm option.

KEY Press Esc R. For the Replace Text option, type **.00**. Press Tab twice to reach the Confirm option (leaving the With Text option blank). Press N, then Enter.

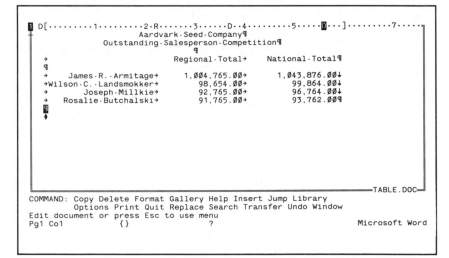

```
1 D[········1········2·R······3·····D·4········5····D···]·········7·····┐
               Aardvark·Seed·Company¶
          Outstanding·Salesperson·Competition¶
                    ¶
    →                     Regional·Total→     National·Total¶
    ¶
    →     James·R.·Armitage→     1,004,765.00→     1,043,876.00↓
    →Wilson·C.·Landsmokker→       98,654.00→       99,864.00↓
    →      Joseph·Millkie→        92,765.00→       96,764.00↓
    →   Rosalie·Butchalski→       91,765.00→       93,762.00¶
    ¶
    ↓


                                                    ──TABLE.DOC──
COMMAND: Copy Delete Format Gallery Help Insert Jump Library
         Options Print Quit Replace Search Transfer Undo Window
Edit document or press Esc to use menu
Pg1 Co1              {}              ?                    Microsoft Word
```

○ **Figure 10.5:** *The format codes displayed on the screen*

```
                    Aardvark Seed Company
               Outstanding Salesperson Competition

                        Regional Total     National Total

       James R. Armitage     1,004,765          1,043,876
         Joseph Millkie         92,765             96,764
     Rosalie Butchalski         91,765             93,762
       Sandra Day Connor        90,541             94,654
```

○ **Figure 10.6:** *The printed reformatted table*

Because you left the With Text option blank, the decimal places will be removed. The numbers, however, will not be aligned with the end of the headings. Figure 10.7 shows how the table looks at this point.

3. Realign the first column. Make sure the cursor is in the table.

   a. Click both on the tab, at position 3.7. The decimal tab stop will be deleted, and the table will not be aligned properly, as shown in Figure 10.8.

   b. Click on the tab type letter until an R appears.

   c. Click left on the 4 on the ruler. The first column will align under the Regional Total heading, as shown in Figure 10.9.

   (With version 4.0, click left on Format, click right on Tab, and then click left on Right for the Alignment option. Click left on 4 on the ruler; then click on the command line title.)

4. Realign the second column.

   a. Click both on the tab at position 5.6.

   b. Click left on the last dot before the right margin indicator.

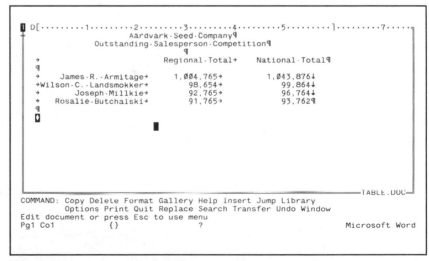

o **Figure 10.7:** *The table with the decimal points and zeros deleted*

(With version 4.0, click left on Format, click right on Tabs, and then click left on Right for the Alignment option. Click left on the last dot before the right margin indicator on the ruler, and then click on the command line title.)

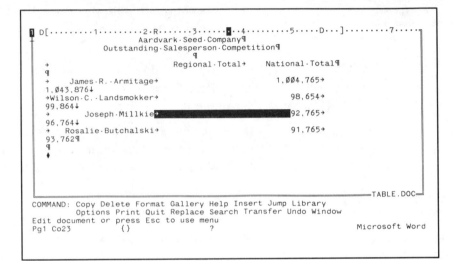

o **Figure 10.8:** *The table after deleting the first decimal tab stop*

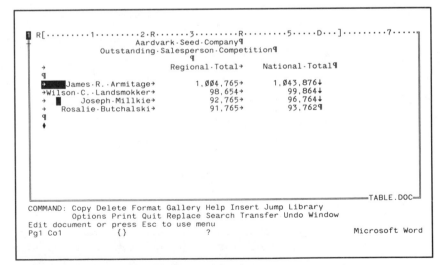

o **Figure 10.9:** *The table with the new right tab stop*

KEY Place the cursor on the line for Wilson C. Landsmokker. Press Shift-F9, and then press Del.

5. Click left in the selection bar next to Wilson C. Landsmokker; then click right on Delete. The line is deleted, and the remaining lines move up.

6. Place the cursor immediately following the last row (after 93,762) and press Shift-Enter. Now you can enter a new last row.

7. Type the new last row. Press Tab before each entry. Press Enter after the last number.

Sandra Day Connor 90,541 94,654

Figure 10.10 shows the revised table on the screen.

KEY Press Ctrl-F10 to save the revised table.

8. Click left on Transfer; then click right on Save to save the revised table.

o **Figure 10.10:** *The revised table*

oADVANCED TABLE MANIPULATION

If you work with tables and numeric documents often, then you're in for a treat—Word provides methods for handling columns of text, sorting lines, totaling columns and rows, and performing four-function math. You can make major changes to a table without retyping text or creating special division formats.

As an example, we'll create a class-ranking system that can be used to produce class lists by name, grade, or attendance. We will also use it to place students in rank order according to their grade, attendance, or both. The techniques you'll use can be applied to any type of table.

CREATING THE CLASS-RANKING TABLE

First, follow these steps to create the table shown in Figure 10.11. You will set left-aligned tab stops at positions .5 and 5, and a decimal tab at position 3.5. But you will also end each line of the table by pressing Tab before pressing Enter. This extra tab setting will make it easier to exchange columns later, without reentering tabs.

1. Press Alt-C to center the cursor.

2. Type

   **Mrs. Neibauer's
   Biology Class**

KEY Press Alt-F1, type **0.5L**, **3.5D**, and **5L**; then press Enter. (With version 4.0, press Alt-F1, type **0.5**, and then press Ins. Type **5** and press Ins. Type **3.5**, press Tab to reach the Alignment option, press D, and then press Enter.)

3. Press Enter twice, then Alt-P to return to the standard paragraph format.

4. Now set the three tab stops.

   a. Make sure the tab type letter is L, and then click left halfway between the left margin and 1 on the ruler.

   b. Click left on 5 on the ruler.

   c. Click on the tab type letter until the D appears.

```
                        Mrs. Neibauer's
                        Biology Class

         Name                      Grade        Days

     1   Sturman, Robert             A           180
     2   Misher, Allan               A           179
     3   Dershaw, Terry              B           175
     4   Chesin, Nancy               C           176
     5   Chesin, Adam                C           150

         Total                                   860
         Number in Class                         5
         Average                                 172
```

○ **Figure 10.11:** *Printed class-ranking table*

d. Click left halfway between 3 and 4.

(With version 4.0, click left on Format, click right on Tab, and then click left halfway between the left margin and the 1 on the ruler. Click left on 5 on the ruler, click left on Decimal for the Alignment option, and then click left halfway between 3 and 4. Click on the command line title.)

5. Type the column headings. Make sure you press Tab before Enter at the end.

   a. Press Tab and type **Name**.

   b. Press Tab and type **Days**.

   c. Press Tab and type **Grade**.

   d. Press Tab.

   e. Press Enter twice to double space between the column headings and the rows of the table.

6. Type the first row of the table. Again, make sure you press Tab before Enter at the end.

   a. Type **1** and press Tab.

   b. Type **Dershaw, Terry** and press Tab.

   c. Type **175** and press Tab.

   d. Type **B** and press Tab.

   e. Press Enter.

7. Now type the remaining lines of the table in the same manner.

8. Click left on Transfer Save and type **Class**.

9. Click on the command line title; then click on SUMMARY. You'll be making some major changes to this document, so if you make a mistake, you'll have an original copy to load again.

KEY Press Ctrl-F10, type **Class**, and then press Enter twice to save the table.

MANIPULATING THE COLUMNS

The first thing we'll do is rearrange the table to stress the student's grade rather than attendance. To do this, you'll exchange the last two columns, Days and Grades.

To select a column, place the cursor in one corner of the block, press Shift-F6, then use the arrow keys to move the cursor to the opposite corner.

KEY Press Esc O. Press Tab three times to reach the Show Non-Printing Symbols option, press A, and then press Enter. (With version 4.0, press C, then Enter.)

To move the columns, we'll use the Column Select key (Shift-F6). This lets you select a rectangular section, or a single column. To select a column, you place the cursor on the character in one corner of the rectangular section, press Shift-F6, move to the opposite corner, and click left. After it is selected, the column can be deleted, copied, or inserted anywhere in the text.

Before you move columns, you must decide if you want to move any tab settings along with the text. First, display the format codes for the class-ranking table. Click on Options; then click right on All for the Show Non-Printing Symbols option (with version 4.0, click right on Complete). Your screen should look like the one shown in Figure 10.12.

Each → represents a tab setting. If you move just the text of the Days column, the tab setting following it will remain, and the last column will stay in its current position, at the 5-inch tab stop. If you include the tab (the right arrow) in the selection, the last column will shift over to the tab stop at 3.5. However, moving a tab does not change the type of alignment it follows, just the tab location.

Because of the potential formatting problems, your saved copy of the document may come in handy.

The table should be on your screen, with the format codes displayed. Follow these steps to rearrange the table:

1. Place the cursor on the first character of *Days*, *D*.

```
 L[····L····1·········2·········3····D····4·········L·········]·········7·····
                        Mrs. Neibauer's¶
                        Biology·Class¶
                            ¶
    →     Name→                    Days→              Grade→      ¶
    ¶
   1→     Dershaw, Terry→           175→              B→     ¶
   2→     Chesin, Nancy→            176→              C→     ¶
   3→     Sturman, Robert→          180→              A→     ¶
   4→     Chesin, Adam→             150→              C→     ¶
   5→     Misher, Allan→            179→              A→     ¶
   ♦



                            ▮


                                                            ═CLASS.DOC═
COMMAND: Copy Delete Format Gallery Help Insert Jump Library
         Options Print Quit Replace Search Transfer Undo Window
Microsoft Word Version 5.Ø release 28
Pg1 Co6              {¶}                ?                    Microsoft Word
```

o **Figure 10.12:** *Format codes in the class-ranking table*

KEY Use the arrow keys to move the cursor to the tab arrow after 179. The column will be selected. Press Del to remove it and place it in the scrap.

KEY Press End to move the cursor to the end of the row. Press Ins to insert the deleted column.

KEY Press Alt-F1, type **3.5C**, and press Enter. (With version 4.0, press Alt-F1, type **3.5**, and press Tab C Enter.)

2. Press Shift-F6. The letters CS appear on the status line, indicating that column select mode is on.

3. Click left on the tab arrow after the number 179. Your screen should look like Figure 10.13.

4. Click right on Delete to remove the column and place it in the scrap.

With the column and the tab deleted, the Grade column shifts to the left and takes on the decimal alignment of the tab stop at position 3.5. The cursor will appear on the word *Grade*.

5. Click left at the end of that row.

6. Click right on Insert.

The columns have been exchanged but not the formats. This doesn't have much effect on the Grades column because it doesn't contain decimal points. So, let's just center the word Grades over that column.

7. Click on the tab type letter until a C appears; then click left halfway between the 3 and 4 on the ruler. (With version 4.0, click left on Format, click right on Tab, and click left on Center for the Alignment option. Click left halfway between the 3 and 4 on the ruler, and then click on the command line title.)

The word *Grade* will shift neatly over the column.

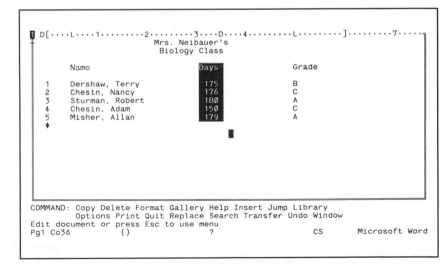

o **Figure 10.13:** *The Days column highlighted on the screen*

SORTING THE TABLE

Notice that the rows of the class-ranking table are not in any particular order. If you were looking for a particular student's name or the student with the highest or lowest grade, you would have to scan the entire list. The table would be more useful if it was sorted into a meaningful order.

The most obvious way to sort this table is in alphabetic order by the student name. Since we entered the last name first, students with the same last name will also be in first name order (placing Adam Chesin before Nancy Chesin). The table can also be sorted by the grade to quickly see who's doing well or poorly, or it can be sorted to evaluate attendance.

But more than that, the table can be used to create a class-rank list that takes both grade and attendance into consideration. This way, the students with the highest grades and best attendance will be ranked the highest.

Word's Library Autosort feature will do this for you. With it, you can sort by any one of the columns at a time, either alphabetically, by name or grade, or numerically, by number of days. The sort can be in either ascending order (from lowest to highest) or descending order (highest to lowest).

To create the class-ranking system, you will sort on three factors, or *keys*. The primary key is the most important element, in this case the grade. The secondary keys are the next most important factors: the days of attendance first and then the students' names. When sorting on more than one key, you must start with the least important secondary key and then work toward the primary key.

Follow these steps to create the ranking system:

1. First you must select the column to sort by for this key. Select the column of names, but do not include the column heading.

   a. Click left on the *D* in *Dershaw*.

   b. Press Shift-F6.

   c. Click left on the tab arrow after the final name.

2. Click right on Library to display the menu

   LIBRARY AUTOSORT by: Alphanumeric Numeric sequence:(Ascending)
   Descending case:Yes(No)   column only:Yes(No)

KEY Place the cursor on the *D* in *Dershaw*. Press Shift-F6 to turn on column select mode. Select the entire column by pressing the down arrow key 4 times, then the right arrow key 15 times—enough to select all the tabs in that column. Press Esc L A to see the Library Autosort menu. Press Enter to sort by the defaults.

3. Click on the command line title to accept the defaults and perform the sort. (We'll review these options after the exercise.)

All the rows in the table will be rearranged according to the alphabetic order of the names. Notice that the two Chesins are also in first name order. Don't worry that the numbering in the first column is not in order. You'll take care of this later. Now we'll sort the table again by the next secondary key, the days.

4. Click left on the *1* in *150* (the number of days for Adam Chesin), press Shift-F6, and click left following the last number, *180*, to select the Days column.

5. Select the sorting options.

   a. Click right on Library.

   b. Click left on Numeric (this column contains only numbers).

   c. Click right on Descending because we want the highest number first.

The students with the best attendance will be listed first. Now we'll sort the table by the primary key: the grades.

6. Click left on the letter *A* (the grade for Robert Sturman), press Shift-F6, and click left on the letter *C* (the grade for Adam Chesin) to select the Grades column.

7. Select the sorting options.

   a. Click right on Library.

   b. Click left on Alphanumeric.

   c. Click right on Ascending. Even though we think of the grades A through F as going from high to low—in descending order—the computer considers this ascending order.

Grades will be listed A through F, with the students with the best grade and highest attendance at the top of the list. All this sorting, however, has also changed the numbers in the leftmost column. To have these indicate rank, we'll sort just that one column numerically.

8. Click left at the start of the first column, press Shift-F6, and click left on the last number in that column to select the ranking column.

9. Select the sorting options.

    a. Click right on Library.

    b. Click left on Numeric.

    c. Click right on Yes for the Column Only option.

The numbers in that column are sorted from 1 to 5. No other column was affected. The table now reflects the class rank of the students by grade and attendance. When you consider that the same technique can be used for a class of any size, the value of sorting becomes apparent.

Sorting Options

Let's review the options on the Library Autosort menu:

o The **By** option default is **Alphanumeric**. Select **Numeric** if the column contains only numbers and the following characters: $, . - ( ).

o The **Sequence** option default is an **Ascending** sort (lowest to highest or A to Z). You can choose **Descending** to sort highest to lowest or Z to A.

o The **Case** option is used for alphanumeric sorts. With the default No option selected, Word ignores the cases of letters, placing *aardvark* before *Zebra*. The letter is used for the sort, regardless of its case. If you select Yes for this option, Word uses the ASCII coding sequence, in which all uppercase letters come before lowercase ones. So in this case, *Zebra* would appear before *aardvark*.

o The **Column Only** option, when set to Yes, will make your sort apply to only the selected column. The other columns in the table will be unaffected.

PERFORMING CALCULATIONS

One useful item still missing from our class-ranking table is the average attendance of the entire class (in many school districts, this is one key factor in allocating funds). To do this by hand, you would add up the total attendance for the class, and then divide the total by the number of students.

Of course, tables are not the only documents that use numbers or that require calculations. For instance, you may be typing an order that lists the quantity and price of an item:

Item	Quantity	Unit Price	Total
Ribbons	10	$2.37	

In this case, you would have to multiply the quantity times the price to compute the total.

You might even be typing more complicated formulas, such as

98 − 32 ∗ 5/9

to convert Fahrenheit to Celsius.

Fortunately, Word can automatically perform four-function math (addition, subtraction, multiplication, and division) and insert the results for you. Calculations can be performed on any column or row of numbers, or on formulas.

To perform math functions, select the numbers you want to calculate, and then press F2. The result will appear in the scrap and can be inserted in the text. To select a column of numbers in a table, be sure to use the Shift-F6 key. If the numbers selected include no operators, such as the multiplication (∗) or division (/) signs, Word will assume that you want to add the numbers together. Numbers with minus signs or in parentheses will be treated as negative numbers. So to total a column, select it using Shift-F6; then press F2.

Let's use the math function for calculating the average attendance for the class.

Using Math Functions

We will perform this process in two parts. First, we will add a row to hold the total attendance using columnar math. Then we will perform the division using four-function math. Here are the steps:

1. Place the cursor at the end of the last row and press Enter twice. This ensures that the new row conforms to the same tab stops.

2. Press Tab and type **Total**.

3. Press Tab twice to reach the tab stop under the Days column.

4. Click left on the *1* in *180*, press Shift-F6, and click left at the end of *150* to select the Days column.

KEY Place the cursor on the *1* in *180*. Press Shift-F6, press the down arrow key four times, and then press the right arrow key twice.

KEY Press Ins to insert the total.

KEY Place the cursor on the *8* in *860*. Press Shift-F6, press the down arrow key, and then press the right arrow key twice.

KEY Press Ins to insert the average. Place the cursor on the division sign (/), and then press Del. Press Ctrl-F8 to print the table. Press Esc Q N to exit Word.

Remember, you do not have to enter plus signs to add numbers.

5. Press F2. The total of the column appears in the scrap.

6. Place the cursor under the Days column, on the line with *Total*.

7. Click right on Insert. The total number of days, 860, will appear under the Days column.

8. Press Enter.

9. Press Tab and type **Number in Class**.

10. Press Tab twice and type **/5**.

11. Press Enter.

12. Press Tab and type **Average**.

13. Press Tab twice.

14. Click left on the *8* in *860*, press Shift-F6, and click left after the *5* in */5* to select the two numbers just above the cursor.

15. Press F2. The result of dividing 860 by 5 appears in the scrap.

16. Place the cursor under the Days column, on the line with *Average*.

17. Click right on Insert to insert the average, 172.

18. Move the cursor to the division sign (/), and then click right on Delete.

19. Click right on Print to print the table.

20. Click left on Quit; then press N.

PERFORMING QUICK ADDITION

You can total numbers in rows (even if they are on more than one line) using the same principles. Select a series of numbers in a row and press F2 to compute their total. Since Word performs addition if no operators are present, you can quickly add a series of numbers by typing them in a row (such as 80 90 35 76), selecting them, and then pressing F2.

OTHER EXAMPLES OF FOUR-FUNCTION MATH

Word's four-function math capabilities can be used to calculate more than one addition or division at a time. If you want to average a series of numbers or grades, or convert Fahrenheit temperature to Celsius, you can have Word perform several math operations in one formula.

To get the correct results, however, you must enter the formula in the proper order. Word follows standard mathematical principles: It performs all multiplications and divisions first, then additions and subtractions.

Take a look at the following two formulas:

98 87 98 / 3   212 − 32 ∗ 5 / 9

The first is intended to calculate the average of three numbers; the other converts 212 degrees Fahrenheit to Celsius. If you selected the formulas just as they are, you would get 217.67 and 194.22—decidedly incorrect. That's because in the average formula, Word first divided 98 by 3, then added it to 98 and 87. In the temperature conversion, Word performed the multiplication and division first, then subtracted that answer from 212.

In order to get the correct answers, enter the formulas like this:

(98 87 98) / 3   (212 − 32) ∗ 5 / 9

ADDING VERTICAL LINES

Vertical tabs stops are not used to align text, but to print vertical lines between columns. The lines neatly separate columns in a table, which makes long tables easier to read.

To add vertical lines, type the table first, setting only those tab stops needed for the columns. If you want a vertical line on the far left of the table, make sure the first column is aligned at a tab stop to the right of the margin.

KEY Press F T S; then set the tab stops using Vertical alignment. Press Enter, and the lines will appear between the columns when you return to the document.

If you used Enter instead of Shift-Enter to end each row, you must then select the entire table. Place the cursor at one corner of the table, press F6, and extend the selection until the table is highlighted. If you used Shift-Enter, just place the cursor somewhere within the table. Click on the tab type letter on the ruler until a | appears. Then click left on the ruler at the positions where you want vertical lines to appear.

In the next chapter, you'll learn how to use Word's features to produce typical financial documents.

CHAPTER 11

- **PRODUCING**
- **FINANCIAL**
- **DOCUMENTS**

4.0

KEY

Letters, memos, reports, and contracts are in constant flow through any business. And hopefully something else flows through the company office, too: money. Financial documents, such as balance sheets and income statements, measure this flow and illustrate (again, hopefully) the financial health of a company. They are used in annual reports and stockholders' meetings, as well as for tax-reporting and legal purposes.

In many respects, balance sheets and income statements are just tables. Like all tables, they require tab stops to align numbers and divide the page into columns. But they often also require very special formatting. Underlining is used to set off headings and major categories. Different levels of indentation are needed for itemizing the lists. The overall appearance must be pleasant and easy to read—even if the numbers are not so encouraging!

In this chapter, we'll prepare a stylesheet and template for a typical balance sheet. Then you'll see how you can use the same techniques to produce a wide range of financial documents, and even import spreadsheets directly into Word.

oCREATING A BALANCE SHEET

Take a look at the sample balance sheet shown in Figure 11.1. It is divided into two major categories: assets and liabilities. Each of these is subdivided even further, with several levels of indentation.

The section headings, such as Current, are at the left margin. The items in the sections are indented $1/2$ inch. They are followed by a line of periods, then either one, two, or three columns of numbers. The subtotal headings, such as Total Current Assets, are indented 1 inch. They are also followed by a row of periods, but they have only one column of numbers on the far right. Finally, the total headings, such as Total Assets, are indented $1 1/2$ inches and followed by a row of periods and one column of numbers.

The amounts are printed in three columns, aligned on the right. The last number in each series is underlined, and the final totals are double-underlined.

By now you should realize that there is a lot of formatting here! Luckily, you can create a stylesheet and template for all these formats.

```
                        Wilson Engine Company
                           Balance Sheet
                           June 30, 1990

─────────────────────────────────────────────────────────────
                              Assets
Current:

        Cash ..........................        $ 25,000
        Accounts Receivable .............        100,000
        Finished Goods Inventory ........         20,000
        Unexpired Insurance .............          1,000
             Total Current Assets .......                   146,000

Parts and Equipment:

        Land ...........................         40,000
        Buildings ...................... 125,000
        Less Depreciation ...............  25,000  100,000
        Machinery ...................... 240,000
        Less Depreciation ............... 120,000  120,000
             Total Plant and Equipment ..                   260,000

             Total Assets ..........                        $406,000

─────────────────────────────────────────────────────────────
                           Liabilities
Current:

        Accounts Payable ................        100,000
        Interest Payable ................          2,000
             Total Current Liabilities ..                   102,000

Long-Term:

        Stockholders Equity .............        250,000
        Retained Earning ................         54,000
             Total Long-Term Liabilities                    304,000

             Total Liabilities .....                        $406,000
```

o **Figure 11.1:** *The printed sample balance sheet*

CREATING THE BALANCE SHEET STYLESHEET

The stylesheet will include the following styles for each specific element of the balance sheet:

- o A standard division with narrower left and right margins to fit the text and three numeric columns on an 8½-inch wide page
- o Level 2 headings, indented ½ inch from the margin

o Level 3 headings, indented 1 inch from the margin

o Level 4 headings, indented 1 ½ inches from the margin

o A tab stop at the 3.8-inch position with leading periods

o A column 1 tab stop at the 4.7-inch position, right-aligned

o A column 2 tab stop at the 5.8-inch position, right-aligned

o A column 3 tab stop at the 7-inch position, right-aligned

o An underlined paragraph for typing horizontal lines

We need the last item, an underlined paragraph style, because Word's built-in speed keys (Alt-U for underlining and Alt-D for double underlining) won't underline an entirely blank line. We'll create our own speed key to produce the underlines in our sample balance sheet. Later in the chapter, you'll learn other techniques for creating ruled financial documents.

Follow these steps to create the stylesheet:

1. Start Word.

2. Click left on Format; then click right on Stylesheet.

3. Type **BSheet**.

4. Click on the command line title, and then click on the message line.

5. Set the division for 3/4-inch right and left margins.

   a. Click left on Gallery Insert.

   b. Click left on Division for the Usage option.

   c. Click right on the Variant option; then click on the command line title to accept the Standard variant.

   d. Click right on Format.

   e. Click on the Left option and type **.75**.

   f. Click on the Right option and type **.75**.

   g. Click on the command line title. Figure 11.2 shows the new standard division.

6. Create the ½-inch indented paragraph format for the level 2 heading.

   a. Click left on Insert.

   b. Type **L2** for the Key Code option.

   c. Click right on Paragraph.

KEY Press Esc F S A, type **BSheet**, and press Enter Y.

KEY Press Esc G I. Press Tab to reach the Usage option, and then press D. Press Tab to reach the Variant option, type **Standard**, and press Enter. Next press F M. Press Tab twice to reach the Left option and type **.75**. Press Tab to reach the Right option, type **.75**, and press Enter.

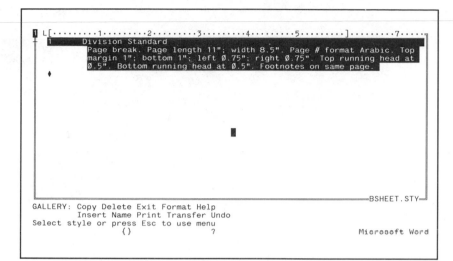

```
 L[·········1·········2·········3·········4·········5·········]·········7····
  1      Division Standard
         Page break. Page length 11"; width 8.5". Page # format Arabic. Top
         margin 1"; bottom 1"; left Ø.75"; right Ø.75". Top running head at
         Ø.5". Bottom running head at Ø.5". Footnotes on same page.



                                    ▮




                                                             ═BSHEET.STY═
 GALLERY: Copy Delete Exit Format Help
          Insert Name Print Transfer Undo
 Select style or press Esc to use menu
                  ()                    ?              Microsoft Word
```

o **Figure 11.2:** *The standard division for the balance sheet*

 From the Gallery menu, press I. Type **L2** as the key code. Press Tab to reach the Usage option, press P, and then press Enter. From the Gallery menu, press F P. Press Tab to reach the Left Indent option, type **.5**, and press Enter.

d. Click left on Format Paragraph.

e. Click on the Left Indent option and type **.5**.

f. Click on the command line title.

7. Set the tab stops for the level 2 heading's leading dots and columns. The L2 paragraph should be highlighted in the Gallery.

a. Click left on the space in front of the tab type character until a period appears.

 Press Alt-F1 and type **3.8L.**, **4.7RB**, **5.8R**, and **7R**. Then press Enter. (With version 4.0, press Alt-F1 and type **3.8**. Press Tab twice, press . (period), and then press Ins. Type **4.7**, press Tab R, Tab B, and then press Ins. Type **5.8**, press Tab R, Tab B, and then press Ins. Type **7**, press Tab R, Tab B, and then press Enter.)

b. Make sure the tab type letter is an L. If not, click on the character until an L appears.

c. Click left on the second dot before the 4 on the ruler, at position 3.8.

d. Click left on the period in front of the tab type character until the space is blank.

e. Click left on the tab type character until an R appears.

f. Click left on the third dot before the 5 on the ruler, at position 4.7.

g. Click left on the second dot before the 6 on the ruler, at position 5.8.

h. Click left on the 7 on the ruler. Figure 11.3 shows the style in the Gallery.

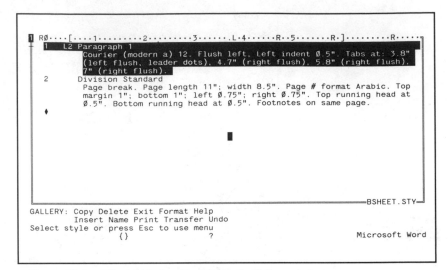

```
1 RØ····[····1·······2·······3······.L·4··R··5······R·]········R·····
       1    L2 Paragraph 1
                 Courier (modern a) 12. Flush left, Left indent Ø.5". Tabs at: 3.8"
                 (left flush, leader dots), 4.7" (right flush), 5.8" (right flush),
                 7" (right flush).
       2    Division Standard
                 Page break. Page length 11"; width 8.5". Page # format Arabic. Top
                 margin 1"; bottom 1"; left Ø.75"; right Ø.75". Top running head at
                 Ø.5". Bottom running head at Ø.5". Footnotes on same page.
       ♦

                                    ■




                                                              ═BSHEET.STY═
    GALLERY: Copy Delete Exit Format Help
             Insert Name Print Transfer Undo
    Select style or press Esc to use menu
                    {}                        ?              Microsoft Word
```

o **Figure 11.3:** *The style for level 2 added in the Gallery window*

(With version 4.0, click left on Format; then right on Tab. Click left as follows: on the period for the leader, on the second dot before the 4 on the ruler, on Blank for the leader, on Right for the alignment, on the third dot before the 5 on the ruler; on the second dot before the 6 on the ruler; on the 7 on the ruler. Finally, click on the command line title.)

8. Create the 1-inch indented paragraph format for the level 3 heading.

    a. Click left on Insert.

    b. Type **L3** for the Key Code option.

    c. Click right on Paragraph for the Usage option.

    d. Click left on Format Paragraph.

    e. Click on the Left Indent option and type **1**.

    f. Click on the command line title.

9. Set the tab stops for the level 3 heading's leading dots and subtotal column. The L3 paragraph should be highlighted in the Gallery.

    a. Click on the tab type character until an L appears.

    b. Click on the space before the character until a period appears.

    c. Click left on the second dot before the 4 on the ruler.

KEY From the Gallery menu, press I and type **L3** as the key code. Press Tab to reach the Usage option, press P, and then press Enter. Press F P. Press Tab to reach the Left Indent option, type **1**, and press Enter.

KEY Press Alt-F1 Type **3.8L.** and **7RB**, and then press Enter. (With version 4.0, type **3.8**, press Tab twice, press . (period), and then press Ins. Type **7**, press Tab R, press Tab B, and then press Enter.

     d. Click left on the tab type character until an R appears.

     e. Click left next to the character until it is blank.

     f. Click left on the 7 on the ruler. Figure 11.4 shows the style for level 3 added in the Gallery window.

(With version 4.0, click left on Format; then click right on Tab. Click left as follows: on the period for the leader, on the second dot before the 4 on the ruler; on Right for the alignment, on Blank for the leader, on the 7 on the ruler. Then click on the command line title.)

```
¶RØ·········[···········2··········3······,│·4··········5,,,,,,,,,]·········R·····
        1    L3 Paragraph 2
                  Courier (modern a) 12. Flush left, Left indent 1". Tabs at: 3.8"
                  (left flush, leader dots), 7" (right flush).
        2    L2 Paragraph 1
                  Courier (modern a) 12. Flush left, Left indent Ø.5". Tabs at: 3.8"
                  (left flush, leader dots), 4.7" (right flush), 5.8" (right flush),
                  7" (right flush).
        3    Division Standard
                  Page break. Page length 11"; width 8.5". Page # format Arabic. Top
                  margin 1"; bottom 1"; left Ø.75"; right Ø.75". Top running head at
                  Ø.5". Bottom running head at Ø.5". Footnotes on same page.
        ◆
                                                   ▮
                                                   ↓

                                                          ─BSHEET.STY─
GALLERY: Copy Delete Exit Format Help
         Insert Name Print Transfer Undo
Select style or press Esc to use menu
         ()                          ?              Microsoft Word
```

o **Figure 11.4:**   *The style for level 3 added in the Gallery window*

KEY From the Gallery menu, press I. Type **L4**. Press Tab P Enter. From the Gallery menu, press F P. Press Tab to reach the Left Indent option, type **1.5**, and press Enter.

10. Create the 1¹/₂-inch indented paragraph format for the level 4 heading.

     a. Click left on Insert.

     b. Type **L4** for the Key Code option.

     c. Click right on Paragraph for the Usage option.

     d. Click left on Format Paragraph.

     e. Click on the Left Indent option and type **1.5**.

     f. Click on the command line title.

KEY Press Alt-F1 and type **3.8L.** and **7RB**. Then press Enter. (With version 4.0, press Alt-F1 and type **3.8**. Press Tab twice, press . (period), and then press Ins. Type **7**, press Tab L, press Tab B, and then press Enter.)

11. Set the tab stops for the level 4 heading's leading dots and total column.

   a. Click left on the tab type letter until an L appears.

   b. Click left on the space next to the character until a period appears.

   c. Click left on the second dot before the 4 on the ruler.

   d. Click left on the tab type character until an R appears.

   e. Click left on the period next to the character until the space is blank.

   f. Click left on the 7 on the ruler. Figure 11.5 shows the style for level 4 added in the Gallery window.

(With version 4.0, click left on Format; then click right on Tab. Click left as follows: on the period for the leader, on the second dot before the 4 on the ruler; on Right for the alignment, on Blank for the leader, on the 7 on the ruler. Then click on the command line title.)

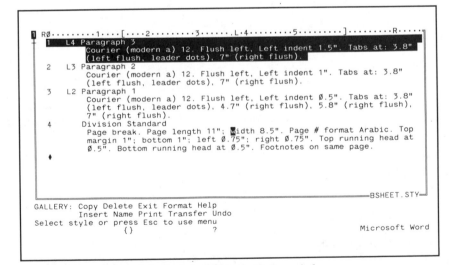

o **Figure 11.5:** *The style for level 4 added in the Gallery window*

12. Create an underlined paragraph format with a tab stop at 7 inches.

KEY From the Gallery, press I and type **un** for the key code. Press Tab to reach the Usage option, press P, and then press Enter. Next press Alt-F1, type **7L_** (remember to press Shift so you get an underline, not a dash), and press Enter. (With version 4.0, press Alt-F1 and type **7**. Press Tab twice, press the underline character, and then press Enter.)

    a. Click left on Insert.

    b. Type **un** for the Key Code option.

    c. Click right on Paragraph for the Usage option.

    d. Click left on the tab type character until an L appears.

    e. Click left on the space before it until an underline appears.

    f. Click left on the 7 on the ruler. Figure 11.6 shows the completed stylesheet.

(With version 4.0, to set the underline tab, click left on Format; then click right on Tab. Click left on the underline for the leader, and then click left on the 7 on the ruler. Click on the command line title.)

KEY Press T S Enter to save the stylesheet. Press E, then Esc Q to quit Word.

13. Click left on Transfer; then click right on Save.

14. Click on Exit; then click right on Quit to exit Word.

```
1 L[..........1.........2.........3.........4.........5.........]........ L.....
1    UN Paragraph 4
        Courier (modern a) 12. Flush left. Tabs at: 7" (left flush, leader
        underscore).
2    L4 Paragraph 3
        Courier (modern a) 12. Flush left, Left indent 1.5". Tabs at: 3.8"
        (left flush, leader dots), 7" (right flush).
3    L3 Paragraph 2
        Courier (modern a) 12. Flush left, Left indent 1". Tabs at: 3.8"
        (left flush, leader dots), 7" (right flush).
4    L2 Paragraph 1
        Courier (modern a) 12. Flush left, Left indent 0.5". Tabs at: 3.8"
        (left flush, leader dots), 4.7" (right flush), 5.8" (right flush),
        7" (right flush).
5    Division Standard
        Page break. Page length 11"; width 8.5". Page # format Arabic. Top
        margin 1"; bottom 1"; left 0.75"; right 0.75". Top running head at
        0.5". Bottom running head at 0.5". Footnotes on same page.
+
                                                         ─BSHEET.STY─
GALLERY: Copy Delete Exit Format Help
         Insert Name Print Transfer Undo
Select style or press Esc to use menu
              ()                    ?            Microsoft Word
```

o **Figure 11.6:** *The completed balance sheet stylesheet*

TYPING THE BALANCE SHEET

4.0 Precede normal speed keys with an X, such as Alt-XC to center text.

KEY Press Esc F S A, type **BSheet**, and press Enter.

You will now use the balance sheet stylesheet to type the balance sheet shown in Figure 11.1. Follow the steps below.

1. Start Word.
2. Click left on Format; then click right on Stylesheet. Type **BSheet**, and then click on the command line title.
3. Press Alt-C to center the title and date.
4. Type

   Wilson Engine Company
   Balance Sheet
   June 30, 1990

5. Press Enter, then Alt-P.
6. Enter the two horizontal lines.

   a. Press Alt-UN, then press Tab.
   b. Press Enter, then press Tab.
   c. Press Enter twice.
   d. Press Alt-P.

7. Enter the Assets heading.

   a. Press Alt-C and type **Assets**.
   b. Press Enter twice.
   c. Press Alt-P. Figure 11.7 shows the screen at this point.

8. Type **Current:**.
9. Press Enter twice.
10. Enter the first three lines of the current assets section at the level 2 position.

    a. Press Alt-L2 and type **Cash**.
    b. Press Tab to insert the line of periods to the 3.8-inch mark.
    c. Press Tab twice more to reach the 5.8-inch mark and type **$25,000**.

    d. Press Enter. Figure 11.8 shows the first entry at the level 2 position.

    e. Type **Accounts Receivable** and press Tab three times.

    f. Type **100,000** and press Enter.

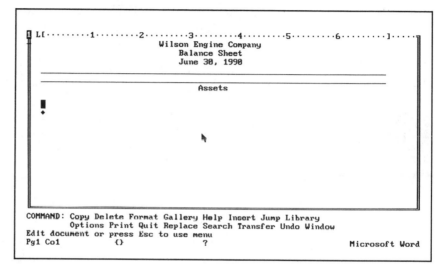

o **Figure 11.7:** *The balance sheet with the title, date, and Assets heading*

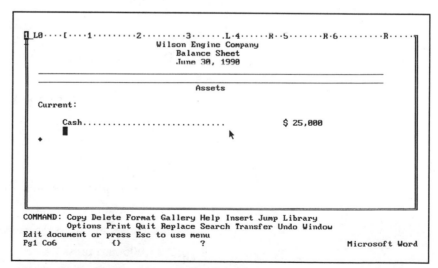

o **Figure 11.8:** *The first entry at the level 2 position*

g. Type **Finished Goods Inventory** and press Tab three times.

h. Type **20,000** and press Enter.

11. Type the next line. Underline the amount.

a. Type **Unexpired Insurance** and press Tab three times.

b. Press Alt-XU. The X is necessary because we created a speed key starting with Alt-U—Alt-UN.

c. Press the spacebar three times to create the underlined spaces.

d. Type **1,000** and press Alt-spacebar.

e. Press Enter.

KEY Place the cursor on the $, then press Shift-F6. Move the cursor to the last zero in 1,000, extending the highlight, and then press F2.

12. We've got four large numbers here, so let's use column math to compute the total of the current asset figures.

a. Click left on the $.

b. Press Shift-F6.

c. Click left on the last zero in 1,000.

d. Press F2.

13. Type the first subtotal at the level 3 position.

a. Place the cursor under the last line you typed and press Alt-L3.

b. Type **Total Current Assets** and press Tab twice to reach the 7-inch mark.

c. Click right on Insert.

d. Press Enter twice. Figure 11.9 shows the completed current assets section.

14. Press Alt-P and and type **Plant and Equipment:**.

15. Press Enter twice.

16. Enter the first two rows of the next category.

a. Press Alt-L2.

b. Type **Land** and press Tab three times.

c. Type **40,000** and press Enter.

d. Type **Buildings** and press Tab twice.

e. Type **125,000** and press Enter.

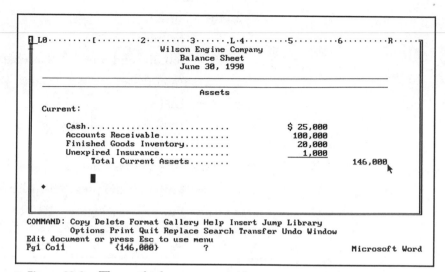

```
⌐ L0·······[······2······3·····.L·4·····5·······6······R····⌐
│                     Wilson Engine Company                  │
│                        Balance Sheet                       │
│                        June 30, 1990                       │
│       ───────────────────────────────────────────────     │
│                                                            │
│                          ──────────                        │
│                            Assets                          │
│                                                            │
│       Current:                                             │
│                                                            │
│           Cash.........................    $ 25,000        │
│           Accounts Receivable..............   100,000      │
│           Finished Goods Inventory........    20,000       │
│           Unexpired Insurance..............    1,000       │
│                 Total Current Assets........       146,000 │
│                                                            │
│        ◆            █                                      │
│                                                            │
│                                                            │
└────────────────────────────────────────────────────────────┘
 COMMAND: Copy Delete Format Gallery Help Insert Jump Library
         Options Print Quit Replace Search Transfer Undo Window
 Edit document or press Esc to use menu
 Pg1 Co11         {146,000}           ?              Microsoft Word
```

o **Figure 11.9:** *The completed current assets section*

17. Enter the next row. Underline the amount.

    a. Type **Less Depreciation** and press Tab twice.

    b. Press Alt-XU, then the spacebar twice.

    c. Type **25,000** and press Alt-spacebar.

    d. Press Tab and type **100,000**.

    e. Press Enter.

18. Complete the level 2 entries for the category.

    a. Type **Machinery** and press Tab twice.

    b. Type **240,000** and press Enter.

    c. Type **Less Depreciation** and press Tab twice.

    d. Press Alt-XU, then the spacebar.

    e. Type **120,000** and press Tab.

    f. Type **120,000** and press Alt-spacebar.

    g. Press Enter.

19. Enter the subtotal and total.

    a. Press Alt-L3.

    b. Type **Total Plant and Equipment** and press Tab twice.

    c. Press Alt-XU.

    d. Press the spacebar twice.

    e. Type **260,000** and press Alt-spacebar.

    f. Press Enter twice.

    g. Press Alt-L4.

    h. Type **Total Assets** and press Tab twice.

    i. Press Alt-D.

    j. Press the spacebar twice.

    k. Type **$406,000** and press Alt-spacebar.

    l. Press Enter twice. Figure 11.10 shows the completed assets portion of the balance sheet.

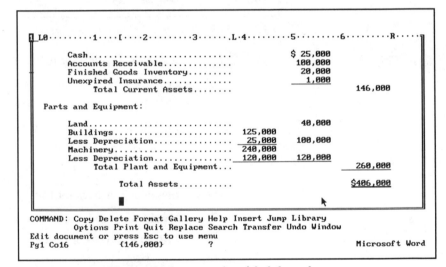

○ **Figure 11.10:** *The completed assets portion of the balance sheet*

20. Enter the horizontal line between the assets and liabilities portions.

    a. Press Alt-UN.

    b. Press Tab.

    c. Press Enter twice.

    d. Press Alt-P.

21. Enter the Liabilities heading.

    a. Press Alt-C.

    b. Type **Liabilities**.

    c. Press Enter twice.

    d. Press Alt-P.

22. Type **Current:**.

23. Press Enter twice.

24. Enter the current liabilities section.

    a. Press Alt-L2.

    b. Type **Accounts Payable** and press Tab three times.

    c. Type **100,000** and press Enter.

    d. Type **Interest Payable** and press Tab three times.

    e. Press Alt-XU.

    f. Press the spacebar three times.

    g. Type **2,000** and press Alt-spacebar.

    h. Press Enter.

    i. Press Alt-L3.

    j. Type **Total Current Liabilities** and press Tab twice.

    k. Type **102,000** and press Enter twice.

    l. Press Alt-P.

25. Type **Long-Term:**.

26. Press Enter twice.

27. Enter the long-term liabilities section.

    a. Press Alt-L2.

    b. Type **Stockholders Equity** and press Tab three times.

    c. Type **250,000** and press Enter.

    d. Type **Retained Earnings** and press Tab three times.

    e. Press Alt-XU.

    f. Press the spacebar twice.

    g. Type **54,000** and press Alt-spacebar.

      h. Press Enter.

      i. Press Alt-L3.

      j. Type **Total Long-Term Liabilities** and press Tab twice.

      k. Press Alt-XU.

      l. Press the spacebar twice.

     m. Type **304,000** and press Alt-spacebar.

      n. Press Enter twice.

28. Enter the total.

      a. Press Alt-L4.

      b. Type **Total Liabilities** and press Tab twice.

      c. Press Alt-D.

      d. Press the spacebar twice.

      e. Type **$406,000** and press Alt-spacebar.

      f. Press Enter. Figure 11.11 shows the completed liabilities portion of the balance sheet.

29. Click right on Print to print the balance sheet.

```
1 L0·········1···[···2·········3······L·4········5·········6·········R·····
                    _____

                               Liabilities

         Current:

                 Accounts Payable................    100,000
                 Interest Payable................      2,000
                        Total Current Liabilities...            102,000

         Long-Term:

                 Stockholders Equity.............    250,000
                 Retained Earning................     54,000
                        Total Long-Term Liabilities.            304,000

                        Total Liabilities......              $406,000
                 █                                      ▶

    COMMAND: Copy Delete Format Gallery Help Insert Jump Library
             Options Print Quit Replace Search Transfer Undo Window
    Edit document or press Esc to use menu
    Pg1 Co16          {146,000}          ?              Microsoft Word
```

o **Figure 11.11:** *The completed liabilities portion of the balance sheet*

30. Click left on Transfer Save and type **Balance**. Click on the command line title, and then click on SUMMARY.

31. Click right on Quit to exit Word.

In this balance sheet, we used Word's math function only once to total a column. If you wanted to use math for all your computations, enter a minus sign before the numbers you want to subtract, such as depreciation amounts. When you're done, delete the minus sign so it doesn't appear on the final printout.

You can compute the numbers as you're typing, inserting them at the appropriate locations. Or, you can enter all the figures except the totals, and then work through the document, adding the appropriate figures and inserting the totals where needed.

oCREATING OTHER FINANCIAL DOCUMENTS

Ask any accountant. There must be hundreds of different financial documents used by a typical business. Each has its own purpose and its own style. This section provides examples of several of these documents and the stylesheets required for their formats.

PRODUCING INCOME STATEMENTS

Income statements detail the source of company income for the year. They can be summaries of the data for the entire company, or they can be detailed lists of the items for each department.

Figure 11.12 shows a typical summary income statement, and Figure 11.13 shows the stylesheet used to create it. Figures 11.14 and 11.15 show an example of a detailed income statement itemized by departments and its stylesheet, respectively. You can create the sample stylesheets or revise them to match the styles that you prefer.

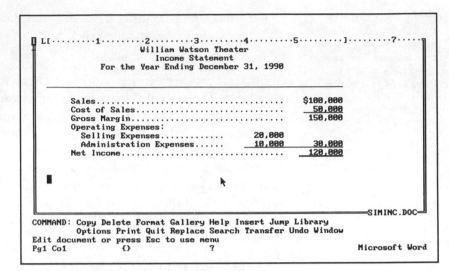

o **Figure 11.12:** *A summary income statement*

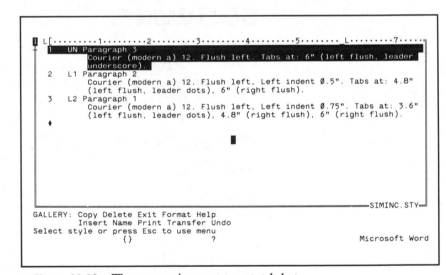

o **Figure 11.13:** *The summary income statement stylesheet*

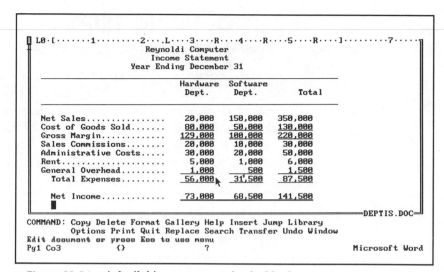

```
▯ L0·[······1········2···L···3···R···4···R···5··R····]·········7····▯
                        Reynoldi Computer
                        Income Statement
                     Year Ending December 31

                             Hardware   Software
                             Dept.      Dept.        Total

         Net Sales...............     20,000    150,000    350,000
         Cost of Goods Sold.......    80,000     50,000    130,000
         Gross Margin............    129,000    100,000    220,000
         Sales Commissions........    20,000     10,000     30,000
         Administrative Costs.....    30,000     20,000     50,000
         Rent....................      5,000      1,000      6,000
         General Overhead.........     1,000        500      1,500
            Total Expenses........    56,000   ▸ 31,500     87,500

            Net Income............    73,000     68,500    141,500
         ▮
                                                           ═DEPTIS.DOC═
  COMMAND: Copy Delete Format Gallery Help Insert Jump Library
           Options Print Quit Replace Search Transfer Undo Window
  Edit document or press Esc to use menu
  Pg1 Co3            {}                   ?              Microsoft Word
```

o **Figure 11.14:** *A detailed income statement itemized by departments*

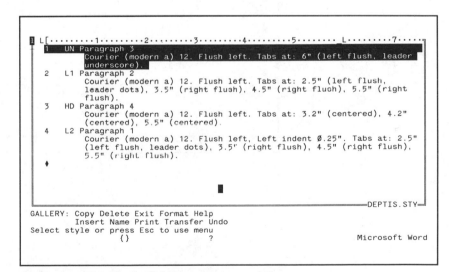

```
▯ L[·········1·········2·········3·········4·········5········L·······7·····
  1    UN Paragraph 3
          Courier (modern a) 12. Flush left. Tabs at: 6" (left flush, leader
          underscore).
  2    L1 Paragraph 2
          Courier (modern a) 12. Flush left. Tabs at: 2.5" (left flush,
          leader dots), 3.5" (right flush), 4.5" (right flush), 5.5" (right
          flush).
  3    HD Paragraph 4
          Courier (modern a) 12. Flush left. Tabs at: 3.2" (centered), 4.2"
          (centered), 5.5" (centered).
  4    L2 Paragraph 1
          Courier (modern a) 12. Flush left, Left indent 0.25". Tabs at: 2.5"
          (left flush, leader dots), 3.5" (right flush), 4.5" (right flush),
          5.5" (right flush).
  ◆


                                 ▮
                                                           ═DEPTIS.STY═
  GALLERY: Copy Delete Exit Format Help
           Insert Name Print Transfer Undo
  Select style or press Esc to use menu
              {}                    ?              Microsoft Word
```

o **Figure 11.15:** *The detailed income statement stylesheet*

PRODUCING TRIAL BALANCES

Trial balances list all general ledger accounts, with the debits or credits pertaining to them. The example trial balance shown in Figure 11.16 includes special paragraphs for underlining the columns and double-underlining the totals. Figure 11.17 shows the stylesheet used to create the sample trial balance.

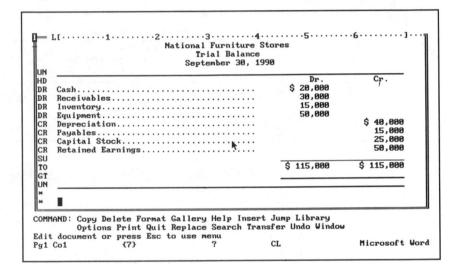

o **Figure 11.16:** *A sample trial balance*

oCREATING RULED FORMS

Most financial documents take forms similar to income statements or balance sheets. They are divided into a number of numeric columns with underlined subtotals and totals. In fact, each of the sample stylesheets in this chapter makes some provisions for underlining.

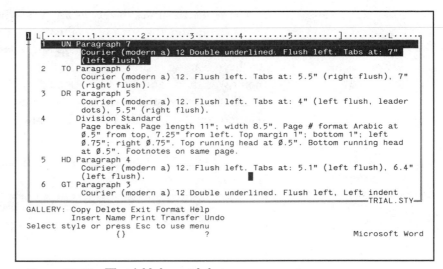

```
1 L[·········1·········2·········3·········4·········5·········]·········L·····
  1    UN Paragraph 7
          Courier (modern a) 12 Double underlined. Flush left. Tabs at: 7"
          (left flush).
  2    TO Paragraph 6
          Courier (modern a) 12. Flush left. Tabs at: 5.5" (right flush), 7"
          (right flush).
  3    DR Paragraph 5
          Courier (modern a) 12. Flush left. Tabs at: 4" (left flush, leader
          dots), 5.5" (right flush).
  4       Division Standard
          Page break. Page length 11"; width 8.5". Page # format Arabic at
          Ø.5" from top, 7.25" from left. Top margin 1"; bottom 1"; left
          Ø.75"; right Ø.75". Top running head at Ø.5". Bottom running head
          at Ø.5". Footnotes on same page.
  5    HD Paragraph 4
          Courier (modern a) 12. Flush left. Tabs at: 5.1" (left flush), 6.4"
          (left flush).
  6    GT Paragraph 3
          Courier (modern a) 12 Double underlined. Flush left, Left indent
                                                              ━━━━━━━━TRIAL.STY━
GALLERY: Copy Delete Exit Format Help
         Insert Name Print Transfer Undo
Select style or press Esc to use menu
             ()                        ?                       Microsoft Word
```

o **Figure 11.17:** *The trial balance stylesheet*

USING UNDERLINE AND DOUBLE-UNDERLINE STYLES

As mentioned earlier, Word's built-in speed keys for underlining and double-underlining won't create a horizontal rule under a blank line. One way to create horizontal lines is to set a tab stop at the far right margin with underlines as its leading characters. This is the method that we used to type the underlines in our example balance sheet. We created an underlined paragraph format with the key code un and pressed Alt-UN and the Tab key to type the underline. We could have created double underlines by pressing Alt-UN Tab twice in a row. This would actually insert two single-underlined lines.

There is a problem with this technique, however. The underline must be by itself on the line. Characters entered before pressing the Tab key will not be underlined. Text inserted after the underline is typed will replace the underline.

This problem can be solved by using another method to create speed keys for single and double underlining. You can then easily create all sorts of ruled forms and documents.

Figure 11.18 shows the styles for producing underlines and double underlines, and Figure 11.19 illustrates a sample ruled form. The single-underline style has a tab stop at the far right. The tab stop does not have leading characters. Instead, the Gallery's Format Character menu was used, and Yes was selected for the Underline option. The double-underline style was created the same way, except that Yes was selected for the Double Underline option on the Format Character menu.

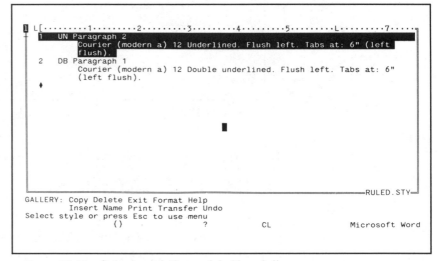

○ **Figure 11.18:** *Styles for underlines and double underlines*

To produce a single- or double-underlined horizontal line, just press the appropriate speed key and the Tab key. To add characters above the line, press the appropriate speed key and type the text, or press the spacebar to reach where you want the text to begin on the line and type it in. After you're finished, press the Tab key to reach the end of the line.

USING GRAPHIC LINES

Another alternative for drawing lines is to use the Format Border Lines menu options, as we did in Chapter 8. Just keep in mind that these graphic lines actually print below the paragraph, not under the words, as shown in Figure 11.20.

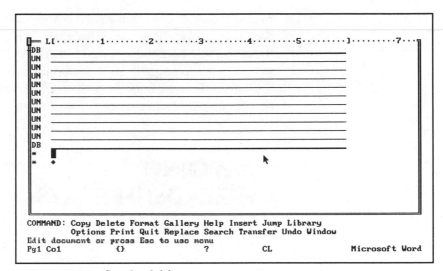

o **Figure 11.19:** *Sample ruled form*

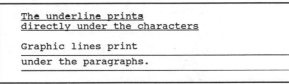

o **Figure 11.20:** *Underline versus graphic lines*

The top of the figure shows two single-spaced paragraphs underlined; the bottom illustrates two single-spaced paragraphs with graphic lines. Notice that the graphic lines take up extra space, so fewer lines will actually fit on the page.

oCREATING YOUR OWN STYLES

If the styles of the financial documents presented in this chapter suit your needs, you can use the sample stylesheets to create your own documents.

If you need to customize a stylesheet, you must first plan how the finished document should look. Decide if your division needs narrower margins to fit all the columns across the page. If so, create a new standard division format for the stylesheet. Then decide on the locations for the columns at each indentation level. Use the Gallery Insert command to create each paragraph style, including those for horizontal lines. Set the tab stops on the ruler. Save the revised stylesheet, and attach it to a new document whenever you want to use it.

oMERGING SPREADSHEET FILES

You may have noticed that these financial documents resemble spreadsheets in that data is formatted into rows and columns. Even with Word's capabilities, it is much easier to create this type of document with a spreadsheet program, such as Lotus 1-2-3, Multiplan, or Excel. In fact, you may already have spreadsheet files containing the data.

You can combine the numeric power of a spreadsheet program and the formatting power of Word by using Word's Library Link command, which allows you to import spreadsheet files directly into Word. You can even update the document to include any changes in the spreadsheet just before printing.

Follow these steps to merge a spreadsheet into Word:

1. Place the cursor where you want to insert the spreadsheet data.

2. Click left on Library Link to display the prompt

   LIBRARY LINK: Document Graphics Spreadsheet

KEY Press Esc L L S. (With version 4.0, press Esc L L.)

3. Click on Spreadsheet. (The other options are discussed in later chapters.) The next prompt appears:

   LIBRARY LINK filename: area:

 **4.0** Click left on Library Link.

4. Type the name (including the directory path if the spreadsheet is not on the default directory) of the spreadsheet file. To display a list of files, type *.*, and then press F1.

5. If you want to import the entire spreadsheet, press Enter. If you want only part of the spreadsheet, click left on the Area option and enter the spreadsheet range. For Lotus files, separate cells with two

To import part of a spreadsheet, press Tab to reach the Area option, enter the range of cells, and then press Enter. To import a named area, press F1 at the Area option, select the name, and press Enter.

periods (A1..C12); for Multiplan and Excel files, use a colon (A1:C12). To import a named area, click right on the Area option to display a list of named ranges, and then click right on the name. After you indicate the whole spreadsheet or a part of it, click on the command line title. If the area of the spreadsheet is protected, Word will prompt you to enter the password.

The spreadsheet will be merged into the document. The hidden code .L. and the file name will be placed at the start of the spreadsheet. Newline characters will end each line, instead of returns, and a .L. code will be placed at the end. Newline codes are used in case you want to reformat the spreadsheet as a paragraph.

If you later move or copy the spreadsheet, include the hidden .L. codes. They will allow you to update the data if you later change it using the spreadsheet program.

When you are importing large spreadsheet areas, you might have to change your margin or switch to a compressed printer font before printing.

UPDATING SPREADSHEETS

If you change and recalculate the data in a spreadsheet after merging it into Word, the Word document will not be current. However, you can use the power of the link (.L.) codes to update the information.

To update a spreadsheet, select it, and press Esc L L S Enter. To update all spreadsheets in the document, press Shift-F10, then Esc L L S Enter. (With version 4.0, press Esc L L Enter.)

Before printing the document, or whenever you want to ensure that the document contains the most recent figures, highlight the spreadsheet in the document (including the .L. codes), click left on Library Link Spreadsheet, and then click on the command line title. If you have more than one spreadsheet that needs updating, click both in the selection bar to select the entire document, click left on Library Link Spreadsheet, and then click on the command line title.

oPRINTING WIDE DOCUMENTS

If your financial document or spreadsheet is wider than a standard 8½-inch page, you'll have to make several adjustments depending on your printer and paper.

Some printers can print on paper up to 22 inches wide, the maximum width that Word can handle. If yours does, just change the page width and margin settings on the Format Division Margins menu, and then print your document as usual.

USING COMPRESSED PRINTING

Many printers, however, can only print on standard 8½-inch paper. Fortunately, most dot-matrix printers can print in compressed mode, using smaller characters. For example, the IBM Graphics Printer can print in 8-point size, fitting 120 characters on each line.

To use this mode, calculate how wide you want the spreadsheet to be, and then change the page-width setting on the Format Division Margins menu. For example, suppose that your widest line will be 100 characters. You would set the page width to 12.5 inches (10 inches for the text, 2½ inches for margins) before typing the document. This way, you would be able to enter the wide lines of text, scrolling horizontally.

After you entered the text, you would select the entire document, use the Format Character menu to select the 8-point type size, and then use the Format Division Margins menu to return the page width to 8½. Finally, you would select Yes for Show Line Breaks on the Options menu. In this mode, the displayed text will still scroll off the right edge of the screen (along with the ruler), but each line will end where it will on the printed page.

USING LASER PRINTERS

Laser printers provide two ways to print wide documents. Most have a Line Printer font of 8.5 points. To print your document in this font in the portrait mode, follow the instructions above for compressed printing and select Line Printer for the font on the Format Character menu.

 In landscape mode, the page is 8½ inches long and 11 inches wide.

You could also print the document in the landscape mode, sideways on the page. Select the landscape PRD file, and change the page margins, length, and width accordingly. By combining landscape mode and the Line Printer font, you can pack a lot of information on each line.

The spaces between characters shown in the sample PCL commands are just to make them easier for you to read—don't type them.

If you want to include a wide financial report within another document, use PCL commands as you did for printing envelopes in Chapter 5. The command for normal print in landscape mode (106 characters per line) is

Alt-27 &l1O

To use landscape mode and Line Printer font (176 characters per line), the PCL command is

Alt-27 &l1O   Alt-27 &k2S

Alt-27 means to hold down the Alt key, then type 27 on the numeric keypad. A small arrow appears when you release the Alt key. Remember to change the page width on the Format Division Margins menu when you are printing wide documents.

We'll cover one more typical application in this part of the book before moving on to more complex operations. The next chapter describes how to produce reports and papers—from the planning stages to the final version.

CHAPTER 12

- **PRODUCING**
- **REPORTS**
- **AND**
- **PAPERS**

4.0

KEY

Long documents such as reports and academic papers present numerous challenges, but Word provides powerful features to make these complex tasks easier. A built-in outlining feature aids in the organization of your thoughts. It provides the same functions as the best stand-alone "thought processors," yet is totally integrated with Word.

After the document is developed, Word allows footnotes to be inserted easily at the proper location and can even prepare a table of contents and index automatically.

In this chapter, you will learn how to use the outlining feature to develop your ideas and begin the process of writing a report. Then you'll complete a sample document by adding footnotes, a table of contents, and an index.

oCREATING OUTLINES

For all but the simplest reports and papers, outlining is a vital first step. The outline provides a framework for organizing and experimenting with the concepts and information that will make up the document. It lets you work with the underlying structure of the document and visualize the inter-relationships of paragraphs and ideas.

Word's outlining function goes even further. It allows you to quickly reorganize that structure and to examine the structure in many levels or views.

SWITCHING BETWEEN VIEWS

To begin with, outlining provides two ways of looking at the document: the document view and the outline view. Figure 12.1 shows an example of text in both views.

The document view is the way the text normally appears on the screen, just as you type it and just as it will appear when printed.

The outline view displays the same document in outline form, with headings indented to their appropriate outline level, as explained in the next section. It is in this view that you can examine and manipulate the basic structure of the document.

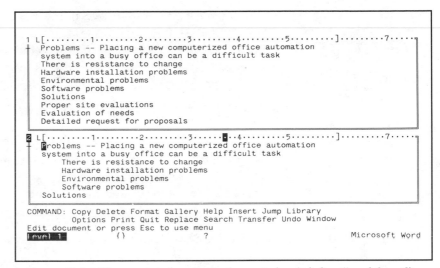

o **Figure 12.1:** *The same text shown in the document view (window 1) and the outline view (window 2)*

You toggle between views by pressing the Shift-F2 key. You can tell you're in the outline view if the word *Text*, *Organize*, or *Level* followed by a number appears on the right side of the status line in place of the page and column position indicators. If you're not using a mouse, Word will automatically display the stylebar when you switch to the outline view.

OUTLINE LEVELS

In Word outlines, entries are indented in levels. The level numbers used and their corresponding outline positions are as follows:

Level Number	Outline Entry
1	I.
2	A.
3	1.
4	a)
5	(1)
6	(a)

You use Alt-9 to raise the level number (such as moving from level 2 to level 1), and Alt-0 to lower the level (changing from level 2 to level 3, for example). Do not use the 9 and 0 keys on the keypad unless the NumLock key has been pressed and the letters NL appear on the status line.

ENTERING AN OUTLINE

Now we'll begin to use the outline feature to organize and write a sample paper. In outlining, it is best to start with the broad, overall topics to be covered, then add text and detail as the subject is refined.

Follow these steps to create the outline:

1. Start Word.

2. Press Shift-F2 to switch to the outline view. The indicator

   Level 1

   appears on the status line, showing that the entry will be a level 1 heading.

3. Type **Introduction**, and then press Enter.

4. Press Alt-0 to lower the level of the next entry. (Do not use the 0 on the keypad.) The indicator

   Level 2

   appears on the status line, as shown in Figure 12.2.

5. Type **Everyone thinks it was Edison**, and then press Enter. The cursor is automatically indented to the same level.

6. Type **There have been other claims**, and then press Enter.

7. Press Alt-9 to raise the next heading back to level 1. (Do not use the 9 on the keypad.)

8. Type **Early Experiments**, and then press Enter.

You now have a very basic outline for a paper on the invention of the motion picture. It will contain two basic sections, a description of the problem, and a discussion of early experiments with the motion picture that may shed some light on the problem.

If you were writing your own paper, you would gather your notes and start to refine the outline, adding short paragraphs to develop the concept. So let's develop this outline a little further.

9. Place the cursor at the end of the line *There have been other claims*, as shown in Figure 12.3.
10. Press Enter.

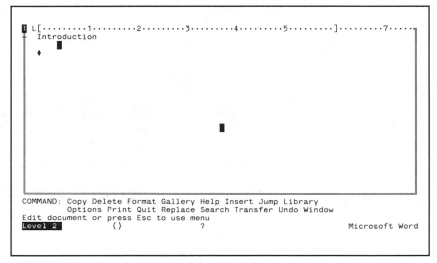

o **Figure 12.2:** *Preparing for the second outline level*

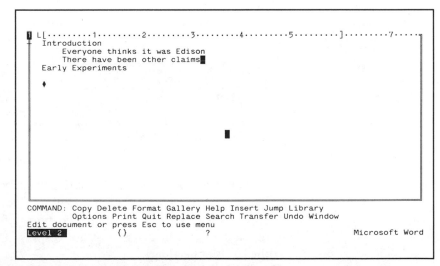

o **Figure 12.3:** *Position of the cursor to develop the outline*

11. Press Alt-0 to lower the level one indentation and type

   Dickson
   Friese-Greene

12. Move the cursor under the last line and press Alt-0.

13. Type

   Dickson
   Flexible film
   Muybridge
   Edison patent

Figure 12.4 shows the completed outline. Now we have a structure to develop for our paper.

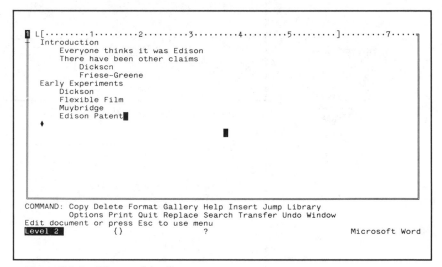

```
  L[·········1·········2·········3·········4·········5·········]·········7·····
  Introduction
        Everyone thinks it was Edison
        There have been other claims
              Dickscn
              Friese-Greene
  Early Experiments
        Dickson
        Flexible Film
        Muybridge
        Edison Patent

COMMAND: Copy Delete Format Gallery Help Insert Jump Library
        Options Print Quit Replace Search Transfer Undo Window
Edit document or press Esc to use menu
Level 2                {}                    ?                      Microsoft Word
```

o **Figure 12.4:** *The sample outline*

The true power of Word's outline feature goes beyond displaying headings at their appropriate indentation levels. While in the outline view, you can select between two types of edit modes, control the amount of text or levels that are displayed and printed, and adjust the levels of headings.

oCONTROLLING THE DISPLAY OF OUTLINE LEVELS

One reason for displaying headings properly indented in the outline view is to visualize the relationship of sections and concepts to others. However, in a long document you would have to scroll up or down to display the headings, making it difficult to see the basic structure of the document.

But you can change the view to show just the major divisions, or subjects, discussed in the paper by *collapsing* selected levels of the outline. When the outline is collapsed, you can easily see the overall organization of the document without having to scroll through several pages. Of course, collapsed headings can be *expanded*, or redisplayed.

Table 12.1 lists the mouse and keyboard methods for collapsing and expanding levels, as well as body text, which we'll discuss shortly. Note that some actions cannot be accomplished with the mouse.

The selection bar, or stylebar if you're not using a mouse, will display a + next to a heading that has additional headings collapsed under it. If there is no symbol next to a heading, it does not have any levels collapsed under it.

Before we save our sample outline, let's see how it looks when some levels are collapsed.

1. Place the cursor on the word *Introduction* in the first line.

2. Press – (the minus key on the keypad), and the subheadings will disappear from the screen, as shown in Figure 12.5. A plus sign appears in the stylebar to indicate that headings are collapsed beneath this one.

3. Place the cursor anywhere on the next major (level 1) heading, *Early Experiments*.

4. Press – . Now only two lines remain. Let's expand each major heading by one level to show more detail.

5. With the cursor still on *Early Experiments*, press + . The collapsed heading reappears.

o **Table 12.1:** *Techniques for Collapsing and Expanding Outline Displays*

Action	Mouse	Keyboard
Collapse headings and body text below the heading	Click both on the heading	Place the cursor on the heading and press – (minus) on the keypad (or press Alt-8)
Collapse body text		Press Shift- – (or Shift-Alt- 8)
Expand next level heading	Click right on the heading	Press + (plus) on the keypad (or Alt-7)
Expand body text		Press Shift- + (or Shift-Alt-7)
Expand all levels below a heading		Press the * (asterisk) key on the keypad (or PrtSc)
Expand all headings to a specific level		Press Ctrl- + (on the keypad) and type the level number to expand to
Expand all headings and body text		Select the entire document, press *, and then press Shift- +

6. Place the cursor on the word *Introduction* and press +. Notice that only the first level of subheadings appeared, not those under the "other claims" section.

7. Place the cursor on that line and press + to reveal the remaining subheadings.

8. Press Shift-F2 to enter the document view. The stylebar and all the level indentations disappear, as shown in Figure 12.6.

KEY Press Ctrl-F10, type **Movies**, and press Enter twice to save the outline.

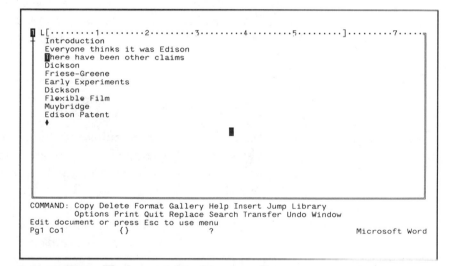

○ **Figure 12.5:** *A partially collapsed outline*

○ **Figure 12.6:** *The document view of the same outline*

9. Press Shift-F2 to return to the outline view.

10. Click left on Transfer Save, type **Movies**, click on the command line title, and then click on SUMMARY to save the outline.

oDEVELOPING THE PAPER

Now we can use our sample outline to create the paper itself. You do this by editing the outline and adding body text to it.

EDITING OUTLINES

In the document view, you have only one way to edit text. But the outline view provides two different edit modes: text edit and outline organize.

You edit text in the default text edit mode as you would make changes in the document view. The same cursor-movement keys, edit commands, and selection procedures apply. In the outline organize mode, however, you work only with sections or paragraphs. So you can move an entire section by moving just the heading it falls under.

You toggle between edit modes by pressing Shift-F5 while in the outline view. Shift-F5 has no effect in the document view—you must be in the outline view for it to work.

ADDING BODY TEXT

You can develop a basic outline by adding body text to it. Body text is text in the default paragraph style, not an outline heading. When you enter body text, a *T* appears next to it in the stylebar.

As with levels, you can collapse body text (see Table 12.1). Only the basic outline will be displayed, and a *t* will appear in the stylebar next to headings with body text collapsed under them.

Now we'll add body text to the sample outline.

1. Place the cursor at the end of the line *Everyone thinks it was Edison* and press Enter.
2. Press Alt-P. The letter *T* appears in the stylebar and the word *Text* is on the status line, as shown in Figure 12.7. These indicate that the section will be body text.

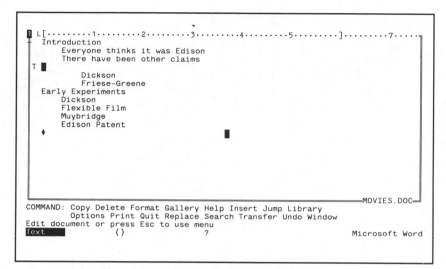

```
 I L[·········1·········2·········3·········4·········5·········]·········7·····
 +  Introduction
         Everyone thinks it was Edison
         There have been other claims
 T ■
             Dickson
             Friese-Greene
     Early Experiments
         Dickson
         Flexible Film
         Muybridge
         Edison Patent
     ♦                               ■


                                                        ┌MOVIES.DOC┐
 COMMAND: Copy Delete Format Gallery Help Insert Jump Library
         Options Print Quit Replace Search Transfer Undo Window
 Edit document or press Esc to use menu
 Text                    {}                 ?              Microsoft Word
```

o **Figure 12.7:** *The stylebar showing the body text format*

3. Type the following paragraphs.

> **The exact origin of the motion picture is not known but has been a subject of controversy for years. However, in the United States, most people give credit for the motion picture to Thomas Edison.**

> **Animated pictures did appear in Europe long before any Edison claim. The toy consisted of two disks mounted parallel on a rod. The front disk contained small slits; the rear disk had a series of pictures. When the child pulled a string, the disks rotated giving the illusion of a moving object.**

4. Now we want to change some level headings and add new levels. First change the first subheading *Everyone thinks it was Edison* to **Problem**, as shown in Figure 12.8.

5. Place the cursor at the end of the first body text paragraph and press Enter to insert a blank line.

6. Press Alt-9 to enter a level 2 heading.

7. Type **Early Toys**.

8. Edit the next subheading to read **Other Claims**.

9. Enter a blank line after that heading, and then press Alt-P to enter body text.

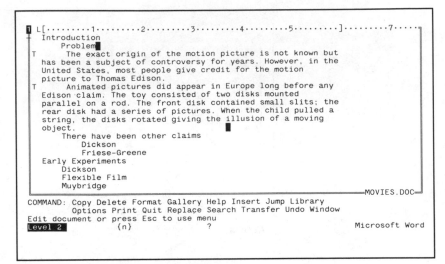

o **Figure 12.8:** *Body text and edited level headings in the outline*

10. Type the following paragraph.

> **Who invented a more sophisticated moving picture device is a question of some doubt. In addition to Edison, both W. K. L. Dickson and William Friese-Greene claim the honor. Both men were Edison's assistant during this period of development.**

11. Since this paragraph mentions the two names listed next as sub-headings, those levels can be deleted. Place the cursor on the subheading *Dickson*.

12. Press Shift-F5 to enter outline organize mode. The entire subheading becomes selected. If the cursor is on body text when you press Shift-F5, the entire paragraph is selected.

KEY Press Del to delete the heading.

13. Click right on Delete to delete the heading. The next heading is selected.

14. Click right on Delete to delete that heading, and then press Shift-F5.

15. Now we'll add body text under the last level 1 heading. Place the cursor after *Early Experiments* and press Enter to insert a blank line.

16. Press Alt-P to enter body text.

17. Type the following paragraph

> **Experiments with moving pictures have been going on for years in both the United States and Europe. But what makes these claims most**

critical is that they came from persons within the Edison idea factory. Perhaps one way to shed light on the subject, however, is to examine the dates when such claims were made.

Now in a similar manner, we'll enter body text under the other subheadings. Remember to press Enter to insert a new line, then press Alt-P for body text.

18. Under the subheading Dickson, type the following text.

> **W. K. L. Dickson, for example, claimed to have worked on the idea himself in 1887, when Edison was away in France. He claimed to have the idea that "it was possible to devise an instrument which could do for the eye what the phonograph does for the ear."**

19. Under the subheading Flexible Film, type the following paragraph.

> **Any earlier equipment was probably doomed because of the lack of good quality flexible film. It wasn't until the end of 1888 that John Carbutt announced a new celluloid-based film. Later publicity, however, gave credit for this invention to the much larger and known Eastman company.**

20. Under the subheading Muybridge, type the following text.

> **Edison himself was reported to have said, in 1888, that photographer Edweard Muybridge proposed to him "a scheme which will afford an almost endless period of instruction and amusement." In fact, later in 1888 he applied for the first motion picture caveat, or patent.**

 Press Shift-F5 Del to delete the subheading.

21. Delete the subheading Edison Patent. Place the cursor on the line, press Shift-F5, and then click right on Delete.

REORGANIZING THE OUTLINE

Because our sample paper is now too long to fit on the screen, editing may appear more difficult, but it is not. Because of Word's outlining abilities, it becomes easier to work with long documents if they are in outline form. Scrolling from section to section becomes quicker, as does moving blocks of text.

To illustrate this, you will exchange two paragraphs. The first problem in doing this with long papers in document view would be scrolling to the desired area. The second would be selecting and moving the proper amount of text without losing track of the desired position. Let's see how much easier these two operations are in outline view.

In this case, you will move the section Flexible Film, the second major section of the paper, to the end of the document.

KEY Press Ctrl-PgUp to reach the first line.

1. Click both under the window number to reach the start of the document, and then click left on the first line.

2. Press Shift-F5 to enter outline organize mode. You must be in the outline view for this to work, so if you hear a warning beep, press Shift-F2 to enter the proper view.

3. Press the down arrow key. Notice that the next level 1 heading is immediately selected. When you are in outline organize mode, the cursor moves the highlight to the next level of the same type.

4. Press F6. This selects the entire section under that heading level, as shown in Figure 12.9.

5. Press Shift- – (on the keypad) to collapse the body text. Only the headings remain for the section Early Experiments.

6. Press Shift-F5 to return to text edit mode.

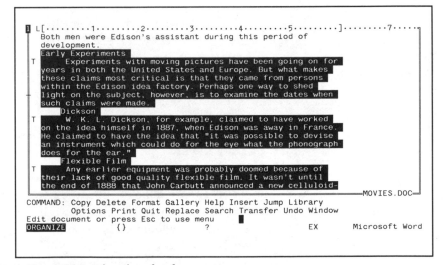

o **Figure 12.9:** *A section selected*

7. Place the cursor at the beginning of the word *Muybridge*.

8. Press Shift-F5 to select the heading and enter the outline organize mode.

KEY Press Del to delete the subheading.

9. Click right on Delete. Not only have you deleted the subheading, but you have also deleted any body text and smaller subheadings between it and the next subheading of the same level. The lower-case t in the stylebar indicates that body text has been collapsed.

10. Press the left arrow key to select the previous heading.

KEY Press Ins to insert the heading.

11. Click right on Insert to insert the heading Muybridge and its associated body text from the scrap.

12. Press the left arrow key twice to select the heading Early Experiments.

13. Press F6 to select the entire section.

14. Press Shift-+ to expand the body text. The text has been moved along with the heading, as shown in Figure 12.10.

You could have made the same move with the body text displayed. However, collapsing the text allows you to view the outline alone for a better overall picture of the structure of the document.

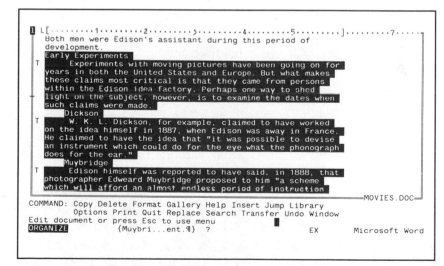

o **Figure 12.10:** *The rearranged outline*

oFORMATTING OUTLINES WITH STYLESHEETS

When you complete the paper, as is often the case with your own work, the outline level headings will become the headings and subheadings for the document itself. Usually the character format and indentation are different for each heading level.

As you saw previously, when you change to the document view, the level indentations disappear. So to use the outline's headings and subheadings in your final document, you have to create your own character and paragraph formats.

The most efficient way to do this is through a stylesheet and Word's built-in paragraph variants. Word has seven special variants that correspond to seven outline levels: the variants Heading Level 1 through Heading Level 7. Character styles assigned to these variants will be used to format the levels in both the outline and document views. Paragraph formats (such as indentations) will be used only in the document view; in the outline view, the normal indentation levels will be displayed.

Let's use these variants to format the outline levels in this document. Since only two outline levels were used in the document, only the first two heading level variants must be formatted. We'll format level 1 to print boldface and underlined. Level 2 will be boldfaced and indented ½ inch from the left margin.

KEY Press Esc G I; then press Tab P. Press Tab to reach the Variant option, and then press F1 to list possible variants. Move the cursor to select the variant Heading Level 1 and press Enter.

1. Click on Gallery; then click left on Insert.

2. Click left on Paragraph for the Usage option.

3. Click right on the Variant option to display a list of possible variants. Variants Heading Level 1 through Heading Level 7 are reserved for the outline entries. The table level and index level variants will be used for the table of contents and index, as described later in the chapter. Figure 12.11 shows the paragraph styles in the Gallery window.

4. Click right on Heading Level 1. The standard paragraph format appears in the Gallery window.

```
Standard              Footnote            Running Head         Heading level 1
Heading level 2       Heading level 3     Heading level 4      Heading level 5
Heading level 6       Heading level 7     Index level 1        Index level 2
Index level 3         Index level 4       Table level 1        Table level 2
Table level 3         Table level 4       Annotation           1
2                     3                   4                    5
6                     7                   8                    9
10                    11                  12                   13
14                    15                  16                   17
18                    19                  20                   21
22                    23                  24                   25
26                    27                  28                   29
30                    31                  32                   33
34                    35                  36                   37
38                    39                  40                   41
42                    43                  44                   45
46                    47                  48                   49
50                    51                  52                   53
54                    55


INSERT key code: {}                          usage: Character(Paragraph)Division
          variant: Standard                  remark:
Enter variant or press F1 to select from list
                 {}                      ?
                                                          Microsoft Word
```

o **Figure 12.11:** *Paragraph styles*

5. Now edit the format to create the desired style.

   a. Click right on Format to display the Format Character menu.

   b. Click left on Yes for the Bold option.

   c. Click right on Yes for the Underline option.

6. Insert and format a paragraph style for level 2.

   a. Click left on Insert.

   b. Click left on Paragraph for the Usage option.

   c. Click right on the Variant option.

   d. Click right on Heading Level 2.

   e. Click left on Format Paragraph.

   f. Click on the Left Indent option and type **.5**.

   g. Click on the command line title.

   h. Click right on Format.

   i. Click right on Yes for the Boldface option. Figure 12.12 shows the complete stylesheet.

7. Click left on Transfer; then click right on Save to save the new styles.

KEY Press F C. Press Y for the Bold option, press Tab twice to reach the Underline option, press Y, and then press Enter.

KEY Press I, press Tab to reach the Usage option, and then press P. Press Tab to reach the Variant option, press F1, and then select Heading Level 2. Press Enter. Next press F P. Press Tab to reach the Left Indent option, type .5, and press Enter. Finally, press F C, press Y to select Boldface, and then press Enter.

KEY Press T S Enter to save the styles. Press E to Exit.

8. Click on Exit to return to the document. As shown in Figure 12.13, outline level 1 entries are now boldfaced and underlined, and level 2 entries are just boldfaced. Because you are still in the outline view, level 2 entries are not indented the full ½ inch, but are at the .4 indentation level for the outline.

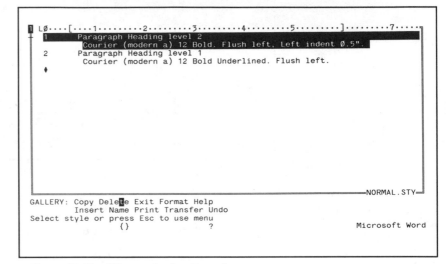

○ **Figure 12.12:** *The completed outline styles*

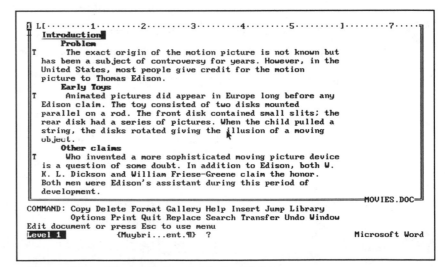

○ **Figure 12.13:** *The outline formatted by the stylesheet*

9. Press Shift-F2 to see the document view. Notice that the level 2 entries shifted to the right to the ½-inch indentation specified in the stylesheet. Keep in mind that paragraph formats for heading variants are only active in the document view.

10. Press Shift-F2 to return to the outline view.

11. Click left on Transfer; then click right on Save to save the formatted document.

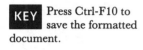 Press Ctrl-F10 to save the formatted document.

You can also record your heading styles by formatting an entry and then selecting Format Stylesheet Record or pressing Alt-F10. Just enter the appropriate heading level variant.

oNUMBERING AND PRINTING OUTLINES

You might just need to print a copy of the finished outline, without any body text and with numbered levels. Numbering can be done automatically with the Library Number command, even in the document view.

Keep in mind that, when you print an outline, whatever appears on the screen is included. You can number the outline headings with the body text on the screen, but to print only the outline itself, you must first collapse all the body text.

As an example, we'll print our sample outline. Follow these steps:

1. You should still be in outline organize mode with the entire second section selected. If not, place the cursor on *Early Experiments*, press Shift-F5, and then press F6.

2. Press Shift- – to collapse the body text in the lower section.

3. Press the up arrow key to select the entire first section.

4. Press Shift- – to collapse the body text.

KEY Press Esc L N to display the menu. Press Enter to accept the defaults.

5. Click left on Library Number to see the menu:

LIBRARY NUMBER: Update Remove   restart sequence:(Yes)No

The Update option and Yes for the Restart option are already selected as the defaults. The Update option numbers or renumbers the document. We'll discuss the Restart option after the exercise.

6. Click on the command line title. The outline entries will be numbered according to their indentation level using the default numbering scheme, as shown in Figure 12.14.

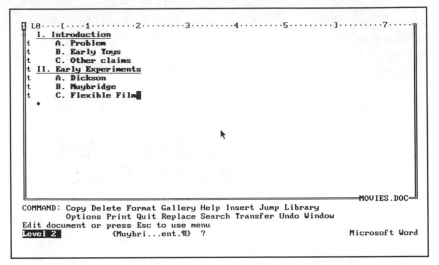

```
 L0···[····1·········2·········3·········4·········5·········]·········7····
    I. Introduction
 t     A. Problem
 t     B. Early Toys
 t     C. Other claims
 t  II. Early Experiments
 t     A. Dickson
 t     B. Muybridge
 t     C. Flexible Film
    ◆

                                                                    MOVIES.DOC
COMMAND: Copy Delete Format Gallery Help Insert Jump Library
         Options Print Quit Replace Search Transfer Undo Window
Edit document or press Esc to use menu
Level 2              {Muybri...ent.¶}  ?                       Microsoft Word
```

o **Figure 12.14:** *The numbered outline*

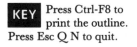

KEY Press Ctrl-F8 to print the outline. Press Esc Q N to quit.

7. Click right on Print to print a copy of the finished outline.

8. Click on Quit, and then press N to exit Word. Do not save a copy of the numbered version.

oUSING OTHER NUMBERING SCHEMES

You can change to another outline numbering scheme by manually entering the first number. For example, if you type

　1.

in front of the first outline entry, the Library Number command will use this scheme:

Level Number	Outline Entry
1	1
2	1.1
3	1.1.1
4	1.1.1.1
5	1.1.1.1.1
6	1.1.1.1.1.1

In each case so far, the numbering automatically started at the first of the scheme, either I. or 1. This will occur whenever you use the default Yes for the Restart option on the Library Number menu. For example, an outline that looks like this:

V. Printers

    A. Dot Matrix

    B. Letter Quality

VI. Input Devices

    A. Mouse

    B. Lightpen

will automatically change to this when numbered:

I. Printers

    A. Dot Matrix

    B. Letter Quality

II. Input Devices

    A. Mouse

    B. Lightpen

To begin numbering at another point, type whatever number you want to start with before the first outline entry, and then select No for the Restart option on the Library Number menu. This way you can work on an outline or another numbered document in sections, and join the parts before printing them.

The Library Number command can be extremely useful when typing and editing numbered paragraphs. If you type a document with numbered paragraphs and later rearrange the paragraphs, you can use the Library Number Update option to renumber them correctly.

The Library Number command works in the document view as well, but it only renumbers text that is already numbered. If you prefer Word to add the initial numbering while you are typing numbered paragraphs, enter the text in the outline view using a level number, not as body text. You can then use the Library Number command to add the numbers. Enter 1. for the first paragraph and select No for the Restart option.

REMOVING NUMBERING

You can use the Remove selection on the Library Number menu to delete the numbering. But be warned: It will delete any numbering that begins paragraphs, not just those placed by the Update command. Any single letter or number followed by a period and space will be deleted from the text. This can be particularly dangerous when you are working with documents that include other text along with the outline.

oADDING A PROFESSIONAL LOOK

You have already used Word's outlining feature to organize and write a document. In the document view, the outline level headings have become document headings and subheadings, and the outline body text is the body of the document itself. That's the easy part. Now you must add the finishing touches that give the document that professional look. You may have footnotes, as well as an index, a table of contents, and a title page. Fortunately, Word can perform much of the work for you.

We'll now begin adding these touches to the document you just created. You will first add the title page and reserve a page for the table of contents. You'll then insert a hidden text annotation, followed by the footnotes, the table of contents, and the index. Before printing the document, you will format the table and index entries using a stylesheet.

CREATING THE TITLE PAGE

Before you create the additional features for a document, you must consider the way you want the pages numbered.

As usual, the title page will be the actual first page of our document, and the table of contents will be the second. But we want the pages numbered so that the first page of text is counted as page 1, not 3. This is not only important for properly printing numbers on the document, but is also necessary to make the proper numbers appear in the table of contents and index. In order to do this, you'll first create a separate division for the body of the document. This division will include page numbers, starting with page 1.

Follow these steps.

KEY Press Esc T L, type **Movies**, and press Enter to recall the document.

1. Click right on Transfer, click right to the right of the command line title, and then click right on Movies.

2. Press Ctrl-Enter to insert a division break at the start of the document. This division will format just the title page and table of contents.

3. Press up arrow, Enter, and then up arrow to place the cursor in the top division.

4. Press Enter six times to position the title.

5. Press Alt-C to center the cursor, then type the title page text.

   Who Really Invented The Movie?
   by
   William Watson

6. Press Ctrl-Shift-Enter to insert a page break.

7. Type **Table of Contents**.

8. Place the cursor anywhere in the body of the text after the division mark, as shown in Figure 12.15.

9. Format the division to start page numbering with 1 and insert the page numbers at the bottom center of each page.

KEY Press Esc F D P Y. Press Tab to reach the From Top option and type **10.5**. Press Tab to reach the From Left option and type **4.25**. Press Tab to reach the Numbering option and press S. Press Tab to reach the At option, type **1**, and press Enter.

   a. Click left on Format Division Page-Numbers.

   b. Click left on Yes.

   c. Click on the From Top option and type **10.5**.

   d. Click on the From Left option and type **4.25**.

   e. Click left on Start for the Numbering option.

   f. Click on the At option and type **1**.

   g. Click on the command line title.

The table of contents page will be used later on, after Word automatically creates the table for you. But first, let's explore how to insert hidden text into the document.

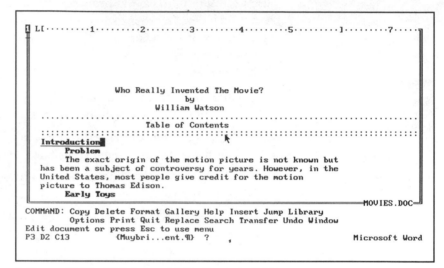

o **Figure 12.15:** *Title page and table of contents divisions*

INSERTING HIDDEN TEXT

Word's hidden text feature, used to keep codes from displaying, can also be used to store your own comments. You can enter informal reminders and messages to yourself into the text, and then choose to hide or display them as necessary.

You designate characters as hidden by using the Alt-E key or selecting Yes for the Hidden option on the Format Character menu. Alt-spacebar returns the text to normal.

To print the document without the hidden text, select No for the Show Hidden Text option on the Window Options menu. If this option is set to No when you enter hidden text, what you type will not appear on the screen. To display hidden text, select Yes for the Show Hidden Text option on the Options menu.

If you are a teacher, you can use the hidden text feature when writing exams. After each question, add the answer as hidden text. Then you can print the student's copies of the test without the answers, and print your own copy with them.

Later, you'll see how to use hidden text to create tables of contents and indexes. For now, we'll add a comment to our sample document.

1. Place the cursor at the end of the first paragraph, the one titled *Problem*.

2. Press Alt-E to format the characters as hidden text.

3. Type **Check facts for Europe**. As you type, each character might appear momentarily, but then it will be covered by the cursor. This is because the display of hidden text is set to No.

4. Press Alt-spacebar to return to normal characters.

5. Click on Options, and then click right on Yes for the Show Hidden Text option to display the comment. (With version 4.0, click left on Window Options, and then select Yes for Show Hidden Text.)

The hidden text appears underlined by a row of dots, as shown in Figure 12.16. (On a monochrome monitor, hidden text is underlined.) If you turned off the hidden text display again and then displayed the document with its format codes (by selecting Show Non-Printing symbols on the Options menu), a small double-headed arrow would appear at the position of the comment.

KEY Press Esc O. Press Tab to reach the Show Hidden Text option, press Y, and then press Enter. (With version 4.0, press Esc W O, press Tab twice, press Y, and then press Enter.)

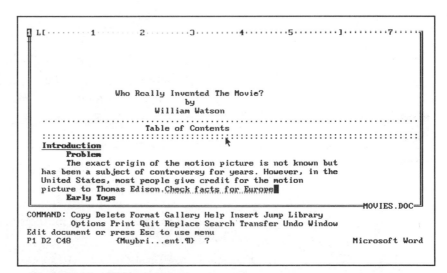

o **Figure 12.16:** *Hidden text*

ADDING FOOTNOTES

Word provides what are known as *floating footnotes*. This means that the footnote can "float," or move from page to page, as text is added or deleted. When the document is printed, the notes will automatically appear at the bottom of the appropriate page. You can also have the notes printed in a group at the end of the document through the Format Division Layout menu.

Regardless of the final placement, footnotes are stored at the end of the document as you type. You can also have them appear in a special footnote window that is synchronized with the document window. As you scroll through the document, the footnote window also scrolls so that footnotes cited in the displayed text will appear.

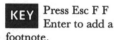 Press Esc F F Enter to add a footnote.

To add a footnote, place the cursor at the desired location, click left on Format Footnote, and then click on the command line title. Word will automatically adjust the numbers of the other footnotes. If you delete a footnote somewhere in the document, Word will automatically renumber the rest.

Now we'll add some footnotes to the paper.

KEY Press Esc W S F, type **12**, and press Enter to display the footnote window.

1. Point to the right window border, about halfway down, hold down the Shift key, and click either mouse button. You will see the footnote window, with a dotted ruler line but no margin indicators at the top, as shown in Figure 12.17.

2. The cursor still remains in the top window. Place it at the end of the second paragraph, the one under the heading Early Toys. This is the location of the first footnote reference.

KEY Press Esc F F to display the prompt line. Press Enter to start at 1.

3. Click left on Format Footnote to display

   FORMAT FOOTNOTE reference mark:

4. Here you can enter the numbering for your footnotes. Since we want our footnotes numbered consecutively starting with 1, click on the command line title to accept the default. The number 1 appears in both the text and footnote windows, and the cursor is now in the footnote window.

5. Type

   "The Electric Tachyscope," Scientific American, November 16, 1889, Vol. 3, No. 6, pg 23.

KEY Press F1 to return the cursor to the document. Press Esc F F Enter to enter the next footnote. Follow this procedure to enter the rest of the footnotes.

6. Click left on the footnote number in the top window to return the cursor to the document, as shown in Figure 12.18.

7. Enter the next footnote at the end of the paragraph titled Dickson.

   a. Place the cursor at the end of the paragraph.

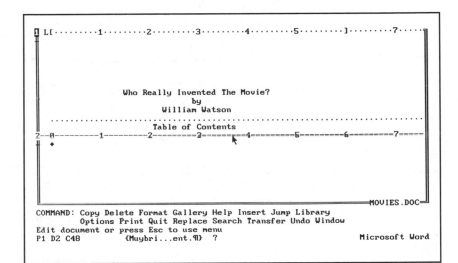

o **Figure 12.17:** *The footnote window*

```
 L[·········1·········2·········3·········4·········5·········]·········7····]
 has been a subject of controversy for years. However, in the
 United States, most people give credit for the motion
 picture to Thomas Edison.Check facts for Europe
      Early Toys
      Animated pictures did appear in Europe long before any
 Edison claim. The toy consisted of two disks mounted
 parallel on a rod. The front disk contained small slits; the
 rear disk had a series of pictures. When the child pulled a
 string, the disks rotated giving the illusion of a moving
 object.1
      Other claims
2--[---------1---------2---------3---------4---------5---------]---------7-----
 1"The Electric Tachyscope," Scientific American, November
 16, 1889, Vol. 3, No. 6, pg 23.
 +

                                                       MOVIES.DOC
COMMAND: Copy Delete Format Gallery Help Insert Jump Library
         Options Print Quit Replace Search Transfer Undo Window
Edit document or press Esc to use menu
P1 D2 C9          {Muybri...ent.¶}  ?               Microsoft Word
```

o **Figure 12.18:** *A footnote with associated text*

b. Click left on Format Footnote, then click on the command line title. The number 2 appears.

c. Type

New York Herald, February 2, 1890, p. 76.

d. Click left on the footnote number in the top window.

8. Follow the same procedure to add the next footnote (number 3) at the end of the paragraph titled Muybridge:

Orange Chronicle, May 23, 1891, p. 111.

9. Enter the final footnote (number 4) at the end of the paragraph titled Flexible Film.

Gordon Hendricks, The Edison Motion Picture Myth, Williams, California, 1961, pg. 45.

Scroll through the text with the arrow keys. Notice that the footnote window will display whatever note is referred to in the part of the text being displayed. While this makes it easy to keep track of your footnotes, you can also move quickly from the note to the appropriate citation without the window.

KEY Press Esc W C, type **2**, and press Enter to close the footnote window. Press Ctrl-PgDn to move to the end.

10. Click both on the right border of the footnote window to close it.

11. Click both on the bottom-left corner to display the end of the document. The footnotes are displayed between two endmarks.

12. Place the cursor anywhere in the second footnote.

KEY Press Esc J F to jump to the next footnote.

13. Click left on Jump Footnote. The cursor moves directly to the second footnote citation in the text.

14. Click left on Jump Footnote again. The cursor moves directly from the citation number in the text to the appropriate footnote at the end of the document.

So you have two ways of displaying the footnote: by opening the footnote window or by jumping between the footnote area and the text. The footnote window displays both the footnote and text at the same time. This is convenient if you move frequently between the text and footnote areas, or need the footnotes displayed for reference. Closing the footnote window, however, displays more lines of text. So if you are mainly working in the document, and only occasionally need to refer to the footnote, use the Jump Footnote command.

FORMATTING FOOTNOTES WITH STYLESHEETS

When you print your document, you'll notice that the footnote reference numbers are not superscripts, the normal style, but plain text. You can tell from the screen, as well, that the footnotes themselves are standard paragraphs.

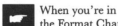 When you're in the Format Character menu, by the way, you'll see Character variants called Page Number and Line Number. You can use these variants to specify how your page and line numbers will appear.

To change the format of the reference numbers and the footnotes, use the Gallery to insert two styles. For example, superscript the citation numbers by inserting a style with Character selected for the Usage option. Display the list of variants and select Footnote Ref. Then use the Format Character menu to select Superscript for the Position option.

Finally, to create hanging indentations, insert a Paragraph style with the Footnote variant. Use the Format Paragraph menu to set the left indent at .5'' and the first line at – .5''. When you exit the Gallery, your footnotes will appear like this:

[1]Neibauer, Barbara E, "Career Opportunities in Clinical Laboratory Sciences," Laboratory Medicine, November 1988.

CREATING A TABLE OF CONTENTS

You can create a table of contents two ways. One method is to manually enter special codes as hidden text around each title you want to include in the table. But if you created your document with the outline feature, Word will produce the table directly from the outline levels. This method is quite effective, but it limits the table to only outline headings and subheadings. We'll use both methods to see how they work.

Compiling a Table with an Outline

When you use the outline to create a table of contents, level headings and subheadings become the entries. Level 2 headings become table subentries under level 1 headings, level 3 under level 2, and so on. No additional codes and formatting are necessary. Just make sure that the headings you want to include in the table of contents are visible.

Follow these steps.

1. Start Word and recall the Movies document.

2. Click left on Library Table to see the menu

KEY Press Esc L T to
display the menu.
Press O, then Enter.

LIBRARY TABLE from: Outline Codes   **index code: C**
   page numbers: Yes No   **entry/page numbers**
                                            separated by: ^t
   indent each level: 0.4"   **Use style sheet: Yes No**

3. Click right on Outline to create the table from the outline. The message

Searching for existing table

will appear for a second; then you will see the message

Formatting Table

on the message line while Word paginates the text and creates the table. If no outline levels exist, you'll hear a beep, and the document will return unchanged.

As shown in Figure 12.19, the table is inserted at the end of the document, following a division break so it appears on its own page. Before the table is the hidden text .Begin Table C.; following it is .End Table C..

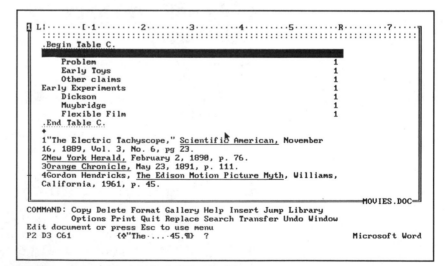

o **Figure 12.19:** *The completed table of contents*

It is now a simple task to select and move the table to the page reserved for it at the beginning of the document. If you do so, however, select the entire table, including .Begin Table C. and .End Table C.. These are used by Word if you later regenerate the table. You'll see the importance of this in a later section.

Other options for tables of contents and procedures for formatting them are discussed later in the chapter.

Creating Tables Using Codes

If you do not use outlining to enter headings and subheadings, you must enter .c. codes into the text to create a table of contents. While this is more time-consuming than the outline method, you have greater con-trol over the design of the completed table.

1. Start Word and recall the Movies document. If you still have the document on the screen from the last exercise, move the cursor to select the first letter of the word *Introduction*.

2. Press Alt-E to turn on hidden text.

3. Type **.c..** (If the characters did not appear on the screen as you typed them, you have the display of hidden text turned off.)

The code .c. tells Word that the following text will be a table level 1 variant, that is, a main entry in the table of contents. This will not affect the actual format of the entry in the table unless you format it yourself through the Gallery, as discussed later.

Unless told otherwise, Word includes all text from the .c. code to the end of the paragraph as the table entry. Since this paragraph is only one word, just that word will be included.

 Because you are inserting the codes into existing text, you do not have to press Alt-spacebar to turn off hidden text.

4. It may be difficult to keep track of your progress, so turn on the display of hidden text by selecting Yes for the Show Hidden Text option on the Options menu.

5. Mark the word *Problem* as a subentry, a table level 2 variant, under Introduction. A single colon after the .c. will identify the second table level.

   a. Place the cursor on the *P* in *Problem*.

   b. Press Alt-E to turn on hidden text.

   c. Type **.c.:.**

6. Mark the words *subject of controversy* as a table level 3 variant. Two colons must be added after the code.

   a. Place the cursor on the *s* in *subject*.

   b. Press Alt-E to turn on hidden text.

   c. Type **.c.::**.

   d. Place the cursor after the word *controversy*.

   e. Press Alt-E to turn on hidden text.

   f. Type **;** (semicolon).

Since this entry is not its own paragraph, the hidden text semicolon is necessary to tell Word where the table entry ends. In fact, without the semicolon, the remainder of the paragraph would be listed in the table of contents.

7. Mark the words *Thomas Edison* as another table level 3 variant.

   a. Place the cursor on the *T* in *Thomas*.

   b. Press Alt-E to turn on hidden text.

   c. Type **.c.::**.

   d. Place the cursor after the word *Edison*.

   e. Press Alt-E to turn on hidden text.

   f. Type **;** (semicolon).

8. Mark the subheadings *Early Toys* and *Other Claims* as table level 2 variants.

   a. Place the cursor on the first letter of the subheading.

   b. Press Alt-E to turn on hidden text.

   c. Type **.c.:**.

9. Mark the words *Early Experiments* as a table level 1 variant. Enter the code *.c.* as hidden text.

10. Mark the subtitles *Dickson*, *Muybridge*, and *Flexible Film* as table level 2 variants by inserting the code **.c.:** as hidden text.

Since all of the entries are marked, you can now generate the table of contents with the Library Table command. Word scans the document collecting text marked with .c. codes. Each entry is placed at the end of the document, indented according to its level, and with its page number.

KEY Press Esc L T, press C, and then press Enter.

11. Click left on Library Table; then click right on Codes to use the default values. (The other options on the menu are described in the next section.) The table will become highlighted on the screen and the status line will display the prompt

Table already exists. Enter Y to replace, N to append, or Esc to cancel

12. Press N to add the new table to the end of the document.

As you saw, table of contents entries can be section headings or sub-headings, or even parts of the text itself. In our example, all the outline entries were also marked as table of contents entries. In fact, level 1 outline entries were marked as table level 1 variants, and level 2 entries as table level 2 variants.

This does not have to be the case, and you should not get confused between the outline levels and the table levels. They are two separate markings. It is true that in a document that is well constructed and planned, there will very likely be a direct relationship between the two. But this is because of the structure of the document, not because it is required by Word.

Other Table of Contents Options

Along with creating a table of contents from either an outline or codes, you can select these options from the Library Table menu:

- The **Index Code** option, by default, has Word scan the document looking for .c. codes. But you can use the Library Table command to create other types of lists and tables, as detailed later on.

- The **Page Numbers** option, when set to the default Yes, includes the page numbers for the table entries. Set it to No, if you don't want page numbers listed in the table.

- The **Entry/Page Numbers Separated By** option, by default, has the page number separated from the table entry with a tab, (^t), at the 5-inch position. Enter your own separator if desired, such as a number of spaces.

- The **Indent Each Level** option, by default, indents sublevels 0.4 inches from each other.

- The **Use Style Sheet** option, with the default No, formats the table according to the indentation and separator settings on this menu.

You can create your own styles, however, including character and paragraph settings to format the table. Insert the formats in the stylesheet, and select Yes for this option.

CREATING AN INDEX

Creating an index with Word is similar to creating a table of contents. Index entries are marked with .i. codes as hidden text, much like .c. is used for table of contents entries. If the entry is not on a line by itself, a semicolon must be entered to mark the end of the entry. You separate the primary entry from its associated subentry with a colon.

Because an index includes not only words but also concepts found in the document, the entire entry can be hidden text. As an illustration, here are several index entries and the document codes that created them. The underline signifies hidden text.

Index	Text
Animals	
Aardvarks 12	.i. Animals:Aardvarks
Bumblebees 13	.i. Animals:Bumblebees
Beagles: See Dogs	.i. "Beagles: See Dogs"
Dogs 14	.i.Dogs
Hounds 16	.1.Dogs:Hounds Among the most popular
Pets 1, 16	.i.Pets; animals are …
Worms 16	.i.Worms;, however, do not make good .i.pets;.

In the first entry, the word *Animals* does not have a page number because it was not listed as an index entry. The entry Dogs, on the other hand, was listed as an index entry. Both Dogs and Hounds are headings that appear alone on a line. The first entry for Pets is entirely hidden. In this case, the word itself is not in the text, so it was entered as hidden text followed by a semicolon. In the last example, both Worms and Pets appear in the text, so only the .i. and closing semicolon must be added.

If a word or phrase is included in both the table of contents and index, only one closing semicolon is needed:

We will not discuss Thomas .c..i.Edison;.

The same semicolon terminates both entries.

Let's add index entries to our sample document, and then generate the index. In a longer document, you would mark each reference to the same word so the index shows each page it is found on. If you paginate the document before marking the index entries, don't bother marking a word more than once on the same page. As an illustration, however, we'll mark several occurrences of key words here that appear on a single page.

1. Place the cursor on the *E* in *Edison* in the second paragraph.
2. Press Alt-E to turn on hidden text.
3. Type **.i.**.
4. Move the cursor after *Edison*.
5. Press Alt-E to turn on hidden text.
6. Type **, Thomas;**. With hidden text displayed, the entry will appear, as shown in Figure 12.20.
7. Follow steps 1 through 6 again, this time marking the occurrence of *Edison* in the third and sixth paragraphs.

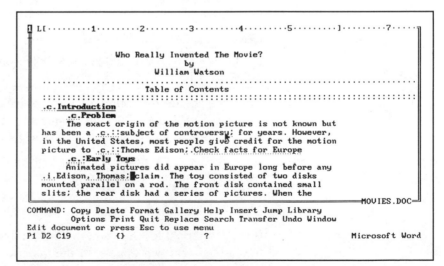

o **Figure 12.20:** *An index entry*

8. Mark the names *Dickson* and *Friese-Greene* in the third paragraph. Use the techniques followed for Edison to enter the name in the index followed by the first name or initials. The entries will appear as follows (underlining indicates hidden text):

   .i.Dickson, W.K.L.;

   .i.Friese-Greene, William

9. Mark the name *Dickson* in the fifth paragraph and *Muybridge* in the sixth paragraph.

10. Mark the names *Carbutt* and *Eastman*, and the word film in the last paragraph.

11. Place the cursor at the start of the second paragraph and enter the hidden text **.i.Animation;**.

Since all the entries are marked, you can now generate the index by using the Library Index command. Word scans the document collecting text marked with .i. codes. Each entry is placed at the end of the document, indented according to its level and with its page number. The hidden text .Begin Index. and .End Index. will surround the index.

12. Click left on Library Index to display the Library Index menu:

LIBRARY INDEX entry/page #	
separated by:	cap main entries:(Yes)No
indent each level: 0.2"	use style sheet:Yes(No)

13. Press Enter to use the default values.

14. Click on the command line title. The completed index is shown in Figure 12.21.

You can change the options on the Library Index menu as necessary. For example, change the default Yes for the Cap Main Entries option to No if you don't want to capitalize the first letter of all primary entries.

KEY Press Esc L I to see the menu. Press Enter to use the defaults.

TABLE AND INDEX COLLISIONS

If text is marked for inclusion in both a table and an index, one set of the hidden text will appear in the generated reference as regular (nonhidden) characters. For example, say the document contains the

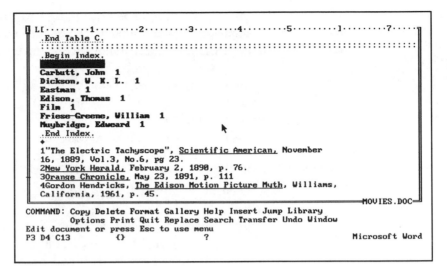

```
 L[·······1········2········3········4········5······]·····7·····
  .End Table C.
  ::::::::::::::::::::::::::::::::::::::::::::::::::::::::::::::::::::
  .Begin Index.
  ██████████████
  Carbutt, John  1
  Dickson, W. K. L.  1
  Eastman  1
  Edison, Thomas  1
  Film  1
  Friese-Greene, William  1
  Muybridge, Edweard  1
  .End Index.
  ◆
  1"The Electric Tachyscope", Scientific American, November
  16, 1889, Vol.3, No.6, pg 23.
  2New York Herald, February 2, 1890, p. 76.
  3Orange Chronicle, May 23, 1891, p. 111
  4Gordon Hendricks, The Edison Motion Picture Myth, Williams,
  California, 1961, p. 45.                              ─MOVIES.DOC─
COMMAND: Copy Delete Format Gallery Help Insert Jump Library
        Options Print Quit Replace Search Transfer Undo Window
Edit document or press Esc to use menu
P3 D4 C13          {}               ?              Microsoft Word
```

o **Figure 12.21:** *The completed index*

following entries:

> **.c..i.Animals**
> **.i..c.Dogs**

The table of contents will include the entry *.i.Animals* and the index will include *.c.Dogs*. The hidden text has been converted into regular text. Hiding the display of the codes, either before generating the table or afterwards, will not correct the situation. The best method is to generate both the table and index, select No for the Show Hidden Text option, and then use the Replace option to delete all occurrences of *.c.* and *.i.*. If you do not hide the display of hidden text, the *.c.* and *.i.* entries in the document will also be deleted. With these gone, you would not be able to regenerate the table or index at some later date. So, be sure to turn off the display of hidden text first.

USING STYLESHEETS TO FORMAT TABLES OF CONTENTS AND INDEXES

When you generate the table of contents or index without the use of a stylesheet, the entries are shown in plain text. Any formatting used within the document is not applied to the reference section. For example, if you mark a boldfaced title for inclusion in the table of contents, it will not appear in boldface in the table.

However, entries in both the table and index can be formatted by a stylesheet if you select Yes for the Use Stylesheet option on the corresponding menu. In this case, Word will ignore the Indent and Entry/Page Number Separated By options on the menu, and any current character formats, so all formatting must be included in the stylesheet.

The stylesheet can include character formats (such as boldfacing or underlining), tabs (to change the position of page numbers or insert dot leaders), and paragraph styles (to change the indentation levels or line spacing).

To format the table of contents, insert formatted styles for Table Heading 1, 2, 3, and 4 variants in the Gallery. The index is formatted through the Index Level 1, 2, 3, and 4 variants.

In this section, you will create a stylesheet for the index and table of contents. The table of contents will have all primary entries boldfaced with dot leaders to the page numbers. Subentries will be indented at 1/2-inch levels. The index will also boldface primary entries, with subentries indented 1/4 inch between levels.

 Press Esc G I. Press Tab P. Press Tab to reach the Variant option; then press F1 to display alternative variants. Highlight Table Level 1 and press Enter.

1. Click on Gallery; then click left on Insert to add a new style to the current stylesheet.

2. Click left on Paragraph for the Usage Option. Because you are formatting a default table entry, you do not have to name the style.

3. Click right on the Variant option. A list of possible variants will appear on the screen. The table and index level variants have been reserved for this use.

4. Click right on Table Level 1. The standard paragraph format appears in the Gallery window.

KEY Press F C. Press Y Enter.

5. Click right on Format to display the Format Character menu.

6. Click right on Yes for the Bold option.

KEY Press Alt-F1, type **5R.**, and press Enter. (With version 4.0, press Alt-F1, type **5**, press Tab R, press Tab ., and then press Enter.)

7. Set the right dot-leader tab at 5 inches.

   a. Click on the tab type letter until an R appears.

   b. Click next to the letter until a period appears.

   c. Click left on the 5 on the ruler.

(With version 4.0, click left on Format; then click right on Tab. Click left on Right at the Alignment option. Click left on the period for the Leader Char option; then click on the 5 on the ruler. Click on the command line title. Follow this procedure to set the tabs for the rest of the exercise.)

8. The formats for the remaining table levels must also be set. Each must be indented ½ inch to the right of the others and a tab stop set at 5. For each of table levels 2, 3, and 4, insert and format a paragraph style. Use the following techniques from the Gallery.

a. Click left on Insert.

b. Click left on Paragraph for the Usage option.

c. Click right at the Variant option.

d. Click right on the appropriate table level, table level 2, 3, or 4.

e. Click left on Format Paragraph.

f. Click on the Left Indent option.

g. Type the desired level indent:

Level	Indent
2	.5
3	1
4	1.5

h. Click on the command line title.

i. To set the tab, click on the period next to the tab type letter until the space is blank; then click left on the 5 in the ruler.

9. The index level formats must now be added to the Gallery using the same techniques. First format the primary entry.

a. Click left on Insert.

b. Click left on Paragraph for the Usage option.

c. Click right on the Variant option.

d. Click right on Index Level 1.

e. Click right on Format.

f. Click right on Yes for the Bold option.

KEY Press I. Press Tab P. Press Tab to reach the Variant option, press F1, and highlight the appropriate table level—2, 3, or 4—then press Enter. Next press F P. Press Tab to reach the Left Indent option, type the desired level indent, and then press Enter. Finally, press Alt-F1, type **5RB**, and press Enter. (With version 4.0, press Alt-F1, type **5**, press Tab R, and then press Enter.)

KEY Press I. Press Tab P. Press Tab to reach the Variant option, press F1, highlight the variant Index Level 1, and then press Enter. Next press F C Y to select Yes for the Bold option, and then press Enter.

KEY Press I. Press Tab P. Press Tab to reach the Variant option, press F1, highlight the appropriate index level—2, 3, or 4—then press Enter. Press F P. Press Tab to reach the Left Indent option, type the desired level indent, and then press Enter.

10. Format the variants index level 2, 3, and 4.

   a. Click left on Insert.

   b. Click left on Paragraph for the Usage option.

   c. Click right at the Variant option.

   d. Click right on the appropriate index level, index level 2, 3, or 4.

   e. Click left on Format Paragraph.

   f. Click on the Left Indent option.

   g. Type the desired level indent:

Level	Indent
2	.25
3	.5
4	.75

   h. Click on the command line title. The completed stylesheet is shown in Figure 12.22.

KEY Press T S Enter E.

11. Click left on Transfer; then click right on Save to save the edited stylesheet.

12. Click on Exit to return to the document.

```
  R0 ·····[··1·········2·········3·········4·········5·········]·········7·····
  ▉
  2         Paragraph Index level 3
            Courier (modern a) 12. Flush left, Left indent 0.5".
  3         Paragraph Index level 2
            Courier (modern a) 12. Flush left, Left indent 0.25".
  4         Paragraph Index level 1
            Courier (modern a) 12 Bold. Flush left.
  5         Paragraph Table level 4
            Courier (modern a) 12. Flush left, Left indent 1.5". Tabs at: 5"
            (right flush).
  6         Paragraph Table level 3
            Courier (modern a) 12. Flush left, Left indent 1". Tabs at: 5"
            (right flush).
  7         Paragraph Table level 2
            Courier (modern a) 12. Flush left, Left indent 0.5". Tabs at: 5"
            (right flush).
  8         Paragraph Table level 1
            Courier (modern a) 12 Bold. Flush left. Tabs at: 5" (right flush,
                                                              NORMAL.STY
  GALLERY: Copy Delete Exit Format Help
           Insert Name Print Transfer Undo
  Select style or press Esc to use menu
                  {}              ?                      Microsoft Word
```

o **Figure 12.22:** *The stylesheet for an index and table of contents*

RECOMPILING THE TABLE AND INDEX

With the stylesheet created, you can regenerate both the table of contents and index. First make sure that hidden text is not displayed. If necessary, select No for the Show Hidden Text option on the Options menu. Then follow these steps.

KEY Press Esc L T. Press Tab five times to reach the Use Stylesheet option, press Y and then press Enter. Press Y to regenerate the table.

1. Click left on Library Table.
2. Click right on Yes for the Use Stylesheet option. Word identifies the existing table by the codes .Begin Table C. and .End Table C. that surround it. If you deleted these lines or failed to move them along with the table to another page, Word will not replace the existing table. It will generate a new one instead. The old one will remain at its present location.
3. Click on the message line to regenerate the table now using the stylesheet. The new table will be in the same position as the original. So if you moved the table to the start of the document, the new table will replace it at that position.
4. Click left on Library Index.
5. Follow steps 2 and 3 to replace the old index with one formatted by the stylesheet.

KEY Press Esc L I to display the Library Index menu.

Figure 12.23 shows the reformatted index and table.

CREATING YOUR OWN LISTS AND TABLES

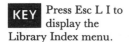

Because it creates a table, the entries are in page number order, not alphabetical order as in an index. Use the Library Sort command on the completed list to create the secondary index.

The Library Table menu can be used to create lists of any type from your document, such as lists of figures or names. It can even create secondary indexes separate from the regular index, such as a list of persons, place names, or vocabulary words.

To create the table, use a letter other than c or i in the hidden code. Then enter the same letter in the Index On option on the Library Table menu.

For example, let's create a vocabulary list for the current document.

1. Place the cursor on the *c* in *controversy* in the first paragraph.
2. Press Alt-E to turn on hidden text.

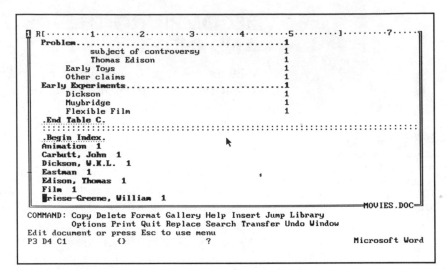

○ **Figure 12.23:** *An index and table formatted with a stylesheet*

3. Type **.n.** to mark the word for inclusion in Table N. A hidden text semicolon is already at the end of the word from its table of contents coding.

4. In the same manner, add the .n. hidden text in front of the words *animated*, *illusion*, *sophisticated*, and *flexible*. Be sure to add a hidden semicolon after each word.

Generating and Sorting Custom Tables and Indexes

You compile your own tables just as you create a regular table of contents marked with .c. codes. It too will be formatted according to the stylesheet (using variants Table Level 1 to 4) if you select Yes for the Use Stylesheet option.

1. Turn off the display of hidden text if necessary.

2. Generate Table N.

   a. Click left on Library Table.

   b. Click on the Index Code option.

   c. Press N.

KEY Press Esc L T. Press Tab; then press N for the Index Code option. Press Tab N to not include page numbers. Press Tab three times to reach the Use Stylesheet option, and then press N Enter.

d. Click left on No for the Page Numbers option.

e. Click right on No for the Use Stylesheet option.

3. Sort the table alphabetically.

KEY Select all the words in the new table. Press Esc L A, and then press Enter. Press Ctrl-F10 to save the table. Press Esc Q to quit.

a. Drag to select the table.

b. Click right on Library; then click on the command line title to activate Autosort.

4. We won't be using this document again, but if you want to save it for reference, click left on Transfer, and then click right on Save.

5. Click on Quit to exit Word.

To make an alphabetized list from your index, just copy the index—but not the Begin and End codes—then sort it with Library Autosort.

In your own work, you may have to delete any .c. or .i. codes that appear when the same text has been marked for more than one list or table. Turn off the display of hidden codes, then use the Replace command to delete the characters .i. and .c. that still may appear in the text.

HINTS FOR INDEXES AND TABLES

If your document is long, formatting headings and marking them for the table of contents can be tedious. Save time by entering document headings and subheadings as outline entries. Format them using heading level variants as you did in this chapter. Then collapse the body text when you are ready to mark the entries for the table of contents. The heading level formats will appear in the text but not in the table of contents.

This concludes our discussion of common word processing tasks that you can perform efficiently with Word. The next part of the book describes more complex Word applications.

PART THREE

POWER-USER APPLICATIONS

The first two parts of this book dealt with general word processing applications. The skills that you learned in the previous chapters can easily be applied to almost any type of document.

The next chapters deal with more demanding word processing tasks, which present challenges to even the most sophisticated user. You'll learn how to use boilerplate and macros to build applications, produce form documents using a database, and create desktop publications with graphics.

CHAPTER 13

○ **USING**
○ **GLOSSARIES**
○ **FOR**
○ **BOILERPLATE**

4.0

KEY

Earlier in the book, you learned how to create form documents. You used a template and inserted or copied text wherever variable information was needed. In all the examples, the variable text was only a word or two. In this chapter, you will learn how to assemble form documents using larger blocks of text, which are called boilerplate.

oINSERTING BOILERPLATE TEXT

A *boilerplate* is a sentence, paragraph, or entire section of text that is used in many different documents. It may be some special legal wording, signature block, advertising message, or contractual term that is used repeatedly.

Boilerplate text can be inserted into the document with a few keystrokes. In fact, some documents may be composed almost entirely of boilerplate paragraphs, with only a few words or lines typed individually.

One method of inserting boilerplate text is by using a glossary. A glossary can hold a number of boilerplate paragraphs. Think of the glossary as a library, with each separate boilerplate paragraph as a book. When you say the name of the book, the librarian gets the book and places it in your hands. In this case, Word serves as the librarian, placing the named boilerplate text into your document.

You create the glossary by typing each boilerplate paragraph once and giving it a name that you can remember. To insert the boilerplate into a document, you just type the name and press F3.

There is one glossary loaded each time that you start a document: the Normal glossary. You can create a library of boilerplate paragraphs and store them in that glossary, and they will be available immediately each time that you begin using Word. Special glossaries can be created and stored on disk and recalled when you're working on specific categories of documents.

oUSING BOILERPLATE IN CORRESPONDENCE

In our first example, we'll see how a legal firm can use boilerplate to simplify production of office correspondence. In such a firm, each attorney typically prefers a certain closing and signature block. By including these as boilerplate in the Normal glossary, they can be instantly inserted when correspondence is being prepared.

CREATING THE BOILERPLATE TEXT

You will create a library of boilerplate paragraphs, which will consist of a closing boilerplate and a signature block boilerplate for each attorney in the firm. You will then save the library in the Normal glossary. Follow these steps:

1. Start Word.

2. Type the boilerplate paragraphs required by each attorney.

> **As always, it has been a pleasure serving you.**
>
> **Sincerely,**
>
> **Mrs. Bernice Koplan**
> **Attorney**
>
> **Best regards.**
>
> **Sincerely yours,**
>
> **William Morris, Esq.**
> **Attorney at Law**
>
> **If I can be of any further service, please do not hesitate to call.**
>
> **Sincerely,**
>
> **Adam Chesin, J.D.**

3. Highlight the first closing:

> **As always, it has been a pleasure serving you.**

4. Click left on Copy to display the prompt

> **COPY to: {}**
> **Enter glossary name or press F1 to select from list**

5. Type **CK**, which stands for the closing for Mrs. Koplan (Closing for Koplan).

6. Click on COPY. The CK boilerplate paragraph has been added to the glossary.

KEY Press Esc C, type **CK**, and press Enter. Repeat this procedure to copy all the closings, giving each its corresponding glossary name.

7. Select the first signature block:

> **Sincerely,**
>
> **Mrs. Bernice Koplan**
> **Attorney**

8. Click left on Copy.

9. Type **SK** as the name for the signature block.

10. Click on COPY.

11. Repeat steps 3 through 10 for all the closing and signature blocks. Name the second closing and signature block **CM** and **SM**, the third as **CC** and **SC**. (No two boilerplate paragraphs in the same glossary can have the same name.)

12. Click left on Transfer Glossary; then click right on Save to save the Normal glossary on the disk.

13. Click left on Quit, and then press N to exit Word without saving the text on the screen.

KEY Press Esc T G S; then press Enter. Press Esc Q N to quit.

USING THE BOILERPLATE TEXT

After the boilerplate text is created, it can easily be inserted into any document.

To see how this works, you will type a sample letter. At the end of the letter, instead of typing the closing and signature block, you will insert them from the Normal glossary. Follow these steps:

1. Start Word.

2. Enter the following letter.

> **Mr. Howard Gorman**
> **2345 Friendship Street**
> **Philadelphia, PA 19115**
>
> **Dear Mr. Gorman:**
>
> **On August 12, I sent a letter to Mrs. Welsh requesting final payment of all funds due the estate. The check for $34,880 was received yesterday and is enclosed.**

3. Press Enter. Since the letter is from Adam Chesin, you want to insert his closing and signature block, which are named CC and SC.

4. Type the name of Adam Chesin's closing: **CC**. Leave the cursor in the space immediately following CC.

5. Press F3. The closing will be inserted in the letter.

6. Press Enter.

7. Type the name of Adam Chesin's signature block: **SC**.

8. Press F3. The signature block will be inserted at the end of the letter.

oUSING SPECIAL GLOSSARIES

You may want to use boilerplate text in special documents, such as bids, proposals, and contracts. In this case, each library of boilerplate paragraphs should be stored in a special glossary, which you can recall from the disk whenever you need that boilerplate text.

CREATING A SPECIAL GLOSSARY

Now you will create a special glossary for preparing bids. You will enter and name the boilerplate text as you did in the previous exercise. However, you will store the library of boilerplate paragraphs in its own glossary. Follow these steps:

KEY Press Esc T C A N to clear the screen.

1. Click left on Transfer, click right on Clear, and then press N to clear the current window, or start Word if you quit after the last exercise.

2. Enter each of the boilerplate paragraphs.

> **This bid is submitted pursuant to the laws of New York State and, if accepted, its terms shall be binding on both parties.**

> **In consideration for the amount of $　　, Fox and Associates will perform the following services:**

> **This proposal represents an estimate of the cost of materials and labor. While every effort has been made to accurately compute all costs involved, the actual price of services, binding on both parties, will be stated in the final contract.**

Fox and Associates will guarantee this price only for the next 60 days. We maintain the authority to adjust the bid if contracts are not formalized in that period.

Fox and Associates greatly appreciates the opportunity to bid on this project.

3. Highlight the first paragraph, including the blank line following the text, as shown in Figure 13.1.

4. Click left on Copy.

5. At the prompt, enter a short name to identify the text: **NYLAW**.

6. Click on the command line title.

7. Highlight, name, and copy into the glossary each of the remaining paragraphs. Name them **AMOUNT**, **EST**, **SIXTY**, and **THANKS**, respectively.

8. Click left on Transfer Glossary Save to see the prompt

   TRANSFER GLOSSARY SAVE filename: C:\WORD5\NORMAL.GLY

9. Type the name for this special glossary: **Bids**.

10. Click on the command line title.

11. Click on Quit; then press N to exit Word without saving the contents or glossary changes.

KEY Press Esc C, enter the name **NYLAW**, and press Enter.

KEY Press Esc T G S to see the prompt, type **Bids**, and press Enter. Press Esc Q N to quit.

```
 L[·········1·········2·········3·········4·········5·········]·········7·····
      This bid is submitted pursuant to the laws of New York
  State and, if accepted, its terms shall be binding on both
  parties.

      In consideration for the amount of $      , Fox and
  Associates will perform the following services:

      This proposal represents an estimate of the cost of
  materials and labor. While every effort has been made to
  accurately compute all costs involved, the actual price of
  services, binding on both parties, will be stated in the
  final contract.

      Fox and Associates will guarantee this price only for
  the next 60 days. We maintain the authority to adjust the
  bid if contracts are not formalized in that period.

      Fox and Associates greatly appreciates the opportunity
  to bid on this project.


COMMAND: Copy Delete Format Gallery Help Insert Jump Library
         Options Print Quit Replace Search Transfer Undo Window
Edit document or press Esc to use menu
Pg1 Co1                  {}              ?                  Microsoft Word
```

○ **Figure 13.1:** *Select the boilerplate paragraph and the blank line beneath it*

USING BOILERPLATE TEXT IN A SPECIAL GLOSSARY

Boilerplate text in a special glossary is inserted in documents in the same manner as boilerplate in the Normal glossary. However, you must first merge the special glossary into the Normal glossary.

You will type the bid shown in Figure 13.2, using the special Bids glossary that you just created. Follow these steps:

1. Start Word.

KEY Press Esc T G M, type **Bids**, and press Enter.

2. Click left on Transfer Glossary Merge.

3. Type the name of the glossary: **Bids**.

4. Click on the command line title. The Bids glossary will be recalled and merged with the Normal glossary.

 4.0 The Glossary Load option is not available.

Any paragraph in the Normal glossary with the same name will be temporarily replaced by the one in the Bids glossary. You could load the glossary instead of merging it, but then any boilerplate paragraphs in the Normal glossary will no longer be available.

5. Type **AMOUNT**, and then press F3. The first boilerplate paragraph is inserted into the document.

6. Highlight the space following the dollar sign, and type **1500.00**. Delete any extra spaces between the number and the comma.

7. Place the cursor on the next line, and type the additional text.

Provide six days of word processing training for five operators at 567 Avenue of the Americas.

The computers and software will be provided by the client. Fox and Associates will supply training manuals.

8. Press Enter twice.

9. Type **SIXTY**, and then press F3 to insert the next boilerplate paragraph.

10. Place the cursor on the line following that boilerplate text.

11. Type **NYLAW**, and then press F3.

12. Place the cursor on the line following that text.

KEY Press Esc Q N N to quit.

13. Type **THANKS**, and press F3. The document is now complete.

14. Click left on Quit, and then press N twice to exit Word.

```
        In consideration for the amount of $1500,00, Fox and
   Associates will perform the following services:

        Provide six days of word processing training for five
   operators at 567 Avenue of the Americas.

        The computers and software will be provided by the
   client. Fox and Associates will supply training manuals.

        Fox and Associates will guarantee this price only for
   the next 60 days. We maintain the authority to adjust the
   bid if contracts are not formalized in that period.

        This bid is submitted pursuant to the laws of New York
   State and, if accepted, its terms shall be binding on both
   parties.

        Fox and Associates greatly appreciates the opportunity
   to bid on this project.
```

o **Figure 13.2:** *A sample document using boilerplate paragraphs in a special glossary*

oVIEWING AND PRINTING GLOSSARIES

Even the best word processor may forget which text is included in a glossary or what the paragraphs are named. In the following exercises, you will learn how to print a copy of a glossary for a quick reference.

But first, let's see how to view the names of the boilerplate entries in the glossary.

1. Start Word.

KEY Press Esc T G M; then press F1.

2. Click left on Transfer Glossary Merge. (You must do this if you want a listing of any glossary other than the Normal glossary.)

3. Click right to the right of the command line title to display the available glossaries. Figure 13.3 shows how this list appears on the screen.

4. Click right on BIDS.GLY. The Bids glossary will be merged with the Normal glossary.

KEY Use the arrow keys to highlight BIDS.GLY, and then press Enter. Press Esc I to insert the text, press F1, and then press Esc.

5. Click left on Insert.

6. Click right to the right of the command line title to display the names of the boilerplate text in the Bids and Normal glossaries, as shown in Figure 13.4.

7. Click both on the message line to return to the text window.

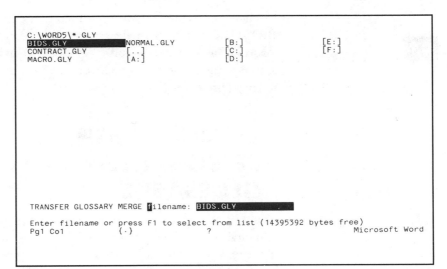

o **Figure 13.3:** *A list of the glossaries available on the disk*

```
page                          nextpage
date                          dateprint
time                          timeprint
footnote                      AMOUNT
EST                           NYLAW
SIXTY                         THANKS




.




INSERT from: page       █
Enter glossary name or press F1 to select from list
Pg1 Co1            (·)               ?              Microsoft Word
```

o **Figure 13.4:** *The names of the boilerplate paragraphs in the glossary*

PRINTING GLOSSARY DIRECTORIES

The names of the paragraphs are not much help if you can't remember the text they represent. A printed listing of each boilerplate name and its associated text would be quite useful.

Press Esc P G to print the glossary.

First, make sure you have returned to the text window after merging BIDS.GLY into the normal glossary. The glossary you want to list must be loaded or merged into the current glossary. Then to print the glossary, click left on Print Glossary. The glossary will print with each glossary entry indented under its name.

o WORKING WITH PERSONALIZED GLOSSARIES

You can create as many special glossaries as will fit on your disk. Although you can't use the same boilerplate name more than once in a glossary, you can use it in as many different glossaries as you want. This allows you to use glossaries for storing and retrieving personal information and for creating a limited number of form documents. (If you need to print a large number of form documents, use Word's powerful merge capabilities, which are described in Chapters 15, 16, and 17.)

CREATING PERSONALIZED GLOSSARIES

You will create two sample glossaries containing information about clients. Since they are separate glossaries, you will use the same boilerplate paragraph names in each one. In actual practice, you can have glossaries for any number of clients.

Follow these steps to create the personalized glossaries:

1. Start Word.

2. Type the following data:

> **Mr. James Lad Widerman**
> **Widerman Construction**
> **453 Jenkintown Road**
> **Jenkintown, PA 19042**

> **Eileen**
> **Rachel, Sarah, and Mikey**
> **single family dwellings**
> **dependability and high quality**
> **expensive and temperamental**

KEY Highlight the four-line address. Press Esc C, type **Client**, and press Enter. Repeat this procedure to save the items, giving each its corresponding name.

KEY Press Esc T G S, type **Widerman**, and press Enter.

KEY Press Esc T G C; then press Enter Y.

3. To save the first item of information in the glossary, highlight the entire four-line address and click left on Copy. Then type **Client** and click on COPY.

4. To save the next item, highlight *Mr.* and click left on Copy. Type **Title** and click on the command line title.

5. Highlight the first name only, *James*, and click left on Copy. Type **First** and click on the command line title.

6. Highlight the last name only, *Widerman*, and click left on Copy. Type **Last** and click on the command line title.

7. Move the cursor down to highlight *Eileen* and click left on Copy. Type **Spouse** and click on the command line title.

8. Highlight the entire next line of names and click left on Copy. Type **Children** and click on the command line title.

9. Highlight *single family dwellings* and click left on Copy. Type **Jobs** and click on the command line title.

10. Highlight *dependability and high quality* and click left on Copy. Type **Good** and click on the command line title.

11. Highlight *expensive and temperamental* and click left on Copy. Type **Bad** and click on the command line title.

12. Click left on Transfer Glossary Save.

13. Type **Widerman** and click on the command line title.

The information about Widerman Construction Company is now stored in its own personal glossary. Now we'll clear the glossary so it's ready for the next set of personal information.

14. Click left on Transfer Glossary Clear, click on the command line title, and then click on the message line to confirm.

15. Repeat steps 3 through 11 for the following data, using the same boilerplate paragraph names.

> **Mr. Joe Gold**
> **Group 2 Architects**
> **265 Rizzo Road**
> **Glenside, PA 19042**
>
> **Elayne**
> **Lee and Michael**
> **residential and commercial architecture**

dependability, high quality, and reasonable rates moderate speed

16. Click left on Transfer Glossary Save.
17. Type **Gold**.
18. Click on the command line title.
19. Click on Quit, and then press N.

USING PERSONALIZED GLOSSARIES

You will now type the letter shown in Figure 13.5, using one of the personalized glossaries that you just created.

Follow these steps:

1. Start Word.
2. Press Alt-C to center the date.
3. Type the date; then press Enter.
4. Press Alt-P.

5. Click left on Transfer; then click right on Glossary. (With version 4.0, click left on Transfer Glossary Clear, and then click on the command line title. Next, click left on Transfer Glossary Merge.)
6. Type **Gold**; then click on the command line title. The personalized glossary is now loaded.
7. Type **Client** and press F3. The client's address will be displayed.
8. Press Enter.
9. Type **Dear**.
10. Type **Title** and press F3.
11. Press the spacebar.
12. Type **Last** and press F3.
13. Type **:** (a colon).
14. Type the body of the letter. Press F3 where it's indicated in parentheses.

It has been some time since we last talked. I hope Spouse(F3) and the children, Children(F3), are fine.

```
┌──────────────────────────────────────────────────────────┐
│   Mr. Joe Gold                                             │
│   Group 2 Architects                                       │
│   265 Rizzo Road                                           │
│   Glenside, PA 19042                                       │
│                                                            │
│   Dear Mr. Gold:                                           │
│                                                            │
│        It has been some time since we last talked. I hope  │
│   Elayne and the children, Lee and Michael, are fine.      │
│                                                            │
│        I appreciate your work in the past. Your work in    │
│   residential and commercial architecture is known for     │
│   dependability, high quality, and reasonable rates. We will│
│   indeed be getting in touch in the future.                │
│                                                            │
│                              Sincerely,                    │
│                                                            │
│                              Warren Harding                │
│                                                            │
└──────────────────────────────────────────────────────────┘
```

o **Figure 13.5:** *The sample letter using boilerplate from a personalized glossary*

I appreciate your work in the past. Your work in Jobs(F3) is known for Good(F3). We will indeed be getting in touch in the future. Sincerely,

Warren Harding

KEY   Press Esc Q N to quit.

15. Click left on Quit, and then press N to exit Word without saving the document or the glossary changes.

Remember to use the Transfer Glossary Clear command to clear the current glossary before using personalized glossaries such as the one in this example. This way, Word can warn you if a particular boilerplate paragraph, such as Spouse or Children, does not exist in a particular glossary.

USING GLOSSARIES FOR FORM LETTERS

If you plan to send the same letter to several persons for whom you have set up personalized glossaries, combine the techniques that you used in this section with those that you learned in Chapter 5.

Write a form letter with variable names that match boilerplate paragraph names in the glossaries. After loading the form letter, use the Transfer Merge command to load the appropriate glossary. Then use the Search command to locate each variable. Press F3 to insert each of the pieces of information from the glossary into the document.

After you print the letter, load the form letter again (to clear the glossary data from the previous letter), load the next appropriate glossary, and repeat the entire process.

oALTERNATIVES FOR BOILERPLATE

There are several methods that you can use to incorporate boilerplate text in documents. Each method is suited for a specific use.

USING GLOSSARIES

Save boilerplate text in glossaries when it will be used in different types of documents. Don't use a glossary if all the boilerplate paragraphs will be used together or always in the same type of document. Templates or the Transfer Merge Command would be more efficient in these cases. Also, avoid using glossaries for frequently printing a large number of form documents.

USING THE TRANSFER MERGE COMMAND

The Transfer Merge command stores the boilerplate paragraphs as separate documents. When you want to use that boilerplate text, each document is merged into the text as an entire unit. Use this method if the boilerplate text is a long section or a collection of paragraphs that are always used together. This way, you can avoid the lengthy process of inserting a number of glossary boilerplate paragraphs one at a time.

With both the glossary and Transfer Merge command methods, the completed document is visible on the screen, and you can edit it before you print or save it.

PRINT MERGING USING THE INCLUDE COMMAND

Word's merge functions (to be discussed later) let you insert text into a document while it is being printed. The name of the boilerplate text is used as part of the INCLUDE command. Use this method when you want the entire contents of another file inserted into the current document.

The main disadvantage of merging documents while printing is that you cannot see the completed version of the document on the screen because the merging is done during the printing. Thus, you cannot review or edit the completed document before you see it in print.

USING TEMPLATES

As you have learned in previous chapters, a template is a formatted document that contains the shell text of the form document. You load the template and add the variable information before printing the final document. Use templates when almost the entire text is repeated.

There is a fine difference between using a template and using the Transfer Merge command. Templates should be reserved for documents that are used often or for those that have complicated or unique format characteristics.

Now we'll move on to explore another one of Word's powerful features: macros.

CHAPTER 14

- BUILDING
- APPLICATIONS
- WITH
- MACROS

In this chapter, you'll learn how to create several types of macros. First, you'll see how they can be used for boilerplate keystrokes and commands. Then we'll describe how to program powerful macros that control the flow of command execution by making decisions and repeating commands.

oUSING MACROS

A *macro* is a special glossary entry that, like regular glossary items, can be instantly inserted into a document. But macros are much more powerful than the glossary items discussed so far because they can repeat keystrokes, not merely contain boilerplate text. The keystrokes can be characters that you type or those used to select and change options in the command area. Macros can perform complex formatting tasks, execute long repetitive commands, or even change the purpose of the function keys to suit your own needs.

You can create a macro two different ways:

o Have Word record your keystrokes as you type. You then name the recorded keystrokes—your macro—adding it to the glossary for recall later on. This type of macro is best reserved for boilerplate text and simple series of commands.

o Write the macro. More complex macros can be written using macro instructions (special commands that have no equivalent) and then saved to the glossary.

The name you give the macro is used to run it later. You can also link the name with a Ctrl or function-key combination. For example, soon you'll create a macro that can be executed by pressing Ctrl-P. Using similar techniques, you can program the ten or twelve function keys to perform your own custom commands.

oRECORDING MACROS

If you want to use a macro for boilerplate text or commands, the simplest way is to record the keystrokes the first time you enter them. Press

Shift-F3, enter the keystrokes, and then press Shift-F3 again. Everything you entered between the Shift-F3 keypresses will have been recorded—even your mistakes, so be careful. Note that you must use the keystrokes; mouse actions will not be recorded.

In this section, we will create two macros. The first will contain text and commands to produce a memo letterhead. The second macro will contain a series of formatting commands.

RECORDING A LETTERHEAD MACRO

Follow these steps to record a macro for a memo letterhead:

1. Start Word.
2. Press Shift-F3. The characters RM (for Record Macro) appear on the status line.
3. Press Alt-C to center the text.
4. Type **MEMORANDUM** and press Enter twice.
5. Press Alt-P.
6. Type **TO:** and press Enter.
7. Type **FROM:** and press Enter.
8. Type **SUBJECT:** and press Enter.
9. Type **DATE:** and press Enter.
10. Press Shift-F3 to end the keystroke recording. On the command line, you'll see the prompt

    COPY to:

    Your screen should look like Figure 14.1.
11. Type **MEMO.MAC**; then press Enter.

Macros are stored in the glossary along with boilerplate paragraphs. Word can automatically distinguish between macros and boilerplate, but adding the optional .MAC extension to the macro name helps you identify which entries are macros.

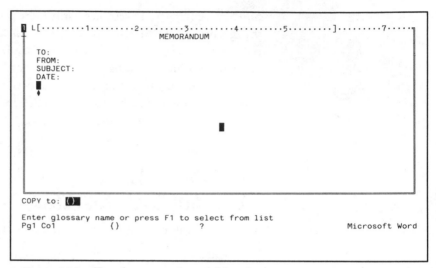

○ **Figure 14.1:** *Text of a macro to be copied into the scrap*

RECORDING A FORMATTING MACRO

Now, let's create a macro with all formatting commands and link it to a Ctrl-key combination so it can be run with a single keystroke. This macro is designed for printing documents on legal-size paper. It formats the proper division, changes the paper feed to manual, and prints the current document. Because you will be entering and recording a printing instruction, make sure your printer is turned on. However, our example is only a few lines, so you don't have to have legal-sized paper in the printer.

1. Press Shift-F3 to begin recording.

2. Format the division for legal-size paper.

    a. Press Esc F D M.

    b. Press Tab four times to reach the Page Length option.

    c. Type **14** and press Enter.

3. Change the paper feed to manual.

    a. Press Esc P O.

Remember, you can't use the mouse when you're recording a macro.

4.0 Press Esc P O. Press the down arrow five times, press M, and then press Enter.

     b. Press the down arrow six times.

     c. Type **Manual** and press Enter.

4. Press P Y to begin printing the document on the first sheet.

5. Press Shift-F3.

6. Type **LEGAL.MAC^**. The ^ (caret) character is Shift-6.

7. Press Ctrl-P to link the name to this key combination. On the status line, you will see the message

      COPY to: LEGAL.MAC^(ctrl P)

8. Press Enter.

    You can also link a macro to one of the function keys, F1 through F12, although this will cancel the built-in function of the key. To do this, name the macro, type the ^ character, and then press the function key you want to use.

oRUNNING MACROS

You should try running these macros, or one you recorded yourself, before going on to writing macros. Depending on how you name a macro, it can be run several ways.

EXPANDING THE MACRO

First, let's run the MEMO.MAC by using the Expand key, F3:

1. Type **MEMO.MAC**.

2. Press F3, the Expand key.

The macro will be executed, and when it is completed, the message

    End of Macro

appears on the status line.

    Notice that the entries in the memo macro are repeated keystroke by keystroke. When you expand a regular glossary entry, the text appears all at once.

INSERTING THE MACRO

You can also run a macro by inserting it from the glossary.

KEY Press Esc I, type **MEMO.MAC**, and press Enter. To select from a list of names, press F1.

1. Click left on Insert.
2. Type **MEMO.MAC**. If you forgot the name of the macro, you can click right to the right of the INSERT command line title, and then click right on the macro you want to run.
3. Click on the command line title.

PRESSING A KEY

Macros linked with Ctrl or a function key can also be run from the glossary, but there is a faster way.

1. Make sure your printer is on.
2. Press Ctrl-P.

The LEGAL.MAC macro, which we linked with Ctrl-P when we named it, will run.

○SAVING MACROS

You can create your own personal glossary, as described in Chapter 13, to hold your macros. Just name it something other than Macro because Word supplies a sample Macro glossary (discussed at the end of this chapter).

The macros you just created have been added to the Normal glossary. If you want to save the macros, use the Transfer Glossary Save command, as described in Chapter 13. If you don't save the glossary, when you quit Word, the message line will display:

Enter Y to save changes to glossary, N to lose changes, or Esc to cancel

Press N if you do not want to save the macros with the Normal glossary.

Now that you know how to record and run macros, let's cover how they can be written.

○WRITING ADVANCED MACROS

One disadvantage of recording macros is that, after you press Shift-F3, all keystrokes, or commands, are recorded, even mistakes and typographical errors. Although you may correct them before saving the macro, the exact series of keystrokes, including the mistakes and corrections, will be repeated when you run the macro.

Another disadvantage of recorded macros is that they cannot contain special macro instructions. We'll discuss some of the tasks you can perform with macro instructions after we write a simple macro.

REPRESENTING NONCHARACTER KEYS

To write a macro, you type the commands to be executed, entering them as you would type regular text. However, function, cursor-movement, and other noncharacter keys are represented in special ways.

When you want to include one of these keystrokes in the macro, type its name within the < and > characters. This way, Word can distinguish between actions and text. For example, the macro to save an already named document would be written like this:

<esc>ts<enter>

When run, this macro repeats the keystrokes Esc T S Enter to perform a Transfer Save.

All the command and noncharacter keys can be designated the same way, as listed in Table 14.1.

To repeat a key more than once, enter the number following the name, but before the closing >. For example, the command <up 5> means to "press" the up arrow key five times; <tab 10> means to "press" the Tab key ten times.

WRITING A FORMATTING MACRO

Let's write and run a simple formatting macro. This macro displays a letterhead in bold characters.

KEY Press
Esc T C W N.

1. Click left on Transfer Clear Window, and then press N to clear the screen.

2. Type **<alt C><alt B>Watson Engine Company<enter>** and press Enter.

○ **Table 14.1:** *Noncharacter Key Representations in Macros*

Key	Representation
Enter	\<enter\>
Esc	\<esc\>
Tab	\<tab\>
⟵	\<backspace\>
←	\<left\>
→	\<right\>
↓	\<down\>
↑	\<up\>
Spacebar	\<space\>
PgUp	\<pgup\>
PgDn	\<pgdn\>
End	\<end\>
Alt	\<alt function-key\>
Home	\<home\>
Shift	\<shift function-key\>
Ctrl	\<ctrl function-key\>

3. Type **435 Baltimore Avenue\<enter\>** and press Enter.
4. Type **Philadelphia, PA 19117\<enter 2\>\<alt space\>**.
5. Press Shift-F10 to select the macro (in this case all the text on the screen), as shown in Figure 14.2.
6. Click left on Delete.
7. Type **HEAD.MAC**, and then click on Delete. Now run the macro.
8. Type **HEAD.MAC**, and then press F3.

 Press Esc D, type **HEAD.MAC**, and press Enter.

When you write macros, you must explicitly include all commands and keystrokes that you want. In this example, you had to type the \<enter\> command to end each line, even though you pressed the Enter key after each line in the macro. It will be the \<enter\> command that

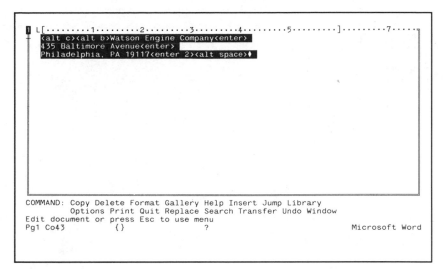

○ **Figure 14.2:** *Text of written macro*

causes the carriage return when the macro is run. In fact, the only reason for dividing the macro into lines is to make them easier to read and edit. You could have typed

<alt C><alt B>Watson Engine Company<enter>435 Baltimore Avenue<enter>Philadelphia, PA 19117<enter 2><alt space>

and the macro would produce the same result.

This macro, by the way, leaves the cursor centered on the screen so you can enter the date. If you want the cursor to return to the left margin, end the macro with Alt-P.

USING MACRO INSTRUCTIONS

Macro instructions can serve many purposes. By including the appropriate instructions, you can have your macros perform more complex tasks, such as prompt the user for keyboard input, set formatting values, and execute instructions based on specified conditions. These instructions are always enclosed in « and » codes, which you insert by pressing Ctrl-[and Ctrl-], respectively.

Table 14.2 summarizes the instructions you can include in your Word macros. It lists the purpose, the syntax, and an example of each instruction.

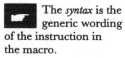 The *syntax* is the generic wording of the instruction in the macro.

o **Table 14.2:** *Macro Instructions*

Instruction	Purpose	Syntax	Example
ASK	Prompts the user to input information while the macro is running (like the INPUT command in BASIC or the READ command in Pascal). The prompt, if any, appears in the status line, and the word RESPONSE: appears in the command area, followed by the cursor.	«ASK *variable-name* = ?» «ASK *variable-name* = ?*prompt*»	«ASK date = ? What is today's date»
SET	Prompts the user to assign a value to a variable. It can also be used to change the value of the variable automatically while the macro is running (like the LET command in BASIC).	«SET *variable* = ?» «SET *variable* = ?*prompt*» «SET *variable* = *expression*»	«SET date = ?What is today's date» «SET top = 6»
COMMENT ... ENDCOMMENT	Add comments within the macro without affecting the macro (similar to the REM instruction in BASIC).	«COMMENT *text-of-comment*» «COMMENT» *text-of-comment* «ENDCOMMENT»	«COMMENT I wrote this macro on June 6» «COMMENT» Ask Sam for help with this «ENDCOMMENT»

o **Table 14.2:** *Macro Instructions (continued)*

Instruction	Purpose	Syntax	Example
IF ... ELSE ... ENDIF	Determines which instructions are to be executed while the macro is running (like the IF ... THEN instruction in BASIC). If the condition is true, and an ELSE is not present, the instructions between the IF and ENDIF are performed. Otherwise, the macro continues at the instruction following ENDIF. If an ELSE instruction is included, and the condition is met, the instructions between the IF and ELSE are performed. Otherwise, the instructions following the ELSE are performed.	«IF *condition*» *more instructions or keys* «ENDIF» «IF *condition*» *some instructions* «ELSE» *do these instructions* «ENDIF»	«ASK date = ?What is today's date?» «IF date = 12/25/90» Merry Christmas «ENDIF» «IF day<>"MON-DAY"» You'll have to wait «ELSE» Merry Christmas «ENDIF»

○ **Table 14.2:** *Macro Instructions (continued)*

Instruction	Purpose	Syntax	Example
MESSAGE	Displays a message of up to 80 characters on the status line while the macro is running.	«MESSAGE *text*»	«MESSAGE You are running the delete macro»
PAUSE	Stops the macro so you can enter keystrokes (text for the document, a response to a screen prompt, or an entry in a menu). Press Enter to continue the macro.	«PAUSE prompt»	‹esc›po«PAUSE enter printer name» ‹enter›p
QUIT	Exits the macro; usually it is included in an IF instruction.	«QUIT»	«IF selection = ''Adam Chesin''»«QUIT» «ELSE»Sorry, wrong number«ENDIF»
REPEAT ... ENDREPEAT	Repeat a set of instructions a specific number of times.	«REPEAT n» *instructions or text* «ENDREPEAT»	«REPEAT 3» ‹esc›pp‹enter› «ENDREPEAT»

Now, let's write a macro that computes the bottom margin setting and sets the proper margins. Follow these steps:

1. Click left on Transfer Clear Window, and then press N to clear the screen.

2. Press Ctrl-[. The « symbol appears.

3. Type **SET length = ?Enter page length**.

4. Press Ctrl-], and then press Enter.

5. Enter the next line.

    a. Press Ctrl-[.

    b. Type **SET top = ?Enter top margin**.

    c. Press Ctrl-], and then press Enter.

6. Enter the next line.

    a. Press Ctrl-[.

    b. Type **SET lines = ?Enter lines of text per page**.

    c. Press Ctrl-], and then press Enter.

7. Enter the next line.

    a. Press Ctrl-[.

    b. Type **SET bottom = length - top - (lines / 6)**.

    c. Press Ctrl-], and then press Enter.

8. Enter the next line without any spaces:

    <esc>fdm«top» <tab> «bottom» <tab 3> «length» <enter>

The completed macro is shown in Figure 14.3.

9. Save the completed macro under the name MARGINS and link it with the Ctrl-M key.

    a. Click both in the selection bar to select the entire document.

    b. Click left on Delete.

    c. Type **MARGINS.MAC^**.

    d. Press Ctrl-M.

    e. Click on DELETE.

 Press Shift-F10, and then press Esc D. Type **MARGINS.MAC^**, press Ctrl-M, and press Enter.

10. Now run the macro.

   a. Press Ctrl-M. The status line changes, as shown in Figure 14.4.

   b. Type **11** and press Enter. The status line now displays the next prompt, for the top margin.

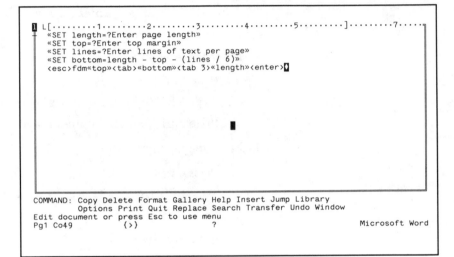

o **Figure 14.3.:** *The completed macro*

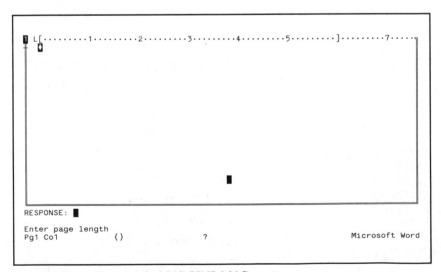

o **Figure 14.4:** *Running the MARGINS.MAC macro*

c. Type **2** and press Enter.

d. Type **42** and press Enter.

COMPONENTS OF MACRO INSTRUCTIONS

If you refer to Table 14.2, you will see that some instructions include variables, and other instructions include conditions. In addition, you can use reserved words, functions, and concatenation in your macros, as described in this section.

Variables

Variable names can be any combination of letters and numbers but they must start with a letter. A maximum of 64 variables are allowed in a single macro.

Conditions

The conditions in IF instructions can include any of the following:

Condition	Example
= Equals	«IF date = 09/09/89» Dates do not have to be in quotation marks.
< > Not equal	«IF name< >"SAM"» Text must be in quotation marks, and the case is ignored.
< Less than	«IF dues<500»
> Greater than	«IF age>65»
< = Less than or equal to	«IF age< = 16»
> = Greater than or equal to	«IF age< = 21»

For example, this macro tests two conditions:

```
«IF num = 2»<esc>ts<enter>«ELSE»«IF num = 5»
<esc>wc2<enter>«ENDIF»«ENDIF»
```

If the value in the variable num is 2, the keystrokes Esc T S Enter are performed and the macro ends. If the value is not 2, the other condition is tested. If the value is 5, the keystrokes Esc W C 2 Enter are performed.

This is called a nested conditional because one IF ENDIF instruction is contained within another. That's why two ENDIF instructions are needed.

Reserved Words

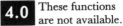 The reserved words Save, Window, Echo, Promptmode, Wordversion, and Zoomedwindow are not available.

There are certain words that cannot be used as variable names because Word assigns them special meaning. However, you can use these reserved words within your own macros to perform their predefined tasks. Table 14.3 lists the reserved words, their purpose, and examples of use.

Functions

4.0 These functions are not available.

In addition to the macro instructions, Word provides three useful functions: INT, LEN, and MID. These functions are described in Table 14.4.

Concatenation

Concatentation combines several strings together in the format:

«SET *newstring = string1 string2 string3*»

You don't have to include plus signs between strings.

In this example:

<esc>po«SET ptr = field»<tab 2>«SET printer = ptr " " field»<esc>Your printer is a «printer»

the macro combines the PRD and model names together into one string, called printer.

TESTING AND EDITING MACROS

Be very careful when writing macros. Make sure that all keystrokes necessary for the function are included and instructions are properly entered. Common errors include having a REPEAT, WHILE, or IF without a matching ENDREPEAT, ENDWHILE, or ENDIF.

o **Table 14.3:** *Reserved Words*

Reserved Word	Purpose	Example
Selection	Refers to whatever text is currently selected.	«IF selection = "Adam Chesin"» <F8> <del> <F8> <del> «ENDIF»—if the words Adam Chesin are selected, they will be deleted.
Scrap	Represents the current text in the scrap area.	«IF scrap = "Adam Chesin"» <ins> «ENDIF»—if the name Adam Chesin is in the scrap, it will be inserted into the text.
Field	Represents the value in the active menu field.	<esc>po<tab>«IF field = "LPT1:"» <esc>p«ELSE» LPT1:<enter>p«ENDIF»—Checks the Setup option in the Print Options menu to make sure it is set to LPT1:; if not, the macro changes it, exits the menu, and then prints the document.
Found and Notfound	Used to test for the results of a search (similar to Boolean variables). If the text was found, the condition Found is true.	«ASK searchphrase = ?Name of person to search for» <esc>s«searchphrase» «IF found» <esc>pp«ENDIF»—the macro requests a name to search for; if the name is found, the document is printed.

o **Table 14.3:** *Reserved Words (continued)*

Reserved Word	Purpose	Example
Save	Detects if the Save message is flashing on the status line (warning you that you're almost out of memory).	«IF save»<esc>ta«ENDIF»—performs a Transfer Allsave if the message is on.
Window	Returns the current active window number.	«SET window =2»—makes window number 2 the active window.
Echo	Turns off or on screen updating as the macro is run. On, the default value, displays each keystroke or screen action as it occurs; off displays all the changes at once after the macro runs.	«SET echo = "on"»—turns screen updating on.
Promptmode	Informs the macro where to accept responses to prompts. It can be set to user (the macro will pause and wait until the user enters the appropriate keystrokes), macro (the response is in the macro itself), or ignore (prompts are ignored and the macro continues).	«SET promptmode = "user"»
Wordversion	Detects the version of Word being used (this is not very useful at this point, but it will be when later versions of Word are released).	«wordversion»
Zoomedwindow	Detects if the window is zoomed.	«IF zoomedwindow» <F1>«ENDIF»

o **Table 14.4:** *Macro Functions*

Function	Purpose	Example
INT	Returns the integer of a number.	«SET average = INT(selection/3»—if the number 175 is selected, average will be assigned the value 58
LEN	Returns the length of the string of characters in the function.	«IF LEN(scrap)>10» All deleted text is not displayed«ELSE»All the deleted text is displayed in the scrap«ENDIF»—determines the number of characters in the scrap.
MID	Returns a substring (part) of a string of characters, using this format: MID (*string, starting position, number of characters*).	<esc>po«SET ptr = MID(field,1,2)»«IF ptr = "HP"» <enter>«ELSE»<F1> «ENDIF»—checks to make sure that the first two characters of the PRD on the Printer Options menu are HP (a Hewlett Packard printer); if so, exits the menu and starts printing; if not, displays a list of available PRD files.

You must also be careful not to include extra spaces within some macros because these may be entered into your document. For example, look at the following macro:

«ASK num = ?»
«REPEAT num» <del> «ENDREPEAT»

In this case, the macro will actually add a space before and after performing each character deletion <del>.

After the macro is completed, you should run it several times to make sure it works properly. If it is asking for a response (using the ASK or SET instructions), try different responses each time. However, if you have difficulties or have to change the macro after it has been written or recorded, you can single step through it or edit it, as described in this section.

Single Stepping Macros

One way to isolate and identify problems in a macro is to run the macro in step mode, one instruction at a time. To do this, press Ctrl-F3. The characters ST appear in the status line. When you run a macro, it will pause after each step. Press Enter to continue with the next step or Esc to stop the macro.

This is an effective tool if your macros are long and complex. At each pause, check the step on the screen to see if it has any errors.

Editing Macros

You can also edit the macro—either recorded or written ones—just like any other text. You must first insert the contents of the macro from the glossary. But, you can't use the normal methods, or the macro will be run instead of displayed.

Instead, follow the name of the macro with the caret (^) character. For example, to display and edit the contents of the MARGINS.MAC^ macro, use one of these methods:

 Press Esc I, type **MARGINS.MAC^**, and press Enter. To select from a list of alternatives, press F1 at the Insert menu.

o **Insert method**: Click left on Insert, type **MARGINS.MAC^**, and click on INSERT.

o **F3 method**: Type **MARGINS.MAC^** and press F3.

o **F1 method**: Click left on Insert, click right to the right of the command line title. Then click left on MARGINS.MAC, type ^, and click on the command line title.

After the macro is on the screen, edit it as necessary. When you copy or delete the macro back to the glossary using the same name, the message line will display

Enter Y to replace glossary entry, N to retype name, or Esc to cancel

Click on the message line, if you wish to replace the old macro with the edited version.

When you recall the contents of a recorded macro, it will appear just as if it had been written. If a you are creating a complex macro that will include a number of command selections, you can record them instead of writing them, and then recall the text and add the instructions that could not be recorded.

SAMPLE MACROS

The macros described in this section illustrate the advanced instructions. Review them carefully if you are unfamiliar with computer programming concepts such as conditionals and loops. Each of the macros perform a specific useful function. To help you understand the instructions, each line of the macros are numbered and discussed. The line numbers are not part of the macro, so do not type them in if you use these macros yourself.

Variable Paragraph Formatting

Take your time and study this complicated paragraph-formatting macro. It formats three consecutive paragraphs, each with a ½-inch wider left and right indentation.

1. «SET leftindent = .5»
2. «SET rightindent = .5»
3. \<F10\>
4. «REPEAT 3»
5. \<esc\>fp\<tab\>«leftindent»\<tab 2\>«rightindent»\<enter\>\<F10\>
6. «SET leftindent = leftindent + .5»
7. «SET rightindent = rightindent + .5»
8. «ENDREPEAT»

Lines 1 and 2 set the initial left and right indentations that will be used to format the first of the three paragraphs. Line 3 selects the first of the paragraphs before starting the repeat in line 4. Line 5 uses the Format

Paragraph command to insert the variables leftindent and rightindent into the appropriate menu options.

Lines 6 and 7 then widen the leftindent and rightindent variables another ½ inch, and the process repeats. After the third repetition, in which the indentations are set at 1.5 inches, the macro stops.

Interactive Paper-Feed Macro

The paper-feed macro is designed for printer owners who often switch between hand-fed and continuous paper. It requests the type of paper feed, changes the Print Options menu accordingly, and then starts printing. Type the lines without any spaces between the instructions.

4.0 For line 2, use *<esc>po<down 5>«IF papertype = "H" »m«ELSE»c«ENDIF» <enter>p.*

1. **«ASK papertype = ?Enter h for hand-fed or c for continuous, then press Enter»**
2. **<esc>po<down 6>«IF papertype = "H"»manual«ELSE»continuous«ENDIF»<enter>p**

Line 1 asks if the paper type (the variable papertype) is hand-fed or continuous. Line 2 enters the Print Options menu and presses the down arrow to reach the Feed option. If hand-fed paper was selected (H or h), Manual is inserted in the field. Otherwise, Continuous is selected.

Notice that line 1 asks for an input of either h or c, however, any key other than H will set the feed to continuous. This is because only an H is "tested" in the condition. If the key was an H (or an h since cases are ignored), Manual feed is selected. If it was not an H—no matter what other key was pressed—the ELSE condition is performed.

Multiple Delete Macro

The delete macro asks for the names of files to delete, and then deletes them. To end the macro, type Stop as the file name.

1. **«ASK filen = ?enter name»**
2. **«WHILE filen<>"stop"»**
3. **<esc>td«filen»<enter>**
4. **«PAUSE Enter Y to delete, N to retain, then press Enter»<enter>**
5. **«ASK filen = ?enter name»**
6. **«ENDWHILE»**

Line 1 asks for the name of the first file to delete. As long as the file name entered is not Stop, the WHILE ENDWHILE repetition loop is started in line 2. Line 3 issues the Transfer Delete command and inserts the contents of the variable filen into the prompt.

Normally when you delete a file, a prompt appears requesting confirmation. Since the macro must account for all keystrokes, the PAUSE instruction is used in line 4. It stops the macro, displays its own prompt, and accepts the Y for confirmation (pressing any other key retains the file).

The user is prompted to press Enter because, after a PAUSE, the Enter key must be pressed to continue the macro.
Line 5 requests the name of the next file to be deleted. The process continues until the file name Stop is entered.

Notice that the ASK line is given twice in the macro. This is standard programming style. The first ASK will obtain the first file name or, if the name entered is Stop, end the macro before continuing. This is necessary in the event the macro was run by mistake.

Delete Macro

This is a delete text macro that creates a general-purpose delete function. It requests the type of text you want deleted, then the number of deletions desired. When naming this macro, it can be linked with the Ctrl-D key or even a function key.

Enter each of the lines as one continuous sentence with no spaces, except if needed between the «QUIT» and «ENDIF». Any other spaces used to separate the commands will appear on the screen, and they may cause the macro to abort prematurely.

1. «ASK delmac = ?Delete (C)haracter, (W)ord, (L)ine, (S)entence, (P)aragraph»
2. «ASK num = ?How many»
3. «IF delmac = "C"»«REPEAT num»<del>«ENDREPEAT»«QUIT»«ENDIF»
4. «IF delmac = "W"»«REPEAT num»<F8><del>«ENDREPEAT»«QUIT»«ENDIF»
5. «IF delmac = "L"»«REPEAT num»<shift F9><del>«ENDREPEAT»«QUIT»«ENDIF»
6. «IF delmac = "S"»«REPEAT num»<shift F8><del>«ENDREPEAT»«QUIT»«ENDIF»
7. «IF delmac = "P"»«REPEAT num»<F10><del>«ENDREPEAT»«QUIT»«ENDIF»

Line 1 presents a custom command line and requests input for the type of deletion required. Line 2 then asks for the number of deletions to be made.

The remaining lines select the type desired, and then repeat the appropriate commands to make the deletion. The QUIT instructions have been added to speed up this macro. Without it, Word would perform the commands on a line, but then still check the remaining conditions, even though they would not be true.

Reverse Printing Macro

Here's a useful macro is you have a laser printer that delivers the pages backward—the last page on top. This macro determines how many pages are in the document, then starts at the end printing the document page by page. This way, the last page out of the printer—and on top of the stack—will be the first.

1. \<esc\>pr\<enter\>
2. \<ctrl pgdn\>
3. \<esc\>JP«SET size = field»\<esc\>
4. «WHILE size \>0»
5. \<esc\>po\<down 4\>p\<tab\>«size»\<enter\>p
6. «SET size = size-1»
7. «ENDWHILE»

4.0 Use \<down 3\> in line 5.

The document is repaginated in line 1; then line 2 moves the cursor to the last page. Line 3 sets the variable size to the number of pages in the document. A WHILE loop is set up in 4 as long as the variable size is greater than zero. Line 5 enters the Print Options menu, sets the Range option to Pages, the Page Numbers option to the last page in the document, exits the menu, and then prints the page. The variable size is reduced by 1 in line 6, and then the process repeats, this time setting the Page Numbers option for the next to the last page. This cycle continues until the first page is printed.

Automatic Startup Macros

If you want a macro to be run automatically when you start Word, name it AUTOEXEC (do not add the .MAC extension) and save it in the Normal glossary. It will run when you start Word, but you can also run it by using the Insert or F3 methods, or even link it with a Ctrl or function key.

oUSING SUPPLIED MACROS

A number of very useful and educational macros come supplied on your Word disks in the glossary MACRO.GLY. Here's how to use them:

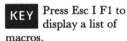 Press Esc T G M, type **Macro**, and press Enter.

1. Start Word.
2. Click left on Transfer Glossary Merge.
3. Type **Macro**.
4. Click on the command line title.

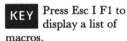 Press Esc I F1 to display a list of macros.

Display a list of the macros by pressing clicking left on Insert; then click right to the right of the command line title. Then load the contents of any that you are interested in examining. If you want to load those macros with every document, use the Transfer Glossary Save command.

This chapter covered a great deal of territory. If you are unfamiliar with computer programming, you might want to reread this chapter several times and carefully examine the sample macros provided.

In the next several chapters, you'll encounter some additional macros. These will be combined with print merging to provide some powerful applications.

CHAPTER 15

- USING
- DATABASE
- MANAGEMENT
- FUNCTIONS

In previous chapters, you learned several ways to produce form documents. In each case, certain variable information was inserted into the shell text. The task of collecting and organizing such information is called *database management*. A database can provide useful information for many business needs. It lets the user quickly find and update information. Specific data can be extracted to study business trends and make key business decisions.

In this chapter, you will learn how Word can provide some database-management functions. You will create a database and learn how to retrieve information and print reports. Even though Word cannot replace the more powerful commercial database programs available, the techniques covered in this chapter are useful if you do not have a separate database program or if you plan to use your database almost exclusively for form documents. One advantage Word does offer, however, is the ability to format database reports using the full powers of your printer, including various font types and sizes.

oDEVELOPING AND MAINTAINING A DATABASE

A database contains all the pertinent information about a certain group of items. For example, it could be the name, address, and other information about clients or employees, or it could be the company's inventory or price list.

IDENTIFYING FIELDS

The database is like an electronic version of an index card file. The information that would be on a single index card is called a *record*. Each item that would be on the card, such as the part name, quantity on hand, supplier, and price, is called a *field*.

The first task in creating a database is to identify what fields are needed for each record. You give each field a name, then enter the specific information.

You can have a maximum of 256 field names in each record. Field names can only be one word up to 64 characters long. They can include letters, numbers, and the underline character, but they must start with a letter. To separate words in a field name, use an underline, as in Sales_Tax or Last_Order. You cannot include spaces or any other punctuation characters.

The first line in the database document must contain the names of the fields, separated by commas. This line is called the *header record*. The number of entries for each record must be the same as the number of fields in the header record. If there is no information for a field of a particular record, insert a comma where the data would appear. Since Word interprets a comma as a blank field, if an entry for a field contains a comma, you must enclose all of it in quotation marks. For example, a company name of Johnson, Inc., must be entered as "Johnson, Inc.".

CREATING A DATABASE

Let's use Word to create a database of clients. Then we'll use this database to produce several reports and extract specific information. In the next chapter, we'll use this same database to produce form letters.

Our database will have the following fields:

Item	Variable Name
Last name	Last
First name	First
Company	Company
Address	Address
City	City
State	State
Zip code	Zip
Telephone	Telephone
Amount due	Due
Total credit	Credit
Credit rating	Rating
Last order	Last_order

Follow these steps to create the client database as a Word document:

1. Start Word.

2. Enter the header record. Press Enter after you've entered the names of all the fields.

   Last, First, Company, Address, City, State, Zip, Telephone, Due, Credit, Rating, Last_order

3. Enter the variable information about the first client, separated by commas. Press Enter after you type all the information. Notice that the date is surrounded by quotation marks because it includes a comma.

   Rogers, Frederick, Williams Shoes, Broad and Locust Streets, Plainfield, MN, 98111, (512) 876-0123, 5.87, 25, B, "December 1, 1990"

4. Enter the information about the next client. Press Enter after you type the data.

   Chesin, Adam, "Shelly Pharmacy, Inc.", 246 Frankford Avenue, Philadelphia, PA, 19106, (215) 555-8765, 45.56, 500, A, "January 12, 1990"

5. Enter the information about the last client. Press Enter after you have typed all the data. Since there is no company name for this client, you will type an extra comma to insert a blank as the entry for that field.

   Gringold, Herman,, 45th Street and 6th Avenue, Oakville, MA, 28612, (412) 666-8765, 100.87, 1000, B, "May 12, 1990"

KEY Press Ctrl-F10, type **Datafile**, and press Enter twice.

6. Click left on Transfer Save, type **Datafile**, click on the command line title, and then click on on SUMMARY.

LOCATING AND EDITING RECORDS

Most database information needs to be updated at some time. Names and addresses change, transactions increase the amount due, and payments affect credit ratings.

Using Word's search function, you can quickly locate specific information, even in a large database file. After you find the correct record, you can edit individual fields using standard editing techniques.

KEY Press Esc S, type **Williams Shoes**, and press Enter.

For example, if you wanted to change the total credit allowed to Williams Shoes in our example database, you would follow these steps:

1. Click left on Search.
2. Type **Williams Shoes**.
3. Click on the command line title. Word locates and displays the record for Williams Shoes.
4. Edit the Credit field to change the amount.

oFUNDAMENTALS OF DATA REPORTING

With the sample database on disk, we can now produce any number of useful reports about our clients. In this section, you will prepare a simple report from the database. The report will list each client's name, telephone number, and amount due.

USING DATABASE INSTRUCTIONS

To create a document to be merged with the database, you must use *merge instructions*. These instructions are enclosed in « and » symbols, just like those used for macro instructions. Press Ctrl-[for « and Ctrl-] for ».

The merge instructions you'll be using in this chapter are summarized in Table 15.1.

CREATING SIMPLE REPORTS

 If you want to merge the document directly to the printer, you must use the NEXT instruction and include merge codes for each record in the database, as discussed in the next section.

You can merge all the data into one report as long as you are merging the data into a new document (not directly to the printer), and the merge document contains no text other than variable names or data to be included between variable names. (Text such as titles and headings can be added later before printing.)

Now we will create a simple report, which will list the first name, last name, telephone number, and amount due fields from the database in

o **Table 15.1:** *Merge Instructions*

Instruction	Purpose	Syntax	Example
DATA	Names the database file that contains the variable information.	«DATA *FILENAME*.DOC»	«DATA DATAFILE.DOC»
IF … ELSE … ENDIF	Determines which text or data varaiable should be inserted into the text (the same IF … ELSE … ENDIF instruction used for macros).	«IF *condition*»*print this*«ELSE»*print this*«ENDIF»	«IF due>50»Please pay today«ELSE»Your credit is still good with us!«ENDIF»
NEXT	Gets the next record from the data file. It is used when merging data to the printer to print more than one record on a page.	«NEXT»	«name» «address» «due» «NEXT»
SKIP	Bypasses data from a particular record in the database.	«SKIP»	«IF rating<B» «SKIP»«ELSE» «due»«ENDIF»
SET	Assigns data to an additional field name when the merge operation begins. The value assigned remains constant during the entire merge operation.	«SET *variable* = *constant*»«SET date = 09/16/88» «SET *variable* = ?» «SET *variable* = ?*prompt*»	«SET date = ?Please enter the date»

three columns. We will begin by splitting the screen into three windows; one to display the database for reference, another to contain the report document, and a third to display the results of the merge operation.

The database that we just created should still be on your screen. Follow these steps to prepare the merge document.

KEY Press Esc W S H, type **10**, press Tab Y, and press Enter. Repeat but type **4** to split the screen again. Press F1 twice to make window 2 active.

1. Click right on the right border, about ten lines down, to create a new window.

2. Click right on the right border of window 2, about four lines down.

3. Click left in window 2.

4. Set tab stops to format the table columns.

KEY Press Alt-F1, type **2L** and **5D**, and then press Enter. (With version 4.0, press Alt-F1, type **5**, and press Ins. Type **2**, press Tab D, and press Enter.)

   a. Make sure that the leader character in the ruler is blank and the tab character is L.

   b. Click left on the 2 on the ruler.

   c. Click on the tab type character until a D appears.

   d. Click left on the 5 on the ruler.

   (With version 4.0, click left on Format; then click right on Tab. Click left on the 2 on the ruler. Click left on Decimal for the alignment; then click left on the 5 on the ruler. Click on the command line title.)

5. Identify the file that contains the database information.

   a. Press Ctrl-[and type **DATA**.

   b. Press the spacebar once.

   c. **DATAFILE.DOC** and press Ctrl-].

   d. Press Enter.

6. Enter the merge codes to print the report line.

   a. Press Ctrl-[, type **FIRST**, and press Ctrl-].

   b. Press the spacebar.

   c. Press Ctrl-[, type **LAST**, and press Ctrl-].

   d. Press Tab.

   e. Press Ctrl-[, type **TELEPHONE**, and press Ctrl-].

   f. Press Tab.

       g. Press Ctrl-[, type **DUE**, and press Ctrl-].

       h. Press Enter.

The completed merge document is shown in Figure 15.1.

The merge document can include any or all of the database fields, and the fields can appear on more than one line. For example, a mailing list could be created using the following form:

    «First» «Last»
    «Address»
    «City», «State»«Zip»

In this case, a comma will print between the city and state.

Printing the Report

After you create the merge document, the information from the database can be added. Word uses the «DATA DATAFILE.DOC» instruction at the beginning of the document to locate the data to be merged into the document.

KEY Press Esc P M D to see the command line.

1. Click left on Print Merge to see the command line

    PRINT MERGE: Printer Document Options

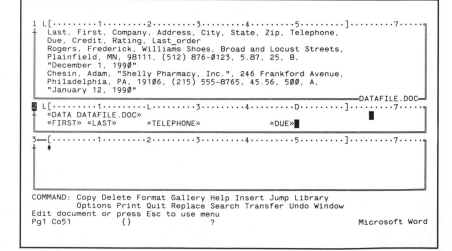

o **Figure 15.1:** *A merge document*

2. Click on Document to show the prompt

PRINT MERGE DOCUMENT filename:

KEY Type **CLIENTS** and press Enter.

3. Type **CLIENTS**, the name of the disk file, and then click on the command line title. (The Printer and Options selections will be discussed later.) The status line will display the prompt

Merging record 1

As the new CLIENTS document is created, the prompt will show the number of the record currently being merged.

Completing the Report

Now let's see the results of the merge and add a title and column headings.

KEY Press F1 to place the cursor in window 3. Press Ctrl-F7, select CLIENTS.DOC, and press Enter.

1. Click left in window 3.

2. Click right on Transfer Load; then click right to the right of the command line title.

3. Click right on CLIENTS.DOC. The merged document will appear, as shown in Figure 15.2. It contains three lines of data, one for each record, but each line is preceded by a blank line and separated with a page break. We'll get rid of the page breaks now, and you'll learn how to avoid the blank lines shortly.

4. Delete all the page break lines.

KEY Press Esc R and type ^d. Press Tab twice, press N, and then press Enter.

a. Click on Replace.

b. Type **^d** for the Text option.

c. Click right on No for the Confirm option.

5. Add a centered report title.

a. Press Enter.

b. Press Alt-C and type **Client Receivable Report**.

c. Press Enter twice; then press Alt-P.

6. Enter the column headings.

a. Type **Name** and press Tab four times.

b. Type **Telephone** and press Tab four times.

c. Type **Due** and press Enter twice.

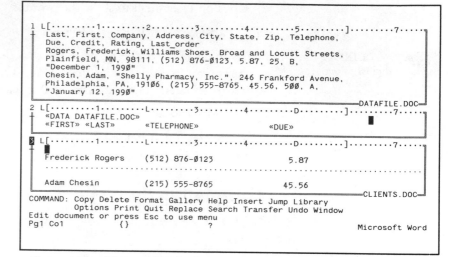

o **Figure 15.2:** *The merged CLIENTS document*

KEY Press Ctrl-F8.
Press Esc T C W
N to clear the window.

7. Click right on Print to print the report.

8. Click left on Transfer Clear Window, and then press N.

MERGING DIRECTLY TO THE PRINTER

You can merge a document directly to the printer, but the procedure is somewhat cumbersome. You can't simply use the Print Merge Printer command to create our sample report because three separate pages, each page with only one line, would have been generated. To produce the report all on one page, the merge document would have to include NEXT commands, as shown in Figure 15.3.

In this case, the NEXT command tells Word to merge the data from the next record before issuing a page-feed command to the printer. The drawback of this method is that the merge code lines must be repeated for every record in the database.

If you are producing a report that will display 20 or more records from a database, you must divide the series of records into pages. Use the Copy command to fill one page with the variable names and the NEXT command. For our example report, you would copy:

«First» «Last» «Telephone» «Due»
«NEXT»

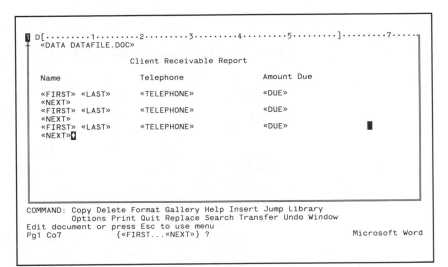

o **Figure 15.3:** *A merge document for merging to the printer*

Copy the entire page until the number of lines matches the number of records in the database, and then paginate the document. Finally, copy the page and column headings from the first page to the remaining pages. When the report is printed, each page will contain the proper headings, followed by a list of records.

Printing a Reference Copy

You should also print a copy of the merge document showing the merge codes and variable names, rather than the actual data. With the document on the screen, click right on Print. You can refer to this copy when you want to edit the report, as well as when you are creating other database reports.

oADVANCED DATABASE REPORTING

The simple report you just created included every record in the database. However, this does not have to be the case. Using the IF...ELSE...ENDIF and SET instructions, you can select specific records to be included in the report.

PRODUCING A CONDITIONAL REPORT

To create the next sample report, you will print only those records that meet a specified condition, and learn how to avoid the extra blank lines that printed before each record.

Conditional printing is performed by using the IF command. The command compares the value of a field with some text or a number. If the condition is true, either a field or some additional text is printed.

The condition can take four different forms:

IF *field name* = *"TEXT"* **(when the field is not a number)**
IF *field name* = *number*
IF *field name* > *number* **(is greater than)**
IF *field name* < *number* **(is less than)**

When you're comparing a field that is not a number, the value must be enclosed in quotation marks, as in the example below:

«IF City = "Los Angeles"»

The IF command must be matched with an ENDIF command. If the IF condition is found to be true, everything between the IF and ENDIF commands is printed. Otherwise, the instructions between the IF and ENDIF commands will be ignored.

The placement of the IF condition is extremely important. Take a look at the following line:

«IF State = "PA"» «First» «Last» «Due» «ENDIF»

If you used this condition, the report would print all three fields only if the State field is PA. While this sounds efficient, there is one problem: Word would print a blank line for all clients not in Pennsylvania.

Preventing Blank Lines

Commands such as DATA, SET, or ASK, do not print anything on the merged document, but the carriage return at the end of the line will cause a blank line to appear. The same is true for an IF command where the entire line is included in the condition—when the condition is not met the carriage return (paragraph end) will still print. So if your form document starts with these lines:

> **«DATA DATAFILE.DOC»**
> **«IF credit>due»«SKIP»«ENDIF»**
> **«client_name» «amount»**

two blank lines will print at the top of every page.

To avoid these extra lines, do not end nonprinting lines with the final » code:

> **«DATA DATAFILE.DOC**
> **«IF credit>due»«SKIP»«ENDIF**
> **«client_name» «amount»**

Word will interpret the carriage return at the end of the line as the closing merge code, and no blank line will appear.

You should still have the text of the first report on the screen. You will use this report to print the names and telephone numbers for all clients, but you will print the amount due only for clients in Pennsylvania (so only the amount due is conditional).

First select window 2; then follow these steps to produce the second report:

1. Delete the closing merge code in the DATA command.

2. Place the cursor in the first record line before the «Due» field.

3. Enter the condition. We will include the closing merge code because something will always print on this line, and we want a carriage return to separate the lines.

   a. Press Ctrl-[, type **IF State = "PA"**, and press Ctrl-]. «Due» will shift past the tab stop but will print correctly.

   b. Move the cursor immediately following the «Due» field.

   c. Press Ctrl-].

   The completed line should look like

   > **«First» «Last» «Telephone» «IF State = "PA"» «Due» «ENDIF»**

KEY Press P M D, type **CLIENTS**, and press Enter. Press Y to replace.

4. Click left on Print Merge Document, type **CLIENTS**, and then click on the command line title. Since you previously created a document with this name, the message line will read

   > **File already exists. Enter Y to replace or Esc to cancel**

5. Click on the message line.

Using Compound Conditions

4.0 The AND, OR, and NOT operators are not available. However, similar results can be performed using the IF...THEN...ELSE instructions described in this section.

By using the AND, OR, and NOT operators, you can include only the records that meet very specific conditions in your report.

For example, the statement

«**IF Rating = "A" AND State = "PA"**» «**Due**» «**ELSE**» N/A «**ENDIF**»

will print the amount due for just the clients in Pennsylvania who have an A rating.

The OR condition is just the opposite. The statement

«**IF Rating = "A" OR State = "PA"**» «**Due**» «**ELSE**» N/A «**ENDIF**»

will print the amount due for all clients in Pennsylvania, as well as all clients with an A rating, no matter where they live.

The results obtained with the AND statement can be duplicated using the IF...ELSE command, using the form:

«**IF** *the condition is true*» *print this* «**ELSE**» *print this* «**ENDIF**»

To expand on the conditions, either action (*print this*, in this case) can be changed to another IF statement, testing for two different conditions. When you use two IF statements, you must also include two ENDIF statements.

For example, to print the amount due for just clients in Pennsylvania with an A rating, you would enter

«**IF Rating = "A"**» «**IF State = "PA"**» «**Due**» «**ELSE**» N/A «**ENDIF**»«**ENDIF**»

Here, we first see if the client has a credit rating of A, the first condition. If this is true, we see if the client is in Pennsylvania. If both conditions are true, we print the amount due. Otherwise, an ELSE instruction will print N/A.

This is called a nested conditional, because one IF...ENDIF statement is completely enclosed within another one. Just make sure that each IF is matched with an ENDIF.

CREATING INTERACTIVE REPORTS

The problem with the conditionals so far is that you have to know which clients you want listed when you write the document. But what if you want clients with an A rating one day, and a B rating the next?

In this case, you can use the SET instruction to prompt the user for the rating and pause until some text is entered.

For example, the report

```
«DATA TEST1.DOC
«SET Rate = ?enter rating desired
«IF rating<>Rate»«SKIP»«ENDIF
«Name» «Address»
```

requests the credit rating of those who should be included in the report. That response is then used in the IF command, where the value of the field rating is compared with the desired rate entered by the user. If the values are not the same, the record is skipped (not merged). This particular example takes advantage of Word's ability to compare one variable directly with another in an IF instruction. Note that the closing merge command was not included in nonprinting lines.

Using field names in this way lets you perform some useful functions. For example, let's say you have an inventory database with the header record:

Item, Stock_Number, Amount_On_Hand, Reorder_Point, Cost, Vendor

You could print a list of items that must be reordered by using the following commands:

```
«DATA INVENTORY
«IF Amount_On_Hand<Reorder_Point »«Item»«Vendor»«ENDIF»
```

By combining this technique with macro functions, you can perform some sophisticated database-management tasks. For example, suppose that you want to update your mailing list by checking which clients still have the old five-digit zipcode. Use these commands:

```
«DATA MAILLIST.DOC
«IF LEN(zipcode) < 9»«SKIP»«ENDIF
```

In the next chapter, you'll see how this feature can be put to even more use for creating form letters.

SELECTING RECORDS

In addition to the methods discussed so far, you can also select records for printing by specifying the record numbers in the Print Merge Options menu.

KEY Press Esc P M O. Press R to select Records, press Tab to reach the Record Numbers option. Type the record numbers and press Enter.

The record number is the position of the record in the database. The first record in the list is record 1, the second record number 2, and so on.

To specify records, click left on Print Merge Options to display the prompt line

PRINT MERGE OPTIONS range: All Records   record numbers:

Click left on Records; then click on the Record Numbers option. You can enter specific records separated by commas (such as 3, 6, 9) or a range of records separated by a hyphen or colon (such as 4-6 or 8:12). Individual records and ranges can be combined (such as 1-6,8,9).

If you plan to use this method, arrange your database in some logical order, placing similar records together. You can also sort the records using Library Autosort, as long as the field you want to sort on is the first. Since you can print the fields in any order, this is not a real limitation.

You can also print a listing of the database with line numbers, which you can refer to when specifying record number ranges. To print line numbers, select Format Division Line-Numbers and choose the Yes option.

MERGING WITH MATH

You can also create database reports based on numeric conditions. Furthermore, numeric fields can be manipulated before you print the report. Just include the entire formula within the « and » codes that bracket the field name.

 Multiplying something by 1.06 is the same as adding 6 percent to the total.

For example, suppose that you want to display the total sale price, including a 6 percent sales tax for all sales over $100. The complete line might appear like this:

«IF Total＞100»«Total∗1.06»«ELSE»«Total»«ENDIF»

For all sales over $100, Word will perform the computation and display the result. If you merely entered «Total∗.06», you would just display 6 percent of the amount, not the percent added to the original. The rules for creating formulas are identical to those discussed in Chapter 14.

Here's a more complex example. Say you want a report consisting of four columns. The first two columns will contain the last name of each client and the amount due. If the client owes more than his or her credit, the third column will list a 10 percent penalty; otherwise, it will be 0.

The last column will contain the total due—the original amount plus any penalty. The merge document would be:

```
«DATA TEST.DOC
«Name» «Due» «IF Due>Credit»«Due*.1» «ELSE»
0«ENDIF» «IF Due>Credit»«Due*1.1»«ELSE»«Due»«ENDIF»
```

In this document, the first IF instruction prints the third column and means: "If the amount due is greater than the credit, print 10 percent of the amount due; otherwise, print 0." The second IF instruction prints the final column and means: "If the amount due is greater than the credit, print 110 percent of the amount due; otherwise, print just the amount due."

DATABASE PUBLISHING

Database publishing means printing the results of your database searches in an attactive and effective format. If your database program doesn't provide formatting and font features, you can use the powers of Word. The first task is to save your database records or reports in a format that can be read by Word. After you load or merge the document into Word, you can use all its character, paragraph, and division commands to format your report.

Most database programs provide some means of saving results in an ASCII, or plain text, format. Using dBASE, for example, enter the command

SET ALTERNATE TO filename

to save output onto the disk.

With Oracle, use the command

SPOOL filename

Whatever program you're using, check for the commands that save screen or report output to a disk file. Then load or merge the disk file into Word.

In the next chapter, we'll cover another application for databases. You'll learn how to automatically merge a database into form documents.

CHAPTER 16

4.0

KEY

- PRODUCING
- FORM
- DOCUMENTS
- USING
- DATA
- FILES

As you learned in the previous chapter, you can create Word data file documents and use them for simple database-management functions. You can also use these data files to produce form documents. Even data files from other programs, such as dBASE, can be merged into Word form documents during printing.

In this chapter, you will learn how to produce any number of form documents directly from data files. You will use many of the same techniques covered in Chapter 15.

oTYPES OF DOCUMENT MERGING

Form documents can be produced using a variety of merge techniques:

o Direct merging, in which variables are inserted by typing their names surrounded by merge codes

o Conditional merging, in which the IF command is used to determine if text or field values will be inserted into the document

o Selective merging, in which certain records in the database are skipped and not merged with the form document

o Interactive merging, in which variable information is accepted from the keyboard during the merging process

DIRECT MERGING

Figure 16.1 is an example of a form letter document that will be directly merged with a data file to produce the individual copies of the letters.

As in the merge documents we created earlier, the command

«DATA DATAFILE.DOC

is at the top of the page. This notifies Word that the DATAFILE.DOC file contains the variable information for the merge operation.

At each place where variable data is to be inserted, the name of the field is surrounded by merge codes. The document does not include

```
▌L[·········1·········2·········3·········4·········5·········]·········7·····▄
  «DATA DATAFILE.DOC

  «FIRST» «LAST»
  «ADDRESS»
  «CITY», «STATE»  «ZIP»

  Dear «SALUTATION»:

       Because of our many fine customers in «CITY», we have
  decided to open a special branch office in your area. We
  would appreciate your input in selecting the exact location.    █
       Enclosed is a list of possible sites available to us.
  Please circle the site which you feel would best serve your
  needs and those of other «CITY» customers. Return the form
  in the enclosed postage-paid mailer.

       Thank you.▌


  ─────────────────────────────────────────────────────────────
  COMMAND: Copy Delete Format Gallery Help Insert Jump Library
           Options Print Quit Replace Search Transfer Undo Window
  Edit document or press Esc to use menu
  Pg1 Co16              {}                  ?            Microsoft Word
```

○ **Figure 16.1:** *Form letter document for direct merging*

NEXT commands because form letters only use information from one
record for each copy.

During the merge operation, Word does the following:

1. It locates the DATA command to find the file containing the variable information.

2. It then reads the header record from the file. Since the record contains 13 fields, it assigns the first 13 data items to each of the field names.

3. It prints the first letter. The appropriate variable information is printed wherever its field name is encountered within merge codes. For example, the name Frederick is printed at every occurrence of «First».

4. After it prints the first letter, Word determines if another record is in the data file. If there is another record, its data is assigned to the field names, and Word prints a second letter.

5. This procedure continues until there are no records left in the data file. You can have 3, 30, or even 300 records in the data file. Word will continue merging the variable items into the letters as long as records exist.

CONDITIONAL MERGING

As discussed in Chapter 15, for conditional merging, you use the IF...ELSE...ENDIF instructions to print different text or field values based on some test or condition. You can also use conditional instructions to prevent Word from printing blank lines if a field is empty.

For example, say that we addressed our form letter document like this:

«First» «Last»
«Company»
«Address»
«City», «State» «Zip»

Since Mr. Gringold's record in our sample database contains no company name, his address would appear as:

Herman Gringold

45th Street and 6th Avenue
Oakville, MN 28612

As you can see, a blank line is printed in place of the empty Company field. You can avoid this by using an IF command on the Company line, as explained shortly.

SELECTIVE MERGING

Through selective merging, you can decide which records in the database are merged with the form document. Perhaps, for example, you only want to send a letter to all clients who have a specific credit rating, or owe you a certain amount of money.

Like conditional merging, you select records using the IF command. If the record doesn't meet the specific requirements, it is skipped—not merged—and the next record is considered.

You can use the Print Merge Options menu to select records, but you have to know in advance which records you want to print. In selective merging, Word makes the determination for you.

INTERACTIVE MERGING

Interactive merging allows you to insert text that is not in the data file itself, so different data can be added to each copy of the letter. The ASK instruction is used for this type of merging.

You've already used the SET instruction, which assigns a value that is used for the entire merge operation—for every set of variable data. The ASK instruction is similar, except that it is performed once for each record in the database.

For example, to enter a different nickname for each letter printed, you could use the command

> **«ASK nickname = ?**

or

> **«ASK nickname = ?Please enter the nickname**

Before each letter is printed, the VALUE? prompt will appear in the command area. Any text that you entered after the question mark in the ASK command will print at the bottom of the screen. Type the data that you want to print for that particular instance of the variable, and then press Enter. If you do not want to enter any variable information, just press Enter.

oA CONDITIONAL FORM LETTER

In the following exercise, you will create a form letter to all the clients in our sample database. The inside address will include a company name if it is available, but Word won't print a blank line when there is no company name.

The first paragraph will also include a company name if one exists. For example, the first letter will begin:

> **Williams Shoes has been a fine and valued customer of Aardvark ComputerWorld.**

However, the last letter, the one for the record without a Company field, will read:

> **You have been a fine and valued customer of Aardvark ComputerWorld.**

If the client owes more than the total credit, the second paragraph will read:

However, your credit limit has been reached and we cannot process any further orders. Please remit full payment as soon as possible.

If the client still has credit remaining, the letter will instead include:

We will be happy to process your orders the same day they are received.

Follow these steps to create the form letter:

1. Start Word.

2. Enter the DATA command. Remember to press Ctrl-[to enter the merge codes. We'll leave the closing » out to avoid a blank line, but press Enter after the data file name.

    «DATA DATAFILE.DOC

3. Press Alt-C to center the date.

4. Type the date, press Enter twice, and then press Alt-P.

5. Enter the first line of the address using the first name and last name fields, and then press Enter.

    «First» «Last»

6. Now use the IF command to print the company line if there is a company name in the field. By placing the ENDIF command on the line after the IF command, the carriage return is included as part of the command, so it will only be printed if a company name is present. Press Enter after each line.

    «IF Company»«Company»
    «ENDIF

7. Complete the address. Don't forget to type a comma after the City field.

    «Address»
    «City», «State» «Zip»

8. Press Enter to insert another blank line, and then type the salutation and first paragraph of the letter.

    Dear «First»:
    «IF Company»«Company» has«ELSE» You have«ENDIF» been a fine and

valued customer of Aardvark ComputerWorld. We are therefore enclosing our new 1990 catalog.

9. Enter the last paragraph. In this case, you want one message to print if there is no credit left, another to print if credit remains.

«IF Due>Credit»However, your credit limit has been reached and we cannot process any further orders. Please remit full payment as soon as possible. «ELSE»We will be happy to process your orders the same day they are received.«ENDIF»

10. Press Enter for another blank line, and then complete the letter.

Sincerely,

**Alvin A. Aardvark
President**

Figure 16.2 shows the completed form letter document.

KEY Press Esc P M P to merge the documents.

11. Click left on Print Merge Printer to produce the form documents.

```
«DATA DATAFILE.DOC
                           November 16, 1990
«First» «Last»
«IF Company»«Company»
«ENDIF
«Address»
«City», «State»   «Zip»

Dear «First»

     «IF Company»«Company» has«ELSE»You have«ENDIF» been a
fine and valued customer of Aardvark ComputerWorld. We are
therefore enclosing our new 1991 catalog.

     «IF Due>Credit»However, your credit limit has been
reached and we cannot process any further orders. Please
remit full payment as soon as possible.«ELSE»We will be
happy to process your orders the same day they are
received.«ENDIF»

Sincerely,


Alvin A. Aardvark
President
```

o **Figure 16.2:** *Complete conditional form letter document*

oUSING SELECTIVE MERGING

It is a simple matter to turn the current form letter into a selective one by adding one line. For example, if you insert this line

«IF credit = 0» «SKIP» «ENDIF

right after the DATA command, no letters will be merged and sent to clients without credit. Any records meeting the condition (the amount of credit is 0) will be skipped.

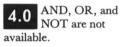

As with database merge documents, you can use the logical operators AND, OR, and NOT to customize your form documents. If you included this statement, for example:

«IF credit = 0 OR due >500» «SKIP» «ENDIF

no letters will be produced for clients who either have no credit or owe more than $500.00.

You can also use the macro functions when merging form letters. Suppose that you have a field called Telephone that has the first three digits representing the area code. You would like to send letters to people living in the same general geographic area, but one single zip code or city doesn't include the whole area. So you decide to send the letter to everyone in the same area code. Use this statement:

«IF MID(telephone, 1,3)< >215» «SKIP» «ENDIF

oAN INTERACTIVE FORM LETTER

Let's use the interactive SET and ASK commands to personalize the form letter that we just created. In this case, we want to insert the date of the letter before each merge operation. We also want the opportunity to place the client's nickname in the salutation. Of course, if the client doesn't have a nickname, then the first name should be printed.

We'll use the SET command to enter the same current date on each letter and the ASK command to enter the individual nicknames. We'll then enter the ASK command after the «DATA DATAFILE command, so the ASK prompt will display the first and last name of the client whose letter will be printed next. If no nickname is entered from the keyboard, Word will insert the first name, as listed in the data file.

Follow these steps to make our form letter interactive:

1. Add a SET command to input the date from the keyboard. Insert this command on its own line under the «DATA DATAFILE instruction.

    «SET date = ?Enter today's date

2. Insert an ASK command to print a nickname at the salutation. Again, insert the line after the «DATA DATAFILE instruction. The » at the end of this line closes off the variable Last, not the ASK command, so no blank line will appear.

    «ASK nickname = ?nickname for «First» «Last»

3. Add the «date» variable in the letter itself. Delete the date that you entered previously and type

    «date»

4. Change the salutation to print the nickname. Delete the current salutation line, and then type

    Dear «IF nickname»«nickname» «ELSE» «First»«ENDIF»:

KEY Press Esc P M P
to merge
the letters.

5. Click left on Print Merge Print; then watch the bottom of the screen. You'll be asked to enter the date, then the nickname for each person on the list as the letters are merged.

As this example shows, Word allows you to create truly "personalized" documents.

oFORMATTING VARIABLES

Variable information can be formatted like any other text. It can be underlined, printed in boldface or italics, or even appear as subscripts or superscripts.

The format of the first character controls the format of the entire variable field. After you type the merge codes and variable name, place the cursor on the first character of the field name. Then use the appropriate speed key. The only difference in the formatting method is that you must press the speed key twice to format the first character. To print the company name in boldface, for example, place the cursor on the *C* in «Company», and then press Alt-B twice.

oMERGING WORD WITH DATABASE PROGRAMS

Word certainly has limitations as a database-management program. But this is no reason to give up its powerful features as a word processor and form-document generator. If you are already using a database-management program, continue to do so. You can use your database files to create form documents and reports with Word.

This section describes how dBASE files can be combined with Word documents. Even if you are using some other database package, take the time to read the information presented here. You'll probably find that your software can be used in the same way.

Combining these two fine programs must be done in several steps:

1. Prepare the database file for merging.
2. Create a header record file.
3. Write the merge document.
4. Print the documents.

PREPARING THE DATABASE FILE

Let's say that you have a monthly transaction file created with the dBASE database program. Each record contains the name and address of the customer, along with a list of items purchased during the month. One field also contains the total of all purchases for that period.

The fields include Customer, Lastname, Firstname, Address, City, State, Zip, Phone, and Total. There is also a series of fields containing the names, quantity, and total price of each customer's purchases. These are called Item1, Amount1, Price1 through Item15, Amount15, and Price15.

At the end of the month, you want to send each client an invoice. You don't want to take the time to create a dBASE command file for this purpose. Anyway, you'd like to use the special features of Word and that new laser printer.

The first step is to convert the database file into a format that Word can use. Follow this procedure:

1. Start your version of dBASE.

2. Type **USE**, and then type the name of the database file (e.g., **USE Clients**).

3. Press Enter.

4. Type

   COPY TO CLIENTS.DOC DELIMITED WITH "

5. Press Enter. dBASE will make a copy of your data file under the name you entered. Each field that does not contain numbers will be enclosed in quotation marks, just in case it contains any commas.

6. Type **QUIT**.

7. Press Enter.

The database file is now ready for merging. The next step is to create a special header file.

CREATING THE HEADER FILE

The only thing missing from the dBASE file is the header record, which Word needs to merge the variable information. Since it is not part of the database file, an external file containing only the header record must be created. Follow these steps:

1. Start Word.

2. Type a paragraph containing only the field names from the database file.

   Customer, Lastname, Firstname, Address, City, State, Zip, Phone, Total, Item1, Amount1, Price1, Item2, Amount2, Price2, Item3, Amount3, Price3, Item4, Amount4, Price4, Item5, Amount5, Price5,

Item6, Amount6, Price6, Item7, Amount7, Price7, Item8, Amount8, Price8, Item9, Amount9, Price9, Item10, Amount10, Price10, Item11, Amount11, Price11, Item12, Amount12, Price12, Item13, Amount13, Price13, Item14, Amount14, Price14, Item15, Amount15, Price15

 Press Ctrl-F10, type **Header**, and then press Enter twice.

3. Click left on Transfer Save, type **Header**, click on the command line title, and then click on SUMMARY.

The final step is to create the merge document.

CREATING THE MERGE DOCUMENT

The final document will contain all the variable names and standard text included in the invoices. If your printer is capable, you can also include the necessary font or color changes to print your letterhead as the invoice is being printed.

Our sample invoice form document will also include a message variable. You can use this to add special remarks such as ''Thank you for your last payment'' or ''Pay up creep'' to individual invoices.

Follow these steps to create the sample invoice merge document:

1. Use Transfer Clear All to clear the current document from the screen.

2. Enter the DATA command. In this case, the instruction must include the name of the separate header file as well as the database document.

    «DATA HEADER.DOC,CLIENTS.DOC

3. Insert a SET instruction to input the date from the keyboard.

    «SET date = ?Enter the date

4. Use an ASK command to insert any special message or reminder at the bottom of the invoice.

    «ASK message = ?Special message for «Customer»

5. If you are not using letterhead paper, enter the name and address of your company. In our sample invoice, this information is centered. Depending on your printer, you may be able to select a larger type size or more elaborate font.

6. Press Alt-C to center the date.

7. Enter the date variable.

   «date»

8. Press Alt-P.

9. Complete the inside address using the field names from the header record.

   «Customer»
   «Address»
   «City», «State» «Zip»

   Attention: «Firstname» «Lastname»

10. Format the name of the client to print boldface.

    a. Place the cursor on the *F* in Firstname and press Alt-B twice.

    b. Place the cursor on the *L* in Lastname and press Alt-B twice.

11. Use the Format Border Lines command, and select Yes for the Below option to separate the billing area from the address.

12. Set tab stops for the Item Purchased, Quantity, and Price columns to appear on the invoice.

    a. Make sure the tab type letter on the ruler is L and the leader character is blank.

    b. Click left halfway between the left margin and the 1 on the ruler.

    c. Click left on the 3 on the ruler.

    d. Click on the tab type character until a D appears.

    e. Click left on the first dot past the 5 on the ruler.

    (With version 4.0, click left on Transfer, then right on Tab. Click left halfway between the left margin and the 1 on the ruler; then click left on the 3 on the ruler. Click left on Decimal for the alignment, click left on the first dot past the 5 on the ruler, and then click on the command line title.)

13. Enter the column headings. Press Tab before you type each one.

    Item Purchased   Quantity   Price

KEY Press Alt-F1. Type **0.5L, 3L,** and **5.1D**; then press Enter. (With version 4.0, press Alt-F1, type **0.5**, and press Ins. Type 3 and press Ins. Type **5.1**, press Tab D, and then press Enter.)

14. Press Enter, then the up arrow. This ensures that the tab stop you just set will be in force when you're ready to enter the merge fields.

15. Use Format Border Lines again to place a line under the headings.

16. Press the down arrow.

17. Enter the first line of the billing area. Remember to press Tab to enter the variables in the correct position.

    «IF Item1»«Item1»«Amount 1»
    $«Price1»«ENDIF»

18. Enter the remaining lines for each of the 15 possible items by copying the first line and pressing Ins. Then, use the Replace command to change the numbers in each line.

19. Enter another line across the page.

20. Add the total line.

    Total $«Total»

21. Place the cursor on the *T* in Total and press Alt-U twice to format the total to print underlined.

22. Insert the message variable.

    «message»

23. Place the cursor on the *m* in message and press Alt-I twice to format the message to print in italics. Figure 16.3 shows the completed invoice merge document.

24. Click left on Print Merge Printer.

25. Respond to the date prompt, and then press Enter.

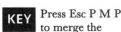 Press Esc P M P to merge the invoices.

26. Respond to the message prompt, and then press Enter. The first invoice will print. You will be prompted for a special message before each invoice is printed.

To avoid printing blank lines when less than 15 items are ordered, delete the closing merge codes on each line.

In this section, you created an invoice form to merge data from a dBASE file. Using the same techniques, you can create form documents

```
«DATA   HEADER.DOC, CLIENTS.DOC
«SET date =?Enter the date
«ASK message =?Special message for «Customer»
                Aardvark ComputerWorld
                412 West Goshen Avenue
                Buckwheat AR 21980

                        «date»

«Customer»
«Address»
«City», «State»   «Zip»

Attention: «Firstname» «Lastname»
```

Item Purhased	Quantity	Due
«IF Item1»«Item1»	«Amount1»	$«Price1»«ENDIF»
«IF Item2»«Item2»	«Amount2»	$«Price2»«ENDIF»
«IF Item3»«Item3»	«Amount3»	$«Price3»«ENDIF»
«IF Item4»«Item4»	«Amount4»	$«Price4»«ENDIF»
«IF Item5»«Item5»	«Amount5»	$«Price5»«ENDIF»
«IF Item6»«Item6»	«Amount6»	$«Price6»«ENDIF»
«IF Item7»«Item7»	«Amount7»	$«Price7»«ENDIF»
«IF Item8»«Item8»	«Amount8»	$«Price8»«ENDIF»
«IF Item9»«Item9»	«Amount9»	$«Price9»«ENDIF»
«IF Item10»«Item10»	«Amount10»	$«Price10»«ENDIF»
«IF Item11»«Item11»	«Amount11»	$«Price11»«ENDIF»
«IF Item12»«Item12»	«Amount12»	$«Price12»«ENDIF»
«IF Itcm13»«Item13»	«Amount13»	$«Price13»«ENDIF»
«IF Item14»«Item14»	«Amount14»	$«Price14»«ENDIF»
«IF Item15»«Item15»	«Amount15»	$«Price15»«ENDIF»
Total$		$«Total»

```
«message»
```

o **Figure 16.3:** *The completed invoice merge document*

with any database file. And it's easier to create a form document than it is to write a database command file.

USING WORD WITH A DATABASE PROGRAM

There are many ways that you can take advantage of the combined powers of Word and your database program. For example, use your database to sort your file by zip code before merge printing. Bulk-rate mail is less expensive when delivered to the post office in zip-code order.

Use the functions of your database to select certain clients for the mailing. Send special mailings to good customers by using

LOCATE FOR Total > 1500

Or mail reminders to customers who haven't ordered for some time with

LOCATE FOR Lastorder < 01/12/86

Word and your database program can be an efficient team.

CHAPTER 17

- **PERFORMING**
- **ADVANCED**
- **MERGING**
- **OPERATIONS**

4.0

KEY

You can use merge codes, templates, and glossaries to assemble a document from various parts. All three methods, however, have limitations:

o Merge codes are most efficient for inserting short variables into form documents. You must prepare the header record carefully and check the data file to ensure that individual records contain the correct number of entries. Within the merge document, the variable names must be spelled exactly as they are spelled in the header record.

o Templates are most efficient when the form document requires a specific format. Using templates is time-consuming because the variable information must be manually typed into each document before it is printed.

o Glossaries can be used to merge boilerplate paragraphs into a document. But again, the assembly process must be done manually. You must first load the correct glossary, type the name of each paragraph (if you remember it), and press F3.

In this chapter, we'll cover more efficient methods for merging documents.

oWORKING WITH LONG DOCUMENTS

Even with a fine program such as Word, it is often difficult to work with long documents. Large documents take longer to save and recall from the disk. Even format changes take longer. But there is a more crucial issue involved for floppy disk users.

As you work on a large document, portions of it are stored in special files on your Word program disk in drive A. These are temporary files that contain parts of your document that do not fit in your computer's memory. When you finally save your text and quit Word, these files are erased from the program disk.

However, the Word program disk does not have a great deal of room for these files. As your document grows larger and these temporary files get near their limit, Word flashes the warning

SAVE

at the bottom of the screen. If you ignore this warning, you may run out of room on the program disk and possibly lose your document.

You can avoid this problem by dividing a large document into smaller sections. Each section is typed and saved as a separate file, and then merged together during printing.

oUSING THE INCLUDE COMMAND

Individual documents are merged into one by using the INCLUDE command. The basic format for this command is

«**INCLUDE** *document name*»

Notice that beginning and ending merge codes (Ctrl-[and Ctrl-]) are used. (With Include, the closing merge code will not cause any blank lines in the merged document.) The INCLUDE command is followed by the name of one of the documents. During a merge operation, Word will insert the document named in the command at that location.

There are four different ways that the INCLUDE command can be used:

o In assembly templates

o Within text

o With multiple data files

o Interactively

This section explains how to use each of these methods.

USING ASSEMBLY TEMPLATES

Perhaps you just completed a major report. Heeding my warnings, you typed each section as a separate document. On your disk are PART1.DOC, PART2.DOC, PART3.DOC, and PART4.DOC.

To print the report as one document, you would create a separate file containing the following text:

«**INCLUDE PART1.DOC**»
«**INCLUDE PART2.DOC**»

```
«INCLUDE PART3.DOC»
«INCLUDE PART4.DOC»
```

Then you would print this document using the Print Merge command. Word would recall each part from the disk in the sequence given and print the report as one document.

USING THE INCLUDE COMMAND WITHIN TEXT

The INCLUDE command can also be used within a document. You can create a series of documents containing standard boilerplate text. Give each document a name relating to its contents. For example, name text about your hours of operation HOURS.DOC and text about your warranty information WARRANTY.DOC. When you need that information in a document, place the cursor at the appropriate place and type «INCLUDE HOURS» or «INCLUDE WARRANTY».

USING THE INCLUDE COMMAND WITH MULTIPLE DATA FILES

For maximum flexibility, the INCLUDE command can be used in conjunction with data files. The "included" document can contain merge commands and variable names. The variable names, however, must reference variables in the data file named in the original document. You cannot have a second «DATA» instruction within the included text. Even with this limitation, the INCLUDE command can be used to efficiently process multiple files during a merge operation.

To demonstrate this flexibility, we'll use the INCLUDE command in conjunction with the data file that we created in Chapter 15. Since this file is used for several merge documents, it contains only basic information about the clients.

The Aardvark ComputerWorld Company also maintains a separate file for each client. The client's last name is used as the file name. This file contains a running account of employee training services that must be reported to the client at the end of every month. As groups of the client's employees attend training seminars, the file is updated.

You will use the data file, the individual files, and the INCLUDE command to process the monthly reports.

Creating Client Files

First, we must create the individual files for each client. Follow these steps:

1. Start Word.

2. Create the client file for Frederick Rogers. Type the following information.

10/15	**2.25**	**Word processing**
10/22	**4.50**	**Database**
10/24	**2.25**	**Word processing**

3. Click left on Transfer Save and type **Rogers**.

4. Click on the command line title; then click on SUMMARY.

5. Click left on Transfer, and then click right on Clear to clear the current document.

6. Create the client file for Adam Chesin. Type the following text.

10/01	**4.50**	**Database**
10/07	**2.25**	**Database**
10/14	**2.25**	**Spreadsheet**
10/21	**2.25**	**Word processing**
10/28	**2.25**	**DOS**

7. Click left on Transfer Save and type **Chesin**.

8. Click on the command line title; then click on SUMMARY.

9. Click left on Transfer, and then click right on Clear to clear the current document.

10. Create the client file for Herman Gringold. Type the following text.

10/02	**2.25**	**Accounting**
10/08	**2.25**	**Ledger**
10/15	**2.25**	**DOS**
10/22	**5.00**	**Graphics**

11. Click left on Transfer Save and type **Gringold**.

KEY Press Ctrl-F10, type **Rogers**, and press Enter twice. Then press Esc T C A.

KEY Press Ctrl-F10, type **Chesin**, and press Enter twice. Then press Esc T C A.

KEY Press Ctrl-F10, type **Gringold**, and press Enter twice. Then press Esc T C A.

12. Click on the command line title, and then click on SUMMARY.

13. Click left on Transfer; then click right on Clear to clear the current document.

Processing the Master File

Notice that the individual client files do not contain the name, address, or any other information about the client. Their only link to the client, in fact, is the name of the document itself. Repeating the client information in each file would be repetitive and defeat the purpose of computerizing such information.

Now that both the data file and the individual client files are created, let's create the merge document to process the monthly reports to all the clients.

1. Enter the data command.

   «DATA DATAFILE

2. Enter a SET command to accept the date of the reports.

   «SET date = ?Enter date of the report

3. Enter a SET command for the month.

   «SET month = ?Enter month ending

4. Enter the date and client variables for the top of the form.

   «date»

   **«First» «Last»
   «IF Company»«Company»
   «ENDIF
   «Address»
   «City», «State» «Zip»**

   Dear «First»:

5. Type the rest of the report.

   In accordance with our contract, Aardvark ComputerWorld has supplied training and consultation services to «IF Company» «Company»«ELSE»your employees«ENDIF» during the month of «month».

**Below is an itemized account of services provided. As always, it has
been our pleasure to work with «IF Company»«Company»«ELSE»your
company «ENDIF» and its employees.**

Date   Hours   Subject

«INCLUDE «Last» »

**Thank you for your continued support. Please keep in mind that our
training should be renewed at the end of this year.**

Sincerely,

**Alvin A. Aardvark
President**

Figure 17.1 shows the completed document.

6. Click left on Print Merge Printer to print the reports.

KEY Press Esc P M P
to print the
reports.

After the Print Merge command is issued, Word prepares for the first
letter. It requests keyboard entry of the date and month. Then it assigns
the data in the first record to the variables in the header record.

The inside address, salutation, and beginning paragraph of the first
letter are printed. Using the IF instruction, either the company name or
some other text is printed at appropriate locations. The three column
headings are printed under the paragraph.

Word then encounters the «INCLUDE «Last» » instruction. When
the first record was read, the name Rogers was assigned to the last name
variable. The program will insert Rogers wherever «Last» is found in
the text. So this instruction really means «INCLUDE ROGERS».

The ROGERS.DOC file is recalled from the disk and printed. Then
the final paragraph and closing are printed. Since this is a merge operation, Word repeats the process. This time, the name Chesin is assigned
to the last name variable. During printing, the CHESIN.DOC file is
included in the document.

Finally, the third and last record is read. The name Gringold is assigned to the variable, and the GRINGOLD.DOC file is printed with the letter.

The key to merging multiple data files is using a variable name inside the INCLUDE command itself. Note the two ending merge codes at the end of the INCLUDE command. One completes the field name, the other the INCLUDE command.

Expanding Data File Uses

The use of data file variables in INCLUDE commands can easily be expanded.

Perhaps you have different pricing structures for geographic areas.

```
«DATA DATAFILE.DOC
«SET date=?Enter date of the report
«SET month=?Enter month ending
                           «date»

«First» «Last»
«IF Company» «Company»
«ENDIF
«Address»
«City», «State» «Zip»

Dear «First»:

     In accordance with our contract, Aardvark Computer-
World has supplied training and consultation services to «IF
Company»«Company»«ELSE»your employees«ENDIF» during the
month of «month».
     Below is an itemized account of services provided.
As always, it has been our pleasure to work with «IF
Company»«Company»«ELSE»your company«ENDIF» and its
employees.

Date              Hours                 Subject

«INCLUDE «Last»»

     Thank you for your continued support. Please keep in
mind that our training should be renewed at the end of this
year.

Sincerely,

Alvin A. Aardvark
President
```

○ **Figure 17.1:** *Completed merge document for use with the data files and the INCLUDE command*

Add a new variable name, such as Location, to the header record. Then add a variable (such as North, South, East, or West) to each record, identifying the geographic location of the client. Finally, create separate price structure documents for each geographic area, and name them North, South, East, and West. Merge the appropriate price structure into a document with the command

«INCLUDE «Location» »

The INCLUDE command can also be combined with IF instructions. You might have a standard pricing schedule and one based on a 10 percent discount for clients who have a better credit rating. This is easily handled with the command

«IF Rating = "A"»«INCLUDE Discount»«ELSE» «INCLUDE Standard»«ENDIF»

INTERACTIVE ASSEMBLY

You can use the SET and ASK instructions with the INCLUDE command to assemble documents interactively.

One use of this combination of commands is to speed up the printing process. Printing a number of documents in one session can be time-consuming. You load each one, and then give the Print command. But there is an easier way. First, create the following document:

«ASK file_to_print = ?Enter document to be printed
«INCLUDE «file_to_print» »

Then click on Print Merge. The command line will display

VALUE?
Enter document to be printed

Type in the name of a document, and it will be inserted into the INCLUDE command and printed. Word will continue to request a document name after each document is printed until you press the Esc key at the VALUE? prompt.

The SET instruction can be used in a similar manner. The document

«SET file_to_print = ?Enter document to be printed
«INCLUDE «file_to_print» »

will request and print only one document with each Print Merge command issued.

oBUILDING LOOKUP TABLES

Lookup tables can be very useful in merging operations. *Lookup table* is a programmer's term for a series of values that can be searched through when needed. For instance, here's a typical shipping rate table:

Area	Charge
1	1.35
2	1.87
3	2.05
4	2.76
5	3.15

An invoicing program would locate the customer's area in the customer record, and then look up the shipping charge in the table. By using a lookup table, rather than placing the shipping charges directly in the customer database, you avoid having to edit all your records if the shipping charges change. You just need to update the figures in the table.

Here are the macro commands that would create the sample shipping rate table:

```
«DATA CLIENTS.DOC
«SET ship«1» = 1.35
«SET ship«2» = 2.35
«SET ship«3» = 3.35
«SET ship«4» = 4.35
«SET ship«5» = 5.35
```

This "loads" the lookup table, placing the value 1.35 in variable ship1, the value 2.35 in variable ship2, and so on.

You can have Word use a lookup table to insert information in form letters. For example, suppose that one of the fields in your database is named Area, and it contains a number from 1 to 5. You could add this line to the form letter:

Shipping Charge $«ship«area»»

and when you merge the documents, Word will insert the proper shipping charge based on the customer's area.

You create lookup tables using Word's array structure.

oCREATING MENUS FOR MERGING

If you produce a number of form letters during the year, keeping track of them all can be a burden. Here is an example of a macro that displays a menu of choices in its own window. It accepts your choice, loads the appropriate document in the other window, merges the documents, and finishes by clearing all windows.

```
<esc>wsv40<tab>y<enter>
<space 5>Macro Menu<enter 2>
1.<tab>Print invoices<enter>
2.<tab>Print request letters<enter>
3.<tab>Print thank you letters<enter>
4.<tab>Print love letters<enter>
5.<tab>End Menu<enter 2>
Make your selection<enter>
then press enter:<space 4>
«ASK which = ?Select macro function»
«IF which = 2»<F1><esc>tlrequests<enter>N<esc>pmp«ENDIF»
«IF which = 3»<F1><esc>tlthanks<enter>N<esc>pmp«ENDIF»
«IF which = 4»<F1><esc>tllove<enter>N<esc>pmp«ENDIF»
<esc>wc2<enter>n
<esc>wc1<enter>n
```

oUSING PREPRINTED FORMS

Insurance forms, invoices, client records, membership records, and patient reports are examples of typical business forms you can create and fill out with Word.

Back in Chapter 9, you learned how to create an alignment grid for printing on preprinted forms. That is a good technique if you are using someone else's form. But if you have your own forms for your business or hobby, you can use the merge operation to great advantage, even if you arc using preprinted blank forms.

Let's say that you want to use Word to both print the basic form and fill it out. You can do this automatically by merging the form template with a database, or manually by entering the data directly into the form at print time. This section will explain both procedures.

AUTOMATIC FORMS GENERATION

Automatic forms generation is really just another application of the standard form document. Create a blank form, inserting the DATA and other merge codes where you want information from the database to be placed. You can use ASK and SET instructions if you want to enter data interactively. Use the Format Border menu options, if desired, to draw a border around the box and lines under the text, as explained in the next chapter. Set tabs for each of the blank fields, taking care to leave enough space to hold the longest possible variable. Figure 17.2 is an example of such a form.

The data file of patients used with the sample form would appear something like this:

> **Last, First, Address, City, State, Zip, Carrier,**
> **Number, Member, Relation, Proc**
> **Chesin, Adam, 365 Spring Street,Dallas, TX, 09812,**
> **BC/BS, 3456A, "Chesin, Nancy", Mother**

To fill out the forms, you would just load the blank form and use the Print Merge Printer or Print Merge Document command. The information from the database would then be inserted into the forms and printed.

```
  D[·········1·········2·········3·········4·········5·········]·········7·····
    «DATA PATIENTS.DOC»█
    ┌──────────────────────────────────────────────────────────┐
    │                      Dr. Frank N. Stein                    │
    │                       Plastic Surgery                      │
    │                    Transylvania, PA 19006                  │
    ├──────────────────────────────────────────────────────────┤
    │  Patient: «Last» «First»                                   │
    ├──────────────────────────────────────────────────────────┤
    │  Address: «Address»                                        │
    ├──────────────────────────────────────────────────────────┤                █
    │  City: «City»            State: «State»     Zip: «Zip»     │
    ├──────────────────────────────────────────────────────────┤
    │  Insurance Data                                            │
    ├──────────────────────────────────────────────────────────┤
    │  Carrier: «Carrier»              Number: «Number»          │
    ├──────────────────────────────────────────────────────────┤
    │  Member's Name: «Member»         Relation: «Relation»      │
    ├──────────────────────────────────────────────────────────┤
    │  Physician's Number: 666         Procedure No.: «Proc»     │
    └──────────────────────────────────────────────────────────┘
  COMMAND: Copy Delete Format Gallery Help Insert Jump Library
           Options Print Quit Replace Search Transfer Undo Window
  Edit document or press Esc to use menu
  Pg1 Co20           {→}                    ?              Microsoft Word
```

o **Figure 17.2:** *A form for merging*

FILLING OUT FORMS MANUALLY

The process for filling out each form manually (not merging them with a database) is very similar to automatic form generation, except that you use only the closing merge code » at each location, with no DATA command or variable names. When you want to fill out a form, press Ctrl-> to move forward from field to field, or Ctrl-< to move backward. Enter all the codes as hidden text. When filling out the form, select Yes for the Show Hidden Text option on the Options menu and No for the Print Hidden Text option on the Print Options menu.

As an example, we'll create a form for a sample membership certificate, and then fill it out.

1. Start Word.

2. Set tabs where you want to print the prompts.

> **KEY** Press Alt-F1, type **3L** and **4.6L**, and then press Enter. (With version 4.0, press Alt-F1, type **3**, press Ins, type **4.6**, and then press Enter.)

    a. Make sure that the tab type character is set to L and the leader character is blank.

    b. Click left on the 3 on the ruler.

    c. Click left on the sixth dot past the 4 on the ruler.

    (With version 4.0, click left on Format; then click right on Tab. Click left on the 3 on the ruler; then click left on the sixth dot after the 4. Click on the command line title.)

3. Type the short form shown in Figure 17.3, pressing Tab to space between entries on the same line.

4. To add the lines and boxes, click both on the selection bar to select the entire document. Then click left on Format Border Box, and click on the command line title.

> **KEY** Press Shift-F10. Press Esc F B B, and then press Enter. Press Ctrl-F10, type **Member**, and then press Enter twice.

5. Click left on Transfer Save and type **Member**.

6. Click on the command line title; then click on SUMMARY.

7. Format each of the codes (») as hidden text. Select each one, and then press Alt-E twice.

Now let's fill out a sample membership certificate for a person who just paid his dues. If you make a mistake after moving to another field, press Ctrl-< to move back a field. If you press Ctrl-> on the last field, the cursor moves to the first field in the document.

```
 D[········1·········2·········3·········4·········5·········]·········7·····
                       Membership Certificate
        ┌─────────────────────────────────────────────────────┐
        │ Name    : »                        Year: »           │
        │ Address: »                                           │
        │ City    : »                   State: »     Zip: »    │
        │                                                      │
        │ Member in good standing for the year stated above    │
        └─────────────────────────────────────────────────────┘     ▮
          ▯



 ───────────────────────────────────────────────────────────────────────
 COMMAND: Copy Delete Format Gallery Help Insert Jump Library
          Options Print Quit Replace Search Transfer Undo Window
 Edit document or press Esc to use menu
 Pg1 Co1            {·}                  ?                Microsoft Word
```

○ **Figure 17.3:** *A form for manual completion*

8. Press Ctrl-PgUp to place the cursor at the start of the document.

9. Press Ctrl->. The cursor moves to the first code.

10. Type **Bill Watson**.

11. Press Ctrl-> to move to the next entry, and type **1990**.

12. Press Ctrl-> and type **45 Oakleaf Road**.

13. Press Ctrl-> and type **OH**.

14. Press Ctrl-> and type **20123**.

15. Click right on Print to print the document. Don't forget to set the Hidden Text option to No in the Print Options menu.

KEY Press Ctrl-F8 to print the form.

If you already created a form using merge codes and variable names, you can still fill it out manually. Just format all the merge codes and variable names as hidden text, and then follow the procedure described above for filling out the form.

Using Preprinted Forms

If you are using a preprinted form, you only want to print the variable information. This is just as easy to do. Start by designing a duplicate of the form on the screen. Use the alignment grid method explained in Chapter 9 if you have to. Test the template by printing several copies directly over your preprinted forms, and adjust the placement of the elements as necessary.

When the blanks on the screen document align with those on the printed form, mark all screen text, markers, titles, and lines as hidden text and select No for the Hidden Text option on the Print Options menu.

Then you can fill out the form (using either the automatic or manual methods explained above) and print it on the preprinted form. The variable information will print in the correct locations.

This chapter has explained how to use Word's merging capabilities to produce any number of form documents. When you're planning form letters, consider the use of database techniques. Create a master data file of variable information. Add more individualized data, such as transaction records, to separate documents saved under the client's name. Use the data file to recall each client in sequence, and then use the INCLUDE command to merge the remaining text.

In the next chapter, you'll learn how to use special characters to create forms and charts.

CHAPTER 18

- USING
- SPECIAL
- CHARACTERS

4.0

KEY

In this chapter, you'll learn how to use the entire IBM character set to print foreign-language and graphic characters, as well as how to draw lines and boxes.

The *character set* is the collection of letters, numbers, and symbols that can be displayed on the screen. This includes the familiar alphabetic, punctuation, and numeric characters found on every standard type-writer. It also includes foreign-language characters, Greek and mathematical symbols, and graphic symbols and characters.

oTESTING YOUR PRINTER

Unfortunately, although the entire character set can be displayed on the screen of your computer, not every printer can reproduce them. Some characters, such as accented foreign-language characters, can be reproduced on most dot-matrix printers and laser printers. But the special graphic characters needed to produce charts are much harder to reproduce. Even some of the more popular "graphics" printers will not reproduce these characters correctly.

Before continuing, test your printer to see what it will reproduce. In the following test procedure, you will be given a series of keystrokes to press. In each case, press and hold down the Alt key while you type the number shown, and then release the Alt key. The special character will not appear until the Alt key is released.

Follow this procedure to test your printer:

 Use only the keys on the numeric keypad to the right of the keyboard. Press NumLock and be sure that the characters NL appear on the status line.

1. Start Word.

2. Press the following keys. Press the spacebar after each Alt-key combination to insert a space in between the characters. After you've entered the codes, your screen should look like Figure 18.1.

Alt-1	Alt-130	Alt-168	Alt-180
Alt-16	Alt-150	Alt-176	Alt-186
Alt-24	Alt-160	Alt-177	Alt-189
Alt-25	Alt-164	Alt-178	Alt-227
Alt-129	Alt-165	Alt-179	Alt-251

KEY Press Ctrl-F8 to print the test.

3. Click right on Print to print the document.

If your printer produced all the characters that appeared on the screen, you'll be able to reproduce the graphics shown in this chapter.

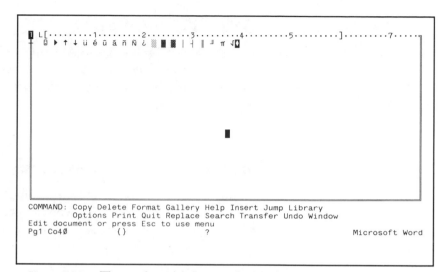

```
█ L[·········1·········2·········3·········4·········5·········]·········7·····
  ╘ ▶ ↑ ↓ ü é û ä ñ Ñ ¿ ▒ ■ ▓ | ┤ ║ ┘ π √█



                                    ▮



COMMAND: Copy Delete Format Gallery Help Insert Jump Library
         Options Print Quit Replace Search Transfer Undo Window
Edit document or press Esc to use menu
Pg1 Co4Ø            {}                  ?                    Microsoft Word
```

o **Figure 18.1:** *The sample special characters for the printer test*

If your printer only produced the accented foreign-language characters, you cannot produce charts or graphs with Word. However, you can print documents using the foreign-language character set.

If your printer didn't produce any of the characters correctly—sorry, but you might as well go on to the next chapter.

oUSING THE CHARACTER SET

Let's take a look at all of the special characters that Word can display. They can be divided into five categories:

- o Special symbols: numbers 1 through 30
- o Regular keyboard characters: numbers 32 through 127
- o Foreign-language characters: numbers 128 through 168
- o Graphic characters: numbers 169 through 223
- o Greek and mathematical symbols: numbers 224 through 255

SPECIAL SYMBOLS

The characters displayed with Alt-1 to Alt-30, shown in Figure 18.2, are special-purpose graphic symbols. Numbers 9 through 14 and 31 aren't shown because they're reserved by the system for special functions. Alt-9, for example, performs a tab function; Alt-12 creates a new page.

REGULAR CHARACTERS

Using Alt-32 through Alt-127 simply displays the normal characters shown on the keyboard. Although you can press Alt-65 to display the letter A, for instance, using the A key is much more efficient.

FOREIGN-LANGUAGE CHARACTERS

The most common use of the special character set is for typing foreign-language and accented characters. With other word-processing programs, accented characters are produced by printing one character, backspacing, and printing the accent. The complete character is usually displayed only on the printed page, not on the screen.

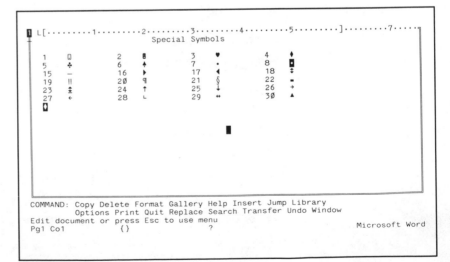

o **Figure 18.2:** *Special symbols*

Word, however, will display every foreign-language character available in the IBM character set. Each accented character will appear on the screen with its accent in the appropriate place.

Alt-128 through Alt-168 will provide the foreign-language characters illustrated in Figure 18.3.

GRAPHIC SYMBOLS

Alt-169 through Alt-223 produce graphic characters, as shown in Figure 18.4. These are used to create line drawings, boxes, and simple charts. Most of them produce a small section of either single or double lines. Word itself combines some of these characters to form the text window border.

GREEK AND MATHEMATICAL SYMBOLS

Alt-224 through Alt-254 produce the Greek and mathematical symbols shown in Figure 18.5. Notice that Alt-244 and Alt-245 can be combined to make one larger character. To create the symbol, press Alt-244, then move the cursor directly under it on the next line, and press Alt-245.

```
L[·········1·········2·········3·········4·········5·········]·········7·····
                     Foreign-Language Characters

     128  Ç        129  ü        130  é        131  â
     132  ä        133  à        134  å        135  ç
     136  ê        137  ë        138  è        139  ï
     140  î        141  ì        142  Ä        143  Å
     144  É        145  æ        146  Æ        147  ô
     148  ö        149  ò        150  û        151  ù
     152  ÿ        153  Ö        154  Ü        155  ¢
     156  £        157  ¥        158  ₧        159  ƒ
     160  á        161  í        162  ó        163  ú
     164  ñ        165  Ñ        166  ª        167  º
     168  ¿



                                        ■


COMMAND: Copy Delete Format Gallery Help Insert Jump Library
         Options Print Quit Replace Search Transfer Undo Window
Edit document or press Esc to use menu
Pg1 Co1              {4}              ?              Microsoft Word
```

o **Figure 18.3:** *Foreign-language characters*

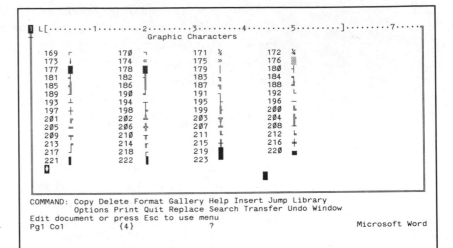

```
 L[········1········2·········3·········4········5········]·········7······
                    Graphic Characters

     169   ┌       170   ┐      171   ½      172   ¼
     173   ┤       174   «      175   »      176   ▓
     177   █       178   ▓      179   │      180   ┤
     181   ┤       182   ▓      183   ┐      184   ┤
     185   ╣       186   ║      187   ┐      188   ┘
     189   ┘       190   ┘      191   ┐      192   └
     193   ┴       194   ┬      195   ├      196   ─
     197   ┼       198   ╞      199   ┟      200   ╚
     201   ╔       202   ╩      203   ╦      204   ╠
     205   ═       206   ╬      207   ╧      208   ╨
     209   ╥       210   ╥      211   ╘      212   ╙
     213   ╒       214   ╓      215   ╫      216   ╪
     217   ┘       218   ┌      219   █      220   ▄
     221   ▌       222   ▐      223   ▀
     ▓

COMMAND: Copy Delete Format Gallery Help Insert Jump Library
         Options Print Quit Replace Search Transfer Undo Window
Edit document or press Esc to use menu
Pg1 Co1              {4}                 ?                  Microsoft Word
```

o **Figure 18.4:** *Graphic characters*

```
 L[········1········2·········3·········4········5·········]·········7······
                 Greek and Mathematical Characters

     224   α      225   β      226   Γ      227   π
     228   Σ      229   σ      230   μ      231   τ
     232   Φ      233   Θ      234   Ω      235   δ
     236   ∞      237   ø      238   ∈      239   ∩
     240   ≡      241   ±      242   ≥      243   ≤
     244   ⌠      245   ⌡      246   ÷      247   ≈
     248   °      249   ·      250   ·      251   √
     252   ⁿ      253   ²      254   ■
     ▓

COMMAND: Copy Delete Format Gallery Help Insert Jump Library
         Options Print Quit Replace Search Transfer Undo Window
Edit document or press Esc to use menu
Pg1 Co1              {4}                 ?                  Microsoft Word
```

o **Figure 18.5:** *Greek and mathematical characters*

oCREATING LINES AND BOXES

You can create lines and boxes in your documents in three ways:

- o Inserting individual graphic characters using the Alt key and the appropriate character set number

You can also import graphic files containing scanned images, photographs, or drawings created with graphics software, as discussed in Chapter 20.

o Using the Format Border command

o Using Word's line-draw mode

Inserting individual characters can be a tedious and time-consuming approach. Since each graphic character is a three-digit character set code, you would have to do a lot of typing and planning to create charts or boxes.

But you can use the Format Border command to quickly create lines and boxes. For example, you can draw a box of either single or double lines around text in as little as four keystrokes. Boxes and horizontal lines extend from the left and right margin settings of the paragraph.

Later you'll learn how to use macros to create a library of graphic shapes that can be quickly and easily incorporated into your drawings.

If you want something other than what the Format Border command offers, you can use Word's line-draw mode. As you move the cursor with the arrow keys, you draw lines of single or double width, or any other character desired.

As an example, we'll use the Format Border command and line-draw mode to create the section of an organization chart shown in Figure 18.6. Note that if you used the Alt-key method to draw the chart, it would take at least ten times the number of keystrokes.

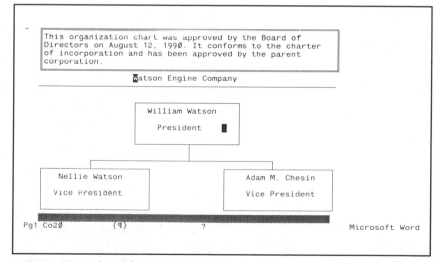

o **Figure 18.6:** *A sample organization chart*

4.0 The Format Border menu does not contain the Color, Background Shading, and Shading options.

Before starting, keep in mind these tips for drawing:

o Boxes and lines created with the Format Border command are usually drawn around existing text.

o Boxes created in line-draw mode should be drawn before adding text in the overtype mode.

o When drawing a complete box, start at the upper-left corner and draw in a clockwise direction. When you reach the upper-left corner again, move once to the right to close off the box.

 You can't use the mouse to draw lines.

Follow these steps to create the chart:

1. Start Word.

2. Type the text that you want included in a box.

> **This organization chart was approved by the Board of Directors on August 12, 1990. It conforms to the charter of incorporation and has been approved by the parent corporation.**

3. Place the cursor anywhere in the paragraph.

4. Click left on Format Border to see the menu

KEY Press Esc F B B. Press Tab to reach the Line Style option, and then press F1. Highlight Double (or Bold, if Double is not listed for your printer); then press Enter. (With version 4.0, press B, press Tab D, and then press Enter.)

> **FORMAT BORDER type: None Box Lines line style: Normal   Color: Black**
> **left: Yes No right: Yes No above: Yes No below: Yes No**
> **background shading: 0   shading color: Black**

5. Click left on Box, click right on the Line Style option to display available styles, and then click right on Double (or Bold, if Double is not listed for your printer). (With version 4.0, click left on Box; then click right on Double for the Line Style option.)

6. Place the cursor on the endmark and press Enter.

7. Press Alt-C to center the cursor, and then type **Watson Engine Company**.

8. Click left on Format Border.

9. Click left on Lines for the Type option.

KEY Press Esc F B L. Press Tab six times to reach the Below option, press Y, and then press Enter.

10. Click right on Yes for the Below option. A horizontal line appears below the text.

11. Place the cursor on the endmark and press Enter. You are now ready to use line-draw mode.

12. Press the spacebar until the cursor is on column position 20 on that line. The column indicator on the status line should read Co20.

13. Draw the first box.

   a. Press Ctrl-F5 to turn on line-draw mode. The characters LD appear in the status line.

   b. Press the right arrow key 21 times.

   c. Press the down arrow key 5 times.

   d. Press the left arrow key 21 times.

   e. Press the up arrow key 5 times.

   f. Press the right arrow. This extra step is needed to close off the upper-left corner of the box.

   g. Press Ctrl-F5 to turn off line-draw mode.

14. Place the cursor on the endmark and press Enter three times.

15. Draw the left box.

   a. Press Ctrl-F5 to turn on line-draw mode.

   b. Press the right arrow key 22 times.

   c. Press the down arrow key 5 times.

   d. Press the left arrow key 22 times.

   e. Press the up arrow key 5 times.

   f. Press the right arrow once.

   g. Press Ctrl-F5 to turn off line-draw mode.

16. Press End, and then press the spacebar until the cursor reaches column position 38, on the same line as the top of the left box.

17. Draw the right box.

   a. Press Ctrl-F5.

   b. Press the right arrow key 22 times.

   c. Press the down arrow key 5 times.

   d. Press the left arrow key 22 times.

   e. Press the up arrow key 5 times.

   f. Press the right arrow key once.

   g. Press Ctrl-F5.

18. Draw the lines connecting the boxes.

    a. Place the cursor on the line above the two boxes, at column position 31.

    b. Press Ctrl-F5.

    c. Press the up arrow key twice.

    d. Press the down arrow key twice. (Drawing over existing lines has no effect, and it's faster than turning off line-draw mode, moving the cursor, and then turning it back on.)

    e. Press the left arrow key 20 times.

    f. Press the down arrow key, then the up arrow key.

    g. Press the right arrow key 40 times.

    h. Press the down arrow key, then the up arrow key.

    i. Press Ctrl-F5.

When typing within graphics, always use the overtype mode (press F5), and never use the Del or Backspace key to erase characters because they will destroy the alignment of the graphics. Instead, delete characters by placing the cursor on them and pressing the spacebar.

19. Now you can enter the text within the boxes.

    a. Press F5 to enter the overtype mode. The letters OT should appear in the status line.

    b. Place the cursor on the first line inside the top box, at column position 23, and type **William Watson**.

    c. Move the cursor (with the mouse or arrow keys, not Enter) down two lines, to column position 25, and type **President**.

    d. Move the cursor to the first line in the left box, at column position 5, and type **Nellie Watson**.

    e. Move the cursor down two lines, to column position 4, and type **Vice President**.

    f. Move the cursor to the first line in the right box, at column position 43, and type **Adam M. Chesin**.

    g. Move the cursor down two lines, to column position 43, and type **Vice President**.

20. The final step is to draw the wide horizontal line under the chart. Since this uses a special graphic character, it must be created in line-draw mode, not with the Format Border Lines command. But

first, you must change the drawing character from the single line to the graphic box.

  a. Click on Options.

  b. Click right on the Linedraw Character option to display a menu of common drawing characters. (We'll discuss this option after the exercise.)

  c. Click right on the graphic box at the beginning of the second line of options.

  d. Place the cursor on the endmark and press Enter.

  e. Press Ctrl-F5 to turn on line-draw mode.

  f. Press End to draw the line to the right margin. (In line-draw mode, you can press End to quickly reach the right margin; press Home to draw to the left margin.)

  g. Press Ctrl-F5 to turn off line-draw mode.

21. Click right on Print to print a copy of the chart. (Remember, line and box characters cannot be reproduced on all printers.)

The Linedraw Character option on Format Border menu lets you select the character you want to draw with. For that option, you can enter any of the standard keyboard characters (such as * to draw lines of asterisks) or a special graphic character by entering Alt and the appropriate number. In addition, you can have Word display a menu of possible choices, as we did in the exercise.

If your printer is capable, you can use the other options on the Format Border menu to add colors to lines and boxes, or shading (darkening) to the inside of boxes. Click right on any of these selections to display a list of available options for your printer.

If you want to change the size or font of the line-drawing character, create a character style in the Gallery using the Line Draw variant.

CREATING RULED FORMS

In Chapter 9, you learned a method of creating ruled forms using the Format Character and Format Set Tab commands; however, forms are much easier to create with the Format Border Box command.

In the previous example, you created boxes around single paragraphs. If you highlight a group of paragraphs, Word will draw a box around each, with a common line between the paragraphs, as shown in Figure 18.7.

You can use this technique to create a ruled form. As an example, we'll create the doctor's appointment form shown in Figure 18.8.

1. Start Word.

2. Type the following:

   Next Appointment
   Name:
   Date: **Time:**   **Doctor:**

KEY Press Shift-F10. Then press Esc F B B Enter.

3. Click both in the selection bar to select the entire form.

4. Click left on Format Border; then click right on Box. Individual boxes are drawn around each line of the document.

If you want several paragraphs to appear in the same box, not separated by a line, end each paragraph by pressing Shift-Enter.

You can now print multiple copies of the form for filling out by hand. Copy the form several times on the page, and then print as many copies as you'll need. You can also use the techniques you learned in Chapter 17 to fill out such forms automatically.

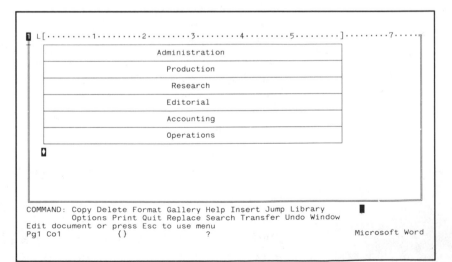

o **Figure 18.7:** *A box around multiple paragraphs*

WORKING WITH BOXES

Boxes around text extend from the left to right margin settings of the paragraph, so the size of the box depends on the indentation settings in the Format Paragraph menu, as shown in Figure 18.9.

```
1 L[·········1·········2·········3·········4·········5·········]·········7·····┐
  ┌──────────────────────────────────────────────────────────────┐
  │                    Next Appointment                          │
  ├──────────────────────────────────────────────────────────────┤
  │ Name:                                                        │
  ├──────────────────────────────────────────────────────────────┤
  │ Date:              Time:              Doctor:                │
  └──────────────────────────────────────────────────────────────┘
  ▯




COMMAND: Copy Delete Format Gallery Help Insert Jump Library        ▮
         Options Print Quit Replace Search Transfer Undo Window
Edit document or press Esc to use menu
Pg1 Co1              {→}                    ?            Microsoft Word
```

○ **Figure 18.8:** *Sample ruled form*

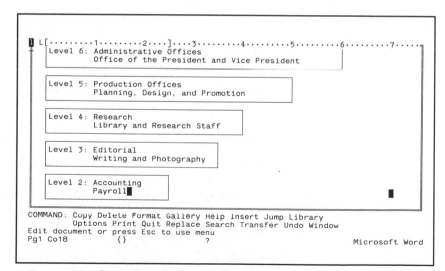

○ **Figure 18.9:** *Boxes align with paragraph margins*

If you use the Format Border Box command on a blank line, a one-line empty box will appear. You can then place the cursor within the box and type. The box will grow to adjust to the text.

After the box is drawn, you do not have to take any special action if you want to change the margins. When you adjust the left or right indentation settings, or add or delete text, the box will automatically expand or contract to conform to the new paragraph size.

Centering text with Alt-C or the Centered Alignment option does not change the margins. If you draw a box around a centered title, the box will extend to the right and left margins. To create a smaller box just around the centered words, change the indentation settings or use the Alt-Q command to bring the margins closer to the centered text.

To delete a box, place the cursor within the box, and then press Alt-P or select Format Border None. This deletes the box without changing the paragraph margins.

If you use boxes often, you may want to create a glossary of commonly used shapes. Use the line-draw mode to draw various sized boxes, and then select and copy them to the glossary individually. Give them names that relate to their shapes and sizes, such as Largebox, Smallbox, and Rectangle. When you need the shape, place the cursor where you want to insert it, type the name of the shape, and press F3.

USING MACROS FOR DRAWING

You can create macros to streamline drawing boxes and lines. For example, the macro:

```
<esc>fbb<enter>
```

will draw a box around the selected paragraph. Link the macro to Ctrl-B to quickly draw a box around text.

You can also create empty boxes on the screen using similar techniques. The following macro, for example, requests the size of the box, and then enters the appropriate keystrokes:

```
«ASK size = ?How big»
«REPEAT size»<shift enter>«ENDREPEAT»
<esc>fbb<enter>
```

To draw a box of a specific size, centered on the screen, use this macro:

```
«SET lines = ?Number of lines»
«SET width = ?How wide»
«SET left = 6-width»
```

```
«SET left = left /2»
«REPEAT lines» <shift enter> «ENDREPEAT»
<esc>fp<tab>«left»<tab 2>«left»<enter>
<esc>fbb<enter>
```

You can also use macros with line-draw mode, so you don't have to keep pressing the arrow keys until the line is drawn. For instance, here are a set of macros for drawing various size lines:

```
«ASK size = ?How long»
<ctrl F5>«REPEAT size»<up>«ENDREPEAT»<ctrl F5>
```

```
«ASK size = ?How long»
<ctrl F5>«REPEAT size»<down>«ENDREPEAT»<ctrl F5>
```

```
«ASK size = ?How long»
<ctrl F5>«REPEAT size»<left>«ENDREPEAT»<ctrl F5>
```

```
«ASK size = ?How long»
<ctrl F5>«REPEAT size»<right>«ENDREPEAT»<ctrl F5>
```

Finally, here is a macro that combines these macros into a Logo-type language:

```
«ASK where = ?U, D, L, R, Q to Quit»
«WHILE where <>"Q"»
«ASK size = ?How long»
<ctrl F5>
«IF where ="U"»«REPEAT size»<up>«ENDREPEAT»«ENDIF»
«IF where ="D"»«REPEAT size»<down>«ENDREPEAT»«ENDIF»
«IF where ="L"»«REPEAT size»<left>«ENDREPEAT»«ENDIF»
«IF where ="R"»«REPEAT size»<right>«ENDREPEAT»«ENDIF»
<ctrl F5>
«ASK where = ?U, D, L, R, Q to Quit»
«ENDWHILE»
```

You could even add diagonal lines to the menu. With the cursor-movement keys turned off (press Num Lock) the numbers could be used for both the size of the lines and the direction. The commands to move diagonally up and to the right might appear like this:

```
«IF where ="9"»«REPEAT size»<right><up>«ENDREPEAT»«ENDIF»
```

Because vertical lines are larger than horizontal ones, the resolution could be improved by using these commands:

«IF where = "9"»«REPEAT size» <right 2> <up> «ENDREPEAT»«ENDIF»

With a little work, you could create a powerful drawing program within Word. In fact, Word can perform many of the functions provided by desktop publishing programs. In the next chapter, you'll learn how to format newsletters and other documents in more than one column.

- CREATING
- MULTICOLUMN
- PAGES

In all the exercises up to this point, you've typed single-column text—each line stretches across the entire page. In fact, most business documents are typed as a single column. No matter what the margins are, there is just one line of text on each line of the page.

This chapter presents the techniques for creating multicolumn documents. Two different types of column layout are discussed here: newspaper and side-by-side columns.

Newspaper columns are those that run continuously from one column to the next, as in a newspaper. Adding text to one column will push existing text to the next column or page. In this type of format, it doesn't matter which text is in adjacent columns.

Side-by-side columns, on the other hand, contain paragraphs that must be kept next to each other. For example, in the following format, it is important that the text in the right column remains next to the corresponding text in the left column.

Type	Purpose
Newspaper Columns	Newsletters, journals, magazines, brochures
Side-by-Side Columns	Instructions, orders, business documents

oWORKING WITH COLUMNS

Although Word gives you a great deal of freedom to choose the measurements of your columns, you shouldn't create columns of text haphazardly. Columns that are too narrow are unattractive and difficult to read. After a certain point, there aren't enough words per line to allow the reader's eye to follow them comfortably. Columns that are too close together are also difficult to read. The text appears as one large block.

As a rule, don't try to fit columns that are too wide into too little space. The white space on a page contributes a great deal to its overall appearance and readability.

Leave enough room for adequate right and left margins. You can make them smaller than Word's default 1¼ inches, but leave a minimum of ½ inch on both sides. The same applies to the space between the columns. Newspapers have at least ¼ inch between columns. A little more space than that will make your columns easier to read.

○CREATING NEWSPAPER COLUMNS

4.0 You cannot combine two divisions on the same page. To print single and multicolumn text on a page, use the special techniques for version 4.0 discussed later in the chapter.

All the text on a page can be multicolumn, or you can combine single and multicolumn text on the same page. However, since page layout is considered a division, you must create a new division style for multicolumn text. As long as the multicolumn division has the same margins and page length as the single-column division, you can print them both on the same page.

To produce newspaper columns of text, use the options on the Format Division menu. You enter the number of columns, the size of the margins, and the space between columns, as illustrated in Figure 19.1. Word computes the width of the columns by dividing the remaining space.

The default margins are 1¼ inch. The default space between columns is ½ inch. If you select two columns, Word divides the remaining 5 inches into 2½-inch columns.

After you select the division options, you simply enter the text. Normally, Word will display just one column at a time on the screen, although the document will be printed in the number of columns that you selected. If you want to see all the columns on the screen, you can switch to show layout mode, as discussed later in the chapter.

CREATING THE NEWS STYLESHEET

Now you will prepare a stylesheet for a two-column page layout. The layout will include 1-inch right and left margins with justified text. Follow the steps below:

1. Start Word.

2. Click left on Format; then click right on Stylesheet.

KEY   Press Esc F S A, type **News**, and then press Enter Y.

KEY   Press Esc G I. Press Tab to reach the Usage option and press P. Press Tab to reach the Variant option, type **Standard**, and press Enter. Press F P J Enter.

3. Type **News**, and then click on the command line title.

4. Click on the message line.

5. Click on Gallery, and then set the format for justified paragraphs.

   a. Click left on Insert.

   b. Click left on Paragraph for the Usage option.

   c. Click right on the Variant option.

   d. Click on the command line title to accept Standard.

   e. Click left on Format Paragraph.

   f. Click right on Justified. The Standard paragraph format will be justified text.

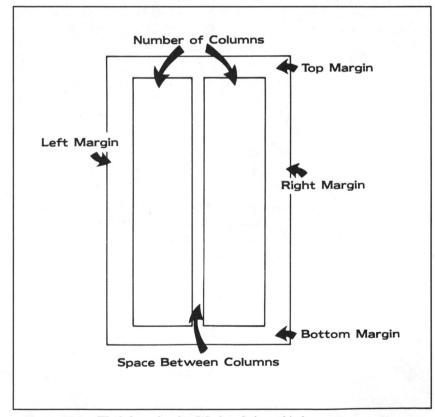

○ **Figure 19.1:** *The information that Word needs for multicolumn text*

KEY Press I and type **CO** as the key code. Press Tab to reach the Usage option, press D, and then press Enter.

6. Prepare to enter a new division style.

    a. Click left on Insert.

    b. Type **CO** for the Key Code option.

    c. Click right on Division for the Usage option.

7. Set the division for 1-inch left and right margins and two columns.

    a. Click left on Format Layout.

KEY Press F L. Press Tab to reach the Number of Columns option and type **2**. Press Tab twice to reach the Division Break option, press the spacebar to highlight Continuous, and then press Enter. Press F M. Press Tab twice to reach the Left option and type **1**. Press Tab to reach the Right option, type **1**, and press Enter.

    b. Click on the Number of Columns option and type **2**.

    c. Click right on Continuous for the Division Break option.

    d. Click right on Format.

    e. Click on the Left option and type **1**.

    f. Click on the Right option and type **1**.

    g. Click on the command line title. Figure 19.2 shows the styles for the two-column format added in the Gallery window.

8. Click left on Transfer; then click right on Save to save the style-sheet.

KEY Press T S Enter. Press E to exit.

9. Click on Exit.

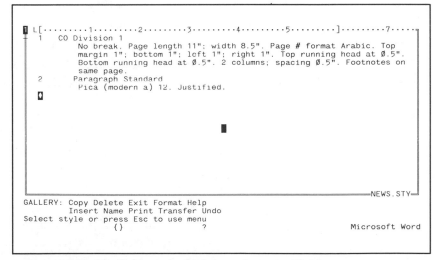

o **Figure 19.2:** *The division styles for the two-column, justified format*

ENTERING AND PRINTING MULTICOLUMN DOCUMENTS

Now we'll use the News stylesheet to create a simple newsletter. The document will have room at the top of the first page for a 2-inch masthead or letterhead, two short paragraphs of introductory material printed in one column across the top of the first page, and the remainder of the first page and subsequent pages in two columns. Figure 19.3 illustrates this format.

Follow these steps:

1. Type the paragraphs that are to be printed in a single column, and then press Enter three times to allow some extra space between the single-column and double-column text.

   This past year has been a productive one for our faculty. Twenty-one faculty members participated in funded research projects representing over $120,000. Twelve of the projects have been published in professional journals.
   Included in this newsletter are summaries of all twenty-one projects.

KEY Press Esc F D L. Press the down arrow twice to reach the Division Break option, press the spacebar to select Continuous, and then press Enter. Press Esc F D M, type **2**, and press Enter.

2. Click left on Format Division Layout.

3. Click right on Continuous for the Division Break option (so Word will not start a new page at this division line).

4. Move the cursor under the division mark; then click left on Format.

5. Click right on Division and type **2** for the top margin.

6. Click on the command line title.

7. Press Alt-CO to format the next division for two columns.

8. Press the up arrow to highlight the division mark, press Enter, and then place the cursor between the two division marks. You'll see that the ruler line changes to reflect the column width, with the right margin at the 3-inch mark.

9. Type the remainder of the newsletter. As you type, the text will appear in one column.

   Factors Involved in French Language Word Processing Utilizing the Standard English Language Keyboard, Dr. Renee Voltaire, French Department.

o **Figure 19.3:** *The format of the sample newsletter*

Dr. Voltaire analyzed several popular word processing programs for their capacity to display and print French language characters. Dr. Voltaire then studied the difficulties encountered in typing French documents using the standard QWERTY keyboard.

The Possible Contributions of Computers to the Creative Writing Process, Dr. Leslie Van Mot, English Department.

Dr. Van Mot tested the effects of using word processing programs on the creative output of students. The writing of student volunteers was measured using several criteria. These included sentence complexity, character development, and grammatical accuracy. The students were divided into test and control groups. The test group was trained in using a word processing program, while the control group was given standard writing practice exercises. The report studies the results of the training.

The Economic Impact of Computer Technology on the Gross National Product, Dr. William Duke, Economics Department.

Dr. Duke abstracted data from the past 10 years supplied by the National Economics Institute. He concludes that starting in 1984 there has been a direct relationship between the GNP and the fortunes of the computer industry.

Art Education and the Computer. Dr. Wilma Stephens, Art Department.

    Dr. Stephens has been researching the use of computer technology in the design process. Her primary interest is in the use of simulated graphics to project light patterns on angular objects and the effects of the projections on color density as observed by the human eye.

KEY Press Ctrl-F9; then press E to exit. Press Ctrl-F10, type **Faculty**, and press Enter twice to save the document.

10. Click left on Print Preview to see how the printed document will appear. Your document should look like Figure 19.4.

11. Click on Exit.

12. Click left on Transfer Save and type **Faculty**.

13. Click on the command line title; then click on SUMMARY.

    When you previewed the newsletter, you saw that Word did not divide all the text into two even columns. It filled the left column, and then placed the remaining text in the right column. If your document were longer than one page, Word would fill both columns on the first page before starting the next page.

    You have also noticed the unsightly gaps between words caused by justifying the columns. You could correct these by using the Library

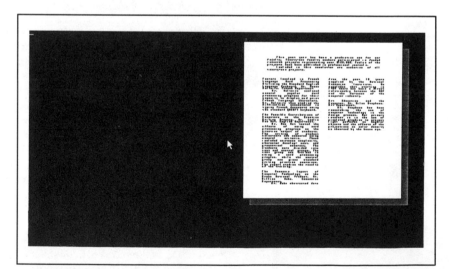

o **Figure 19.4:** *Newsletter in the preview mode*

Hyphenate command or returning the paragraph format to left alignment, as we'll do in the next chapter.

○USING SHOW LAYOUT MODE

4.0 Show layout mode is not available.

Working with columns that are underneath each other is inconvenient. You can use the Print Preview option to see how the printed page will appear, but you can't make any changes to the document in that mode. Instead, you can switch to show layout mode, which allows you to type, edit, or format the text while seeing it as it will appear on the printed page. Figure 19.5 shows the sample newsletter in show layout mode.

Notice that the top border closes in so the ruler line is only over the active column, the one in which the cursor is placed. Click left in a column to make it active and display the ruler over it.

KEY To move from column to column, press Ctrl-5, and then press the right or left arrow key. To move between entries in the same column, press Ctrl-5, and then press the up or down arrow key.

Word will respond slowly in the show layout mode, so use it just to visualize how your document will appear. Do most of your typing, editing, and formatting in the regular mode, and then switch to show layout mode for an overall impression and minor adjustments.

Press Alt-F4 to toggle in and out of the show layout mode.

```
 L[·········1·········2·········]
       This past year has been  a  productive  one  for  our
    faculty. Twenty-one faculty members participated  in  funded
    research projects representing over $120,000. Twelve of  the
    projects have been published in professional journals.
       Included  in  this  newsletter  are  summaries  of  all
    twenty-one projects.


    ::::::::::::::::::::::::::::::::::::::::::::::::::::::::::::::::
    Factors Involved  in  French       Dr. Duke abstracted  data
    Language   Word   Processing    from  the  past  10  years
    Utilizing the Standard English    supplied   by   the   National
    Language Keyboard,  Dr.  Renee    Economics   Institute.    He
    Voltaire, French Department.     concludes  that  starting  in
       Dr.   Voltaire   analyzed    1984 there has been  a  direct
    several   popular   word    relationship between  the  GNP
    processing programs for  their    and  the  fortunes  of  the
    capacity to display and  print    computer industry.
                                                       ═FACULTY.DOC═
    COMMAND: Copy Delete Format Gallery Help Insert Jump Library
            Options Print Quit Replace Search Transfer Undo Window
    Edit document or press Esc to use menu
    P1 D2 C8          {¶}              ?          LY      Microsoft Word
```

○ **Figure 19.5:** *The newsletter in show layout mode*

○CREATING SINGLE AND DOUBLE COLUMNS IN VERSION 4.0

Version 4.0 will not print two different divisions on the same page. Instead, you can use a running head to hold the single-column text within a division set for more than one column. But because Word treats running heads in a special way, a number of format changes must be made.

For example, the running head always prints in the division margin. So the top margin must be made large enough to accommodate it. If the full running head will not fit in the margin, Word won't print it.

In addition, remember that running heads in version 4.0 automatically print at the left edge of the paper. So you'll also have to change their paragraph format to align them with the regular text margin. Finally, each paragraph of the single-column text must be defined individually as a running head.

To create a multicolumn layout like the one illustrated in Figure 19.4, you would follow these steps:

1. Type the single-column text that you want to appear at the top of the page.

2. Using the Format Running-Head menu, format the text as top running heads. Select No for the Odd pages and Even Pages options, but Yes for the First Page option. Be sure to format the blank lines following the second paragraph as a running head as well.

3. For each of the running heads, set the paragraph indentations to match the margins of the text. For our example, set the running heads with 1-inch left and right paragraph indentations.

4. Compute the total margin required to hold the running heads, including any preprinted letterhead. In this example, the running head includes six lines of text, two blank lines, plus a 2-inch pre-printed letterhead; so you should set aside $3^{1}/_{2}$ inches for the top margin.

5. Format the division margins. Set the top margin at $3^1/2$ inches, the left and right margins at 1 inch, and the Running-Head Position from Top option at 2.

6. Using the Format Division menu options, format the division layout. Set the number of columns at 2 and the Break option at Column.

7. Type the two-column text.

8. After you finish typing, repaginate the document.

9. Scroll through the paginated text. Starting at the top of the document, you'll see the column 1 indicator (1»), the column 2 indicator, and another column 1 indicator. The second column 1 indicator marks the beginning of the first column of the second page.

10. Place the cursor next to the second column 1 indicator, and then press Ctrl-Enter. This division marks the end of the first page of text.

11. Place the cursor on the division mark at the end of the document. Change the top margin to 1 inch and return the running-head position from top to .5.

12. Print a copy of the document.

For your own work, always start by typing the single-column text. Format it as a running head with the correct left and right indentations to match the division margins. Combine the size of the text with any top margin you want, add some space between it and the multicolumn material, and make that total your division top margin. Make sure that the Running-Head Position From Top option is set wide enough to leave the correct amount of blank paper (your real top margin). Be sure to set the running head for the first page only; otherwise, it will appear on every page of the newsletter.

If this is a format you use often, create a separate stylesheet for it. Set one division format for the first page (complete with a wide top margin and running-head position) and another for subsequent pages with a normal top margin. You can then attach the stylesheet and insert the division style easily.

Using similar techniques, you can place single-column text at the bottom of the page. Just designate the running-head position for the bottom and make sure that the bottom margin is wide enough to hold the text.

○CREATING SIDE-BY-SIDE COLUMNS

Side-by-side columns are typed one under another, each formatted with an appropriate left and right indentation, so that they are printed next to each other on the page.

USING STANDARD STYLES

There are several special styles provided on the Sideby stylesheet on the Word utility disk. These are already formatted for two- and three-column formats. You can use them as they are or customize them to suit your own needs.

Here are five styles on the Sideby stylesheet:

2L   Paragraph 1   LEFT
Courier (modern a) 12. Flush left, right indent 3.25". Place side by side.
2R   Paragraph 2   RIGHT
Courier (modern a) 12. Flush left, left indent 3.25". Place side by side.
3L   Paragraph 3   LEFT
Courier (modern a) 12. Flush left, right indent 4.3". Place side by side.
3C   Paragraph 4   CENTER
Courier (modern a) 12. Flush left, left indent 2.15", right indent 2.15".
Place side by side.
3R   Paragraph 5   RIGHT
Courier (modern a) 12. Flush left, left indent 4.3". Place side by side.

Figure 19.6 shows an example of two paragraphs, one formatted using style 2L, and the other with style 2R.

Word prints side-by-side columns following these simple rules:

○ If a paragraph's left indentation is larger than the previous paragraph's, it prints to the right.

○ If a paragraph's left indentation is smaller than the previous paragraph's, it prints to the left.

○ If a paragraph's left indentation is the same as the previous paragraph's, it prints below it.

To use the styles, follow these steps:

1. Attach the Sideby stylesheet or insert the styles shown above in the Normal stylesheet or another one.

```
▌━ LØ·········1·········2·········3·[·······4·········5·········]·········7···┐
▕2L  Word processing, database,
     graphics, and spreadsheet
 2R                                    These are the most popular
                                       types of application
                                       software.█
 *    ◆

                                                                        █




 COMMAND: Copy Delete Format Gallery Help Insert Jump Library
          Options Print Quit Replace Search Transfer Undo Window
 Edit document or press Esc to use menu
 Pg1 Co42          {}                  ?                    Microsoft Word
```

○ **Figure 19.6:** *Side-by-side columns*

2. Type the document in the following manner:

   a. Type the first paragraph that is to appear on the left.

   b. Type the paragraph that you want to the right of the first one on the left.

   c. Type the next paragraph that is to appear on the left.

   d. Type the next right-column paragraph.

   e. Continue entering the paragraphs, alternating between the left- and right-column text.

3. Now format the paragraphs so they print on the appropriate sides.

   a. Place the cursor anywhere in the first left-column paragraph, and press Alt-2L. The paragraph will adjust to the right-indentation setting.

   b. Place the cursor anywhere in the next paragraph, which you want to print to the right of the one above it, and press Alt-2R. Although it appears underneath the left-column text, it will print beside it.

   c. Continue formatting the remaining paragraphs. Press Alt-2L for left-column text and Alt-2R for right-column text. If you want more than one consecutive paragraph printed on the left or right, just format it with the Alt-2L or Alt-2R style.

KEY Press Ctrl-F8 to print the text.

4. Click right on Print to print the text.

If you want three side-by-side columns, type them in the same manner: first the left column, then the middle, then the right. Format them with the Alt-3L (left), Alt-3C (center), and Alt-3R (right) styles.

CUSTOMIZING SIDE-BY-SIDE COLUMNS

The styles in the Sideby stylesheet produce three evenly sized columns. But in many instances, one column may be smaller than the other, as in the following example:

Application	Programs that are used for one specific function such as word processing, database management, graphics, or spreadsheets.
System	Programs that are required to make the computer operate, such as disk operating systems (DOS), or utilities.
Languages	Programs that are used to write other programs. These can be assemblers, compilers, or interpreters. The most popular languages include C, COBOL, Pascal, and BASIC.

Creating this side-by-side format requires changing the 2L and 2R styles or creating entirely new ones. After you set up the styles, type the text and then format it the same way as you would evenly sized columns.

As an example, here are the steps required to create the side-by-side columns shown above:

1. Compute the total typing space available to the two columns. Using the default settings, you would subtract the 1.25-inch left and right margins from 8.50-inch paper, leaving 6 inches.

2. Start Word and, if necessary, set the left and right margins that you used in the calculations above.

3. Determine the width of the left and right columns, and the amount of space you want between them. Take your time and compute

 Remember, columns that are too narrow can result in paragraphs that are unattractive and difficult to read.

these measurements exactly. The best way to determine the column widths is to first calculate the size of the narrower column.

  a. Type a paragraph or two of the smaller of the two columns. Try right indentations of various sizes until you find the one that leaves enough room for the larger column but is also suitable for the narrow one.

  b. Determine how much space you want between columns ($\frac{1}{2}$ inch is the most common).

  c. Subtract the narrow column width and the space from the total space available. The remainder is the width of the other column. If this does not leave enough space, reduce the left and right margins slightly. In our example, the longest word in the left column, *Application*, requires 1.1 inch at the default type size. We'll leave 0.4 inch between columns, so the right column would start at position 1.6.

4. Determine the left and right indentations necessary for columns of those sizes.

  a. Compute the right indentation needed for the left column by subtracting the column width from the total space. In this example, the right indentation would be 4.9 ($6 - 1.1 = 4.9$ inches).

  b. Compute the left indentation needed for the right column by adding the width of the left column plus the space between columns. In our example, $1.1 + 0.4 = 1.5$ inches.

5. Create two paragraph styles in the Gallery:

   2L   Paragraph 1   LEFT
   Courier (modern a) 12. Flush left, right indent 4.9". Place side by side.

   2R   Paragraph 2   RIGHT
   Courier (modern a) 12. Flush left, left indent 1.5". Place side by side.

6. Type the side-by-side columns and then format them using the procedure described in the previous section.

7. Press Alt-F4 to see the columns in show layout mode.

You can also customize the font type and size for your side-by-side columns by using the Format Character menu options. Just keep in mind that if you use a font size other than 12, you'll have to compensate for this when computing the column widths.

You can use the techniques described in this chapter to print any combination of division styles on one page. Just remember that you must carefully define your divisions. They must take into account the measurements of the full length of the paper, including top and bottom margins and any space between the two divisions.

In the next chapter, you'll learn how to enhance your multicolumn (or single-column) documents with pictures, drawings, and charts.

CHAPTER 20

- USING
- GRAPHICS
- AND
- DESKTOP
- PUBLISHING
- WITH
- WORD

4.0

KEY

4.0 These graphic functions are not available. To print graphics with Word documents, you need a utility program such as Microsoft Pageview or Softcraft Laser Graphics.

Special characters, lines, and boxes certainly add interest to your document, but drawings, charts, and pictures can really make a difference. This chapter covers Word's true desktop publishing applications. You'll learn how to merge graphics, such as spreadsheet graphs and scanned images, into your text, and how to use layout tools to design publication-quality documents. If you have a laser printer, you'll see how to use downloadable fonts.

But first the small print: Not all printers are capable of reproducing all the effects that you can create with Word. Daisywheel printers, and dot-matrix printers without graphic capabilities, won't be very useful here. If you were able to print the graphic characters, line drawings, and boxes discussed in Chapter 18, your printer will probably reproduce other graphics with the same quality. But the only way to tell is to try the exercises here and see how your printer reproduces the samples.

oWORKING WITH GRAPHICS

In this chapter, we'll be merging a number of graphic files and images and using a variety of type styles. If you have a drawing or another type of graphics program, you can create several sample files to use here. You might even have a PIC file created with Lotus 1-2-3 that you can merge into the document. If you don't have any graphic files available, you can use the Capture program supplied on the Word utilities disk to store an image on disk, as described shortly.

COMPATIBLE GRAPHIC FILE FORMATS

You can link the following types of graphic files to Word documents:

- o CAPTURE.COM files
- o Hewlett-Packard HPGL files
- o Lotus PIC files
- o Microsoft Pageview files
- o PC Paintbrush PCX and PCC files

- PostScript printer files
- TIFF (tag image file format) files
- Windows Clipboard files

You can use scanned images by capturing them in one of these formats.

MANIPULATING GRAPHICS

Before you begin working with graphics, you need to know how Word lets you manipulate these images. Every paragraph of text, and every graphic image, is contained in an invisible frame. Using all the default settings, the frame extends from the left to right margins—the full 6 inches across the page—for the depth of the paragraph, selected text, or graphic.

You can control the size of each frame and its position on the page through the Format Position menu. To adjust the size and position of a graphic image relative to its frame, you use the Library Link Graphics menu options.

oCAPTURING SCREENS

The Capture program "captures" screen images into a disk file. You can then merge the image on the disk with your Word document and print them together.

To use the Capture program, return to the DOS prompt, type **Capture**, and then press Enter.

CAPTURING TEXT MODE SCREENS

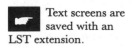
Text screens are saved with an LST extension.

When you want to capture a text image, press Shift-Prtscr. You'll be prompted to accept Word's suggested file name or enter your own. If you press Enter, the screen will be saved under the name CAPT0001.LST.

Each time you capture an image and accept the default file name, Capture will automatically increment the number in the name to avoid overwriting existing files.

CAPTURING GRAPHIC SCREENS

Graphic screens are saved with the extension SCR.

When you capture a graphic screen, you can *clip*, or crop, the image before saving it. Word surrounds the screen with *clipping lines*, which you adjust to enclose just the part of the screen you want to capture. Clip the image as desired, and then press Enter.

To clip the image, use the following keystrokes:

arrow keys	Move the top and left clipping lines
Tab	Activates the bottom and left clipping lines
Ins	Moves the top and bottom clipping lines toward each other simultaneously
Del	Returns to single clipping line control
+ (plus on the keypad)	Increases the distance the clipping lines move when you press an arrow key
– (minus on the keypad)	Decreases the distance the clipping lines move when you press an arrow key

oLAYING OUT A NEWSLETTER WITH GRAPHICS

Figure 20.1 shows a sample newsletter created using the Faculty document that we entered in Chapter 18. The entire page was printed on a Hewlett-Packard LaserJet Plus printer.

The masthead is a graphic image created using Spinfont, a program that creates curved and rotated graphic files from softfont outline files. All the text was printed in type styles that are supplied with the Font Solution Pack. (Both Spinfont and the Font Solution Pack are products of Softcraft, Inc.)

Underneath the masthead is the text of the newsletter. Each of the paragraphs is in its own frame. The large initial capital (called a *stick-up capital*) in the first sentence was formatted in 30-point Cooper Black; the remaining text is in a proportionally spaced 12-point Times.

FACULTY NOTES
News About Faculty Research

This past year has been a productive one for our faculty. Twenty-one faculty members participated in funded research projects representing over $120,000. Twelve of the projects have been published in professional journals. Included in this newsletter are summaries of all twenty-one projects.

Factors Involved in French Language Word Processing Utilizing the Standard English Language Keyboard, Dr. Renee Voltaire, French Department.

    Dr. Voltaire analyzed several popular word processing programs for their capacity to display and print French language characters. Dr. Voltaire then studied the difficulties encountered in typing French documents using the standard QWERTY keyboard.

The Possible Contributions of Computers to the Creative Writing Process, Dr. Leslie Van Mot, English Department.

INSIDE THIS ISSUE:
More important news about research and grants,

    Dr. Van Mot tested the effects of using word processing programs on the creative output of students. The writing of student volunteers was measured using several criteria. These included sentence complexity, character development, and grammatical accuracy. The students were divided into test and control groups. The test group was trained in using a word processing program, while the control group was given standard writing practice exercises. The report studies the results of the training.

The Economic Impact of Computer Technology on the Gross National Product, Dr. William Duke, Economics Department.

    Dr. Duke abstracted data from the past 10 years supplied by the National Economics Institute. He concludes that

starting in 1984 there has been a direct relationship between the GNP and the fortunes of the computer industry.

Art Education and the Computer. Dr. Wilma Stephens, Art Department.

    Dr. Stephens has been researching the use of computer technology in the design process. Her primary interest is in the use of simulated graphics to project light patterns on angular objects and the effects of the projections on color density as observed by the human eye.

o **Figure 20.1:** *Sample newsletter*

The next paragraph is in a normal, single-column, frame. This is followed by double columns, with each paragraph in each column in its own frame.

The box with small type (8.5-point Line Printer) is in a separate boxed paragraph with a frame width of 1.15 inches. Since the frame is smaller than the column width, the other text in the document wraps around it.

The second column contains a frame holding an imported spreadsheet graph. This frame is centered relative to the column. (Later, we'll see how it looks centered between the two columns.)

Figure 20.2 illustrates the frames in the sample newsletter. Although the figure shows each frame as a box, only two of the frames in the document are actually enclosed in boxes. Even so, the other elements are still contained in invisible Word frames.

> You can place a box around a frame by using the Format Border menu options, but frames do not have to be boxed. The frame exists whether or not you see actual lines around it.

ADDING THE GRAPH

Now we will begin laying out the newsletter by adding the graph to the document. Use your own graphic, PIC, or captured file for the exercise. Even if you don't have a graphic image (or the various font sizes) right now, follow the steps so you'll be ready when you do.

The sample newsletter uses several different type styles and sizes, which you might not have available in your own system. In the remaining figures, most of the newsletter text is in a fixed-spaced 12-point Courier type style, so that it more closely corresponds to what you'll see on your own screen.

Follow these steps to place the graphic in the document:

1. Recall the Faculty document you created in Chapter 18.

2. When we add the graphic features to the newsletter, the justified columns will include unsightly extra spaces. Rather than hyphenate the text, let's return the paragraphs to left alignment.

   > **KEY** Press Shift-F10. Press Esc F P L Enter; then press the up arrow to reach the top of the document.

   a. Click both in the selection bar to select the entire document.

   b. Click left on Format Paragraph.

   c. Click right on Left.

   d. Click both on the left border just under the window number to reach the start of the document.

   e. Click before the first line.

3. Press Enter twice to add blank lines at the start of the document. Later, we'll add the masthead to the top of the newsletter.

4. Place the cursor in the blank line before the paragraph starting *Art Education and the Computer*.

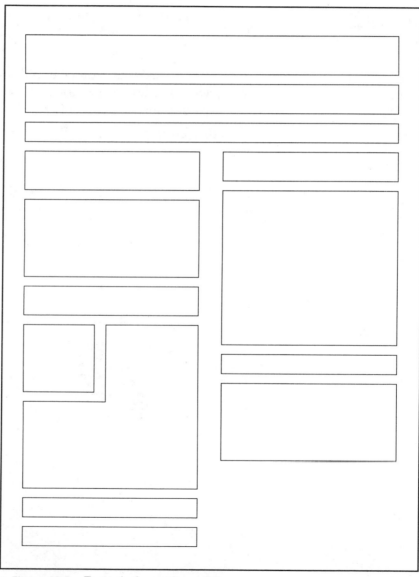

○ **Figure 20.2:** *Frames in the sample newsletter*

KEY Press Esc L L G to display the menu.

5. Click left on Library Link Graphics to display the menu shown in Figure 20.3. Except for the Filename and File Format options, this menu controls the size of your graphic and its placement in the frame. Table 20.1 summarizes the options on the Library Link Graphics menu.

6. Type the full path and name of your graphic file, and then press Enter. Word checks for the presence of the file, determines its format, and inserts that information as the File Format option.

Next, you will see the document with the graphic link command inserted. For example, if you're using a Lotus PIC file named Research, the command in the text would be

If Word can't locate the graphic file on your disk, it will beep and display the message *file does not exist.* Reenter the file name and the complete path, or press Esc to cancel the operation.

\RESEARCH.PIC;3";2.165";Lotus PIC

When printing or previewing the document, the command tells Word to merge this file into the column. The size is automatically set at the column width (3 inches) and scaled for the proper length. (Note that the code .G. is entered as hidden text before the graphic link command.)

KEY Press Ctrl-F9 to preview the document.

7. Click left on Print Preview to see the document. Figure 20.4 shows the newsletter in preview mode. Notice that there is no space between the text and the graphic, so the document looks cluttered. Let's take care of this now.

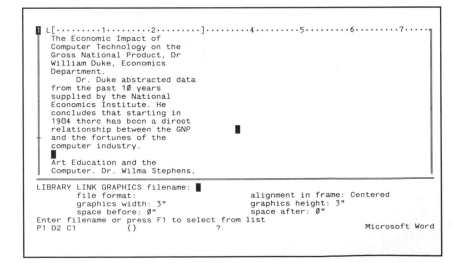

o **Figure 20.3:** *Library Link Graphics menu*

Press E, then Esc L L G. Press the down arrow three times to reach the Space Before option and type **.15**. Press Tab to reach the Space After option and type **.15**. Then press Enter.

8. Add space above and below the graphic.

   a. Click on Exit.

   b. Click left on Library Link Graphics.

   c. Click on the Space Before option and type **.15**.

   d. Click on the Space After option and type **.15**.

   e. Click on the command line title.

o **Table 20.1:** *Library Link Graphics Menu Options*

Option	Function
Filename	Enter the name of the graphic file to be merged, including its path and extension.
File Format	After reading the graphic file, Word will insert its format type for this option. If none appears, select this option and press F1 to see a list of possible formats.
Alignment in Frame	To position the graphic in relation to the left edge of the frame, enter a specific measurement or press F1 to see alternatives.
Graphics Width	To change the default width, enter a measurement or press F1 to see alternatives.
Graphics Height	To change the default height, enter a measurement or press F1 to see alternatives.
Space Before	To set the amount of blank space between the graphic frame and preceding text, enter a measurement.
Space After	To set the amount of blank space between the graphic frame and the following text, enter a measurement.

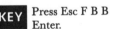

o **Figure 20.4:** *Document with Lotus picture file*

KEY Press Ctrl-F9, then E to exit.

9. Click left on Print Preview. You'll see that about one line of space has been added above and beneath the chart.

10. Click on Exit to return to the document.

11. Now let's surround the chart in a box.

KEY Press Esc F B B Enter.

    a. Place the cursor anywhere in the graphic link command line.

    b. Click left on Format Border; then click right on Box.

12. Click left on Print Preview. The preview shows that the chart is now surrounded in a box.

13. Click on Exit.

KEY Press Ctrl-F9, then E to exit.

You may have noticed that each time you previewed the document, Word accessed the disk containing the PIC file. This is because the linked file is not really added to the document, just the graphic link command. Whenever you print or preview a document containing a linked graphic, the file must be on the drive or subdirectory specified on the Library Link Graphics menu.

ADDING SPECIAL ENHANCEMENTS

Later, we'll experiment with the position of the graphic. But now let's add the masthead, the initial capital letter, and the small box in the first column. The sample masthead is a graphic file in TIFF format. It is approximately 6 inches wide and 1 inch deep.

Follow these steps to add the elements:

1. Place the cursor at the start of the document.

 Press Esc L L G, type the file name, and then press Enter.

2. Click left on Library Link Graphics, type the name and path of your graphic file, and then press Enter.

3. Now create the initial letter with a larger sized font.

    a. Place the cursor on the first letter of the paragraph.

    b. Click on Format Character.

    c. Select a font name and size that will look appropriate.

4. Next add the box and its text.

    a. Place the cursor at the beginning of the paragraph starting *Dr. Van Mot*.

    b. Press Enter, and then move the cursor to the blank line.

    c. Type the text **INSIDE THIS ISSUE:**.

    d. Press Shift-Enter.

    e. Type the text **More important news about research and grants**.

    f. Select the paragraph and format it in a small typeface.

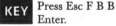 Press Esc F B B Enter.

    g. Click left on Format Border; then click right on Box to box the paragraph.

5. We want to make the box smaller so the other text wraps around it in the column. This is done by changing the frame width in the Format Position menu.

 Press Esc F O, press the down arrow twice, type **1.15**, and then press Enter.

    a. Click left on Format Position to see the menu shown in Figure 20.5. The options on the Format Position menu are summarized in Table 20.2.

    b. Click left on the Frame Width option and type **1.15**.

Press Ctrl-F9 to preview, and then press E to exit.

    c. Click on the command line title.

6. Click left on Print Preview.

7. Click on Exit.
8. Press Alt-F4 to see the newsletter in show layout mode, as shown in Figure 20.6. The graphic boxes are outlined on the screen,

```
L[·······1·······2·······]·······4·······5·······6·······7·····
the standard QWERTY keyboard.

The Possible Contributions of
Computers to the Creative
Writing Process, Dr. Leslie
Van Mot, English Department.

      ▆▆▆▆▆▆▆▆▆▆▆▆▆▆▆▆

        Dr. Van Mot tested the
effects of using word
processing programs on the
creative output of students.
The writing of student
volunteers was measured using

FORMAT POSITION
    horizontal frame position: Left        relative to:(Column)Margins Page
    vertical frame position: In line       relative to:(Margins)Page
    frame width: Single Column             distance from text: 0.167"
Enter measurement or press F1 to select from list
P1 D2 C21        {INSIDE...ants¶}  ?                      Microsoft Word
```

o **Figure 20.5:** *Format Position menu*

```
L[·······1·]
The Possible Contributions of          relationship between the
Computers to the Creative              and the fortunes of the
Writing Process, Dr. Leslie            computer industry.
Van Mot, English Department.
                    Dr. Van Mot
INSIDE THIS        tested the
ISSUE:             effects of using
More important     word processing
news about         programs on the
research and       creative output
grants.            of students. The

writing of student volunteers
was measured using several
criteria. These included
sentence complexity, character
development, and grammatical
accuracy. The students were            RESEARCH.PIC;3";
divided into test and control          PIC
                                       FACULTY.DOC

COMMAND: Copy Delete Format Gallery Help Insert Jump Library
        Options Print Quit Replace Search Transfer Undo Window
Microsoft Word Version 5.0
P1 D2 C2        {}              ?         LY       Microsoft Word
```

o **Figure 20.6:** *Newsletter in show layout mode*

showing their relative position and size. Scroll through the document and watch the changes on the ruler.

9. Press Alt-F4 to return to the normal view.

o **Table 20.2:** *Format Position Menu Options*

Option	Function
Horizontal Frame Position	Sets the horizontal position of the frame on the page in relation to the column, the left and right margins, or the edges of the page (as determined by the Relative To option). Enter a specific measurement or press F1 to select from left, centered, right, inside (toward center of facing pages), or outside (toward outside of facing pages).
Relative To	Selects columns, margins, or page for relative horizontal positioning.
Vertical Frame Position	Sets the vertical position of the frame in relation to the top margins or the edges of the page, as determined by the Relative To option. Enter a specific distance or press F1 to select from inline (normal position within the text), top, centered, or bottom.
Relative To	Select margins or page for relative vertical positioning.
Frame Width	Adjust the width of the frame. Enter a specific size or press F1 to select from alternatives. The options vary with the layout of the document, but may include single-column width, the width of the graphic, or multicolumn width for multicolumn documents.
Distance From Text	Sets the amount of white space between the frame and surrounding text.

CENTERING THE GRAPH ON THE PAGE

Now that the graphic links are created, let's see how we can control the appearance on this page. We'll begin by changing the size and position of the text and graphic frames.

Our goal is to position the graph in the center of the two columns. If we try to do this with the current layout, Word will instead push the graph onto the next page because the new position would conflict with the small text box. Therefore, our first step is to lower the frame position of the text box so there's enough room for the chart above it.

Follow these steps to reposition the graphics:

1. Place the cursor in the text box in the first column.

2. Click left on Format Position.

3. Click left on the Vertical Frame Position option and type **6.5**.

4. Click on the command line title. This positions the frame 6½ inches from the top margin.

5. Place the cursor somewhere in the graphic link command in the second column.

6. Click left on Format Position.

7. Click right on the Horizontal Frame Position option to see possible settings: left, centered, right, inside, or outside.

8. Click left on Centered.

9. Click left on Margins for the Relative To option.

10. Click left on the Vertical Frame Position option and type **2.5**.

11. Click on the command line title.

12. Click left on Print Preview to see the new position of the frame, as shown in Figure 20.7. With these settings, the frame is positioned under the single-column text, between the two columns. Of course, this placement affects the position of the other text on the page.

13. Click on Exit.

 KEY Press Esc F O. Press the down arrow, type **6.5**, and press Enter.

KEY Press Esc F O; then press F1 to display alternatives. Press the right arrow to select Centered. Press Tab M. Press Tab, type **2.5**, and then press Enter.

KEY Press Ctrl-F9 to preview; then press E to exit.

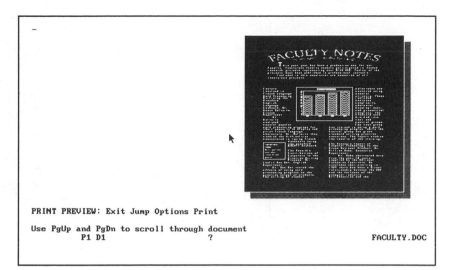

```
PRINT PREVIEW: Exit Jump Options Print

Use PgUp and PgDn to scroll through document
         P1 D1                            ?                    FACULTY.DOC
```

o **Figure 20.7:** *Graph centered on page*

14. Now let's adjust the size of the graph. The cursor should still be in the graphic link command for the graph.

 KEY Press Esc L L G, then the down arrow twice. Type **2**, and press Enter. Press Ctrl-F9 to preview, then E to exit.

    a. Click left on Library Link Graphics.

    b. Click left on the Graphic Width option and type **2**.

    c. Click on the command line title.

15. Click left on Print Preview to see the new position of the frame. Changing the size of the graphic does not affect the frame size. In fact, if we made the graph larger than the frame, it would extend beyond the frame's borders. So, let's make the frame smaller.

16. Click on Exit.

17. Decrease the frame's size.

KEY Press Esc F O, then the down arrow twice. Press F1 to list alternatives. Select Width of Graphic, and then press Enter. Press Ctrl-F9 to preview, then E to exit.

    a. Click left on Format Position.

    b. Click right on the Frame Width option to display the possible selections.

    c. Click right on Width of Graphic.

18. Click left on Print Preview to see the new position of the frame, as shown in Figure 20.8.

19. Click on Exit.

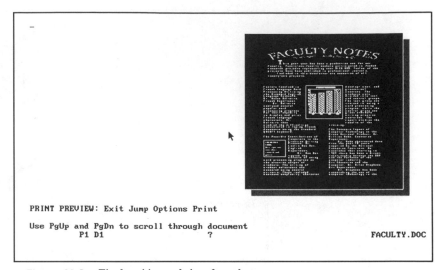

```
PRINT PREVIEW: Exit Jump Options Print

Use PgUp and PgDn to scroll through document
        P1 D1                              ?                      FACULTY.DOC
```

o **Figure 20.8:** *Final position and size of graph*

MANIPULATING FRAMES

Our example illustrates how changing the size and position of a graphic image and frame can affect the placement of other elements on the page. Text and graphics will be pushed up or down as necessary to adjust to the changes. If you make a frame too large, however, it might be pushed to the next page. So experiment with the various options on the Library Link Graphics and Format Position menus. Use Print Preview to see how your adjustments affected the layout.

You can also generate a quick draft copy of graphic documents. Select the lowest Graphics Resolution setting in the Print Options menu and print the document. After the layout is finalized, change the setting to a higher resolution for the final copy.

oCREATING DROP CAPITAL LETTERS

The large initial letter in the newsletter could also have been formatted as a *drop capital*, as shown in Figure 20.9. It takes a little trial and error to properly align drop capitals, and the exact settings depend on the character's point size. The 30-point letter in the figure, for instance, is in a frame 0.4 inches wide with the Distance From Text option set at zero. The line spacing (in the Format Paragraph menu) is set at 2 lines.

To create your own drop capitals, follow this general procedure:

1. Place the letter in its own paragraph directly above the remaining text in the paragraph. Just place the cursor on the character next to it and press Enter.

2. Format the letter in the type style and size desired.

3. Use the options on the Format Position menu to adjust the letter's frame width to the size of the character. Keep checking the page in preview mode until the remaining text and drop character are positioned correctly. Make sure you set the Distance From Text option to zero.

4. Print a sample to see how the character aligns with the rest of the text. If the letter is too high, reduce the line spacing option in the Format Paragraph menu, using a point size slightly smaller than the point size of the letter.

5. Keep reviewing the alignment in preview mode, and adjust the line spacing and frame size until the character appears properly spaced.

○USING LASER FONTS

In order to use downloaded fonts with your laser printer, you need two files on your disk: the proper PRD file and a matching one with the extension DAT. The second file tells Word the name and path of the fonts. When you use the Setup program to install Word, the proper files will be copied onto your hard disk. If you don't have the softfonts supported

---

This past year has been a productive one for our faculty. Twenty-one faculty members participated in funded research projects representing over $120,000. Twelve of the projects have been published in professional journals.
Included in this newsletter are summaries of all twenty-one projects.

○ **Figure 20.9:** *Paragraph beginning with drop capital*

in Word's PRD and DAT files, you can use other software, such as the Font Solution Pack or Bitstream Fontware, to create the proper files.

When you print a document using a PRD file that contains softfonts, you'll see the message

> This prompt appears even if your document is not using any of the PRD file downloadable fonts.

Enter Y to download New Fonts, A to download All Fonts, N to skip

If this is the first time in the current session that you're using the softfonts, press either Y or A. In this case, all the fonts needed for the document are new and will be downloaded to the printer.

After the fonts are downloaded, however, you don't have to download them again (unless you've turned off your printer). The next time you want to use the same fonts, press either Y to just download any new ones, or N if the document uses just fonts previously downloaded.

Unfortunately, fonts take up quite a bit of your printer's memory; the more fonts and sizes you use in a document, the more memory required.

PRINTER MEMORY LIMITATIONS

> Set the resolution of printed graphics by using the Graphic Resolution option on the Print Options menu.

Graphic images also take up your printer's memory. When you print a document with a laser printer, the entire page—including all the font and graphic information—must be stored in the printer's memory before the page is printed. Graphics printed in a high resolution require more memory than those reproduced at lower resolutions.

If your printer does not have enough memory to hold all the fonts and graphics, you'll see some sort of error message on its control panel. Consider some of the following steps to reduce the amount of memory required:

- o Select internal or cartridge fonts rather than softfonts.

- o Reduce the size of characters using softfonts.

- o Reduce the size or resolution of the graphics.

- o Print the page in sections. For example, print just the masthead in high resolution, adjust the margins, and then print the remainder of the page.

In the next chapter, you'll learn how to manage all your Word applications. We'll also cover networking techniques.

CHAPTER **21**

- MANAGING
  - YOUR
  - SYSTEM

4.0

KEY

All the techniques and applications you've learned so far can be used in any type of word processing environment. But working with a network, or in a busy office that generates a great deal of paperwork, has its own special set of problems.

In this chapter, you'll learn how to handle Word in these environments. We'll discuss differences in a network system and techniques for writing and reviewing documents with other people. Finally, we'll cover document management, including how to easily archive and batch print documents.

oACCESSING FILES ON A NETWORK

There are only a few differences between using Word on a single computer and on a network. The main one is that you may not be able to access a document or glossary that is already being used by another person. In general, only one workstation can access a file in the read/write mode—a document or glossary retrieved with the Read Only option set to No.

Store your personal glossary and a copy of the Normal one on your own workstation disk. This way, you'll have access to them at all times.

If you try to load or merge a document or glossary and see a warning message that the file is already in use, you'll just have to wait. After the user saves the document, you'll be able to retrieve it into your own workstation.

When you just want to review a document, not modify it, load it with Read Only set to Yes so others will be able to access it at the same time.

On a network, don't select Yes for the Queued option on the Print Options menu. Your network software will take care of queuing print jobs for you.

oWORKING WITH MULTIPLE AUTHORS AND REVIEWERS

Electronic mail and network systems are excellent tools when you're working on a document with other individuals. Rather than using copies of the document for review and revision, all the participants can access the file on their own system. But even if you're not on a network, you can take advantage of Word's features to streamline the review and revision process.

You can use Word's revision marks to display changes on the screen and annotations to show reviewer's comments.

EDITING WITH REVISION MARKS

Suppose that you're working on a document with someone else. You access the file on the network and want to make some changes to the text. But in the spirit of cooperation, you want to retain the original text until all the changes have been reviewed and accepted by your coauthor. After the changes are agreed upon, the final document can be printed.

You can keep track of editing using revision marks. They show what was selected for deletion and what has been added during the revision process. Deleted text remains in the document but appears crossed out; inserted text appears in a special format, such as underlined or bold.

You can also display a revision bar in the margin as a quick reference to where changes have been made. A *revision bar* is a small vertical line in the margin next to lines that have been revised. You can place the bar in the left or right margin, or on the outside margin, alternating on odd and even pages.

Adding Revision Marks

Here's how to add revision marks during the editing process:

KEY Press Esc F M O to see the Format Revision-Marks Options menu.

1. When you are ready to edit the document, click left on Format Revision-Marks to see the command line

    FORMAT REVISION-MARKS: Options accept-Revisions Undo-revisions Search

2. Click on Options to display the menu

    FORMAT REVISION-MARKS OPTIONS
    add revision marks: Yes No
    inserted text: Normal Bold(Underlined)Uppercase
    Double-underlined
    revision bar position:(None)Left Right Outside

If you want to display this menu without seeing the intermediate Format Revision-Marks command line, click left on Format, and then click right on Revision-Marks.

KEY Press Y. Press the down arrow key, then the spacebar to select your choice of format. Press the down arrow key to select the position of the revision bar. Press Enter after selecting options.

3. For the Add Revision Marks option, click right on Yes to accept the default values. If you want to change the other options (discussed below) click left on Yes.

4. Click on the command line title after selecting your options.

By default, newly inserted text will appear underlined. To change the setting, click on your choice for the Inserted Text option.

If you also want Word to display a revision bar on the screen, select where you want it to appear for the Revision Bar Position option.

4.0 The Outside option on the Format Revision-Marks menu is replaced with Alternate.

As you edit the document, Word will strike through text that has been selected for deletion and show inserted text in the style you selected from the Format Revision-Marks Options menu. With a monochrome system, deleted text is underlined, so select some other format, such as boldface, for inserted characters. Figure 21.1 shows a sample of edited text with a revision bar.

Undoing and Searching for Revisions

KEY Press Esc F M U to undo revisions.

If you change your mind about some revisions, you can quickly return the text to the unedited version. Select the text, and then click left

```
1L[·······1·······2·······3·······4·······5·······]·······7····
  July 23, 1989


       On behalf of the Faculty Council of the Philadelphia
  College of Pharmacy and Science, let me welcome you to our
  college.
       We appreciate the contribution made to our students by
  part-time instructors like yourself. Adjunct faculty add
  unique insights to the learning environment and contribute
  greatly to the overall academic program.
       Enclosed is the 1989-90 1990-91 Faculty Handbook and
  Academic Calendar. Our first Faculty Council meeting will be
  September 5, 1989 September 21, 1990█ in Whitecar Hall, at
  noon. I am looking forward to seeing you there.

  Sincerely,


  G. Victor Rossi
                                                      ROSSI.DOC
COMMAND: Copy Delete Format Gallery Help Insert Jump Library
         Options Print Quit Replace Search Transfer Undo Window
Edit document or press Esc to use menu
Pg1 Co37          {}                  ?              MR   Microsoft Word
```

o **Figure 21.1:** *A revised document*

on Format Revision-Marks Undo-Revisions. Word deletes any text you inserted, removes the strike through from deleted text, and removes the revision bar. Then you will see the word Search on the prompt line. Press Esc to return to the document.

You may need to undo some particular revision you made several places in a document, or you might just want to quickly review the revisions rather than the entire document. To search the document for revisions, click left on Format Revision-Marks Search.

Completing Revised Documents

After the document has been reviewed and the revisions are finalized, the changes can be incorporated into the text.

To accept the revisions and remove the special marks (the strike through, inserted text format, and revision bar), first select the text (click both in the selection bar for the entire document). Next click left on Format Revision-Marks; then click right on Accept-Revisions.

ADDING ANNOTATIONS

Like revision marks, annotations are useful when you're working on a document with someone else or reviewing another person's work. They allow you to add notes without changing the text. For example, you may want to refer to a certain passage and comment on its context or style.

In many ways, Word's annotations are like footnotes. They have the following features in common:

o Consecutively numbered

o Linked with a reference number in the text

o Automatically renumbered as other annotations are inserted or deleted

o Displayed in the footnote window

o Stored at the end of the document, but print at the location indicated by the Footnote option on the Format Division Layout menu

In addition, you can add the date and time and a name or other characters next to the reference number and the annotation itself.

KEY Press Esc F M S to search for revisions.

4.0 The Accept-Revisions option is replaced with Remove-Marks.

KEY Press Shift-F10; then press Esc F M R.

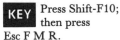 Annotations are not available.

KEY Press Esc F A.
Complete the
menu, and then press
Enter.

Adding a name is
particularly useful
when a document is
reviewed by several
people. Each annotation
can be followed by
the reviewer's name
or initials.

KEY Press Esc J A or
press F1 to return
to the document from a
footnote window.

To add an annotation, place the cursor where you want to insert the reference number, and then click left on Format Annotation to see the menu:

FORMAT ANNOTATION mark:
        insert date:Yes(No)   **insert time:Yes(No)**

If you want a name or some other mark to display along with the annotation number, such as your initials, enter it for the Mark option. To include the date or time in the annotation, select Yes for those options. Then click on the command line title.

Word will display the end of the document, or it will jump to the footnote window if you created one. The annotation number, and if you entered one, your selection for the Mark option, will appear. They will be followed by the date and time if you selected those options.

Now type your annotation just as you would enter a footnote. To return to the document, click left on Jump Annotation or, if the footnote window is displayed, click left in the document window.

Like footnotes, annotations can be formatted through the Gallery. Insert a character or paragraph style using the Annotation Ref variant.

oDOCUMENT MANAGEMENT

Keeping track of documents—especially on a hard disk—can be tedious. This is a particular problem in an office or network environment, where documents with similar names but from several different individuals may exist on the same disk. If you must manage many documents, you can take advantage of Word's Library Document-Retrieval command to ease your burden. You can combine this command's power with document summary sheet information to quickly locate and perform operations with specific files.

Using the Library Document-Retrieval command, you can locate and batch print documents, archive or delete files, and even custom design your own directory listings that display only files that meet certain criteria. A law firm could list just the documents relating to a specific client or type of case; a word processor could select documents from a specific administrator or print archive copies of all memos written that week.

RETRIEVING DOCUMENTS

Begin document retrieval by clicking left on Library Document-
Retrieval. Figure 21.2 shows a typical retrieval screen.

The top of the screen shows the default path name and a directory of
the .DOC files on that path. The directory is shown in the default view,
listing only the names of the files. At the bottom of the screen are the
eight options that can be selected and the prompt line

**Press Spacebar to mark-unmark file, Ctrl + Spacebar to mark all, or esc
for menu**

Some of the command line options, such as Load and Update, act on
only one file at a time. To select the file and perform the action, click left
on the file name and then click on the command line option. Other
options, such as Print, Delete, and Copy, can work with one or more
files. So you must first mark the files you want to include before selecting
the option.

To mark a file, click right on its name. An asterisk will appear before
the name, showing that it has been marked. To unmark a file, click right
on its name again. (To mark all the files listed, press Ctrl-spacebar.)

```
Path: C:
C:\WORD5\ADD.DOC            C:\WORD5\FIG17-2.DOC
C:\WORD5\AM12-18.DOC        C:\WORD5\FIG17-3.DOC
C:\WORD5\ANAPP.DOC          C:\WORD5\FIG5-12.DOC
C:\WORD5\APADD.DOC          C:\WORD5\FIGS.DOC
C:\WORD5\BALANCE.DOC        C:\WORD5\FIGURES.DOC
C:\WORD5\BUSTEM.DOC         C:\WORD5\FONTS.DOC
C:\WORD5\CH1.DOC            C:\WORD5\FORM1.DOC
C:\WORD5\CH10.DOC           C:\WORD5\FORMLET.DOC
C:\WORD5\CH10A.DOC          C:\WORD5\FTEST.DOC
C:\WORD5\CH11.DOC           C:\WORD5\LENV.DOC
C:\WORD5\CH12.DOC           C:\WORD5\LIST.DOC
C:\WORD5\CH13.DOC           C:\WORD5\M12-14.DOC
C:\WORD5\CH14.DOC           C:\WORD5\M15-18.DOC
C:\WORD5\CH15.DOC           C:\WORD5\M4-10.DOC
C:\WORD5\CH16.DOC           C:\WORD5\MACROCNV.DOC
C:\WORD5\CH17.DOC           C:\WORD5\MEMO.DOC
C:\WORD5\CH2.DOC            C:\WORD5\MEMO2.DOC
C:\WORD5\CH21.DOC           C:\WORD5\MEYERS.DOC
C:\WORD5\CH3.DOC            C:\WORD5\MN2.DOC

DOCUMENT-RETRIEVAL: Query Exit Load Print Update View Copy Delete

Press Spacebar to mark-unmark file, Ctrl+Spacebar to mark all, or Esc for menu
                              ?                          Microsoft Word
```

o **Figure 21.2:** *A document-retrieval screen*

For example, to print several files, click right on their names, and then click on Print. (You can use either button when clicking on these command line options.)

Keep in mind the differences between *listed files* and *marked files*. You can list all the document files on the disk or use the Query option to display certain ones. But to print, copy, or delete files, they must first be marked. If none are marked, Word sounds a warning beep and displays the message

No marked files in list

The Document-Retrieval command line contains the following options:

o **Query**: Lets you set retrieval criteria

o **Exit**: Returns to the text window

o **Load**: Recalls the highlighted document to the screen

o **Print**: Prints marked files

o **Update**: Allows you to edit the summary sheet of the highlighted document

o **View**: Lets you customize the way documents are listed on the document-retrieval screen

o **Copy**: Copies marked files from one disk or directory to another

o **Delete**: Deletes marked files from your disk (Word prompts you to confirm the deletion)

The Exit, Load, Update, and Delete options are straightforward. The other options are explained in the remainder of this chapter.

SETTING RETRIEVAL CRITERIA

KEY Press Q to display the Query menu.

Using the Query option on the Document-Retrieval command line, you can list only the files that meet certain criteria. Click on Query to display the Query menu, as shown in Figure 21.3.

Most of the fields on this menu are the same as the summary sheet fields. This allows you to list just those files whose summary sheets contain the same information you enter in the Query menu. In addition,

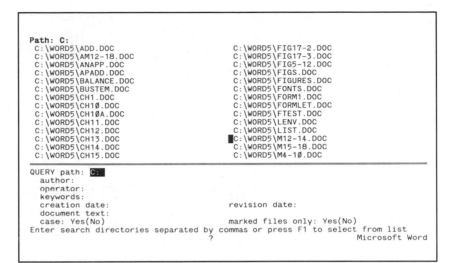

```
Path: C:
  C:\WORD5\ADD.DOC                    C:\WORD5\FIG17-2.DOC
  C:\WORD5\AM12-18.DOC                C:\WORD5\FIG17-3.DOC
  C:\WORD5\ANAPP.DOC                  C:\WORD5\FIG5-12.DOC
  C:\WORD5\APADD.DOC                  C:\WORD5\FIGS.DOC
  C:\WORD5\BALANCE.DOC                C:\WORD5\FIGURES.DOC
  C:\WORD5\BUSTEM.DOC                 C:\WORD5\FONTS.DOC
  C:\WORD5\CH1.DOC                    C:\WORD5\FORM1.DOC
  C:\WORD5\CH10.DOC                   C:\WORD5\FORMLET.DOC
  C:\WORD5\CH10A.DOC                  C:\WORD5\FTEST.DOC
  C:\WORD5\CH11.DOC                   C:\WORD5\LENV.DOC
  C:\WORD5\CH12.DOC                   C:\WORD5\LIST.DOC
  C:\WORD5\CH13.DOC                  ■C:\WORD5\M12-14.DOC
  C:\WORD5\CH14.DOC                   C:\WORD5\M15-18.DOC
  C:\WORD5\CH15.DOC                   C:\WORD5\M4-10.DOC

QUERY path: C:
  author:
  operator:
  keywords:
  creation date:                       revision date:
  document text:
  case: Yes(No)                        marked files only: Yes(No)
Enter search directories separated by commas or press F1 to select from list
                                 ?                        Microsoft Word
```

o **Figure 21.3:** *Query menu to set retrieval criteria*

you can extend the search to any word or phrase in the document itself by entering it in the Document Text field.

The Case field on the Query menu determines if the case of the words you're looking for must match the ones you entered. The Marked Files Only field limits the search to marked files, not all the files listed. To speed up your search, mark the files that will most likely meet your criteria and select Yes for this option.

After you enter your retrieval criteria, click on QUERY. Word will list the files that meet the criteria.

The retrieval criteria can be simple, such as a single author's name or a creation date. But you can also make the criteria more complex by using logical operators. A , (comma) represents the OR operator, a & or space represents the AND operator, and a ˜ (tilde) stands for the NOT operator. In the Creation Date and Revision Date fields, < and > represent less than and greater than, respectively. Here are some examples of complex retrieval criteria:

o To locate a document created between January 1, 1989, and June 3, 1989, enter **>12/31/88&<6/4/89** in the Creation Date field.

o To list all invoices for John Smith, enter **invoice & John Smith** in the Keywords field (assuming you already entered the appropriate key words in the document summary sheet).

 4.0 The Marked Files Only option is not available.

KEY Press Enter to list the files that meet the retrieval criteria.

○ To list files that contain references to either Washington or Jefferson, enter **Washington, Jefferson** in the Document Text field.

○ To list references to New York, the state, but not New York City, type **New York ~ City** in the Document Text field.

By entering criteria in more than one Query menu field, you can be very specific about the documents you're trying to locate. For instance, to list only wills prepared by Koplin after March, enter **Koplin** as the author, **Will** as a key word, and **>03/01/90** as the revision date.

PRINTING DOCUMENTS

Select the Print option on the Document-Retrieval command line to see the command line

PRINT: Summary Document Both

Indicate whether you want to print just the summary sheet, the document, or both, for all marked files.

4.0 The command line also includes the prompt *range: selection all*. Choose Selection to print just the highlighted document or All to print all those listed on the screen. To print multiple files, use the Query menu to list the files, and then select All as the range.

To print a group of related documents at one time, mark them all, then click on Print.

CUSTOMIZING THE LISTING

Select the View option on the Document-Retrieval command line to display the prompt line

VIEW: Short Long Full
        Sort by:(Directory)Author Operator Revision_date
        Creation_date Size

The View options display the list as follows:

○ **Short**: Just the document name (not the title) appears.

○ **Long**: The name, title, and the field used to sort the list appear.

○ **Full**: The summary sheet for the selected document appears on the bottom of the screen.

You can sort the display by any item listed for the Sort By option. For example, to see the name, title, and creation date of all documents in the order of their creation, select the Long view sorted by Creation Date.

COPYING DOCUMENTS

Select the Copy option from the Document-Retrieval command line to see the menu

COPY marked files to drive/directory:
delete files after copy: Yes(No)   copy style sheets: Yes(No)

Make your selections from the menu, and then click on the command line title. To move the document from one disk or directory to another, not just copy it, select Yes for the Delete Files After Copy option.

You can use the Copy command in combination with the Query command to archive documents. For instance, say you want to make a backup copy of all the documents you created or revised during the day. Start by entering the date in the Revision Date field of the Query menu. Click on QUERY to list all those files; then press Ctrl-spacebar to mark them all. Click on Copy to display the Copy menu, enter the destination disk or directory, and then click on the command line title.

You can archive files in the same way. Perhaps you're done with all the correspondence regarding a certain project, whose name you listed as a key word. Use the Query menu to list the documents. Then use the Copy command to move them to another disk for storage, selecting Yes for the Delete Files After Copy option.

KEY To back up files, press Q, enter the retrieval criteria, and press Enter. Press Ctrl-spacebar to mark the files, and then press C. Designate the destination disk and directory; then press Enter.

DOCUMENT-RETRIEVAL TECHNIQUES

Library Document-Retrieval is a very powerful command that can be used to manage your files. You can recall, print, copy, and delete individual documents using the Transfer menu, but the Document-Retrieval command line options allow you to manipulate groups of files.

If you have a hard disk or a network system in a busy office, this command can save you a great deal of time. It's quicker than using the DOS directory, copy, and delete commands. Even if you have just a few files, take advantage of these powers by completing the summary sheet when you first save a document and updating it as necessary. Figure 21.4 illustrates the basic techniques for using the Library Document-Retrieval command.

You're now thoroughly prepared to get the most out of Word. If you need help completing you own work, refer back to the appropriate

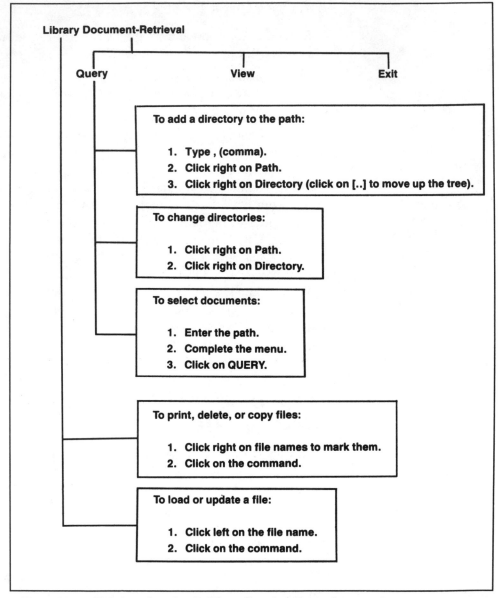

Library Document-Retrieval

Query   View   Exit

To add a directory to the path:

1. Type , (comma).
2. Click right on Path.
3. Click right on Directory (click on [..] to move up the tree).

To change directories:

1. Click right on Path.
2. Click right on Directory.

To select documents:

1. Enter the path.
2. Complete the menu.
3. Click on QUERY.

To print, delete, or copy files:

1. Click right on file names to mark them.
2. Click on the command.

To load or update a file:

1. Click left on the file name.
2. Click on the command.

o **Figure 21.4:** *Techniques for using the Library Document-Retrieval command*

chapter or section in this book. By carefully following the steps, but adjusting the measurements or settings to your own needs, you'll be able to handle even the most complicated word processing tasks.

APPENDIX

- USING
- THE
- SPELL
- AND
- THESAURUS
- COMMANDS

Word provides two powerful commands for improving your writing: Library Spell and Library Thesaurus. The Spell command compares each word in your document with those stored in its own dictionary. The Thesaurus command displays synonyms for your words, helping to vary your writing and improve your vocabulary.

○CHECKING YOUR SPELLING

4.0 Spell in version 4.0 is much different than the newer releases. Refer to the section about checking spelling with version 4.0 later in the appendix.

After you complete a document, you can use the Spell command to review the text for spelling errors. When it encounters a word not in its own list, it reports the word as not found. This does not necessarily mean the spelling is incorrect. For example, names and technical and foreign words that are spelled correctly will be reported as possible errors because they are not in Word's dictionary. However, you can add terms to the dictionary so that Spell will accept them.

Spell also cannot determine if you used the wrong word if it is a correctly spelled one. For instance, it won't report if you used too instead of to or two. It also doesn't report typographical errors that resulted in a word found in the dictionary, such as typing *doing* instead of *going*.

Even though the Spell command doesn't eliminate the need for proofreading, it can still help you catch errors.

To begin checking spelling, type your document or load it using the Transfer Load command, and then move to the start of the document.

Word begins checking spelling at the position of the cursor. But if the cursor isn't at the start of the document when you start the process, you'll see the prompt

Enter Y to continue spelling from top of document or ESC to exit

when Word reaches the end of your text. Press Y to "wrap around" to the beginning of the document to complete the process or Esc to stop.

You can also check the spelling in a specific section of text by selecting it first.

After you've positioned the cursor, click left on Library Spell. If you are using a floppy disk system, Word will display the prompt

Enter Y when Spell disk is ready

 KEY Press Alt-F6. If you're using floppy disks, insert the Spell disk, and then press Y.

Replace the program disk in drive A with the Spell disk, and then click on the message line.

Next you'll see the message

Loading dictionary ...

Then Word will display

Checking document ...

as it starts comparing the words in your document with those in its dictionary.

When the program finds a word that is not in its dictionary, one that is repeated twice in a row, or incorrect punctuation or capitalization, the screen will divide into two windows: the text window above and the Spell window below.

The message

Checking dictionaries...

might appear for an instant as Word looks up some suggested spellings. If found, they are displayed in the bottom window, along with a new command line:

SPELL: Correct Add Exit Ignore Options Undo

You can select to correct the word, add it to the dictionary, or accept it as spelled. You can also undo the last correction or even customize the way the Spell command works. Choose the option you want for each word, as explained in the following sections. You can select Exit at any time to stop the checking process.

When the spelling check is complete, Word reports the total number of words checked and the number of unknown words.

CORRECTING WORDS

KEY Select the correctly spelled word with the arrow keys, then press Enter. If the correct spelling isn't shown, press C, type the word, and press Enter.

To correct a misspelled word, click right on the proper spelling if it is shown on the screen. If the correct spelling doesn't appear on the screen, click left on Correct, type the word again, and then click on the command line title. If the word you type is not in the dictionary, you'll see this prompt:

Not in dictionary. Enter Y to retype or N to make your correction

If Word can't locate any words similar to the one in question, you'll see the prompt

No alternative words found

Click on Correct or Ignore to leave it as spelled.

If a word is found twice in a row, you'll see the message

is repeated

Click right on Correct to delete one of the words.

Accepting Words as Spelled

KEY Press I to accept the word as spelled.

When the word is spelled correctly, even though it's not in Word's dictionary, click on Ignore to leave it as is and continue checking the rest of the document. Alternatively, you can add the word to the dictionary, as explained below.

Adding Words to the Dictionary

KEY Press A to add a word to the dictionary.

If you will be frequently using a word that's not in Word's dictionary, you may want to add it. This will speed up the checking process.

The first time Word locates the word, click on Add to add the word to a dictionary. You'll see the prompt

Add word to: Standard User Document

Select the dictionary you want to add the word to:

For greatest efficiency, create a new user dictionary (as you'll soon learn how) and add words to it when you need to. Leave SPE-CIALS.CMP empty to quicken the checking process for documents that won't contain these words.

o **Standard** is the file UPDAT-AM.CMP, a separate dictionary file that Word will use with every checking process.

o **User** is the dictionary for technical words, foreign phrases, and other uncommon words that you don't want to use for every document. The user dictionary is also checked with every document. The default user dictionary is called SPECIALS.CMP.

o **Document** is the dictionary linked only with the current document. For example, suppose that while checking a document called Report, you add words to the document dictionary. A file named REPORT.CMP will be created and automatically used when you check the spelling in that document.

UNDOING CORRECTIONS

KEY Press U to return to and undo the last correction.

If you change your mind about a correction you just made, or you just want to return to the previous error, click on Undo. The last correction will return to its original form and appear on the screen.

CHANGING THE WAY SPELL WORKS

KEY Press O to see the Options menu.

Click on Options to see the Options menu and select from the following choices:

o **User Dictionary:** Enter the name of the user dictionary. For example, if you use technical terms that aren't in Word's dictionary, enter something like TECHNICAL.CMP, and then add those terms to this dictionary. This new dictionary will be used as the default the next time you start Word. So if you want to check a document that doesn't contain technical words, reenter the original default, SPECIALS.CMP, when the first unknown word is found.

o **Lookup:** A Quick lookup assumes the first two letters of the word are correct. This speeds up (but limits) the dictionary search. A Complete lookup is the default.

To save time, use Manual when you know there are many correctly spelled words in the document that aren't in the dictionary.

o **Alternative:** Using the default Auto setting, Word looks up each misspelled word before displaying the command line. Manual displays the command line without looking for alternative words in the dictionary (you have to select Correct for the dictionary search).

o **Ignore All Caps:** Select Yes to have Word skip words that are all capital letters.

o **Check Punctuation:** Select Yes to have Word report improper punctuation—the characters @ # % & * + = _ and all numbers that immediately precede or follow words. If you select No, these characters are treated as spaces and ignored, so something like *hello#there* will be viewed as *hello there*.

○CHECKING SPELLING WITH VERSION 4.0

 Press Alt-F6 to select Library Spell.

To use the Spell command with version 4.0, type or load your document, and then click left on Library Spell.

You'll see the message

Saving work file ...

in the command area while Word saves a special working copy of your document to use during the spelling checking process.

If you're using floppy disks, you should always keep some extra space on your document disk for this working copy. Before starting Word, use the DOS DIR command to display a list of files on the disk and the amount of free space. Make sure the number of free bytes (characters) shown at the end of the directory listing is large enough to hold a duplicate copy of any document you wish to check.

After saving a copy of the file, Word begins the checking process. If you are using a floppy disk system, Word will display the prompt

 Insert the Spell disk, and then press Y.

Enter Y when Spell disk is ready

Replace the program disk in drive A with the Spell disk, and then click on the message line.

The screen will divide into three smaller windows with a new command line:

COMMAND: Dictionary Help Lookup Options Proof Quit

Press P to begin checking the spelling.

Click on Proof to begin checking your document. (We'll review the other options is a moment.)

Next you'll see the message

reading document

while the document is loaded into the computer's memory. Then the message

Checking document

appears in the status line while Word begins comparing the words in your document with those in the dictionary.

When the program finds a word that is not in its dictionary, or one that is repeated twice in a row, the word appears in the bottom window, and the text in which it was found is at the top. A new command line also appears:

COMMAND: Add Correct Lookup Help Ignore Mark Options Quit Resume Next Previous

 Select the correctly spelled word, and then press Enter. If it is not in the list, press C, type the word correctly, and press Enter.

To correct the word, click right on the proper spelling if it is shown on the screen. If the correct spelling doesn't appear on the screen, click left on Correct, type the word again, and then click on the command line title. If the word you type is not in the dictionary, you'll see the prompt

Not in dictionary. Enter Y to retype or N to make your correction

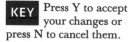 Press C or I to accept the word as spelled.

If Word can't locate any words similar to the one in question, you'll see the prompt

No alternative words found

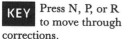 Press I to leave the word as spelled. Press A to add the word to your own dictionary.

Click on Correct or on Ignore to accept the word as spelled.

If the word is spelled correctly, but not in Word's dictionary, you can click on Ignore to accept it as is and continue the checking process. If it's a word you will be using often, you may want to add it to your own dictionary. Click on Add to place the word in the dictionary. You can select a personal dictionary using the Options command, as discussed shortly.

KEY Press Y to accept your changes or press N to cancel them.

When the entire document has been checked, you'll see the prompt

Enter Y to process, N to discard changes

Click on the message line to accept your changes or press N to cancel them.

KEY Press Q to quit.

If you want to stop the spelling checking process before the whole document has been checked, click on Quit.

You can also make the following selections while a document is being checked:

KEY Press N, P, or R to move through corrections.

o **Next**: Skips ahead to the next incorrect word.

o **Previous**: Moves back to the last incorrect word.

o **Resume**: Returns to the original word after Next or Previous has been selected.

KEY Press L to look up other words.

o **Lookup**: Searches the directory for the correct spelling and displays a list of possible words. However, you cannot select from this list as you can from the Correct option's listing; it is provided only for reference.

Press H for help instructions.

o **Help**: Displays instructions for using the spelling checker.

o **Mark**: Inserts a special marking character (an asterisk by default) in front of the word. You can check the proper spelling of the word, return to the document, and locate the word using the Search command, and then correct it. You can select a marking character from the Options menu.

 Press M to mark words.

o **Options**: Displays a menu of choices that allow you to change the way the spelling checker works. From this menu, select Quick for the Lookup option to have the program assume the first two letters of the word are correct (this speeds up but limits the dictionary search). Select Yes for the Ignore All Caps option to skip words that are all capital letters. If you want to change the character for marking words, select one for the Marking Character option. Select Manual for the Alternative option if you want to be able to retype the word yourself before Word searches the dictionary and displays a list of alternative spellings.

 Press O to see the Options menu.

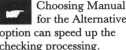 Choosing Manual for the Alternative option can speed up the checking processing. Looking up alternatives can be time consuming, particularly if you made typographical errors and can easily retype the word yourself. You can change this option during the checking process.

OTHER SPELLING CHECKER OPTIONS

In addition to Proof, the initial Spell command line has several selections. You can select Help for instructions, Options to display the Options menu, or Quit to return to the document. The two other options are Dictionary and Lookup, which are described below.

Select the Dictionary option to use a personal dictionary along with the primary one. The dictionary Word uses to check spelling is the SPELL-AM.LEX file, which contains the most common words found in the English language. If you use names, technical words, foreign phrases, or uncommon words in your writing, these will be reported as possible misspellings. By selecting the Dictionary option, you can create and use your own personal dictionary. The first time a word is reported as unknown, add it to the personal dictionary, and that word will not be reported as misspelled again.

To use or create a dictionary, press D to see the prompt

DICTIONARY: Specials.CMP

Press ← to use the default name as your personal dictionary, or type another name and then press ←. You can have as many personal dictionaries as you want.

The Lookup option allows you to search for a word in the dictionary. Type the word you're searching for at the prompt WORD, and then press ←. The program will report if the word is found or display a list of words with similar spellings.

oUSING THE THESAURUS

When you are looking for just the right word, use Word's Library Thesaurus command. It can recommend alternative words so you can avoid repeating a word or phrase in the same sentence or paragraph. This not only builds your vocabulary, but enhances the quality of your documents.

 KEY Press Ctrl-F6 to activate the Thesaurus.

To use the Thesaurus command, place the cursor anywhere in the word you want to replace, and then click left on Library Thesaurus. If you are using a floppy disk system, you will be prompted to replace the Word disk in drive A with the Thesaurus disk.

Word will look for a word with similar meaning while displaying the message

Looking up *your-word*

If synonyms are found, they are displayed in a second window. When there are more words than can fit on the screen, the message MORE PgDn or MORE PgUp will appear. If you don't see the word you want, press PgUp or PgDn to display the additional choices.

 KEY Use the arrow keys to select a new word, and then press Enter to replace it for the one in the text. Press Ctrl-F6 to look up other synonyms.

Click right on the word you want to select. If no words seem exactly appropriate, select one that's close, and then click on Ctrl-F6: Look Up. Word will display another list of suggestions.

If your word is not in its thesaurus list, Word will try to locate its root word and display synonyms of it instead. Root word synonyms may or may not be appropriate. For example, looking up *pretentious* will display synonyms for *pretense*. However, looking up *cursor* will present synonyms for *curse*. If Word can't even find a root word, it displays a list of words similar in spelling.

KEY Press Esc to
return to the
document.

To return to the document, click on ESC: Exit. You can select this option at any time to stop the search for synonyms.

If you are trying to think of a word but don't know where to begin, type a word with a similar meaning—even if you know it's not the one you want. This will be a starting place for your search.

oSPECIAL CHARACTERS INDEX

oALPHABETICAL INDEX

o A

o B

o C

Selections from The SYBEX Library

WORD PROCESSING

The ABC's of WordPerfect 5
Alan R. Neibauer
283pp. Ref. 504-2

This introduction explains the basics of desktop publishing with WordPerfect 5: editing, layout, formatting, printing, sorting, merging, and more. Readers are shown how to use WordPerfect 5's new features to produce great-looking reports.

The ABC's of WordPerfect
Alan R. Neibauer
239pp. Ref. 425-9

This basic introduction to WordPefect consists of short, step-by-step lessons—for new users who want to get going fast. Topics range from simple editing and formatting, to merging, sorting, macros, and more. Includes version 4.2

Mastering WordPerfect 5
Susan Baake Kelly
709pp. Ref. 500-X

The revised and expanded version of this definitive guide is now on WordPerfect 5 and covers wordprocessing and basic desktop publishing. As more than 200,000 readers of the original edition can attest, no tutorial approaches it for clarity and depth of treatment. Sorting, line drawing, and laser printing included.

Mastering WordPerfect
Susan Baake Kelly
435pp. Ref. 332-5

Step-by-step training from startup to mastery, featuring practical uses (form letters, newsletters and more), plus advanced topics such as document security and macro creation, sorting and columnar math. Includes Version 4.2.

Advanced Techniques in WordPerfect 5
Kay Yarborough Nelson
586pp. Ref. 511-5

Now updated for Version 5, this invaluable guide to the advanced features of Word-Perfect provides step-by-step instructions and practical examples covering those specialized techniques which have most perplexed users--indexing, outlining, foreign-language typing, mathematical functions, and more.

WordPerfect Desktop Companion
SYBEX Ready Reference Series
Greg Harvey/Kay Yarbourough Nelson
663pp. Ref. 507-7

This compact encyclopedia offers detailed, cross-referenced entries on every software feature, organized for fast, convenient on-the-job help. Includes self-contained enrichment material with tips, techniques and macros. Special information is included about laser printing using WordPerfect that is not available elsewhere. For Version 4.2.

WordPerfect 5 Desktop Companion
SYBEX Ready Reference Series
Greg Harvey/Kay Yarborough Nelson
1000pp. Ref. 522-0

Desktop publishing features have been added to this compact encyclopedia. This title offers more detailed, cross-referenced entries on every software features including page formatting and layout, laser printing and word processing macros. New users of WordPerfect, and those new to Version 5 and desktop publishing will find this easy to use for on-the-job help. For Version 5.

WordPerfect Tips and Tricks (Third Edition)
Alan R. Neibauer
650pp. Ref. 520-4

This new edition is a real timesaver. For on-the-job guidance and creative new uses, this title covers all versions of WordPerfect up to and including 5.0—covers streamlining documents, automating with macros, new print enhancements, and more.

WordPerfect 5 Instant Reference
Greg Harvey/Kay Yarborough Nelson
316pp. Ref. 535-2

This pocket-sized reference has all the program commands for the powerful WordPerfect 5 organized alphabetically for quick access. Each command entry has the exact key sequence, any reveal codes, a list of available options, and option-by-option discussions.

WordPerfect Instant Reference SYBEX Prompter Series
Greg Harvey/Kay Yarborough Nelson
254pp. Ref. 476-3

When you don't have time to go digging through the manuals, this fingertip guide offers clear, concise answers: command summaries, correct usage, and exact keystroke sequences for on-the-job tasks. Convenient organization reflects the structure of WordPerfect.

Mastering SAMNA
Ann McFarland Draper
503pp. Ref. 376-7

Word-processing professionals learn not just how, but also when and why to use SAMNA's many powerful features. Master the basics, gain power-user skills, return again and again for reference and expert tips.

The ABC's of Microsoft WORD
Alan R. Neibauer
321pp. Ref. 497-6

Users who want to wordprocess straightforward documents and print elegant reports without wading through reams of documentation will find all they need to know about MicroSoft WORD in this basic guide. Simple editing, formatting, merging, sorting, macros and style sheets are detailed.

Mastering Microsoft WORD (Third Edition)
Matthew Holtz
638pp. Ref. 524-7

This comprehensive, step-by-step guide includes Version 4.0. Hands-on tutorials treat everything from word processing basics to the fundamentals of desktop publishing, stressing business applications throughout.

Advanced Techinques in Microsoft WORD
Alan R. Neibauer
537pp. Ref. 416-X

The book starts with a brief overview, but the main focus is on practical applications using advanced features. Topics include customization, forms, style sheets, columns, tables, financial documents, graphics and data management.

Mastering DisplayWrite 4
Michael E. McCarthy
447pp. Ref. 510-7

Total training, reference and support for users at all levels--in plain, non-technical language. Novices will be up and running in an hour's time; everyone will gain complete word-processing and document-management skills.

Mastering MultiMate Advantage II
Charles Ackerman
407pp. Ref. 482-8

This comprehensive tutorial covers all the capabilities of MultiMate, and highlights the differences between MultiMate Advantage II and previous versions--in pathway support, sorting, math, DOS access, using dBASE III, and more. With many practical examples, and a chapter on the On-File database.

The Complete Guide to MultiMate
Carol Holcomb Dreger
208pp. Ref. 229-9

This step-by-step tutorial is also an excellent reference guide to MultiMate features and uses. Topics include search/replace, library and merge functions, repagination, document defaults and more.

Advanced Techniques in MultiMate
Chris Gilbert
275pp. Ref. 412-7
A textbook on efficient use of MultiMate for business applications, in a series of self-contained lessons on such topics as multiple columns, high-speed merging, mailing-list printing and Key Procedures.

Introduction to WordStar
Arthur Naiman
208pp. Ref. 134-9
This all time bestseller is an engaging first-time introduction to word processing as well as a complete guide to using WordStar--from basic editing to blocks, global searches, formatting, dot commands, SpellStar and MailMerge.

Mastering Wordstar on the IBM PC (Second Edition)
Arthur Naiman
200pp. Ref. 392-9
A specially revised and expanded introduction to Wordstar with SpellStar and MailMerge. Reviewers call it "clearly written, conveniently organized, generously illustrated and definitely designed from the user's point of view."

Practical WordStar Uses
Julie Anne Arca
303pp. Ref. 107-1
A hands-on guide to WordStar and MailMerge applications, with solutions to comon problems and "recipes" for day-to-day tasks. Formatting, merge-printing and much more; plus a quick-reference command chart and notes on CP/M and PC-DOS.

Practical Techniques in WordStar Release 4
Julie Anne Arca
334pp. Ref. 465-8

A task oriented approach to WordStar Release 4 and the DOS operating system. Special applications are covered in detail with summaries of important commands and step-by-step instructions.

Mastering WordStar Release 4
Greg Harvey
413pp. Ref. 399-6
Practical training and reference for the latest WordStar release--from startup to advanced featues. Experienced users will find new features highlighted and illustrated with hands-on examples. Covers math, macros, laser printers and more.

WordStar Instant Reference
David J. Clark
314pp. Ref. 543-3
This quick reference provides reminders on the use of the editing, formatting, mailmerge, and document processing commands available through WordStar 4 and 5. Operations are organized alphabetically for easy access. The text includes a survey of the menu system and instructions for installing and customizing WordStar.

Understanding WordStar 2000
David Kolodney/Thomas Blackadar
275pp. Ref. 554-9
This engaging, fast-paced series of tutorials covers everything from moving the cursor to print enhancements, format files, key glossaries, windows and MailMerge. With practical examples, and notes for former WordStar users.

Advanced Techniques in WordStar 2000
John Donovan
350pp. Ref. 418-0
This task-oriented guide to Release 2 builds advanced skills by developing practical applications. Tutorials cover everything from simple printing to macro creation and complex merging. With MailList, StarIndex and TelMerge.

SPREADSHEETS AND INTEGRATED SOFTWARE

The ABC's of 1-2-3 (Second Edition)
Chris Gilbert/Laurie Williams
245pp. Ref. 355-4

Online Today recommends it as "an easy and comfortable way to get started with the program." An essential tutorial for novices, it will remain on your desk as a valuable source of ongoing reference and support. For Release 2.

Mastering 1-2-3 (Second Edition)
Carolyn Jorgensen
702pp. Ref. 528-X

Get the most from 1-2-3 Release 2 with this step-by-step guide emphasizing advanced features and practical uses. Topics include data sharing, macros, spreadsheet security, expanded memory, and graphics enhancements.

Lotus 1-2-3 Desktop Companion (SYBEX Ready Reference Series)
Greg Harvey
976pp. Ref. 501-8

A full-time consultant, right on your desk. Hundreds of self-contained entries cover every 1-2-3 feature, organized by topic, indexed and cross-referenced, and supplemented by tips, macros and working examples. For Release 2.

Advanced Techniques in Lotus 1-2-3
Peter Antoniak/E. Michael Lunsford
367pp. Ref. 556-5

This guide for experienced users focuses on advanced functions, and techniques for designing menu-driven applications using macros and the Release 2 command language. Interfacing techniques and add-on products are also considered.

Lotus 1-2-3 Tips and Tricks
Gene Weisskopf
396pp. Ref. 454-2

A rare collection of timesavers and tricks for longtime Lotus users. Topics include macros, range names, spreadsheet design, hardware considerations, DOS operations, efficient data analysis, printing, data interchange, applications development, and more.

Lotus 1-2-3 Instant Reference SYBEX Prompter Series
Greg Harvey/Kay Yarborough Nelson
296pp. Ref. 475-5; 4 3/4x8

Organized information at a glance. When you don't have time to hunt through hundreds of pages of manuals, turn here for a quick reminder: the right key sequence, a brief explanation of a command, or the correct syntax for a specialized function.

Mastering Lotus HAL
Mary V. Campbell
342pp. Ref. 422-4

A complete guide to using HAL "natural language" requests to communicate with 1-2-3—for new and experienced users. Covers all the basics, plus advanced HAL features such as worksheet linking and auditing, macro recording, and more.

Mastering Symphony (Fourth Edition)
Douglas Cobb
857pp. Ref. 494-1

Thoroughly revised to cover all aspects of the major upgrade of Symphony Version 2, this Fourth Edition of Doug Cobb's classic is still "the Symphony bible" to this complex but even more powerful package. All the new features are discussed and placed in context with prior versions so that both new and previous users will benefit from Cobb's insights.

The ABC's of Quattro
Alan Simpson/Douglas J. Wolf
286pp. Ref. 560-3

Especially for users new to spreadsheets, this is an introduction to the basic concepts and a guide to instant productivity through editing and using spreadsheet formulas and functions. Includes how to print out graphs and data for presentation. For Quattro 1.1.

Mastering Quattro
Alan Simpson
576pp. Ref. 514-X

This tutorial covers not only all of Quattro's classic spreadsheet features, but also its added capabilities including extended graphing, modifiable menus, and the macro debugging environment. Simpson brings out how to use all of Quattro's new-generation-spreadsheet capabilities.

Mastering Framework II
Douglas Hergert/Jonathan Kamin
509pp. Ref. 390-2

This business-minded tutorial includes a complete introduction to idea processing, "frames," and software integration, along with its comprehensive treatment of word processing, spreadsheet, and database management with Framework.

The ABC's of Excel on the IBM PC
Douglas Hergert
326pp. Ref. 567-0

This book is a brisk and friendly introduction to the most important features of Microsoft Excel for PC's. This beginner's book discusses worksheets, charts, database operations, and macros, all with hands-on examples. Written for all versions through Version 2.

Mastering Excel on the IBM PC
Carl Townsend
628pp. Ref. 403-8

A complete Excel handbook with step-by-step tutorials, sample applications and an extensive reference section. Topics include worksheet fundamentals, formulas and windows, graphics, database techniques, special features, macros and more.

Mastering Enable
Keith D. Bishop
517pp. Ref. 440-2

A comprehensive, practical, hands-on guide to Enable 2.0—integrated word processing, spreadsheet, database management, graphics, and communications—from basic concepts to custom menus, macros and the Enable Procedural Language.

Mastering Q & A (Second Edition)
Greg Harvey
540pp. Ref. 452-6

This hands-on tutorial explores the Q & A Write, File, and Report modules, and the Intelligent Assistant. English-language command processor, macro creation, interfacing with other software, and more, using practical business examples.

Mastering SuperCalc 4
Greg Harvey
311pp. Ref. 419-4

A guided tour of this spreadsheet, database and graphics package shows how and why it adds up to a powerful business planning tool. Step-by-step lessons and real-life examples cover every aspect of the program.

Understanding Javelin PLUS
John R. Levine
Margaret Levine Young
Jordan M. Young
558pp. Ref. 358-9

This detailed guide to Javelin's latest release includes a concise introduction to business modeling, from profit-and-loss analysis to manufacturing studies. Readers build sample models and produce multiple reports and graphs, to master Javelin's unique features.

DATABASE MANAGEMENT

Mastering Paradox (Third Edition)
Alan Simpson
663pp. Ref. 490-9

Paradox is given authoritative, comprehensive explanation in Simpson's up-to-date new edition which goes from database basics to command-file programming with PAL. Topics include multiuser networking, the Personal Programmer Application Generator, the Data-Entry Toolkit, and more.

The ABC's of dBASE IV
Robert Cowart
300pp. Ref. 531-X
This superb tutorial introduces beginners to the concept of databases and practical dBASE IV applications featuring the new menu-driven interface, the new report writer, and Query by Example.

Understanding dBASE IV (Special Edition)
Alan Simpson
880pp. Ref. 509-3
This Special Edition is the best introduction to dBASE IV, written by 1 million-reader-strong dBASE expert Alan Simpson. First it gives basic skills for creating and manipulating efficient databases. Then the author explains how to make reports, manage multiple databases, and build applications. Includes Fast Track speed notes.

dBASE III PLUS Programmer's Reference Guide (SYBEX Ready Reference Series)
Alan Simpson
1056pp. Ref. 508-5
Programmers will save untold hours and effort using this comprehensive, well-organized dBASE encyclopedia. Complete technical details on commands and functions, plus scores of often-needed algorithms.

The ABC's of dBASE III PLUS
Robert Cowart
264pp. Ref. 379-1
The most efficient way to get beginners up and running with dBASE. Every 'how' and 'why' of database management is demonstrated through tutorials and practical dBASE III PLUS applications.

Mastering dBASE III PLUS: A Structured Approach
Carl Townsend
342pp. Ref. 372-4
In-depth treatment of structured programming for custom dBASE solutions. An ideal study and reference guide for applications developers, new and experienced users with an interest in efficient programming.

Also:
Mastering dBASE III: A Structured Approach
Carl Townsend
338pp. Ref. 301-5

Understanding dBASE III PLUS
Alan Simpson
415pp. Ref. 349-X
A solid sourcebook of training and ongoing support. Everything from creating a first database to command file programming is presented in working examples, with tips and techniques you won't find anywhere else.

Also:
Understanding dBASE III
Alan Simpson
300pp. Ref. 267-1

Understanding dBASE II
Alan Simpson
260pp. Ref. 147-0

Advanced Techniques in dBASE III PLUS
Alan Simpson
454pp. Ref. 369-4
A full course in database design and structured programming, with routines for inventory control, accounts receivable, system management, and integrated databases.

Simpson's dBASE Tips and Tricks (For dBASE III PLUS)
Alan Simpson
420pp. Ref. 383-X

A unique library of techniques and programs shows how creative use of built-in features can solve all your needs--without expensive add-on products or external languages. Spreadsheet functions, graphics, and much more.

Expert dBASE III PLUS
Judd Robbins/Ken Braly
423pp. Ref. 404-6
Experienced dBASE programmers learn scores of advanced techniques for maximizing performance and efficiency in program design, development and testing, database design, indexing, input and output, using compilers, and much more.

dBASE Instant Reference
SYBEX Prompter Series
Alan Simpson
471pp. Ref. 484-4; 4 3/4x8
Comprehensive information at a glance: a brief explanation of syntax and usage for every dBASE command, with step-by-step instructions and exact keystroke sequences. Commands are grouped by function in twenty precise categories.

Understanding R:BASE
Alan Simpson/Karen Watterson
609pp. Ref.503-4
This is the definitive R:BASE tutorial, for use with either OS/2 or DOS. Hands-on lessons cover every aspect of the software, from creating and using a database, to custom systems. Includes Fast Track speed notes.

Also:
Understanding R:BASE 5000
Alan Simpson
413pp. Ref. 302-3

Understanding Oracle
James T. Perry/Joseph G. Lateer
634pp. Ref. 534-4
A comprehensive guide to the Oracle database management system for administrators, users, and applications developers. Covers everything in Version 5 from database basics to multi-user systems, performance, and development tools including SQL*Forms, SQL*Report,

and SQL*Calc. Includes Fast Track speed notes.

DESKTOP PUBLISHING

Mastering Ventura (Second Edition)
Matthew Holtz
600pp. Ref. 581-6
A complete, step-by-step guide to IBM PC desktop publishing with Xerox Ventura Publisher. Practical examples show how to use style sheets, format pages, cut and paste, enhance layouts, import material from other programs, and more.

Ventura Tips and Techniques
Carl Townsend/Sandy Townsend
424pp. Ref. 559-X
Packed with an experienced Ventura user's tips and tricks, this volume is a time saver and design booster. From crop marks to file management to using special fonts, this book is for serious Ventura users. Covers Ventura 2.

Ventura Instant Reference
Matthew Holtz
320pp. Ref. 544-1
This compact volume offers easy access to the complex details of Ventura modes and options, commands, side-bars, file management, output device configuration, and control. Written for versions through Ventura 2, it also includes standard procedures for project and job control.

Mastering PageMaker on the IBM PC (Second Edition)
Antonia Stacy Jolles
400pp. Ref. 521-2
A guide to every aspect of desktop publishing with PageMaker: the vocabulary and basics of page design, layout, graphics and typography, plus instructions for creating finished typeset publications of all kinds.

Mastering Ready, Set, Go!
David A. Kater
482pp. Ref. 536-0

This hands-on introduction to the popular desktop publishing package for the Macintosh allows readers to produce professional-looking reports, brochures, and flyers. Written for Version 4, this title has been endorsed by Letraset, the Ready, Set, Go! software publisher.

Understanding PostScript Programming
(Second Edition)
David A. Holzgang
472pp. Ref. 566-2

In-depth treatment of PostScript for programmers and advanced users working on custom desktop publishing tasks. Hands-on development of programs for font creation, integrating graphics, printer implementations and more.

COMPUTER-AIDED DESIGN AND DRAFTING

The ABC's of AutoCAD
(Second Edition)
Alan R. Miller
375pp. Ref. 584-0

This brief but effective introduction to AutoCAD quickly gets users drafting and designing with this complex CADD package. The essential operations and capabilities of AutoCAD are neatly detailed, using a proven, step-by-step method that is tailored to the results-oriented beginner.

Mastering AutoCAD
(Third Edition)
George Omura
825pp. Ref. 574-3

Now in its third edition, this tutorial guide to computer-aided design and drafting with AutoCAD is perfect for newcomers to CADD, as well as AutoCAD users seeking greater proficiency. An architectural project serves as an example throughout.

Advanced Techniques in AutoCAD
(Second Edition)
Robert M. Thomas
425pp. Ref. 593-X

Develop custom applications using screen menus, command macros, and AutoLISP programming--no prior programming experience required. Topics include customizing the AutoCAD environment, advanced data extraction techniques, and much more.

DOS

The ABC's of DOS 4
Alan R. Miller
250pp. Ref. 583-2

This step-by-step introduction to using DOS 4 is written especially for beginners. Filled with simple examples, *The ABC's of DOS 4* covers the basics of hardware, software, disks, the system editor EDLIN, DOS commands, and more.

ABC's of MS-DOS
(Second Edition)
Alan R. Miller
233pp. Ref. 493-3

This handy guide to MS-DOS is all many PC users need to manage their computer files, organize floppy and hard disks, use EDLIN, and keep their computers organized. Additional information is given about utilities like Sidekick, and there is a DOS command and program summary. The second edition is fully updated for Version 3.3.

Mastering DOS
(Second Edition)
Judd Robbins
700pp. Ref. 555-7

"The most useful DOS book." This seven-part, in-depth tutorial addresses the needs of users at all levels. Topics range from running applications, to managing files and directories, configuring the system, batch file programming, and techniques for system developers.

MS-DOS Handbook
(Third Edition)
Richard Allen King
362pp. Ref. 492-5
This classic has been fully expanded and revised to include the latest features of MS-DOS Version 3.3. Two reference books in one, this title has separate sections for programmer and user. Multi-DOS partitons, 3 1/2disk format, batch file call and return feature, and comprehensive coverage of MS-DOS commands are included.

MS-DOS Power User's Guide,
Volume I
(Second Edition)
Jonathan Kamin
482pp. Ref. 473-9
A fully revised, expanded edition of our best-selling guide to high-performance DOS techniques and utilities--with details on Version 3.3. Configuration, I/O, directory structures, hard disks, RAM disks, batch file programming, the ANSI.SYS device driver, more.

MS-DOS Advanced
Programming
Michael J. Young
490pp. Ref. 578-6
Practical techniques for maximizing performance in MS-DOS software by making best use of system resources. Topics include functions, interrupts, devices, multitasking, memory residency and more, with examples in C and assembler.

Essential PC-DOS
(Second Edition)
**Myril Clement Shaw/
Susan Soltis Shaw**
332pp. Ref. 413-5
An authoritative guide to PC-DOS, including version 3.2. Designed to make experts out of beginners, it explores everything from disk management to batch file programming. Includes an 85-page command summary.

DOS User's Desktop Companion
Judd Robbins
969 pp. Ref. 505-0 Softcover
459-3 Hardcover

This comprehensive reference covers DOS commands, batch files, memory enhancements, printing, communications and more information on optimizing each user's DOS environment. Written with step-by-step instructions and plenty of examples, this volume covers all versions through 3.3.

MS-DOS Power User's Guide,
Volume II
Martin Waterhouse/Jonathan Kamin
418pp, Ref. 411-9
A second volume of high-performance techniques and utilities, with expanded coverage of DOS 3.3, and new material on video modes, Token-Ring and PC Network support, micro-mainframe links, extended and expanded memory, multitasking systems, and more.

The IBM PC-DOS Handbook
(Third Edition)
Richard Allen King
359pp. Ref. 512-3
A guide to the inner workings of PC-DOS 3.2, for intermediate to advanced users and programmers of the IBM PC series. Topics include disk, screen and port control, batch files, networks, compatibility, and more.

DOS Instant Reference
SYBEX Prompter Series
Greg Harvey/Kay Yarborough Nelson
220pp. Ref. 477-1; 4 3/4x8
A complete fingertip reference for fast, easy on-line help:command summaries, syntax, usage and error messages. Organized by function--system commands, file commands, disk management, directories, batch files, I/O, networking, programming, and more.

OTHER OPERATING SYSTEMS AND ENVIRONMENTS

Essential OS/2
Judd Robbins
367pp. Ref. 478-X

This introduction to OS/2 for new and prospective users offers clear explanations of multitasking, details key OS/2 commands and functions, and updates current DOS users to the new OS/2 world. Details are also given for users to run existing DOS programs under OS/2.

Programmer's Guide to OS/2
Michael J. Young
625pp. Ref. 464-X
This concise introduction gives a complete overview of program development under OS/2, with careful attention to new tools and features. Topics include MS-DOS compatibility, device drivers, services, graphics, windows, the LAN manager, and more.

Programmer's Guide to GEM
Phillip Balma/William Fitler
504pp. Ref. 297-3
GEM programming from the ground up, including the Resource Construction Set, ICON Editor, and Virtual Device Interface. Build a complete graphics application with objects, events, menus, windows, alerts and dialogs.

Understanding Hard Disk Management
Jonathan Kamin
500pp. Ref. 561-1
Put your work, your office or your entire business literally at your fingertips, in a customized, automated MS-DOS work environment. Topics include RAM disks, extended and expanded memory, and more.

Programmer's Guide to Windows
(Second Edition)
David Durant/Geta Carlson/Paul Yao
704pp. Ref. 496-8
The first edition of this programmer's guide was hailed as a classic. This new edition covers Windows 2 and Windows/386 in depth. Special emphasis is given to over fifty new routines to the Windows interface, and to preparation for OS/2 Presentation Manager compatibility.

Graphics Programming Under Windows
Brian Myers/Chris Doner
646pp. Ref. 448-8
Straightforward discussion, abundant examples, and a concise reference guide to graphics commands make this book a must for Windows programmers. Topics range from how Windows works to programming for business, animation, CAD, and desktop publishing. For Version 2.

LANGUAGES

Mastering Turbo Pascal 5
Douglas Hergert
595pp. Ref. 529-8
This in-depth treatment of Turbo Pascal Versions 4 and 5 offers separate sections on the Turbo environment, the new debugger, the extensive capabilities of the language itself, and special techniques for graphics, date arithmetic, and recursion. Assumes some programming knowledge.

Advanced Techniques in Turbo Pascal
Charles C. Edwards
309pp. Ref. 350-3
This collection of system-oriented techniques and sample programs shows how to make the most of IBM PC capabilities using Turbo Pascal. Topics include screens, windows, directory management, the mouse interface, and communications.

Turbo BASIC Instant Reference
SYBEX Prompter Series
Douglas Hergert
393pp. Ref. 485-2
This quick reference for programmers offers concise, alphabetical entries on every command--statement, metastatement, function, and operation--in the Turbo BASIC language with descriptions, syntax, and examples cross-referenced to related commands.

Introduction to Turbo BASIC
Douglas Hergert
523pp. Ref. 441-0

A complete tutorial and guide to this now highly professional language: Turbo BASIC, including important Turbo extras such as parameter passing, structured loops, long integers, recursion, and 8087 compatibility for high-speed numerical operation.

Advanced Techniques in Turbo Prolog
Carl Townsend
398pp. Ref. 428-3

A goldmine of techniques and predicates for control procedures, string operations, list processing, database operations, BIOS-level support, program development, expert systems, natural language processing, and much more.

Introduction to Turbo Prolog
Carl Townsend
315pp. Ref. 359-7

This comprehensive tutorial includes sample applications for expert systems, natural language interfaces, and simulation. Covers every aspect of Prolog: facts, objects and predicates, rules, recursion, databases, and much more.

Turbo Pascal Toolbox (Second Edition)
Frank Dutton
425pp. Ref. 602-2

This collection of tested, efficient Turbo Pascal building blocks gives a boost to intermediate-level programmers, while teaching effective programming by example. Topics include accessing DOS, menus, bit maps, screen handling, and much more.

Introduction to Pascal: Including Turbo Pascal (Second Edition)
Rodnay Zaks
464pp. Ref. 533-6

This best-selling tutorial builds complete mastery of Pascal--from basic structured programming concepts, to advanced I/O, data structures, file operations, sets, pointers and lists, and more. Both ISO Standard and Turbo Pascal.

Introduction to Pascal (Including UCSD Pascal)
Rodnay Zaks
420pp. Ref. 066-0

This edition of our best-selling tutorial on Pascal programming gives special attention to the UCSD Pascal implementation for small computers. Covers everything from basic concepts to advanced data structures and more.

Celestial BASIC: Astronomy on Your Computer
Eric Burgess
300pp. Ref. 087-3

A complete home planetarium. This collection of BASIC programs for astronomical calculations enables armchair astronomers to observe and identify on screen the configurations and motions of sun, moon, planets and stars.

Mastering Turbo C
Stan Kelly-Bootle
578pp. Ref. 462-3

No prior knowledge of C or structured programming is required for this introductory course on the Turbo C language and development environment by this well-known author. A logical progression of tutorials and useful sample programs build a thorough understanding of Turbo C.

Systems Programming in Turbo C
Michael J. Young
365pp. Ref. 467-4

An introduction to advanced programming with Borland's Turbo C, and a goldmine of ready-made routines for the system programmer's library: DOS and BIOS interfacing, interrupt handling, windows, graphics, expanded memory, UNIX utilities, and more.

Understanding C
Bruce H. Hunter
320pp. Ref. 123-3

A programmer's introduction to C, with special attention to implementations for microcomputers--both CP/M and MS-DOS. Topics include data types, storage management, pointers, random I/O, function libraries, compilers and more.

Mastering C
Craig Bolon
437pp. Ref. 326-0

This in-depth guide stresses planning, testing, efficiency and portability in C applications. Topics include data types, storage classes, arrays, pointers, data structures, control statements, I/O and the C function library.

Data Handling Utilities in Microsoft C
Robert A. Radcliffe/Thomas J. Raab
519pp. Ref. 444-5

A C library for commercial programmers, with techniques and utilities for data entry, validation, display and storage. Focuses on creating and manipulating custom logical data types: dates, dollars, phone numbers, much more.

HARDWARE

The RS-232 Solution
Joe Campbell
194pp. Ref. 140-3

A complete how-to guide to trouble-free RS-232-C interfacing from scratch. In-depth coverage of concepts, techniques and testing devices, and case studies deriving cables for a variety of common computers, printers and modems.

Mastering Serial Communications
Peter W. Gofton
289pp. Ref. 180-2

The software side of communications, with details on the IBM PC's serial programming, the XMODEM and Kermit protocols, non-ASCII data transfer, interrupt-level programming and more. Sample programs in C, assembly language and BASIC.

Microprocessor Interfacing Techniques (Third Edition)
Austin Lesea/Rodnay Zaks
456pp. Ref. 029-6

This handbook is for engineers and hobbyists alike, covering every aspect of interfacing microprocessors with peripheral devices. Topics include assembling a CPU, basic I/O, analog circuitry, and bus standards.

From Chips to Systems: An Introduction to Microcomputers (Second Edition)
Rodnay Zaks/Alexander Wolfe
580pp. Ref. 377-5

The best-selling introduction to microcomputer hardware--now fully updated, revised, and illustrated. Such recent advances as 32-bit processors and RISC architecture are introduced and explained for the first time in a beginning text.

Mastering Digital Device Control
William G. Houghton
366pp. Ref. 346-5

Complete principles of system design using single-chip microcontrollers, with numerous examples. Topics include expanding memory and I/O, interfacing with multi-chip CPUs, clocks, display devices, analog measurements, and much more.

TO JOIN THE SYBEX MAILING LIST OR ORDER BOOKS
PLEASE COMPLETE THIS FORM

NAME _____ COMPANY _____

STREET _____ CITY _____

STATE _____ ZIP _____

☐ PLEASE MAIL ME MORE INFORMATION ABOUT **SYBEX** TITLES

ORDER FORM (There is no obligation to order)

PLEASE SEND ME THE FOLLOWING:

TITLE	QTY	PRICE
_____	_____	_____
_____	_____	_____
_____	_____	_____
_____	_____	_____

TOTAL BOOK ORDER _____ $_____

CUSTOMER SIGNATURE _____

SHIPPING AND HANDLING PLEASE ADD $2.00 PER BOOK VIA UPS _____

FOR OVERSEAS SURFACE ADD $5.25 PER BOOK PLUS $4.40 REGISTRATION FEE _____

FOR OVERSEAS AIRMAIL ADD $18.25 PER BOOK PLUS $4.40 REGISTRATION FEE _____

CALIFORNIA RESIDENTS PLEASE ADD APPLICABLE SALES TAX _____

TOTAL AMOUNT PAYABLE _____

☐ CHECK ENCLOSED   ☐ VISA
☐ MASTERCARD   ☐ AMERICAN EXPRESS

ACCOUNT NUMBER _____

EXPIR. DATE _____ DAYTIME PHONE _____

CHECK AREA OF COMPUTER INTEREST:

☐ BUSINESS SOFTWARE

☐ TECHNICAL PROGRAMMING

☐ OTHER: _____

THE FACTOR THAT WAS MOST IMPORTANT IN YOUR SELECTION:

☐ THE SYBEX NAME

☐ QUALITY

☐ PRICE

☐ EXTRA FEATURES

☐ COMPREHENSIVENESS

☐ CLEAR WRITING

☐ OTHER _____

OTHER COMPUTER TITLES YOU WOULD LIKE TO SEE IN PRINT:

_____

_____

OCCUPATION

☐ PROGRAMMER   ☐ TEACHER

☐ SENIOR EXECUTIVE   ☐ HOMEMAKER

☐ COMPUTER CONSULTANT   ☐ RETIRED

☐ SUPERVISOR   ☐ STUDENT

☐ MIDDLE MANAGEMENT   ☐ OTHER:

☐ ENGINEER/TECHNICAL   _____

☐ CLERICAL/SERVICE

☐ BUSINESS OWNER/SELF EMPLOYED

CHECK YOUR LEVEL OF COMPUTER USE

☐ NEW TO COMPUTERS

☐ INFREQUENT COMPUTER USER

☐ FREQUENT USER OF ONE SOFTWARE

   PACKAGE:

   NAME _____

☐ FREQUENT USER OF MANY SOFTWARE

   PACKAGES

☐ PROFESSIONAL PROGRAMMER

OTHER COMMENTS:

_____

_____

_____

_____

_____

_____

_____

PLEASE FOLD, SEAL, AND MAIL TO SYBEX

– – – – – – – – – – – – – – – – – – –

SYBEX, INC.
2021 CHALLENGER DR. #100
ALAMEDA, CALIFORNIA USA
             94501

SEAL

SYBEX Computer Books
are different.

Here is why . . .

At SYBEX, each book is designed with you in mind. Every manuscript is carefully selected and supervised by our editors, who are themselves computer experts. We publish the best authors, whose technical expertise is matched by an ability to write clearly and to communicate effectively. Programs are thoroughly tested for accuracy by our technical staff. Our computerized production department goes to great lengths to make sure that each book is well-designed.

In the pursuit of timeliness, SYBEX has achieved many publishing firsts. SYBEX was among the first to integrate personal computers used by authors and staff into the publishing process. SYBEX was the first to publish books on the CP/M operating system, microprocessor interfacing techniques, word processing, and many more topics.

Expertise in computers and dedication to the highest quality product have made SYBEX a world leader in computer book publishing. Translated into fourteen languages, SYBEX books have helped millions of people around the world to get the most from their computers. We hope we have helped you, too.

For a complete catalog of our publications:

SYBEX, Inc. 2021 Challenger Drive, #100, Alameda, CA 94501
Tel: (415) 523-8233/(800) 227-2346   Telex: 336311
Fax: (415) 523-2373

ALPHABETIC LISTING OF KEY COMMANDS BY FUNCTION

○FUNCTION	○KEY
Index	Esc L I
Insert mode	F5 (toggle)
Italic	Alt-I
Justify	Alt-J
Left flush	Alt-L
Line draw	Ctrl-F5
Line number	Esc F D L
Line spacing	Esc F P
Lines	Esc F B L
Link	
Document	Esc L L D
Graphic	Esc L L G (5)
Spreadsheet	Esc L L S
Macros	
Record	Shift-F3
Step	Ctrl-F3
Margins	Esc F D
Merge codes	Ctrl-{ and Ctrl-}
Merge text	Esc T M
Move text	Esc D ⏎ Ins or Del Ins
New line	Shift-⏎
New page	Shift-Ctrl-⏎
Open paragraph spacing	Alt-O
Outline	
Collapse	– (--on keypad)
Collapse body text	Shift- –(minus)
Expand all headings	* (asterisk)
Expand body text	Shift- +
Expand heading	+ (on keypad)
Lower heading level	Alt-0
Organize	Shift-F5
Raise heading level	Alt-9
View	Shift-F2
Overtype mode	F5 (toggle)
Page break	Shift-Ctrl-⏎
Page numbering	Esc F D P

○FUNCTION	○KEY
Page size	Esc F D M
Paginate	Esc P R
Pagination toggle	Esc O (5)
Paragraph numbering	Esc L N
Pitch	Esc F C
Printer display	Alt-F7
Printing	
Paper feed	Esc P O
Print direct	Esc P D
Print document	Ctrl-F8
Print glossary	Esc P G
Print merge	Esc P M
Print pages	Esc P O
Print preview	Esc P V (5)
Print to file	Esc P F
Printer model	Esc P O (5)
Printer type	Esc P O
Queue printing	Esc P O
Resolution	Esc P O (5)
Queue files	Esc P Q
Quit	Esc Q
Recall text	Ctrl-F7
Record style	Alt-F10
Rename file	Esc T R
Repaginate	Esc P R
	Ctrl-F9 (4)
Repeat	
Edit	F4
Search	Shift-F4
Replace	
Format	Esc F L
Text	Esc R
Required space	Ctrl-spacebar